# AUTONOMY
# SOLIDARITY
# POSSIBILITY

## THE COLIN WARD READER

EDITED BY CHRIS WILBERT & DAMIAN F. WHITE

AK PRESS PUBLISHING & DISTRIBUTION
2011

*Autonomy, Solidarity, Possibility:*
*The Colin Ward Reader*
Edited by Chris Wilbert & Damian F. White

Introduction © 2011 Chris Wilbert & Damian F. White

This edition © 2011 AK Press (Edinburgh, Oakland, Baltimore)

ISBN-13: 978-1-84935-020-4
Library of Congress Control Number: 2010925770

AK Press
674-A 23rd Street
Oakland, CA 94612
USA
www.akpress.org
akpress@akpress.org

AK Press UK
PO Box 12766
Edinburgh EH8 9YE
Scotland
www.akuk.com
ak@akdin.demon.co.uk

The above addresses would be delighted to provide you with the latest AK Press
distribution catalog, which features several thousand books, pamphlets, zines, audio and
video recordings, and gear, all published or distributed by AK Press. Alternately, visit our
websites to browse the catalog and find out
the latest news from the world of anarchist publishing:
www.akpress.org | www.akuk.com
revolutionbythebook.akpress.org

Printed in the United States on 100% recycled, acid-free paper with union labor.

This book was made possible in part by a generous donation from
the Anarchist Archives Project.

Cover by Josh MacPhee | www.justseeds.org
*Interior by Carey Chiaia & Kate Khatib*

RECYCLED
Paper made from
recycled material
FSC® C068106

# TABLE OF CONTENTS

# SECTION THREE: DESIGN, ARCHITECTURE AND CREATIVITY

# SECTION FOUR: WORK, LEISURE, EDUCATION AND PLAY

# SECTION FIVE: INFLUENCES AND ALTERNATIVES

# NOTES

# PREFACE AND ACKNOWLEDGEMENTS

Colin Ward, who died in February 2010 at the age of eighty-five, was Britain's most persistent and articulate defender of the libertarian Left in the second half of the twentieth century. For over six decades, this gentle anarchist bucked conventional wisdom by arguing that those who wish to see the emergence of a more compassionate, humane society need to think beyond the dogma of centralised state planning and the 'free' market. As a man of the Left, Ward insisted progressives and radicals should not cede to conservatism the ideas of 'self reliance' and 'autonomy', 'mutual aid' or 'enterprise'. As an environmentalist, Ward recommended that we should put aside the 'cult of wild nature' to develop an environmentalism that values working landscapes and the built environment. As a writer, journalist and social critic he counselled against being enthralled to experts and maintained that we can learn much from the day-to-day creativity of ordinary people.

Drawing inspiration from a neglected tradition of libertarian, decentralist, regionalist and anarchist thinkers (from Peter Kropotkin and Lewis Mumford, to Ebenezer Howard and Martin Buber, Patrick Geddes and Paul Goodman), the starting premise of Ward's writings is that we are first and foremost creative and resourceful beings and that given the right circumstances we are fully capable of organizing our own affairs in humane, co-operative ways. Such a bold position might strike some as startling, perhaps curious, romantic or simply naïve. Yet Ward responds to such critics by suggesting that the curious mixture of cynicism, hopelessness and misanthropy that passes for a refined intelligence has itself long been a poor guide to organizing human affairs.

Across some thirty books and hundreds of articles Ward counters cynicism about the possibility of developing social institutions that maximise solidarity *and* autonomy by bringing to light a range of self-organized and self-managed social practices—in housing, work and leisure, urban policy, architecture and design. His work explores community gardens, allotments and credit unions, housing co-operatives and participatory design, self-build dwellings and multiple other grassroots ventures organised around mutual aid and communal support. Such writings argue that we should attend seriously to the history and politics of such activities because they can facilitate autonomy, build new solidarities and like 'seeds beneath the snow'[1], open new possibilities for living differently.

*Autonomy, Solidarity, Possibility* provides a wide ranging overview of Colin Ward's six decades of writings. For the first time in one volume, it brings together a selection of Ward's journalism, seminal essays, extracts from his most important books (and some more obscure ones), as well as examples of his final writings.

The hope is that this collection will trigger interest amongst the uninitiated and remind older readers of the richness of his practical thoughts and writings. Minimally from this, some will be left suitably provoked and annoyed. Others though may well head off on their own, and more hopefully with others, to plot their own engagements with his work, and perhaps explore further the traditions and practice of self-organization he describes and defends.

This anthology is the product of many years of work and it has concurrently incurred many debts along the way. The editors would firstly like to thank the late Colin Ward and his wife Harriet Ward, Charles Weiss and David Goodway for all their help in envisaging this project. Colin and Harriet Ward helped to develop this project in its early stages. They gave their time on numerous occasions to answer requests for interviews and they helped trace difficult to find articles. It was a pleasure to engage with Colin, and as Harriet has let us know, Colin's checking of the introduction to this anthology for accuracy (with her aid) was his last engagement with writing. David Goodway's help in developing this project from start to finish was invaluable. Ken Worpole, Peter Hall and David Crouch also swiftly responded to queries. Virtually all of Colin's original writings were produced on a typewriter and most pre-date the rise of word processing (and in any case, he had no truck with computers). As such, assembling this anthology took many hours of transcribing and typing Colin's prose into word processing formats. The British Library Reading Rooms, the library staff at James Madison University, Anglia Ruskin University, and the Rhode Island School of Design proved invaluable in locating materials and in copying and scanning of texts and microfiche.

At a more general level, the writing and editing of books invariably draws support from a much broader circle of intellectual, academic and personal support systems. As such Chris would like to thank all those who had to put up with him when holidays beckoned and libraries took over. It seems to go with the terrain that this was work, but a lot was learned from Dennis Hardy and David Crouch at various times. We might not have always agreed, but then that is the way of conversations, and respect is due. Thanks also to Martin Spaul and Rikke Hansen for diffuse conversations on and around this work.

Damian would like to thank Andrew Lainton, and Gideon Kossoff for introducing him to the work of Colin Ward many years ago. He would like to acknowledge helpful conversations he has had over the years with Geoff Robinson, Alan Carter, Neil Curry, Eamon Nolan, Mike Small, Alan Rudy, Liam Buckley, Caroll Ann Friedmann, John Ott, Sarah Warren, Joe Rumbo, Fletcher Linder, Joe Spear, Mark Collins and Jennifer Kaufman. He would like to thank the multiple student cohorts that have moved through his seminars in 'The Sociology of Design' and 'Cities, Urbanization, Nature' at the Rhode Island School of Design and new colleagues there, notably Anne Tate, Charlie Cannon, David Bogen, Chris Rose and Markus Berger for helping him think more clearly about the relations between society and design. He would additionally like to thank and acknowledge the sustenance and support of Sarah Friel, Finbar, Cormac and Xavier White, Mary and Mark White.

# AUTONOMY, SOLIDARITY AND POSSIBILITY: THE WORLDS OF COLIN WARD'S ANARCHISM

## CHRIS WILBERT & DAMIAN F. WHITE

There are good reasons to feel that the writings of Colin Ward have made a significant, if still under-appreciated, contribution to post-1945 culture, intellectual life and politics in Britain and further afield. As a co-editor of the newspaper *Freedom* through the 1950s, the editor of the influential monthly periodical *Anarchy* through the 1960s, a columnist for *Town and Country Planning, New Society* and *The New Statesman & Society* from the late 1970s to the mid-1990s and the author of some thirty books, Ward's writings persistently champion the politics of self-organization and radical democratic self-management.

Across these numerous books and articles, Ward's writings have variously explored the social histories of allotments and community gardens, squatting, housing co-operatives and the holiday camp for workers and families. He has recovered the histories of mutual aid and self-help that run through the labour movement and many other community and co-operative movements. Assorted books reflect deeply on the tensions that exist between architecture, design, democracy and human creativity. Award-winning works also emphasise the rights of children to play and experiment in the city and stress the virtues of a form of environmental education that attends to the design, histories, uses, and politics of the built environment.[2]

Such agendas might seem disparate, but what is striking about this body of work is the connecting threads. Ward's writings draw 'bottom up' cultures of self-organization into a dialogue with the thinking of Peter Kropotkin and Martin Buber, Ebenezer Howard and Patrick Geddes and many more. In doing so his work not only constitutes a sustained attempt to write multiple histories of popular sovereignty but is a bold attempt to envisage alternative futures.

If there is a core theme running through Ward's writings, it is the suggestion that we often succumb to pessimistic, passive views of human being's capacities, not simply because such cynicism suits the interests of the powerful (as it nearly always does) but because we read the present and the past in a partial and limited fashion. While most conventional history is preoccupied with the rise and consolidation of authoritarian institutions from above, Ward maintains there is a much more interesting tale that can be told from below of the rise of autonomous and fraternal institutions.

This is an often 'hidden history' of men and women—relatively free of officials, managers, experts and employers—practically and intelligently resolving their own problems through acts of social creativity, 'bottom up' institution building and voluntary collective action. Ward suggests that when this past is obscured, the multiple examples of mutual aid, solidarity and voluntary collective action that are constantly going on in the present are obscured. Running though all of his writings is the sense that these examples of the day-to-day inventiveness of ordinary people suggest that 'doing things differently' is a possibility always lingering in social life—no matter how unpromising the political terrain might feel.

If 'doing things differently' to get somewhere more liberatory is a guiding thread in Ward's work, the central locus of his writings has been the day-to-day spaces and places of life and living. Long before environmentalism was a mass social movement, Ward argued for a politics of the environment.[3] But what will be clear in the pages ahead is that this is not an environmentalism that constantly problematises human action for its impact on an abstract, static, external entity called 'Nature'. Rather, Ward's understanding of society and nature is much more dynamic, historical and specific. It is concerned with the everyday environments we inhabit, co-create and constantly transform and the everyday politics of life that potentially make these spaces vital sites of creativity and social transformation.

Maurice Blanchot has argued that 'everyday life' is a deeply spatial realm, but the everyday most often goes unnoticed because we are ensconced within it. By exploring and drawing attention to different social practices, we can see the everyday *again* in different ways, and this opens up new possibilities.[4] Such an observation resonates with Ward's project. Ward's writings maintain that the politics of the spaces and places we live within—our shared environments—cannot be adequately read from the vantage point of governments, from guiding analyses of Marx's *Capital* or simple dogmas about the functioning of the 'free' market. On the contrary, he documents a politics made and remade by people who are often twisting new uses out of periodic gaps, margins and spaces—whether these are creative possibilities that emerge from financially unproductive land and housing or falling land prices, cultural shifts or changes in sensibilities that allow new possibilities for living. His writings demonstrate how 'some of these innovations disappear, others survive, but the challenge remains to find them, encourage people to articulate, expand and connect them.'[5]

It is this that lies at the root of Colin Ward's political philosophy: anarchism. To be sure, his commitment to anarchism is deeply rooted in Kropotkin, Godwin and Goodman and based on a firm libertarian distrust of state institutions, party vanguards, bureaucrats and managers. What makes these writings refreshing to read though, is that they are uncluttered by bombast or theoretical jargon. Indeed, they are marked by a certain realism and humility.

Starting from Malatesta's premise that 'we are, in any case, only one of the forces acting in society'[6] and that that is likely to be the case in any foreseeable future, Ward maintains that the human condition is characterised by irreducible social and political pluralism. To deny this, or seek to eradicate such plurality, Ward believes, would be profoundly un-anarchist. The case for anti-authoritarian politics has to be *argued for*. As such, Ward argues that anarchists should not only engage respectfully with non-anarchists, but that coalitions reflecting a wide range of different opinions have to be built for an anti-authoritarian politics to move forward. Indeed, Ward's reflections on his influences nicely capture his own ethics of writing and politics. He notes:

> My influences sought as wide an audience as possible. They did not all write particularly well, but they did address the reader as a serious person to be debated with, not as an ignoramus to be bullied or hectored. Still less did they pander to or flatter the prejudices or superstitions of their prospective readership. My influences founded no parties. None of them started wars nor took part in governments. None of them inspired people to hate each other.[7]

What follows from this is that Ward's form of social criticism is less concerned with providing a 'head on' critique of the stupid brutality of the state that obsessed so many of the classical anarchist thinkers of the nineteenth century. Rather, his writings attempt to win 'reasonable people' round to recognising the positive benefits of self-organizing social practises, self-managing solutions and anti-authoritarian politics. Through this, he seeks to undermine the self-evident virtues of statist, technocratic, centralist and coercive solutions to specific social problems. His work additionally seeks to demonstrate that what 'the State' and informed opinion deem social problems may not always converge with what people in their everyday lives see as social problems.[8]

## CONTEXT AND CONCERNS

As the extracts that make up this anthology will demonstrate, Ward's writings are clearly situated, historically and geographically, in the curve of British history that begins with the enormous transformations of the post World War Two era; of decolonialisation and the disintegration of Empire, social and economic rebuilding, and the triumph of the post-war Labour government and Fabian social democracy. His writings move through Butskellism, Butlins and The Beatles, the cultural experimentation of the 1960s and the political turbulence of the 1970s through to the rise of Thatcherism. They conclude in the era of post-Thatcherism's partial consolidation and transformation under New Labour.

Many of these writings are preoccupied with the new lords of the post-war era of technocracy and social engineering, the rise of the professional expert and the institutionalization of experience. Ward is by no means dismissive of expert knowledges; all his writings draw heavily from his own experience as a draughtsman and an educator, and from his own deep engagement with the disciplines of sociology, anthropology and psychology, geography, art history and poetry, philosophy and literature. Nevertheless, these writings do rail against a generalized technocratic domination that is presented as a deep-seated feature of modern social life: the architect who, in his belief that he 'knows best', derides local knowledge and, along with the urban planner and politician, 'benignly' replaces pre-war slums with post-war 'rationally' designed new slums; or the faith of the social engineering professionals 'that bigger and better schools, or bigger and better units of housing, or more expert and intensive social work will modify the culture of poverty.'[9] His writings make a persistent claim that the voices, creativity, expertise and agency of the marginalized and the ignored—most obviously rural and urban working class men and women, but also the unemployed and underemployed, squatters, travellers and most strikingly working class children in the city and the countryside—should be heard and listened to. Perhaps his most celebrated work—*The Child in the City*—warns of and describes a city that forecloses freedom for children—due to motor cars (and the uncritical embrace of the car economy), parental anxiety, poverty or petty authoritarianism. Such a set of arrangements, he maintains, can simply ensure that 'self confidence and purposeful self-respect drain away from children as they grow up because there is no way which makes sense to them, of becoming involved, except in a predatory way, in their own city'.[10]

In terms of solutions, Ward's work is interesting in that it is committed to a vision of anarchism that is both pragmatic and potentially multiple. Again, it is very different to dominant conceptions of the anarchist tradition that associate it either with chaos (usually in terms of lack of state control, police and military institutions) or a revolutionary romanticism.

Long before the critique of grand narratives and 'totalising theory' was mounted by the likes of Lyotard and Foucault, Ward argued that radical politics was all but useless if conceptualized simply as an end point that has to be built by an act of purgation by fire. In contrast, Ward's writings present anarchism as a constant subjective desire that appears in social life characterised by creative forms of self-organization and expression, a libertarian current that, following Kropotkin, he sees as always in competition with the forces of authoritarianism, bureaucracy and state power. As he argues:

> The choice between libertarian and authoritarian solutions is not a once-and-for-all cataclysmic struggle, it is a series of running engagements, most of them never concluded, which occur, and have occurred, throughout history.

This leads Ward to argue for a central aspiration: to search for anarchist solutions to social problems in the here and now. As he says:

> one of the tasks of the anarchist propagandist is to propagate solutions to contemporary issues which, however dependent they are on the existing social and economic structures, are *anarchist* solutions: the kind of approaches that would be made if we were living in the kind of society we envisage. We are much more likely to win support for our point of view, in other words, if we put anarchist answers in the here and now, than if we declared that there are no answers until the ultimate answer: a social revolution which continually disappears over the horizon.[11]

The problem with the view that there can be no solutions to people's problems 'until *the* social revolution that will change everything', is that 'they solve no problems for me or anyone else'.[12] Here, Ward has a more nuanced account of driving forces within society (broadly conceived) and change than many might associate with anarchism, overlapping with some of the other writers and theorists of the everyday and politics in the twentieth century, such as Gramsci or Lefebvre.[13]

To be sure, Ward's body of work is heavily in debt to a range of influences that he constantly acknowledges and seeks to promote: from the writings of Peter Kropotkin, Ebenezer Howard and Patrick Geddes to Paul Goodman, Alexander Herzen, Gustav Landauer, Martin Buber, Walter Segal, Alex Comfort and Lewis Mumford. Yet this group of anti-authoritarian, decentralist and regionalist thinkers provide a seam of political thought that remains neglected and too poorly understood. Ward draws the insights of these thinkers and practitioners together in a unique fashion, building on them and often situating their more valuable insights within the context of the contemporary life he sees around him.

In this anthology, we attempt to provide a flavour of this work. We begin this book, though, with a sketch of Ward's personal, political and intellectual background, followed by an introduction to the five thematic sections of this anthology.

## TALKING ABOUT ANARCHISM: LIFE AND POLITICS

Colin Ward was born in Wanstead, in the east London suburbs on the 14th August 1924, the son of Arnold Ward, an elementary school teacher, and Ruby West, a shorthand typist and housewife.[14] While he was artistically orientated and politically curious, the formal education system failed to ignite his interests. He attended the prestigious Ilford County High School, in Barkingside, Ilford, but left at the age of fifteen. After a brief period working for the Borough Surveyor of Ilford Council, he 'drifted into' architecture.[15] For some twenty-five years following this—interrupted by a period of conscription in the British Army—he worked as an assistant architect in his day job and developed his interests in journalism, writing and editing in the evening, through his involvement with the anarchist movement.

As an architect's assistant, Ward got his 'start' in 1941 working on the drawing board for the architect Sydney Caulfield. Though drafted in 1942, he returned to architecture after the end of the war working variously for The Architects Co-Partnership; Bridgwater, Shepheard and Epstein; and finally Chamberlin, Powell and Bon—where he became director of research in 1961.[16] As a journalist, Ward began writing pieces for *War Commentary: For Anarchism* whilst in the British Army in 1943.[17] He joined the editorial collective of the anarchist newspaper *Freedom* after the war, and initiated (with the agreement of the Freedom Press group) and became the editor of the influential monthly journal *Anarchy* in 1961.[18]

After a career shift from architecture to teaching, as Head of Liberal Studies at Wandsworth Technical College (1966–1971), Ward returned to the worlds of architecture and planning by taking a post as the education officer of the Town and Country Planning Association (TCPA).[19] Here, he edited the *Bulletin of Environmental Education* and wrote a column for *Town and Country Planning*. In 1979, he resigned from the TCPA and moved with his wife, Harriet, to rural Suffolk to become a prolific full-time author, a columnist for the *New Society* and, later, *The New Statesman & Society* and a contributor to innumerable magazines, journals and newspapers from *The Raven* to *Prospect* magazine. Though, according to Harriet Ward, this rural life, existing on freelance writing, was not at all an easy life economically. In 2000, he was appointed the visiting centenary Professor of Social Policy at the London School of Economics. He died at the age of eighty-five on the 11th February, 2010.

As Ward tells David Goodway, in a rich, extended interview—with which we begin this anthology—reflecting on his early life, a range of influences can be identified. Ward's family clearly played an important role in introducing him to progressive politics. Arnold Ward was active in the Labour Party and when he was scarcely fourteen, Colin heard the anarchist and feminist orator Emma Goldman speak at a May Day rally in Hyde Park in 1938.[20] As Goodway has discovered, Ward's architecture mentor Sydney Caulfield also played an important role in his intellectual development. Caulfield had studied under the influential architect and critic W.R. Lethaby, John Loughborough Pearson (the architect of Truro Cathedral in south west England) and other central figures of the Arts and Crafts movement, and Ward soaked up such influences.[21] Caulfield left the young Ward with a lifelong interest in lettering and typography,[22] and it was through these connections, alongside Ward's growing engagements with radical and bohemian currents around the London political scene of the 1940s, that ensured exposure to the work of William Morris and the arts and crafts movements, and authors such as Proust and Gide, Orwell and Trotsky, Lorca and Canetti, Mann and Brecht. As this interview demonstrates, though, it was his wartime experiences, and encounters with 'real' anarchists in Glasgow and London, that proved formative of his politics and subsequent career.

At the age of eighteen, Ward was conscripted into the Royal Engineers where he was 'taught to build bridges' and 'make explosions'. Fortunately for him, he was posted to Glasgow and so avoided combat. Encounters with the grinding poverty of the city and contact with the Glaswegian anarchist movement was to prove decisively important to his development. Extracts in the first chapter of this reader outline Ward's first journalistic pieces, written for the publication *War Commentary—For Anarchism* whilst still a young soldier. These are short propaganda pieces dealing with the politics of post-war reconstruction that have now mostly been forgotten, yet, they provide a flavour of the emerging politics of the young Colin Ward. In these articles he criticizes the disturbing willingness of the allies to work with 'ex'-fascists to put in place 'a capitalist elite' to re-organize the economies of the liberated regions of Italy. These writing are additionally interesting because of the biographical role they played in contributing to Ward's redeployment from Glasgow to a 'maintenance unit' in the Shetland and Orkney Islands, (where he eventually ended up spending time in a Military Detention Camp for insubordination) and for their role in strengthening Ward's links with the anarchist movement. In April 1945, the four editors of *War Commentary* were prosecuted for conspiring to cause disaffection in the military and three were imprisoned for nine months as a result.[23]

In 1947, after being demobilized from the army, Ward returned to London and found his political home amongst the anarchist intellectuals and bohemian radicals that clustered around Freedom Press. Situated in Whitechapel, Freedom Press was founded in 1886 by the group centred around Kropotkin. Ward found in its post-1945 regrouping a convivial political, intellectual and personal space.[24] As he documents both in his interview and in the two articles we excerpt in this section from his *Freedom* writings, this was a Britain still defined by rationing and crudely authoritarian attitudes to free speech, sexual mores and civil liberties, by anti-colonial wars in east Africa and Asia and a series of increasingly dangerous proxy wars being fought by new nuclear armed superpowers speaking the language of 'acceptable nuclear warfare'. As part of *Freedom*'s editorial collective from 1947 to 1960, and as the sole editor of the monthly journal *Anarchy* from 1961, Ward (along with the Freedom Press group more generally) sought to rail against such currents and, in doing so, they played an important role in generating a wider renewal of interest in anarchist and broader left-libertarian thought and action.

Deeply influenced by Kropotkin, Freedom Press supported the emerging peace movement but they also culturally anticipated, to a large degree, many counter-cultural concerns of the 1960s. Ward's *Anarchy* in particular won plaudits from an early point—being described by Colin MacInnes as providing 'the liveliest social commentary in Britain'. Ward sought to develop *Anarchy* as a journal that would avoid parochialism and sectarianism and be open to a broad range of voices and topics and oriented to the 'outside world rather than the in-group'.[25] As such, as well as publishing the work of critical figures in the British anarchist movement, such as Nicolas Walter, George Woodcock, Alex Comfort and Geoffery Ostergaard, the journal became the first British publisher of the writings of the American social ecologist Murray Bookchin on environmental issues and radical technology. *Anarchy* published some of Paul Goodman's seminal pieces on child psychology, and it provided an important forum for the dissemination of the new sociology of deviance developed by Jock Young, Stan Cohen and Laurie Taylor. It also opened itself up to a broader range of contributions on culture and politics from sources as diverse as the author Alan Sillitoe and jazz musician George Melly.

We have drawn on extracts from Ward's writings in *Anarchy* and *Freedom* throughout this anthology. In this first section we focus on Ward's key theoretical statements of why he views anarchism—and specifically the Kropotkin communitarian anarchist tradition—as such a fruitful source of inspiration for thinking and practicing politically. In extract two, we provide a lengthy account of Ward's articulation of the anarchist critique of the state, managerialism and bureaucracy. This passionate piece demonstrates that, for all his pragmatism, Ward is committed to the classic anarchist critique of the state. The piece begins by restating the prophetic critiques of the political limitations of political Marxism by classic anarchist thinkers such as Bakunin and Kropotkin. Long before the rise of State Socialism, as Ward articulates, it was these anarchists who explicitly warned the socialist movement that Marxist 'state worship' was all but inevitably going to generate an authoritarian political system. Ward goes on in this article to reflect on the insanity of a state system that has generated a stockpile of nuclear weapons equivalent to ten tons of TNT for every person alive today. It is this bare fact, he argues, that makes it necessary to be involved in forms of politics that strengthen *other* loyalties, generate *alternative* foci of power, and develop *different* modes of human behaviour. In the final extract of section one, Ward reflects on the extent to which anarchism as a theory of organization might provide some guidance for thinking about how we could generate richer forms of autonomy and solidarity.

## CULTURE, PLACE AND HOUSING

In the second section of this anthology, we present a selection of Ward's pieces on housing, place and culture. His writings on housing reach back to the social and cultural history of housing and land use and move forwards to sustained and active attempts to influence contemporary housing policy practice. What is immediately striking about this body of writing is not simply the ongoing interest in documenting unofficial uses of land but the grounding of such writings in a commitment to the virtues of 'dweller control'. What follows from this is that Ward's writings on housing do not play to the easy orthodoxies of left, right or indeed much contemporary green thinking. Whilst Ward relentlessly critiqued the 'free' market model of housing provision, he is equally a biting critic of various left wing romances—from state collectivization of land to the 'local council as landlord model' of housing provision that dominated housing policy from 1945 until the 1980s in Britain and in many other western European countries. His writings are also sharply critical of what he sees are class interests and biases that inform the thinking and practices of the countryside preservation lobby.

We begin this section with two fascinating moments in British housing history that would have been widely forgotten if not for Ward's research—in tandem with Dennis Hardy. In "Plotlands", Ward draws on his longer work from 1984 with Hardy (*Arcadia for All: The Legacy of a Makeshift Landscape*) to provide a succinct history of the explosion of self-built housing that spread across much of rural Britain not too far from major cities during the long agricultural depression that began in the mid-1870s. The agricultural depression saw a dramatic stagnation of land prices. Land for building became available—from a variety of entrepreneurs who bought up cheap farmland—at prices that even some urban working class families could afford. Many took advantage of this and began to build a variety of structures that became known as plotlands. The spread of 'the plotlands' as Ward notes, were looked upon with horror by politicians of the left and right and the liberal intelligentsia as marking a 'vulgar desecration of the rural landscape by the wrong kind of people'. Nevertheless, Ward argues that the plotlands not only provided a vital weekend, holiday or retirement space of rural respite for many working-class city dwellers, but they generated built structures sometimes marked by real innovations. Struggles over the plotlands, as this extract reveals, also generated some interesting class dynamics. As he notes:

> At the end of the century we may smile at the way the shapers of policy took it
> for granted that *they* were entitled to a rural retreat, while wanting to deny on

aesthetic grounds the same opportunity to people further down the hierarchy of chance and income.

This kind of upper and middle class moralisation of urban working class use of the countryside can also be found in wider leisure uses of the countryside in the early-twentieth century—as the geographer David Matless has documented in his book *Landscape and Englishness* (1998). As such, this social history of plotlands demonstrates to good effect how land use, class, ideas of an appropriate landscape and ideas of 'preservation' can be bound up together in all kinds of complicated, troubling ways, but also ways full of potential.

In "The People Act", a series of reports that were first published in *Freedom* in 1946, Ward provides us with a vivid account of the post war British squatters' movements. In these powerful pieces of journalism, Ward documents the explosion of direct action that unfolded across the UK in 1946, as returning servicemen—either homeless or living in squalid conditions—took over empty air force and army bases, as well as empty houses and hotels across Britain to provide shelter for their families. The scale of this response to one of the worst housing crises in the post-war era—one that was not just the result of the destruction of housing through bombings—is remarkable. Ward notes how, by October 1946, 1,038 army and air force camps in England and Wales had been occupied by 39,535 people. What is additionally remarkable is how little this incident is remembered today. Such stories—like the histories of industrial disputes in wartime[26]—do not fit the dominant British narratives of the Second World War, with its emphasis on a nation united beyond class.

In "The DIY New Town" and "Fiction, Non-Fiction and Reference", we turn to consider a moment in urban history that many would seemingly prefer to forget—the New Towns policy experiment in Britain.[27] The development of New Towns, such as Milton Keynes, Harlow and Runcorn, is seen by many as a moment in post-war urban history that marks a highpoint of the confidence that urban planners and architects could significantly define urban futures for mass-populations, and a low point in terms of many of the results. Whilst Ward is critical of the execution of these projects, perhaps surprising for some, he suggests that it is too often forgotten that the New Town experiment (and many other social housing redevelopments in cities) provided many working class people, who had been horrifically oppressed by the squalor and over-crowding of the inner city, with real opportunities for a better life. He also seeks to defend the idea of urban dispersal that informed the development of the New Towns. In "The DIY New Town", he goes on to advocate a new experimental urban form, arguing that a relaxing of building and planning regulations in certain spaces could make it possible (if carefully done) for people to experiment with alternative ways of building and servicing houses.

"Self Help in Urban Renewal" provides some surprising views on gentrification. Both urban gentrification and squatting in certain contexts are presented as potential drivers of self-help in urban renewal. He notes 'A comparison of the bizarre prices that the rescued houses fetch today with the sorry state of the estate opposite is interesting in pondering the conclusion reached some time ago by Dr Graham Lomas (formerly deputy strategic planner for the Greater London Council) that in London more *fit* houses had been destroyed by public authorities than had been built since the war (*The Inner City*, 1975). Ward continues to explore the potentially productive role that squatters—turned into members of housing co-operatives—can play in generating urban renewal. In contrast to the public views of squatting, as Ward observes, the typical modern squatter often 'actually hopes for the security of a rent book'.

Our extract from *Cotters and Squatters* deepens our understanding of Ward's views on the disasters that have often resulted from state collectivisation of land. In dispossessing the peasants of their right to farm common land, he argues that the state—whether this is in Britain or the Soviet Union—has often created the conditions of a completely dysfunctional countryside. As he notes, in the former USSR, the disastrous dispossession of the peasantry by Stalin gave rise to the anomaly of private farmed land contributing a hugely disproportionate share of agricultural production to national food supply in contrast to the lacklustre experience of collectivization. In the UK, on the other hand, Ward argues that excessive state control of land policy—through the various Town and Country Planning Acts from the 1940s onwards—has helped generate an increasing marginalisation of the urban poor from the rural hinterland. Ward maintains here that planning measures, informed by a romantic conservation movement (which seems to view all housing for the poor as a blot on the landscape), along with a stubborn belief in encouraging privately owned housing developments and practice, not only helped generate a housing crisis for the poor, but ensured that large areas of the British countryside have been transformed into spaces where increasingly only the well off can afford to live. These same planning measures, which 'protect' the green belt from building around cities have had further repercussions. Today's gypsies and travellers, who for years have been hounded off temporary sites of living—and as a tactical reaction have taken to buying up cheap green belt tracts to live on—have found themselves often violently removed by local authorities (and the bailiffs they employ) for supposedly despoiling this green belt land on the edges of towns and cities.[28]

In our final extracts for this section, Ward outlines general values that he thinks should more fully inform our attitudes to housing, and he also defends some specific policy proposals that he believes could open up spaces for more libertarian approaches. In "Self-help and Mutual Aid", he argues that these terms, along with the concept of 'self reliance' are popularly associated with conservative politics. Ward maintains though that these terms are not only widely misunderstood—'mutual aid' in Kropotkin's sense referring to the manner in which all species involve themselves in co-operative relations and 'self help' by definition involving help of neighbours—but these values have a long history within the politics of the Left. Reviewing the history of the Left, he argues 'self help' and 'mutual aid' provided 'the dominant characteristic of the emerging working-class organizations of the nineteenth century, whether we are thinking of the co-operative movement, the trade union movement, the friendly society movement or the adult education movement'. He goes on to observe, 'It is ironical that the twentieth-century political heirs of these organizations have put their faith exclusively in the governmental bureaucracy and have not only ignored this heritage, but despise it'.

What Ward says, in examining a number of successful contemporary examples of housing renovations such as the Black Road Action Group in Macclesfield—which resisted a projected housing clearance project and then proposed, implemented and subsequently managed housing by the residents themselves—is that much official housing legislation:

> demonstrates the extent to which the procedures introduced by government to improve the housing situation have unwittingly complicated it and made it unresponsive to the aspirations of ordinary citizens. The habit of self-help and mutual aid have been deliberately repressed by inducing the habit of reliance on the bureaucratic organization of housing.

We conclude this section with *High Density Life*, an article that Ward wrote for the monthly magazine *Prospect* in 2006. Here, Ward returns to the issue of density in the light of discussions about sustainability. Whilst much contemporary green urbanism has argued that maximising densities in urban areas will optimise solutions for sustainability, Ward argues that we should be careful about embracing this new orthodoxy lest we repeat all the failures of post war urban policy.

## DESIGN, ARCHITECTURE AND CREATIVITY

The topics of 'design' architecture and creativity have become voguish in sociology and the social sciences of late,[29] and it is striking how much of the literature on design is understood in conventional ways—as exploring the professional practice engaged by trained individuals who are involved in the construction of artefacts, buildings and so on.[30] Colin Ward's writings, in contrast, explore lay people's capacity and practices of creativity, and outline how these practices are often stifled. In this section, we draw together a selection of Ward's broad ranging writings on architecture and design with his work on the importance of creativity in day-to-day life and the potential resourcefulness of children more generally. Once again, this section demonstrates how Ward's left libertarian approach to these issues starts from very different premises from conventional professionalized and bureaucratized organizations and ends with very different conclusions.

Ward's basic starting point for a discussion of design—drawing from the spirit of such central figures of the arts and crafts movement like William Morris—is that design creativity is much more widely possessed than is generally acknowledged by professional designers. He moves on to remind us that the rise of the professional expert in design, architecture and creativity is, in fact, a recent phenomenon and that indeed historically it has been the layperson who did (and often still does) most of the building construction that has gone on in the world.[31] As will be apparent from the two lectures with which we begin this chapter, as a working architect's assistant of twenty-five years, Ward takes seriously the dilemmas that architects and designers face in their professional lives. Yet, equally, he has some significant concerns about how the design professions have been conceived and have conceived themselves. Central worries flagged in these lectures include a concern about the dismissive attitude that has been adopted by professional architecture to vernacular architecture, the broader effects that bureaucratization has had on design—particularly in facilitating state-sponsored dreary and often cheap modernism in the post-war era—and more generally in the narcissism of much design culture and 'design ideology'. Such concerns run through his writings on urban design. As he observes:

> Take one hilarious example: for generations, in municipal housing, the kitchen became smaller and smaller, in order to cure people of the reprehensible habit of eating in the kitchen. The result is that, up and down the land, you can meet families, squashed in a corner, taking turns at eating their meals on a table as big as a shelf. Meanwhile the socially conscious architect of the 'scheme' they have been obliged to inhabit, eats in his kitchen, surrounded by his family, off a scrubbed deal table, and his wife prides herself that their kitchen looks exactly like that of a Provençal peasant. There's a string of onions hanging from the beam of *her* kitchen ceiling in a house which is two miners' cottages joined together into one, in a Category D village to which Durham County Council has denied improvement grants.

His full attitude to architecture and design is perhaps best captured by his reaction to the explosion of the professions in the post war era. Ward, in 'Self-help and Mutual Aid', quotes Peter Hall:

> It's chastening to ask what would have happened if we'd never trained the architects, but had spent all that slum clearance money quite differently. Suppose, in the Liverpool of 1955, we hadn't said: 'a problem of replacing 88,000 unfit houses', but rather: 'a problem of making 88,000 houses fit', we could have given very generous improvement grants, encouraged small builders, opened DIY shops. The whole environment would have been improved piecemeal. It wouldn't have been very efficient—small-scale work never is—and besides, a good deal of the basic infrastructure would have had to be renewed. But it would have involved ordinary people in fixing up their own houses and helping improve their own neighbourhoods. It wouldn't have caused the enormous disruption, physical and social, that gave us the Everton Piggeries and the vandalized streets of Kirkby.

Ward suggests that Hall is wrong just to blame the architects for post-war urban blight. 'The whole coalition of politicians, experts and administrators had a vested interest in not enabling people to find their own solutions.' His critique of design professionals in these two extracts is nevertheless severe. So what are his solutions?

Ward asks us to envisage a future where design professionals do not exist as separate 'expert' entities involved in master building but more as 'enablers'. He invokes here the Belgian architect Lucien Kroll as showing the beginnings of an enabler (one working in the constraints of the late-capitalist ways of building), an architect who does not 'finish' his designs or conceive social space with a prede-termined objective. Instead, Kroll emphasises diversity, social relationships, self-management; he leaves builders with some ability to work creatively with residents to produce places to inhabit that suit their present and future needs.[32]

Our fourth and fifth extracts in this section provide reflections on the life and work of the architects Walter Segal and John F.C. Turner, both key figures in instigating the self-build housing method. Segal was a hugely influential figure for Ward, who returns again and again to Segal's practices in his writings. Examples of Segal-method self-build designs can be found in only a few places in England, such as Honor Oak, Lewisham in south London,[33] but his designs and ideas have inspired many other projects. John F.C. Turner's work on the potential for self-build in developing countries also had a big impact on Ward.[34] We include here Ward's preface to Turner's book *Housing By People* (1976), which sets out what he sees as Turner's philosophy and politics of housing through discussion of the creativity of urban dwellers of shanty towns in Latin America. It should be evi-dent from these chapters that many of the examples of preferable practices that Ward would like to see proliferate operate in the interstices of mainstream land and housing policy in the market economy.

In our sixth excerpt, we draw from Ward's writing on the medieval Goth-ic masterpiece of architecture that is Chartres Cathedral in France. Originally published for the Folio Press, one of Ward's works as a freelance writer, it is a hugely interesting study of medieval building that still has some lessons today for architecture. In this extract Ward argues that the Gothic cathedrals of medieval France and other countries were the product of many travelling workers, not some 'individual genius' as is currently celebrated in architecture and city development and regeneration projects.

This section moves on from considering creativity in architecture and design to Ward's writings on creativity more broadly in daily life. We provide two excerpts from Ward's award-winning writings on the potential creativity of the child in the city. His writings on this topic have been hugely influential in the ways human geographers have developed studies of children's engagements in urban and rural spaces. In 'How the Child Sees the City' Ward outlines the research done by a variety of academics to demonstrate to students and policy makers the very dif-ferent ways children of different classes, ethnicities and genders engage with city spaces—and he documents how these forms of engagement subtly change as chil-dren age. From this, Ward argues that the child's perspective is rarely factored into the design of cities and urban places, nor has it been of enough interest to planners and designers. Obviously many things have changed since *The Child in the City* was written in 1976. Ongoing suburbanisation, sprawl, cell phones, the ubiquity of the car and extended mobilities of many people in cities has continued to trans-form the spatial possibilities and understandings many children and parents have of their urban environments. Yet Ward's writings in this subject are of continued interest because they suggest that if we valued play, and had some regard for the re-sourcefulness of children then we might see a much greater unleashing of human possibility. These points may sound simplistic to some, but such concerns work as alternative challenges to neo-liberal city governance and developments that work in tandem—in more day-to-day practical terms, with political-economic critiques of city life, economies, and social-ecologies.

We conclude this section with Ward's thoughts on design futures. In "The Anarchist House", Ward outlines his thoughts on the extent to which anarchism may or may not offer a specific building aesthetic. In general, he does not feel there is such a thing, and his conclusion, building on what Green movements have encouraged is that: 'The technical criterion for the anarchist house is "Long life, loose fit, low energy", but the political demand is the principle of Dweller Control.'

## WORK, LEISURE, PLAY AND EDUCATION

The idea that leisure, work and education should involve play has not been greatly developed by leftist or even anarchist political analysis. It is however a theme that runs through many of Colin Ward's writings. Play, leisure, and holidays have nearly always been seen as subservient to the study and politics of work. Throughout the history and geographies of industrialism and modernization, whether in the UK, France, India, China or beyond, play and leisure has been of crucial importance to people's everyday lives. Moreover, there has been a marginal, but substantive, argument put forward by a variety of writers that play, rather than work, is a formative element of the culture of peoples through history—indeed, for Mumford it is the key driver of social evolution—a view that we are sure Ward would share.[35]

The morality and politics of leisure, play and holidays has long been an area of everyday life that has been seen as potentially subversive, in need of control, like education and work. Yet, what is 'appropriate play', or leisure, or education, is contested and subjected to often-bitter moral and political policies and impositions that are often resisted, or played with and transformed. This can be seen, for example in the rational recreation movements of the mid- to late-nineteenth century engaged in by philanthropists in Britain and elsewhere who sought to 'improve' the lives of the poor, or religious and temperance groups that emphasised the good of team sports (muscular Christianity), back-to-nature activities, arts and culture for personal improvement, or indeed any activities that stopped the working classes drinking alcohol, engaging in 'unruly' activities or gambling. Such 'reformists' were of course often partly driven by the same aims of factory owners and other employers: to make the working classes better workers, families more effective reproductive units for work, fitter bodies as fighters in armies, and less potentially 'unruly' revolutionists or criminals. Moreover, the notion of leisure and play as 'free-time' has to be seen as too simple. Leisure is not free, it is always practiced and performed within the constraints of the social, technological and ecological relations people are living within. People's engagement in leisure and play also co-make spaces, sometimes resistant spaces, more often conventional spaces of consumption.

As such, in section four we consider how Ward expands the quest to do things differently into the realms of work, education and leisure. The section begins with

"The Factory We Never Had", an essay written as a preface to William Morris's "The Factory As It Might Be". For Ward, Morris emerges as the most important socialist of the nineteenth century—more important than Karl Marx. Ward argues that Morris was unusual as a male radical of the period in being very much concerned with the factory but also the home, housework and seemingly banal technologies such as cups, furniture and cutlery. For Morris, all of life, including factories, should aspire to be art, and the modernist spatial and temporal division between work and leisure should be arrested, so that leisure fed in to work, and work in to leisure, with education conjoining these. Moreover, modern technology had a role to play here. Ward argues that Morris was only against technology and factories that enslaved people in monotonous routines (and was not as such against these forms), whereas Ward searched for social forms that would liberate people. Repetitive work could be restful, but only if done for a short period, it should not be all there is to work. Ward mentions that a few 'enlightened' entrepreneurs took on some of Morris's notions to create 'model factories', though it must be said, it was in very partial ways that look like the above mentioned reforms of philanthropists.

In the second extract from this section, entitled "In the Sandbox of the City", Ward outlines the need for environmental education of children in cities, and the need for cities to be re-made to emphasise play, not just for children but for adults too. In our third extract, we outline Ward and Dennis Hardy's work on the social history of self-organised workers' leisure. *Goodnight Campers: The history of the British holiday camp* explores numerous examples of small-scale cooperative, trades union and family-run holiday camps that pre-date the commercial mass-holiday camps of the early decades of the twentieth century. In "Pioneer Camps"—the name given to forerunners of the more commercial holiday camps—Ward and Hardy show a simpler sense of the early holidays often paid for through mutual societies or membership schemes. This work has complimented many social histories of leisure that developed in the 1970s and a wider focus on the importance of examples of self-organized leisure that show other ways of living, playing and learning.

In "Images of childhood", Colin and Tim Ward argue that the humble postcard was, for a short while, a mode of communication where orders to shops, or announcements of one's arrival at the railway station could be made with remarkable speed because postal deliveries were so frequent in the early decades of the twentieth century. Though this period of relatively speedy communication did not last long in the UK, the postcard went on to become a kind of accidental documentary of social life, especially around leisure pursuits. It quickly developed its own rituals of sending and receiving and later changed into a form of communication that seemingly has no inherent content. Moreover, the postcard existed before images appeared in newspapers, and when newspapers did incorporate pictures, postcards featuring the same image would still be available first. And, as in the early history of film, entrepreneurs pictured locals, families, winners of prizes in festivals and fetes as a deliberate way to encourage friends and families, and others caught in these images to consume them.

In "Streetwork", Ward and Anthony Fyson provide us with a vision of the city as potentially a vital and useful centre of learning for children. This piece explores the idea of environmental education and considers how the school should also be a community resource for adults. Ward and Fyson advocate an 'exploding school' that moves outwards to the people and environments around them, where students engage in education in spaces outside of the classroom and engage with community problems from which knowledges can be passed through to adults. They argue that we need less to protect children from urban life, but to get children into the urban and rural world so they can explore the local politics of the built environment, land use and aesthetics, and critically engage with how social relations might be organized differently than how they are told they are or must be.

With the final two extracts of this section we find Colin Ward focusing further on schools, schooling and anarchism. In the first part "Anarchism and Schools", Ward explores William Godwin's educational writings from the eighteenth century. After outlining Godwin's arguments against national education policies and for small schools, Ward argues against the compulsory State education initiated in the nineteenth century in Britain. As he also argues with welfare policies, he controversially suggests that private, but community-run schools worked much better for working class families than did the authoritarian teaching methods of the new State schools. These schools did not segregate children by age or gender and tolerated irregular absences, and most importantly: 'they belonged to and were controlled by the local community rather than being imposed on the neighbourhood by an alien authority.' Ward goes on to briefly discuss other anarchist ideas and practices of schooling, supporting their practical rather than intellectual focus— Fourier's ideas of primary school focused on Cookery and Opera is one example, that he says may sound strange but were based on fun and enjoyment.

## THINKING THROUGH A PRAGMATIST ANARCHY: ANARCHY IN ACTION

In the final section of this reader, we gather together Ward's assorted writings on his political influences, his own thoughts on political theory and possible political future scenarios. This section moves from essays that discuss the importance of Martin Buber as a political thinker to extracts from different decades of his writings that map out Ward's vision of possible futures. Central to this section though is a key chapter from his main programmatic book, *Anarchy in Action*.

In 'Anarchy and a Plausible Future', Ward begins by reflecting on the nature of an Anarchist society. He then boldly suggests that such an outcome in our modern world is not only unlikely but most probably undesirable. This is because:

> The degree of social cohesion implied in the idea of 'an anarchist society' could only occur in a society so embedded in the cake of custom that the idea of *choice* among alternative patterns of social behaviour simply did not occur to people. I cannot imagine that degree of unanimity and I would dislike it if I could, because the idea of *choice* is crucial to any philosophy of freedom and spontaneity. So we don't have to worry about the boredom of utopia: we shan't get there.

Ward goes on to argue that if we are committed to human pluralism, it is both undesirable and unlikely that any society can be run by a single cohesive logic whether capitalist (the market), 'communist' state-socialist (the plan) or anarchist (through mutual aid). Ward argues that all societies, apart from the most totalitarian end, are plural societies that rely on diverse logics to coordinate themselves—often in contradictory ways. Where does this leave us then? An Anarchist society, with a capital 'A', is a social form that we need not be troubled with. However, Ward wants to argue that anarchism as a form of everyday life, is in fact always present in the self-organizing projects and decentralized institutions that constantly emerge to challenge the grip of authoritarian ideas and institutions. As such, having dispensed with the politics of absolutism and absolute utopia, Ward reformulates the basic politics of the libertarian left:

> The project then is to work in the here and now to facilitate and support the role of the huge array of decentralizing projects and forms of self organization which will 'widen the scope of free action and the potentiality for freedom in the society we have'. The point then of an anarchist politics is not a systematic installation of a new society but a substantial shifting of the balance in society towards self organizing social forms.

## ENGAGEMENTS

How can we interpret, evaluate and assess the influence and impact of Colin Ward's work? Early assessments of his contributions were divided. Ward's pragmatism left some anarchists distinctly uncomfortable with his work and he was criticised for being overly reformist.[36] Others have argued that his writing in the 1960s played a critical role (following on from the work of Paul Goodman, E.P. Thompson, David Wieck, Geoffery Oostergaard and others) in helping prefigure the move that the New Left took from state socialism to a more libertarian politics.[37] The reception to Ward's thinking though has steadily warmed over the decades, with the urban researcher and former editor of *New Society*, Paul Barker describing him as 'an environmentalist before most people knew what it meant'.[38] His revisions in anarchist political theory have been commended by Oxford political theorist Stuart White as playing a critical role in making anarchism respectable as a social philosophy.[39]

There is a sense though that outside the UK context Ward's writings have yet to generate the kind of sustained attention that has been accorded to the likes of post-war anarchists or libertarian socialists such as Murray Bookchin, Cornelius Castoriadis, André Gorz, Guy Debord or Henri Lefebvre. Perhaps this is related to the very distinct pedigree of Ward's writings. Ward's theoretical influences are cosmopolitan and wide-ranging. He draws from examples around the world to bolster arguments for anarchism, and there is a certain Italophilia running through much of his thought.[40] At the same time, his interest in documenting the histories of shanty towns and allotments, holiday camps and friendly societies, his interest in English rural and urban history, English local government, and changes in planning legislation clearly give a strong, and quite uniquely English flavour to many of his writings. There is a certain English pragmatism to Ward's reading of anarchism as a body of thought that recognises the virtues of the socialist critique of liberalism and the liberal critique of socialism. Despite his constant acknowledgements of the classic anarchist thinkers, Ward's writings seem far from the theatrics of Bakunin and arguably much closer to a trajectory of English radicalism that begins with the Levellers and the Diggers and moves through to Tom Paine, William Morris and George Orwell.

In terms of evaluating Ward's world view, a range of critical issues emerge. Perhaps the first matter that numerous friendly critics have pressed is the extent to which his critique of the state is entirely compelling and consistent.[41] As this anthology demonstrates, Ward's critique of technocracy, bureaucracy and centralism is well developed, and his writings provide many examples of the brutalism of the administrative state. His broader claims that state-centralised welfare systems can disempower individuals, create cultures of dependency, unravel systems of mutual aid and undermine incentives for engagement with self-organization are issues that liberals and socialists have all too often ignored—with damaging consequences. More generally, his critique of the damning effects of the institutionalization of experience—particularly as this pertains to contemporary experiences of childhood and the undermining of adult competencies—deserves serious reflection. His attempt to outline the historical insights of anarchism as 'a theory of organization', with its preference for institutions that take the form of flat networks rather than hierarchically organized pyramids, has taken on a curious life of its own —becoming a stock axiom of net culture as well as new management theory.[42] Yet, one might still wonder how far this defence of civil society and his critique of the state and centralism can be successfully pressed?

Some readers of this anthology may feel that Ward's writings too quickly sideline some of the positive aspects of the social-democratic welfare state and the deficiencies of nineteenth-century institutions like the friendly societies, particularly in terms of their limited social cover or their capacities to address poverty and inequality. Many will argue that comprehensive state provision of services in Britain and in other social democracies—in terms of health care, mental health and schooling—generated real gains that were indeed hard fought for and should not be so easily dismissed. Nevertheless, Ward's claim that a more effective and humane decentralized welfare system—one built upon and augmented by local strengths—could have been developed in the post-1945 era is intriguing. His claim that possibilities still exist for a more decentralised, democratic and locally grounded welfare system continues to shape contemporary debates in social policy.[43] His claim that patching together social welfare arrangements from the bottom up could well describe how many developing countries could proceed with their welfare strategies in the years to come.[44] His work more generally points to the continual frustrating inability to try to creatively think and practice forms of institutional innovation that are located neither in the realms of the state, the market, or non-democratic non-governmental organizations such as charities.[45]

Ward's observation that systems of mutual aid still play vital social roles in sustaining social bonds and the vitality of civil society in all societies, from rural peasant contexts to even the most free market driven societies, is indisputable. How such systems can be expanded and enriched though has long been a challenging question for the committed mutualist. Thick systems of mutual-aid have tended to flourish in socially and ethnically homogeneous groups, in communities of fate that have few exit options. An ongoing issue is how far such systems can be expanded across individuals, groups and communities in highly pluralist societies where multi-culturalism and expanded mobility can ensure that social ties and senses of social obligation are weak. The honest mutualist would have to concede that many institutions with roots in mutualist thinking from the Co-operative Movement to Building Societies in the UK have been disappointingly susceptible to market colonization.

It also has to be recognised that discourses of 'self-help', 'self-organization' and 'mutual aid' are regularly deployed by conservative forces—not only to embed a politics of 'personal responsibility' (which obscures the role that embedded structural/cultural advantages and pure luck plays in the reward system of contemporary society) but also to facilitate the withdrawal of state support from some of the most vulnerable members of society. Boltanski and Chapello have argued that the move in business organizations from hierarchical models of the Fordist era to new post-Fordist network models has indeed sought to expand employee initiative and relative work autonomy, but this has been at the cost of material and psychological security.[46] They maintain—somewhat ironically—that what they call the 'New Spirit of Capitalism' with the demand to be endlessly flexible, autonomous and self-organizing in networked workplaces, constitutes a remarkable recuperation of what they refer to as the "artistic critique" (what we might understand as the left libertarian critique) of capitalism, which, after May 1968, attacked the alienation of everyday life by capitalism and bureaucracy. Recent discussions of 'The Big Society' in British Conservative thought and praxis have sought to make value out of mutualist and associative language to push forward economic austerity.

Nevertheless, Ward, as a persistent optimist argues that the ongoing popularity of LETS (Local Exchange Trading Systems) schemes, free-cycle sites, urban community gardens, free art projects and the mass of voluntary labour more generally that sustains a range of vital services and resources from parent–teachers associations to blood donations, from clubs and co-ops to voluntary services abroad, suggests that mutualism is alive and well. Indeed, even in our fluid digital age numerous currents in Internet culture—from the rise of 'web 2.0' collaborative developments such as Wikipedia, open source software projects such as Linux to 'free cycle' sites, file sharing communities and beyond—suggest that a resilient and productive mutualism can re-emerge in the most free market of contexts.[47]

As this anthology demonstrates, Ward's work persistently seeks to make the case for the importance of local control and decentralisation. At the most basic level, his arguments are based in the anarchist moral insistence on the central value of human autonomy and the critique of the pernicious effects of standardization, bureaucracy and hierarchy. Ward also seeks to further convince non-anarchists by offering supplementary arguments: notably his writings stress the importance of vernacular cultures, the importance of a vital localism to foster grassroots democracy, mutual aid and community, and indeed the importance of marginality so as to foster social innovation.[48] Such arguments are important and are well made by Ward. The work of Nobel Prize winning political scientist Elinor Ostrom, which focuses on the many ways in which common resources can be successfully managed at the community level without privatization or government regulation, partially validates some elements of Ward's thinking.[49] However, the stronger argument that Ward sometimes pushes—that 'the local' offers intrinsically progressive spaces for political activity and that decentralized social and political forms are almost always optimal—are harder to sustain. A degree of spatial fetishism seems to enter into Ward's thinking here, which does not fully confront Doreen Massey's observation that a simple walk down a London High Street reveals not only that there is much of 'the global' bound up in 'the local', from foods to people, cultural flows to financial flows and that some of this is all to the good, but that the politics of these relational concepts can take on very different meanings in different contexts. Strong defences of 'the local' can as easily play as parochial, xenophobic and forms of closure, as they can self-empowerment and self management.[50] We are invariably 'for' some 'locals' (some forms of community empowerment) and some 'globals' (some defences of human rights and environmental justice) and against other 'locals' (xenophobia, Jim Crow) and other 'globals' (humanitarian intervention), etc.

To be fair to Ward, it has to be recognised that he is not an advocate of a simple localism. His writings invariably emphasise the importance of the local being connected through overlapping and diverse confederal networks that would serve many forms and move from the local to the global to encourage a type of democratic cosmopolitanism and multi-tiered interconnected localism. The extent to which this envisaged forms of institutional innovation could provide a check against parochialism, narrow-mindedness, racism, or indeed viable forms of co-ordinating mechanisms to replace state and other forms of organization such as transport networks, food production and distribution, and much more besides, is something the reader of this anthology will have to judge.

Beyond this, it could be wondered in what sense does Ward's defense of self-organized social forms actually aggregate up to substantive *political* forces pushing for social change? Two issues that deserve greater reflection emerge here. Firstly, as will be apparent from Ward's engagement with the work of Martin Buber,[51] Ward has a tendency to view 'the political' as a realm of manipulation in contrast to the realm of 'the social', which is seen as the site of real community reconstruction. This suppression of the political though might make readers wonder where political contestation, antagonism and the ongoing clash of different opinions is located in Ward's mutualist and communitarian vision of the future?[52] Second, Ward's vision of a pragmatic anarchism would seem to rely, somewhat ironically, on state structures and protection to prosper. For example, his concept of the 'DIY New Towns' attempts to envisage a facilitated form of self-organized urbanism where the state provides basic facilities, tools and infrastructure then withdraws to allow a diverse range of DIY or do-it-yourself self-build and low-impact activities to emerge from interested parties. It is a provocative idea. His view that strategic use can be made of local authority-based planning systems to deflect the prowl-ing development of private capital—but also to allow other possibilities for self-organized practices—is interesting. The local state is often appealed to in Ward's writings as a mechanism that could facilitate the transfer of squats to the status of housing co-operatives. Yet in all these contexts, it is striking that to prosper, the self-organizing projects that he would like to see flourish would seem to rely on the existence not simply of a 'night watchman' state[53] but of a benign liberal-social democratic interventionist state.[54/55]

Ward's work to be sure has its limitations.[56] Such critical issues pushed too far can also miss much. Colin Ward does not provide us with a form of anarchism marked by philosophical pyrotechnics produced by long years in graduate school obsessing about the latest ethical or ontological conundrums posed by continental philosophy. Nor does his work present us with a total theory that dogmatically demands allegiance.[57] Informed by a pragmatic empirical humanism, whether supporting the idea of the DIY new town, housing co-operatives or self-build, he is defending 'the freedom to experiment' and, as such, his work as a whole allows and indeed invites anarchists and non-anarchists alike to read and reflect, engage and argue with him.

## THE VALUE AND IMPACT OF WARD'S WORK

An evaluation of the impact of Ward's work is a complex matter. As an anarchist theorist, his presence with the Freedom Press group has loomed large over the landscape of British anarchism over the last five decades. As a journalist and a columnist for such general interest publications as *Town and Country Planning*, *New Society*, *New Statesman*, *The Guardian*, *Prospect*, and so on, there is no doubt that Ward's reach (in the UK at least) has been much more extensive than many of his cherished influences. Ward's writings have also had a diffuse but significant impact in the academy. Most notably he has had a significant influence on pro-gressive and radical planners, housing specialists and human geographers in the UK. Urban sociologists and sociologists of everyday life have been drawn to his work, as have scholars working in British rural studies.

Ward's work on environmental education at the TCPA with Anthony Fyson (who worked with him there for several years) and Eileen Adams (on the project 'Art and the Built Environment') opened up new lines of engagement with teach-ers and school students. His accessible books and articles (and his engagement in public meetings over the decades) have been taken up and read by an assorted range of community and environmental activists. There are good reasons to feel that his writings on housing played an important role in humanising and historicising (at least in some quarters) what we now call squatting. It is worth noting that his ear-liest writings on squatting were enthusiastically reprinted by the London Squat-ters Campaign in the late 1960s onwards. In the 1970s and 1980s, he was an in-demand public speaker, contributing to many public meetings on a huge range of housing issues. From these experiences he stated: 'My proudest moment as a writer came when the chair holder of a tenant's co-operative in Liverpool held up a copy of *Tenants Take Over*, falling to bits in his hands, and said. "Here's the man who wrote the Old Testament, but *we built* the new Jerusalem".[58] His advocacy of ten-ants' self management, whilst heretical to socialists at the time, has now become something of a new orthodoxy in progressive housing policy circles.[59] More gener-ally, an enormous range of social movements from farmers markets and land trusts to individuals involved in LETS schemes and community centres have expressed, and acted on, the politics of self-management that he has defended and sought to popularise in his books and columns for various journals and magazines.

## FUTURES

What then is the legacy of Ward's work? What future discussions might it pro-ductively engage with and prompt? Ward has suggested that a defining feature of all of his writings is the relationship between people and their environments, and there are good reasons for feeling that, in terms of the politics of the 'environ-ment', his writings offer much. His form of environmentalism, as will be evident from this book, is of a rather different variety than either early-twentieth century preservation-orientated currents or the influential 'ecocentric' forms of environ-mentalism that have been more influential of late.

Rather than work through the realm of formal ethics or deploy moralism to develop an environmental sensibility towards the abstract of a singular 'nature' which then ushers in a set of 'dos and don'ts' towards environmental protection, Ward's work has emphasised the importance of listening to, encouraging and de-veloping people's material and 'embodied knowledge' of their environments. In this he emphasises the importance of environmental and design education and attending to the range of ways in which people productively work within, aes-thetically engage with and transform the environments they are wholly ensconced within, but can all too easily be alienated from. It is an 'environmentalism' that is much less interested in 'protecting' or viewing the countryside as a 'green mu-seum'[60] and much more concerned with obtaining 'popular sovereignty' over what are always seen as dynamically transformed landscapes. It is a set of writings that, following Kropotkin, provocatively emphasises the virtues of the worked environ-ment, both in terms of rural and urban life. It is also a form of environmentalism that maintains a keen eye to the politics of misanthropy—whether buried in the narratives of preservationists or in neo-Malthusian arguments about the tragedy of the commons.[61]

There are many virtues of these aspects of Ward's thinking. Most obvious is that he provides a way of thinking about society-nature relations that accepts that we live in thoroughly modified worlds.[62] The central question then is not whether we should transform or produce nature but how and with what consequences. Ward's thinking is also useful because he provides us with an environmental poli-tics that is not afraid to break from orthodox ideas. For example, whilst increas-ing urban density has now become something of an orthodoxy in much of the literature and policy on sustainability, Ward has long held to the view that the push *out* of the city had a clearly liberating effect.[63] For Ward, the experiments in a redeveloped high-density inner-city living of the modernist period has not worked and what needs to be worked on is what has worked. Controversially, he argues that one aspect that has partially worked are the New Town social policies of the post-1945 period in the UK. "Indeed one of the best kept secrets of social policy is that the post-war New Towns, by comparison with suburban expansion or high-density inner-city redevelopment, were a social and financial success and were far more economical in land use than any other form of urban expansion."[64]

Moreover, Ward's work is provocative in arguing that the British countryside should be a 'peopled place' not some overly protected heritage-cum-theme-park landscape. He argues for a countryside that is not just for tourism and the wealthy, mingled with intensive agriculture, but a place where conservation, diversity of people and ecology is part of life.

Ward's writing focusing on children has spanned many decades and it is a body of work that continues to hold insights. The very idea we should aim to construct cities and urban places that allow children to have the freedom to roam, to play on the streets, to have time for autonomous play and doing nothing in particular (with no adults around) is prescient. The argument that they should have time for adventure with other children in the city—so that they can learn to be street smart, develop their sociability, a basic sense of social justice and indeed develop some elementary sense of aesthetics for (what are erroneously separately termed) the built and natural environment—is an idea and group of practices that are in serious danger of extinction in some parts of the USA, the UK, and beyond. Ward's work should prompt reflection on the extent to which, in many parts of the affluent world, we have now constructed a tightly controlled and domesticated experience of childhood where children are coddled, protected, controlled and increasingly groomed for economic and social 'success'. Ward observes in his essay 'In the Sandbox of the City' that:

> We no longer cow our children into submission, in fact we indulge them as consumers, with the powerful aid of the advertising industry, but we fail to induct them into a world of adult decision-making, perhaps just because as adults we have delegated to others the habit of deciding.[65]

This simple observation continues to resonate in a time where paranoid parenting[66] is so commonplace. Ken Worpole could well be correct with his statement that: "Putting childhood centre-stage, may perhaps be anarchism's (and Ward's) single most important contribution to social policy and political thought."[67]

In terms of the politics of left and right, Ward's work is interesting because it does buck some traditional left-right distinctions. His writings address social pathologies generated by the state and the market. Somewhat interestingly for a person of the left, Ward has suggested that the desire to be self-employed is deeply rooted in a desire for autonomy. Small local businesses have also often been viewed as playing a potentially positive role in promoting social change.[68] These commitments may well be seem as examples of petit-bourgeois Proudhonism to some, but the notion that the self-employed and indeed small business could play an important role in a progressive coalition for social change has been raised again most recently by social and political theorists such as Roberto Unger.[69]

Colin Ward's work does not offer all the answers. He would never have claimed it could or should. His work is both necessary and refreshing to read though because at the root of his writings lies a deep commitment to defending the values of autonomy and solidarity. In an age when the capable subject, and the possibilities for building rich cultures of solidarities, are too often placed in doubt, Ward's writings invite us to think and practice differently.

# Section One

Life, Politics and Journalism

# 1. TALKING ANARCHY:
# COLIN WARD IN CONVERSATION
# WITH DAVID GOODWAY

**David Goodway:** *First and most obviously, tell me about how you became an anarchist?*

**Colin Ward:** I came from a Labour Party family in one of the East suburbs of London and I knew about the existence of anarchism because of the Spanish war. My father was the youngest of a family of ten from the East India Dock Road, where his father was described as a "general dealer."[1] In his early teens, he became a "pupil teacher" at the school he attended and subsequently won a place at a teacher-training college. After the First World War, whilst teaching at the London docklands, he earned a degree in geography at the London School of Economics, one of the few institutions catering for that kind of part-time study. My mother was the daughter of a carpenter from the same area of London.

I passed what is known as the scholarship examination to the local High School, but left at the end of the fourth year at 15 in 1939. I must have been a disappointment to my parents, and I am sure that my father felt that, if I was not capable of the sustained effort he had imposed on himself, there was no point in pushing me to succeed. One of my big interests as a boy was in printing ... I bought an old treadle operated press, and a friend of my brother who worked for a newspaper used to bring home old parcels of old type for me. Later when I wanted to show him the results of his kindness, I learned that he had been killed in an air raid.

I failed to find a job in the printing trade, but my third job in 1941 was working on the drawing board for an elderly architect[2] whose own history went back to William Morris and the Arts and Crafts Movement of the 1890s. His own work had dwindled to temporary repairs to factories in the East End of London, very familiar to me, which had been destroyed in the blitz of September 1940.... I drifted into the world of architecture when a boy, in a way that would be impossible today when training is dominated by the schools of architecture and professional qualifications ...

But, like any young worker in the centre of London for the first time, I spent a lot of time exploring the city itself, and remember discovering the Socialist Book

---

Originally printed in Colin Ward and David Goodway, *Talking Anarchy*. (Nottingham: Five Leaves, 2003), 21–24, 33–49.

Centre in Essex Street, off the Strand, run by Orwell's friend Jon Kimche. It was there that I discovered Orwell's writings, hard to find elsewhere, and journals like *Tribune* and the *New Leader*.

Like any 18-year-old (for I knew no war-resisters), I was conscripted into the army in 1942 and, because of my occupation, was automatically sent to join the Royal Engineers. I was taught how to build bridges and how to make explosions, but there must have been a sudden shortage of draftsmen because, in the extraordinary way that military strategy works, I was sent to the Army School of Hygiene, to make large scale drawings of latrines and of deadly insects, as a guide to camp builders and sanitary engineers.

... In the Autumn of 1943, the same vagaries of military strategy sent me to Glasgow in Scotland, to work in a requisitioned mansion in Park Terrace with a wonderful panorama of the smoky city below us, where heavy industry was booming for the first time since the First World War. My Sundays were free, and I would spend them exploring the city, and its wonderful ... Mitchell Library, until it was time to hear the open air political orators. Glasgow had a long tradition of political oratory, and at this time, anarchism was represented by two remarkable witty and sardonic speakers, Eddie Shaw and Jimmy Dick. They handed out leaflets directing us to the anarchist bookstore in George Street ...

*They were working men, weren't they, and ideologically, managed to combine individualism and syndicalism?*

Yes, you are right. Both the propagandists I mentioned linked the most apparently incompatible versions of anarchism. But for me, the most impressive of the Glasgow anarchists was Frank Leech. He was an Irishman, not from Ireland, but from Lancashire in England, a Navy boxing champion in the First World War. He had a general shop in one of the housing estates on the fringe of the city. There he had housed refugees from Germany and from Spain, and operated a printing press. When I told him about the material from official American publications that I had read in the Mitchell library describing plans for post-war Europe, he urged me to put it together in articles for the London publication *War Commentary—for Anarchism* ... I did this and the material appeared in ... December, 1943[3].

By that time Frank Leech was in trouble with the law and was anxious to make propaganda out of staging a hunger strike in Barlinnie Prison. He was a much-loved character, and his friends, worried about his health, urged me to attempt to visit him at the prison to persuade him to abandon his hunger strike. They thought that a soldier in uniform, with a London rather than a Glasgow accent would be more likely to be admitted by the prison governor. My visit to the prison was evidently noted, because immediately afterwards I was posted by the army to a maintenance unit in the Orkney and Shetland Islands ...

There is an irony here. My suspected unreliability kept me in safety for the rest of the war, while many other conscripts of my generation died in forgotten and meaningless battles in South-East Asia.

But I had been won for anarchism by the busy self-educated Glasgow propagandists, who had put me in touch with their bookshop, selling the range of anarchist literature and, by post, with the Freedom Press bookshop in London.

*Why did anarchism so appeal, at a time when enthusiasm for Soviet Communism was at its zenith?*

I am not quite sure how I managed not to be swept up into the Stalin-worship that infected the British left. But the literature on sale at the anarchist bookshop in Glasgow included the writings of Emma Goldman and Alexander Berkman. Frank Leech himself printed and published Emma Goldman's pamphlet *Trotsky Protests Too Much*. I was influenced very early by the writings of Arthur Koestler and George Orwell. Lilian Wolfe, a veteran from earlier years of Freedom Press, put me on her mailing list for copies of several dissenting journals, like for example, Dwight Macdonald's *Politics* from 1944, whose common factor was hostility to the blanket Stalinism of the regular left-wing press. Also in 1944, Freedom Press first published Marie Louise Berneri's book *Workers in Stalin's Russia....* It argued that the fundamental test of any political regime was "How do the workers fare under it?" and that, by this test, the Soviet regime was a disaster, with the same extremes of wealth and poverty as the capitalist world....

*You were belatedly released from the army in 1947 and you were immediately asked to join the Freedom Press Group, weren't you? Who were the most important figures of this extremely talented group and how did they influence you?*

They certainly were an extremely talented group, and they made a deep impression on me, becoming lifelong friends.... Early in 1946, I was moved from Orkney (no longer a threat to national security) to another unit of the Royal Engineers, camped on a polo ground in South West London, where our task was to dig latrines for the soldiers, sailors and airmen taking part in a Victory Parade in Hyde Park (which had been populated by sheep all through the war.) This enabled me to write a series of reports on the squatters' movement that emerged, with the seizure by homeless families of empty military camps,[4] but also to attend the meetings organised by the London Anarchist Group and by the Freedom Defence Committee, which was organising meetings to focus attention on the plight of at least a hundred refugees from the Spanish war, who had been used as forced labour during the German occupation of France, and were treated by the British as prisoners of war and imprisoned in Lancashire.

The key figures were undoubtedly Vero [Vernon Richards] and Marie Louise [Berneri], simply because they had been involved with the task of producing an anarchist journal since 1936, when he was aged 21, and she since she came to live in England in 1937 at the age of 18, after her father was murdered in Barcelona. Their knowledge of international anarchism, its trends and personalities, as well, of course, as their easy use of four languages, added weight to their opinions.

Vero had great charm and relished the art of cooking delicious meals with simple ingredients. He had trained as a civil engineer and until his arrest[5] had been working on railway building. His conversation on railway design was fascinating, although he never wrote on the subject. Sadly, he has died, at the age of 86, during the course of our conversations. I have always regretted that I was never able to persuade him to write about the aspects of life, whether as a city child, or about railways or horticulture, where he had direct personal experience to share.

And of course *everyone* fell in love with Marie Louise. There is a famous English diarist, Frances Partridge, who on 22 January 1941 described a visit to the writer Gerald Brenan and his wife: "They had staying with them their Italian anarchist friend, Maria Luisa, wife of the son of King Bomba, the Soho grocer. She is, I think, the most beautiful girl I ever saw, and with this goes great sweetness, a low husky voice and apparent intelligence". And when Lewis Mumford, himself the author of a survey of utopias, reviewed Marie Louise's *Journey Through Utopia*, he found it to be "such a book as only a brave intelligence and an ardent spirit can produce".

Another immensely useful member of the Freedom Press Group in those days was George Woodcock. He was born in Canada in 1912 and had been brought to England as a child. In 1949 he returned to Canada, where he became one of that country's best-known writers. He had begun the Second World War as a pacifist and had started a literary magazine *Now* in 1940, and in 1942 had become one of the busy writers and editors of *War Commentary*.

He was by far the most prolific of the new pamphleteers, writing a series of pamphlets in that area where anarchist propaganda in English, and probably in other languages, has been weakest: the application of anarchist ideas to specific social issues. I was drawn to his writing because among these was his study of *Railways and Society* and his pamphlet on housing *Homes or Hovels*? But especially important for me was his study of regionalism in a series of articles in *Freedom* (later subsumed, I suppose, in his biography of Kropotkin) where he made the connections between the French regional geographers like Réclus, by way of Kropotkin and Patrick Geddes, with Ebenezer Howard's decentralist ideology and the Regional Planning Association of America and the work of Lewis Mumford. ...

My colleagues in the Freedom Group influenced me greatly, not only about the interpretation of anarchism, but also about most other things. You must remember that I had been in the army from the age of 18 to that of 23, much of that time spent in a remote part of Britain, and was suddenly part of, by my standards, a sophisticated and cosmopolitan milieu. One of these new joys was food, and especially the French and Italian cuisine....

Another was music. Like most English children of my generation, I had been educated in music by the BBC, and it was a joy to have friends like Vero and John Hewetson who would discuss the chamber music of Beethoven, Haydn and Mozart, and the operas of Verdi with immense enthusiasm, rushing to the gramophone to illustrate the arguments from their big collections of 78 rpm discs. Unlike them, I was also, like Philip, a devotee of New Orleans jazz. In the late 1940s, Philip was working part-time, together with the jazz and blues singer George Melly, for the surrealist dealer E.L.T. Mesens at the London Gallery in Brook Street.

George Melly, who is the same age as me, is still giving pleasure to jazz audiences and never fails to declare his allegiance to anarchism. He was brought to anarchist ideas by the penny pamphlet by George Woodcock, *What is Anarchism?*, when he was in the Navy.

But perhaps the most important influence on me from the Freedom Press Group was in its attitudes to sexual freedom and enlightenment. This was most certainly not on the agenda of any other political group, least of all the Marxists. Marie Louise's article "Sexuality and Freedom" in George Woodcock's magazine *Now* (No. 5, in 1945) was one of the earliest discussions anywhere in the British press of the theories of Wilhelm Reich. And John Hewetson was a well-known pioneer among male doctors, both for freely available contraception and for abortion on demand....

*Would you give me some idea of the Group's way of life? I'm thinking of producing* Freedom*; selling* Freedom*; public meetings and oratory; friendships and relationships; summer schools and camps and holidays; children; families; and education; and the relation between the central core and a wider group of supporters and sympathisers.*

When I was invited to join the Freedom Press Group in 1947, it had leased the Freedom Bookshop in central London and had bought the Express Printers in an alley off Whitechapel High Street in the East End. Editorial meetings ... were merry, social occasions.... Current events were discussed and responsibility to write about them was distributed around the group.

Most of us knew, or learned, how to mark up material for the typesetter, how to correct proofs and how to paste-up the "dummy" of the paper....Within the group there was absolute trust. We did not read each other's contributions to check on their ideological acceptability.

Most of us developed some experience of indoor and outdoor speaking ...

*But tell me more about the anarchist culture of the 1940s and 1950s.*

In the 1950s the idea of an anarchist club in central London was explored, and it started with a cellar in Holborn, not far from the Freedom Bookshop. By 1954 it had moved, as the Malatesta Club, to Percy Street, near Tottenham Court Road, an area where German, Russian and Italian anarchists had settled almost a century earlier. Malatesta had lived there, working as an electrician. The club attracted traditional jazz and a long series of interesting speakers....

Burgess Hill School was a progressive school in North London, with several anarchists, Tony Weaver, Tony Gibson and Marjorie Mitchell, on its teaching staff, and so far as I can remember, it was there that the first postwar Anarchist Summer School was held in 1947....

There was, in fact, more anarchist social life in London than the people whose Sundays were devoted to writing anarchist propaganda could possibly become engaged in....

As an anarchist propagandist I have been interested for many years in the sociology of autonomous groups, and the Freedom Press Group as I first knew it seems to me to be an interesting example, having a secure internal network based on friendship and shared skills, and a series of external networks of contacts in a variety of fields....

It was at Burgess Hill that I first met Herbert Read, who was one of that school's directors. His book *Poetry and Anarchism*, first published by Faber in 1938, and followed by his *The Philosophy of Anarchism*, from Freedom Press in 1940, were among the vital books whose influence led people of my generation, as well as those a little older, to describe themselves as anarchists. This is true of a great variety of readers including Murray Bookchin. ...

I first met Alex Comfort when I was still in the army, but was free to attend Sunday night meetings of the London Anarchist Group in 1946; and I met George Orwell, drinking tea in an ante-room of the Holborn Hall in Grays Inn Road, when George Woodcock persuaded him to talk at a meeting to demand the release of those unfortunate Spaniards detained first by the Germans and then by the British in France, who were still interned in a prison camp in Lancashire.

*Read and Comfort were the best-known British anarchists of the time. How did you react to them as individuals? And what is your assessment of their work?*

Read was a quiet, gentle person and, if we ever met, I was hesitant to approach him because I knew he was continually harassed by unpublished poets or novelists who were soliciting his help in getting their great works published. My only concern was to ask his permission to reprint a broadcast of his in *Freedom* or *Anarchy*.

I valued Read because his anarchist propaganda reached a wider audience than most of us could expect. And his *Education Through Art*, together with his Freedom Press pamphlet *The Education of Free Men*, were important, not for themselves, but for giving a climate of respectability to teachers I met, fighting on their own for the recognition of the role of the arts in education. In the late 1970s I was employed to propagate (among other things) the role of art in environmental education and I found Read's writings an important certificate of intellectual respectability. You may smile, but this was very valuable to me at the time. ...

Relations with Alex Comfort were easier, because he had a jolly, joking nature. As you know, his first public advocacy of sexual freedom was in his Freedom Press book *Barbarism and Sexual Freedom*, in 1948, built around his lectures to the London Anarchist Group. No modern reader, half a century later, can appreciate the stifling sexual climate of ordinary life in those days, and can see how subtle a liberator Comfort was, in using ridicule to undermine authoritarian attitudes ...

*You once mentioned to me how small groups can have an influence entirely disproportionate to their actual numbers. You named, to my surprise, the French Impressionists as an example. Would you care to elaborate on this?*

Yes, I spoke of Alex Comfort's advice that we anarchists should learn from the sociologists. I took his advice more seriously than most of his admirers and one of the documents I studied was the 1959 (final) issue of the American bulletin, *Au-*

*tonomous Groups*, which contained an account of "The Batignolles Group—Creators of Impressionism" by Maria Rogers, and another of "The Old Gang, Nucleus of Fabianism" by Charles Kitzen.

The French Impressionists were a group of painters, mostly excluded by the Paris Salon, who included anarchists, for example Pissarro, and right-wingers, for example, Degas. They formed an influential informal network built around the cafés where they met.

> In their meetings at the Café Guerbois, the painters expressed themselves freely, gained understanding of one another's aims, ideas, theories, and techniques, formulated criteria for judging their contemporaries, and jointly explored new influences ...

The group, with its ever-widening circles of influence, disintegrated, but not before it had conquered the art market, and achieved recognition: the aim that brought them together in the first place.

In Britain, the nickname "the Old Gang" was given to a small group (George Bernard Shaw, Sidney and Beatrice Webb, Sydney Olivier and Graham Wallas) who dominated the socialist organisation, the Fabian Society, from 1886 until 1911, and established the character of the Labour Party for most of the subsequent hundred years. Originally, the Society had held a wider view of socialism and had included the anarchist Charlotte Wilson, who in 1886 had, with Kropotkin, founded the journal *Freedom*. Obviously, as anarchists, we deplore the statist, bureaucratic version of socialism that the Fabian Old Gang bequeathed to Britain. They came together, initiated a programme, and separated, not before achieving their original objective. Like the Impressionists, they exercised an influence far beyond their numbers. Both these groups, in totally different spheres of life were remarkably effective as autonomous groups.

*And their importance for anarchists?*

It is because, traditionally, anarchists have conceived of the whole of social organisation as a series of interlocking networks of autonomous groups. So we should pay serious attention to studies of effective ones. In the journal *Anarchy* I twice drew attention to these particular studies. (In *Anarchy* no 8, Oct 1961, pp. 230–231, and in *Anarchy* no 77, July 1967, pp. 206–208, where I condensed Dorothy Blitzen's conclusions from that bulletin *Autonomous Groups*.)

My personal experience of the dynamics of autonomous groups has been as a close observer of housing co-operatives in the 1970s, and as an active member of the Freedom Press Group from the late 1940s to the 1960s. Dr Blitzen distinguished autonomous groups from other forms of organisation associated with hierarchies of relationships, fixed divisions of labour, and explicit rules and practices.

In autonomous groups she noted "the degree of individual autonomy, the complete reliance on direct reciprocities for decisions for action affecting them all" which are not characteristic of larger organisations, and she observed "the flux of temporary leadership by one or another member." And she remarks that "it would be difficult to imagine a voluntary group made up of anything but peers. The range of inequality between members cannot be too great. Even in the instance of a voluntary association of a master and his students, the students manifest a fair repertoire of the master's skills, must approach or even equal his level of intelligence and, over time, narrow the gap between his abilities and theirs."

She also observed that in both the cases studied, the Impressionists and the Fabian "Old Gang", the groups began and ended with a series of friendships, while "similar interests, goals, skills, talents, or anything else, do not of themselves evoke associations. We often overlook the simple fact that people have to meet"; and she added that,

> It strikes me that autonomous groups do not so much promote friendship and sentiments that are friendly as organised them when circumstances bring them together, or particular goals required grouping for the achievement of particular ends. In the end, when the group no longer existed, the individuals and their friendships persisted.

One of the characteristics of those two disparate groups, the Impressionists and the Fabians, was that individual members provided links with a series of other specialist networks and interest groups. The Freedom Group in the days when I was asked to join it had links with the literary world through George Woodcock, with the world of the emergent Health Service and the field of contraception and sexual politics through John Hewetson, with the anarchist publishing groups in other languages through Marie Louise and Vero, with trade unionism and syndicalism through Philip, through several of us with the field of progressive education, and with me to those of architecture, housing and planning.

These links were of lasting importance to me and they certainly affected the quality of *Freedom* and of Freedom Press publications.

*You developed a great empathy for all things Italian, didn't you? How did this originate?*

... I was a keen reader of the novels of Ignazio Silone during the war, and reviewed the English version of Carlo Levi's *Christ Stopped at Eboli* in *Freedom* in 1948 ... Predictably I was attracted by the postwar Neo-Realism of the Italian cinema. I remember meeting Riccardo Argno, then the London correspondent of *La Stampa*, who remarked that the interesting thing about London was that the poor formed queues in the East End to see bad films about the rich, while the rich formed queues in the West End to see good films about the poor....

In 1948 I translated (badly) from *Volontà*, Giancarlo [DeCarlo]'s article on housing problems in Italy....

You are right that I do feel a great empathy with some aspects of Italian life.... One is in attitudes to children.... Another aspect of Italy which I find attractive ... is the small workshop economy that we can observe in regions like Emilia-Romagna, which I had the opportunity to examine in ... *Welcome, Thinner City*....

*Your own conception of anarchism was surely very different from that of the rest of the Freedom Press Group. How did you come to develop it? ...*

We all have our characteristic ways of thinking. My mode of thinking has its limitations and its advantages. I tend to think in terms of practical examples or actual experiences rather than theories or hypotheses. This has its useful aspects, but it also means that there is a whole range of theoretical literature that I find too tedious to read. Another aspect of the way I think, and in spite of what I have just said, is that, although I have no background in sociology, my way of looking at most things is a sociological approach....

Two big influences on me in the 1950s were Martin Buber's essay "Society and the State" published in English in 1951 and Alexander Herzen's *From the Other Shore* published in English in 1956. Other influences were ... Paul Goodman and David Wieck who related anarchism to ordinary decisions of daily life, in such journals as *Resistance* and *Liberation* and, earlier, *Politics*.

Speculating about "The Unwritten Handbook" in *Freedom* for 28 June 1958, I wrote that

> To my mind the most striking feature of the unwritten handbook of twentieth century anarchism is not its rejection of the insights of the classic anarchist thinkers, Godwin, Proudhon, Bakunin, Kropotkin, but its widening and deepening of them. But it is selective, it rejects perfectionism, utopian fantasy, conspiratorial romanticism, revolutionary optimism; it draws from the classical anarchists their most valid, not their most questionable ideas. And it adds to them the subtler contribution of ... Landauer and Malatesta. It also adds the evidence provided in this century by the social sciences, by psychology and anthropology, and by technical change.
>
> It is still an anarchism of present and permanent protest—how could it be anything else in our present peril? But it is one which recognises that the choices between libertarian and authoritarian solutions occurs every day and in every way. And the extent to which we choose, or accept, or are fobbed off with, or lack the imagination or inventiveness to discover alternatives to, authoritarian solutions to small problems is the extent to which we are their powerless victims in big affairs. We are powerless to change the course of events over the nuclear arms race, imperialism and so on, precisely because we have surrendered our power over everything else....

I don't think my fellow members of the Freedom Press Group would have found this opinion objectionable from an anarchist point of view.

# 2. THE STATE

*"As long as today's problems are stated in terms of mass politics and 'mass organ-
isation', it is clear that only States and mass parties can deal with them. But if the
solutions that can be offered by the existing States and parties are acknowledged
to be either futile or wicked, or both, then we must look not only for different
'solutions' but especially for a different way of stating the problems themselves."*
—Andrea Caffi

If you look at the history of socialism, reflecting on the melancholy difference
between promise and performance, both in those countries where socialist parties
have triumphed in the struggle for political power, and in those where they have
never attained it, you are bound to ask yourself what went wrong, when and why.
Some would see the Russian revolution of 1917 as the fatal turning point in the
socialist history. Others would look as far back as the February revolution of 1848
in Paris as 'the starting point of the two-fold development of European socialism,
anarchistic and Marxist', while many would locate the critical point of divergence
as the congress of the International at the Hague in 1872, when the exclusion of
Bakunin and the anarchists signified the victory of Marxism. In one of his prophetic criticisms of Marx that year Bakunin previsaged the whole subsequent history of Communist society:

> Marx is an authoritarian and centralising communist. He wants what we
> want, the complete triumph of economic and social equality, but he wants it
> in the State and through the State power, through the dictatorship of a very
> strong and, so to say, despotic provisional government, that is by the nega-
> tion of liberty. His economic ideal is the State as sole owner of the land and
> of all kinds of capital, cultivating the land under the management of State
> engineers, and controlling all industrial and commercial associations with
> State capital. We want the same triumph of economic and social equality
> through the abolition of the State and of all that passes by the name of law
> (which, in our view, is the permanent negation of human rights). We want
> the reconstruction of society and the unification of mankind to be achieved,
> not from above downwards by any sort of authority, not by socialist officials,
> engineers, and other accredited men of learning—but from below upwards,

Originally printed in Colin Ward, *Anarchy in Action,* Second Edition. (London: Freedom
Press, 1988), 17–27.

by the free federation of all kinds of workers' associations liberated from the yoke of the State.

The home-grown English variety of socialism reached the point of divergence later. It was possible for one of the earliest Fabian Tracts to declare in 1886 that 'English Socialism is not yet Anarchist or Collectivist, not yet defined enough in point of policy to be classified. There is a mass of Socialistic feeling not yet conscious of itself as Socialism. But when the unconscious Socialists of England discover their position, they also will probably fall into two parties: a Collectivist party supporting a strong central administration and a counterbalancing Anarchist party defending individual initiative against that administration.' The Fabians rapidly found which side of the watershed was theirs and when a Labour Party was founded they exercised a decisive influence on its policies. At its annual conference in 1918 the Labour Party finally committed itself to that interpretation of socialism which identified it with the unlimited increase of the State's power and activity through its chosen form: the giant managerially-controlled public corporation.

And when socialism has achieved power what has it created? Monopoly capitalism with a veneer of social welfare as a substitute for social justice. The large hopes of the nineteenth century have not been fulfilled; only the gloomy prophecies have come true. The criticism of the state and of the structure of its power and authority made by the classical anarchist thinkers has increased in validity and urgency in the century of total war and the total state, while the faith that the conquest of state power would bring the advent of socialism has been destroyed in every country where socialist parties have won a parliamentary majority, or have ridden to power on the wave of a popular revolution, or have been installed by Soviet tanks. What has happened is exactly what the anarchist Proudhon, over a hundred years ago, said would happen. All that has been achieved is 'a compact democracy having the appearance of being founded on the dictatorship of the masses, but in which the masses have no more power than is necessary to ensure a general serfdom in accordance with the following precepts and principles borrowed from the old absolutism: indivisibility of public power, all-consuming centralisation, systematic destruction of all individual, corporative and regional thought (regarded as disruptive), inquisitorial police.'

Kropotkin, too, warned us that 'The State organization, having been the force to which the minorities resorted for establishing and organising their power over the masses, cannot be the force which will serve to destroy these privileges,' and he declared that 'the economic and political liberation of man will have to create new forms for its expression in life, instead of those established by the State.' He thought it self-evident that 'this new form will have to be more popular, more decentralised, and nearer to the folk-mote self-government than representative government can ever be,' reiterating that we will be compelled to find new forms of organisation for the social functions that the state fulfils through the bureaucracy, and that 'as long as this is not done, nothing will be done'.

When we look at the *powerlessness* of the individual and the small face-to-face group in the world today and ask ourselves *why* they are powerless, we have to answer not merely that they are weak because of the vast central agglomerations of power in the modern, military-industrial state, but that they are weak *because* they have surrendered their power to the state. It is as though every individual possessed a certain quantity of power, but that by default, negligence, or thoughtless and unimaginative habit or conditioning, he has allowed someone else to pick it up, rather than use it himself for his own purposes. ('According to Kenneth Boulding, there is only so much human energy around. When large organisations utilise these energy resources, they are drained away from the other spheres.')

Gustav Landauer, the German anarchist, made a profound and simple contribution to the analysis of the state and society in one sentence: 'The state is not something which can be destroyed by a revolution, but is a condition, a certain relationship between human beings, a mode of human behaviour; we destroy it by contracting other relationships, by behaving differently.' It is *we* and not an abstract outside identity, Landauer implies, who behave in one way or the other, politically or socially. Landauer's friend and executor, Martin Buber, begins his essay *Society and the State* with an observation of the sociologist, Robert MacIver, that 'to identify the social with the political is to be guilty of the grossest of all confusions, which completely bars any understanding of either society or the state.' The political principle, for Buber, is characterised by power, authority, hierarchy, dominion. He sees the social principle wherever men link themselves in an association based on a common need or a common interest.

What is it, Buber asks, that gives the political principle its ascendancy? And he answers, 'the fact that every people feels itself threatened by the others gives the state its definite unifying power; it depends upon the instinct of self-preservation of society itself; the latent external crisis enables it to get the upper hand in internal crises ... All forms of government have this in common: each possesses more power than is required by the given conditions; in fact this excess in the capacity for making dispositions is actually what we understand by political power. The measure of this excess which cannot, of course, be computed precisely, represents the exact difference between administration and government.' He calls this excess the 'political surplus' and observes that 'its justification derives from the external and internal instability, from the latent state of crisis between nations and within every nation. The political principle is always stronger in relation to the social principle than the given conditions require. The result is continuous diminution in social spontaneity.'

The conflict between these two principles is a permanent aspect of the human condition. Or as Kropotkin put it: 'Throughout the history of our civilisation, two traditions, two opposed tendencies, have been in conflict: the Roman tradition and the popular tradition, the imperial tradition and the federalist tradition, the authoritarian tradition and the libertarian tradition.' There is an inverse correlation between the two: the strength of one is the weakness of the other. If we want to strengthen society we must weaken the state. Totalitarians of all kinds realise this, which is why they invariably seek to destroy those social institutions which they cannot dominate. So do the dominant interest groups in the state, like the alliance of big business and the military establishment for the 'permanent war economy' suggested by the Secretary of Defence Charles E. Wilson in the United States, which has since become so dominant that even Eisenhower, in his last address as President, felt obliged to warn us of its menace.

Shorn of the metaphysics with which politicians and philosophers have enveloped it, the state can be defined as a political mechanism using force, and to the sociologist it is *one* among many forms of social organisation. It is, however, 'distinguished from all other associations by its exclusive investment with the final power of coercion.' And against whom is this final power directed? It is *directed* at the enemy without, but it is *aimed* at the subject society *within*.

This is why Buber declared that it is the maintenance of the latent external crisis that enables the state to get the upper hand in internal crises. Is this a conscious procedure? Is it simply that 'wicked' men control the state, so that we could put things right by voting for 'good' men? Or is it a fundamental characteristic of the state as an institution? It was because she drew this final conclusion that Simone Weil declared that 'The great error of nearly all studies of war, an error into which all socialists have fallen, has been to consider war as an episode in foreign politics, when it is especially an act of interior politics, and the most atrocious act of all.' For just as Marx found that in the era of unrestrained capitalism, competition between employers, knowing no other weapon than the exploitation of their workers, was transformed into a struggle of each employer against his own workmen, and ultimately of the entire employing class against their employees, so the state uses war and the threat of war as a weapon against *its own* population. 'Since the directing apparatus has no other way of fighting the enemy than by sending its own soldiers, under compulsion, to their death—the war of one State against another State resolves itself into a war of the State and the military apparatus against its own people.'[11]

It doesn't look like this, of course, if you are a part of the directing apparatus, calculating what proportion of the population you can afford to lose in a nuclear war—just as the governments of all the great powers, capitalist and communist, have calculated. But it does look like this if you are part of the expendable population—unless you identify your own unimportant carcase with the state apparatus—*as millions do.* The expendability factor has increased by being transferred from the specialised, scarce and expensively trained military personnel to the amorphous civilian population. American strategists have calculated the proportion of civilians killed in this century's major wars. In the First World War 5 per cent of those killed were civilians, in the Second World War 48 per cent, in the Korean War 84 per cent, while in a Third World War 90–95 per cent would be civilians. States, great and small, now have a stockpile of nuclear weapons equivalent to ten tons of TNT for every person alive today.

In the nineteenth century T. H. Green remarked that war is the expression of the 'imperfect' state, but he was quite wrong. War is the expression of the state in its most perfect form: it is its finest hour. War is the health of the state—the phrase was invented during the First World War by Randolph Bourne, who explained:

> The State is the organisation of the herd to act offensively or defensively against another herd similarly organised. War sends the current of purpose

and activity flowing down to the lowest level of the herd, and to its most remote branches. All the activities of society are linked together as fast as possible to this central purpose of making a military offensive or a military defence, and the State becomes what in peacetime it has vainly struggled to become ... The slack is taken up, the cross-currents fade out, and the nation moves lumberingly and slowly, but with ever accelerated speed and integration, towards the great end, towards that *peacefulness of being at war* ... [12]

This is why the weakening of the state, the progressive development of its imperfections, is a social necessity. The strengthening of *other* loyalties, of *alternative* foci of power, of *different* modes of human behaviour, is an essential for survival. But where do we begin? It ought to be obvious that we do *not* begin by supporting, joining, or hoping to change from within, the existing political parties, by starting new ones as rival contenders for political power. Our task is not to gain power, but to erode it, to drain it away from the state. 'The State bureaucracy and centralisation are as irreconcilable with socialism as was autocracy with capitalist rule. One way or another, socialism must become more popular, more communalistic, and less dependent upon indirect government through elected representatives. It must become more self-governing.'[13] Putting it differently, we have to build networks instead of pyramids. All authoritarian institutions are organised as pyramids: the state, the private or public corporation, the army, the police, the church, the university, the hospital: they are all pyramidal structures with a small group of decision-makers at the top and a broad base of people whose decisions are *made for them* at the bottom. Anarchism does not demand the changing of the labels on the layers, it doesn't want different people on top, it wants *us* to clamber out from underneath. It advocates an extended network of individuals and groups, making their own decisions, controlling their destiny.

The classical anarchist thinkers envisaged the whole social organisation woven from such local groups: the *commune* or council as the territorial nucleus (being 'not a branch of the state, but the free association of the members concerned, which may be either a co-operative or a corporative body, or simply a provisional union of several people united by a common need,'[14]) and the *syndicate* or worker's council as the industrial or occupational unit. These units would federate together not like the stones of a pyramid where the biggest burden is borne by the lowest layer, but like the links of a network, the network of autonomous groups. Several strands of thought are linked together in anarchist social theory: the ideas of direct action, autonomy and workers' control, decentralisation and federalism.

The phrase 'direct action' was first given currency by the French revolutionary syndicalists of the turn of the century, and was associated with the various forms of militant industrial resistance—the strike, go-slow, working-to-rule, sabotage and the general strike. Its meaning has widened since then to take in the experience of, for example, Gandhi's civil disobedience campaign and the civil rights struggle in the United States, and the many other forms of do-it-yourself politics that are spreading round the world. Direct action has been defined by David Wieck as that 'action which, in respect to a situation, *realises the end desired,* so far as this lies within one's power or the power of one's group' and he distinguishes this from indirect action which realises *an irrelevant or even* contradictory end, presumably as a means to the 'good' end. He gives this as a homely example: 'If the butcher weighs one's meat with his thumb on the scale, one may complain about it and tell him he is a bandit who robs the poor, and if he persists and one does nothing else, this is *mere talk*; one may call the Department of Weights and Measures, and this is *indirect action*; or one may, talk failing, insist on weighing one's own meat, bring along a scale to check the butcher's weight, take one's business somewhere else, help open a co-operative store, and these are *direct actions.*' Wieck observes that: 'Proceeding with the belief that in every situation, every individual and group has the possibility of *some* direct action on *some* level of generality, we may discover much that has been unrecognised, and the importance of much that has been underrated. So politicalised is our thinking, so focused to the motions of governmental institutions, that the effects of direct efforts to modify one's environment are unexplored. 'The habit of direct action is, perhaps, identical with the habit of being a free man, prepared to live responsibly in a free society.'[15]

The ideas of autonomy and workers' control and of decentralization are inseparable from that of direct action. In the modern state, everywhere and in every field, one group of people makes decisions, exercises control, limits choices, while the great majority have to accept these decisions, submit to this control and act within the limits of these externally imposed choices. The habit of direct action is the habit of wresting back the power to make decisions affecting *us* from *them*. The autonomy of the worker at work is the most important field in which this expropriation of decision-making can apply. When workers' control is mentioned, people smile sadly and murmur regretfully that it is a pity that the scale and complexity of modern industry make it a utopian dream which could never be put into practice in a developed economy. They are wrong. There are no *technical* grounds for regarding workers' control as impossible. The obstacles to self-management in industry are the same obstacles that stand in the way of any kind of equitable share-out of society's assets: the vested interest of the privileged in the existing distribution of power and property.

Similarly, decentralisation is not so much a technical problem as an approach to problems of human organisation. A convincing case can be made for decentralisation on economic grounds, but for the anarchist there just isn't any other solution consistent with his advocacy of direct action and autonomy. It doesn't occur to him to seek centralist solutions just as it doesn't occur to the person with an authoritarian and centralising frame of thought to seek decentralist ones. A contemporary anarchist advocate of decentralisation, Paul Goodman, remarks that:

> In fact there have always been two strands to decentralist thinking. Some authors, e.g. Lao-Tse or Tolstoy, make a conservative peasant critique of centralised court and town as inorganic, verbal and ritualistic. But other authors, e.g. Proudhon or Kropotkin, make a democratic urban critique of centralised bureaucracy and power, including feudal industrial power, as exploiting, inefficient, and discouraging initiative. In our present era of State-socialism, corpo-

rate feudalism, regimented schooling, brainwashing mass communications and urban anomie, both kinds of critique make sense. We need to revive both peasant self-reliance and the democratic power of professional and technical guilds.

Any decentralisation that could occur at present would inevitably be post-urban and post-centralist: it could not be provincial ... [16]

His conclusion is that decentralisation is 'a kind of social organisation; it does not involve geographical isolation, but a particular sociological use of geography'.

Precisely because we are not concerned with recommending geographical isolation, anarchist thinkers have devoted a great deal of thought to the principle of federalism. Proudhon regarded it as the alpha and omega of his political and economic ideas. He was not thinking of a confederation of states or of a world federal government, but of a basic principle of human organisation.

Bakunin's philosophy of federalism echoed Proudhon's but insisted that only socialism could give it a genuinely revolutionary content, and Kropotkin, too, drew on the history of the French Revolution, the Paris Commune, and, at the very end of his life, the experience of the Russian Revolution, to illustrate the importance of the federal principle if a revolution is to retain its revolutionary content.

Autonomous direct action, decentralised decision-making, and free federation have been the characteristics of all genuinely popular uprisings. Staughton Lynd remarked that 'no real revolution has ever taken place—whether in America in 1776, France in 1789, Russia in 1917, China in 1949—without *ad hoc* popular institutions improvised from below, simply beginning to administer power in place of the institutions previously recognised as legitimate.' They were seen too in the German uprisings of 1919 like the Munich 'council-republic', in the Spanish Revolution of 1936 and in the Hungarian Revolution of 1956, or in the Spring days in Prague in 1968—only to be destroyed by the very party which rode to power on the essentially anarchist slogan 'All Power to the Soviets' in 1917. In March 1920, by which time the Bolsheviks had transformed the local soviets into organs of the central administration, Lenin said to Emma Goldman, 'Why, even your great comrade Errico Malatesta has declared himself for the soviets.' 'Yes,' she replied, 'For the *free* soviets.' Malatesta himself, defining the anarchist interpretation of revolution, wrote:

Revolution is the destruction of all coercive ties; it is the autonomy of groups, of communes, of regions, revolution is the free federation brought about by a desire for brotherhood, by individual and collective interests, by the needs of production and defence; revolution is the constitution of innumerable free groupings based on ideas, wishes and tastes of all kinds that exist among the people; revolution is the forming and disbanding of thousands of representative, district, communal, regional, national bodies, which without having any legislative power, serve to make known and to co-ordinate the desires and interests of people near and far and which act through information, advice and example. Revolution is freedom proved in the crucible of facts—and lasts so long as freedom lasts, that is until others, taking advantage of the weariness that overtakes the masses, of the inevitable disappointments that follow exaggerated hopes, of the probable errors and human faults, succeed in constituting a power which, supported by an army of mercenaries or conscripts, lays down the law, arrests the movement at the point it has reached, and then begins the reaction.[17]

His last sentence indicates that he thought reaction inevitable, and so it is, if people are willing to surrender the power they have wrested from a former ruling elite into the hands of a new one. But a reaction to every revolution is inevitable in another sense. This is what the ebb and flow of history implies. The *lutte finale* exists only in the words of a song. As Landauer says, every time after the revolution is a time before the revolution for all those whose lives have not got bogged down in some great moment of the past. There is no final struggle, only a series of partisan struggles on a variety of fronts.

And after over a century of experience of the theory, and over half a century of experience of the practice of the Marxist and social democratic varieties of socialism, after the historians have dismissed anarchism as one of the nineteenth-century also-rans of history, it is emerging again as a coherent social philosophy in the guerilla warfare for a society of participants, which is occurring sporadically all over the world. Thus, commenting on the events of May 1968 in France, Theodore Draper declared that 'The lineage of the new revolutionaries goes back to Bakunin rather than to Marx, and it is just as well that the term "anarchism" is coming back into vogue. For what we have been witnessing is a revival of anarchism in modern dress or masquerading as latter-day Marxism. Just as nineteenth century Marxism matured in a struggle against anarchism, so twentieth-century Marxism may have to recreate itself in another struggle against anarchism in its latest guise.'[18] He went on to comment that the anarchists did not have much staying-power in the nineteenth century and that it is unlikely that they will have much more in this century. Whether or not he is right about the new anarchists depends on a number of factors. Firstly, on whether or not people have learned *anything* from the history of the last hundred years; secondly, on whether the large number of people both east and west—the dissatisfied and dissident young of the Soviet empire as well as of the United States who seek an alternative theory of social organisation—will grasp the relevance of those ideas which we define as anarchism; and thirdly, on whether the anarchists themselves are sufficiently imaginative and inventive to find ways of applying their ideas today to the society we live in, in ways that combine immediate aims with ultimate ends.

# 3. ALLIED MILITARY GOVERNMENT

*"The presence of a soldier in a state that is new to freedom is a danger, however disinterested he may appear."*

—Simon Bolivar

*"There is nothing on earth so stupid as a gallant officer."*

—The Duke of Wellington

Let us examine the first organisation set up by the Allies in "Liberated" Europe. It is called AMGOT ['Allied Military Government of Occupied Territories' set up in 1943 with the Allied invasion of Sicily and the Italian mainland—Editors] and who is at its head? Baron Rennell of Rodd. And who is he?

> Lord Rennell is a Managing Director of the international banking firm of Morgan, Grenfell & Co., another of whose directors is:
> J. Pierpoint Morgan.
> A director of Courthaulds, the artificial silk combine.
> A former member of the Stock Exchange.
> A former manager of the Bank of International Settlements.
> "A former friend of Volpi, big business backers of Italian Fascism" ... *New Statesman*, 24ᵗʰ July, 1943.
> "An English banker who has expressed his admiration for Mussolini"
> ... *L'Adunata dei Refrattari*, 25ᵗʰ September, 1943.

Lord Rennell's Chief Deputy is the American Brig. Gen. Frank L. McSherry, a professional soldier for 26 years.
Lord Rennell's assistants are—

> Lt.-Col. C.R.S. Harris, directors of six companies.
> Former editor of the anti-socialist *Nineteenth Century*.
> Former Tory candidate.
> And
> Group-Capt. C.E. Benson, Director of eleven companies including Lloyds Bank, Robert Benson's Bank, Montague Burton, and Marks & Spencer.

---

Originally printed in *War Commentary* (Mid-December 1943).

The Finance Section of AMGOT is in the hands of Col. A.P. Grafftney Smith of the Cashier's Department of the Bank of England, dealing with exchange control—and he can certainly deal with it:

> "The lira has been fixed at 400 to the £ compared with 75 to the £ before the war". "In Tunis too, the lira was fixed at an unfavourable rate for the native population—at 480 to the £—*War Commentary*, August, 1943.

How like the Nazi method in the territory they plunder!

We can only find out who else is concerned with this organisation from incidental comment in the press and thus we learn from the *Evening Citizen* of 11th November, 1943, that one of the AMGOT officers in charge at Isernia on the road to Rome is Keith Erskine, son of Sir James Erskine, Tory ex-M.P. Sir James says that his son, who stumped his father's constituency making Conservative speeches at the age of 13, "has his eyes on Parliament, after the war".

So much for Amgot personnel. But what is its administration like? Have the Italian people been helped to rid themselves of their Fascist legacy? As Winston Churchill announced "no political action by the inhabitants can be countenanced". He added that it was "the earnest hope of His Majesty's government that when thus delivered from the Fascist régime, the people of Sicily will of their own accord turn towards Liberal and democratic ideas". Thus, in Churchill's view a liberal and democratic regime is compatible with no political activity by its people. Fascism must indeed be in accordance with liberalism and democracy.

Perhaps that is the reason why Amgot hasn't stamped out Fascism in its territory. A citizen of Ferla wrote to Amgot denouncing the mayor who was co-operating with the Allies yet continued to run the town in the same old "corrupt Fascist tradition", and a British soldier, writing at first hand in the *Observer* for 24 Oct., 1943, told how two officers of OVRA—the Fascist Gestapo—were arrested one day only to walk out of prison 24 hours later as qualified Amgot officials in the very town "which they had bossed for the Fascists".

Then the name. Amgot was shortened to AMG. This was for two reasons. Firstly, it was discovered that "Amgot" is Turkish for "a heap of Dung" and the Allied governments didn't see that many a true word is spoken in jest; and secondly in order to fob off enlightened British and Allied opinion which was apprehensive about the reactionary nature of Amgot and of proposals, mentioned in the *New Statesman* of 21 August, 1943, that Amgot and other allied organisations "should in effect take over the government of these countries for an indefinite period, controlling for instance, such important instruments of administration as the whole broadcasting and propaganda system".

But the European dungheap by any other name would smell as foul, and no-one was re-assured. The Soviet Magazine *War and the Working Classes* said that there was no freedom of speech in Sicily, that high Fascists were on the Allied pay list and that Amgot was "not undertaking the necessary measures for the actual destruction of Fascism", " ... the Administration itself is of a military government based on principles which have nothing in common with the principles of democracy".

Despite all criticism, AMG continued. The American *Christian Science Monitor* for 3 September, 1943, quotes the OFFICIAL handout of British Information Services:

> "AMG in Sicily is doing two things: it is providing the Allies with a testing ground for their administrative organisation, which will enable them to adjust the training of future AMG officers, and, more important—in setting up a régime which stands for justice and respects personal liberty—it is placing at the very door of Fortress Europe, a living example of the war aims of the United Nations."

Take notice, unhappy Continent! Massacred and torn from your homes by the Axis, bombed and blockaded by the Allies, here is a living example of our war aims:

We employ your old oppressors.
We refuse you freedom of speech.
We prohibit all political activity.
We reduce the rate of exchange,
but we respect the sacred rights of property and open up a bank on the second day of our administration.

# 4. POLITICAL USE OF RELIEF

To many of us who do not accept the brutal standards of our materialist era it seems incredible that any government could exploit a famine for political purposes. But looking at recent history it is the only conclusion we can draw.

That is the lesson of the great Irish potato famine of the last century, when potatoes were still exported to England. And it is most certainly the lesson of the present famine in India, as this paper has continually pointed out.

It is well-known that, after the last war, the blockade of revolutionary Germany and Austria was continued for 7 months after the armistice. As Gen. Smuts recently admitted: " ... we actually allowed the position in enemy countries to grow worse, the existing famine conditions to spread, until the Armistice period inflicted in some respects greater injury and suffering on the civilian populations than the war itself, and became a more bitter memory."

Even worse was the Allied attitude to Russia:

> "The Supreme Economic Council would not contemplate the supply of relief to Hungary, while the Communist régime of Bela Kun lasted. When relief to the U.S.S.R was urged in 1919, one of the conditions proposed was that hostilities against the invaders of Union should cease. In 1921 when finally relief was granted, this condition had become inoperable as the invaders had disappeared."
>
> —Prof. John Marrack in *When Hostilities Cease.*

The writer goes on to point out that goods were supplied without any conditions to the White adventurers Yudenitch and Denikin.

In the Spanish civil war, the insurance companies refused to insure ships going to Government ports to bring food to the starving people. Remember "Potato Jones" and his brave era of blockade runners?

It is significant that in the recently published *When Hostilities Cease*—Fabian Papers on Relief and Reconstruction, almost all the writers stress the dangers in this respect. Prof. Harold Laski writes:

> "This is the language of sober fact and not of defeatism. It is what happened after the last war; in a large measure it is what happened during the Russian Revolution, in an even larger measure, it is what happened during the Spanish

Originally printed in *War Commentary* (March 1944).

Civil War. It is imperative for us to take to heart the lesson of the Russo-Finnish war. There it was obvious that the flow of relief derived not merely from the desire to aid the suffering, but from the anxiety to strike a blow in an ideological conflict ... Only as we are united by a system of common values can we construct relief institutions that are the agents of hope and not the instruments of fear."

Prof. Laski's "system of common values" will never be achieved by our society which has rejected all values except those of the jungle.

From the study of UNRRA in the January *War Commentary*, it looks as though that organisation will have just as bad a record as its counterparts of the last war. There remain the voluntary relief organisations. Will they be able to help starving revolutionary Europe? ...

# 5. CONTRARY TO OUR INTERESTS

In a letter in last week's *New Scientist*, Edward Hyams discussing the difference between human and animal intelligence, concluded: "A didactic rationalist with whom I was discussing this very subject, driven at last into a corner, did, however, produce a definition of intelligence which, I confess, persuaded me that men and beasts are not in the same category in this respect. *'Intelligence,'* he said, in desperation, *'is that quality of the mind which enables a living being to act contrary to its own interests.'* A glance at the morning paper will convince any reader that my friend was right."

A glance at any newspaper will also reveal our complete inability to prevent those who rule us from acting contrary to our interests. Take three examples from recent events in British politics. When the British and French governments began their invasion of the Suez Canal Zone last Autumn, a demonstration was held in Trafalgar Square. It was attended by 30,000 people. On the same day two million people turned out to watch the annual London-to-Brighton run of veteran cars. This is the relative importance we give to the preservation of our own interests. Then there is the conscription issue. For years anarchists and pacifists have carried on a campaign against conscription, without the slightest influence. Then suddenly last month the government announced it was going to bring conscription to an end. This did not bring joy to the abolitionists; it was simply the automation principle applied to warfare: a routine administrative decision recognising as a matter of course that future wars will be nuclear wars, which makes large armies of cannon-fodder superfluous. Finally there are the current British hydrogen bomb tests in the Pacific. The warnings from scientists, the protests of the Japanese, or world figures like Albert Schweitzer or Bertrand Russell, quite apart from the agitation of insignificant left-wingers, pacifists and anarchists, were brushed aside by the government which simply brought tests forward a month and presented protesters with a *fait accompli* ('The Government did not want the world to know when the H-bomb tests would begin'—*Star*, 16/5/57).

The protesters are impotent; they are therefore ridiculous; they are not so much opposed as ignored. But they are not wrong, as those who try to persuade themselves that protest is useless, imply. The only thing that is wrong is that there are not enough of them. But why are we unable to persuade men to act in defence of their own interests, and why are governments able so easily to mobilise them to act contrary to their own interests?

---

Originally printed in *Freedom* Volume 18, No. 21 (May 25, 1957).

One can find answers of every kind. Some people will point to the irrationality of man, some to the 'death wish', some to original sin. But the most obvious and near-at-hand explanation is the hypnotic effect of authority in modern society, which has destroyed our faith in our power as individuals; we don't believe in our power, and we have in consequence become powerless. "The irresistible is often only that which is not resisted".

And this is why when people say, "But what can we *do*?", the suggestion which they may find most rewarding is the quite unrevolutionary and unspectacular one that they should seek to develop those forms of social organisation which are the alternative to the governmental and authoritarian social structure which has resulted in such incredible irresponsibility in those who have power and such suicidal indifference in the governed.

A Reader asks in our last issue, "How can we live out our beliefs, as anarchists, every one of us, here and now, in the particular environment in which we happen to be?"

The answer is of course that it's up to him. "The State," said Landauer, "is a condition, a certain relationship between human beings, a mode of human behaviour; we destroy it by contracting other relationships, by behaving differently." This means, it seems to me, by lending our support to whatever tendencies we can find towards workers' control in industry, towards local autonomy in social affairs and public services, towards greater freedom and responsibility for the young, towards everything that makes for more variety, more dignity and quality in human life.

It isn't a matter of anarchism as a substitute religion, a creed or a dogma, but simply as an attitude to life and human affairs, of ceasing to act contrary to our own interests. We live only once and our lives are inevitably full of compromises between the way we would like to live and the way our society works. There is no judge or arbiter to tell us where to draw the line, but if all we have to look back on is a life of sordid and trivial conformity, we have only ourselves to blame.

# 6. THE UNWRITTEN HANDBOOK

Continually you meet people who heartily agree with anarchist arguments but declare sadly that in the complex conditions of modern society, anarchy would never work. When they say that the whole historical trend of the last hundred years has been towards ever more government they are right; it is in their assumption that this *must* go on indefinitely, that it is some inevitable law of history, that they are wrong. But who can blame them for thinking as they do?

For the brains, like the military ironmongery, are sold to the big battalions. In the last few years an immense amount of study, research, investigation, tabulation, statistical analysis, and PhD mongering has been done on the growth of government; while a pathetic quantity of amateur journalism, after-dinner flippancy and wishful thinking has gone into the search for those "new forms of organisation for the social functions which the State now fulfils through the bureaucracy."

The last *nine months* have seen the publication of:

*The Growth of Public Employment in Great Britain* by M. Abramoviez & V. Eliasberg (National Bureau of Economic Research, Princeton University Press).

*The Organisation of British Central Government 1914–1956*, ed. by D.N. Chester (Study Group of the Royal Institute of Public Administration, Allen & Unwin).

*Central Administration in Britain* by W.J. MacKenzie and J.W. Grove (Longmans).

*The Growth of Government* (Political and Economic Planning).

Between them they have 1,128 pages, cost £4 14s.6d., and weigh 4lb.2 oz. It is sad to think of the tiny percentage of all this thought, scholarship, and sheer weight of learning that has gone in the same period to the elaboration of the alternatives to government, and the news that during these nine months Kropotkin's *Conquest of Bread* has been published in Polish in Warsaw, Bakunin's *Selected Works* in Yiddish in Buenos Aires, and Kropotkin's *Anarchism: Its Philosophy and Ideal* in Hebrew in Jerusalem, would be rather more welcome if we thought that

Originally printed in *Freedom* Volume 19, No. 26 (June 28, 1958).

they would be accompanied by an exposition of anarchism written in the twentieth century and in terms of the twentieth century. And not only in those cities and those languages.

To my mind the most striking feature of the unwritten handbook of twentieth century anarchism is not in its rejection of the insights of the classical anarchist thinkers, Godwin, Proudhon, Bakunin, Kropotkin, but its widening and deepening of them. But it is selective, it rejects perfectionism, utopian fantasy, conspiratorial romanticism, revolutionary optimism; it draws from the classical anarchists their most valid, not their most questionable ideas. And it adds to them the subtler contribution of later (and neglected because untranslated) thinkers like Landauer and Malatesta. It also adds the evidence provided in this century by the social sciences, by psychology and anthropology, and by technical change.

It is still an anarchism of present and permanent protest—how could it be anything else in our present peril? But it is one that recognises that the conflict between authority and liberty is a permanent aspect of the human condition and not something that can be resolved by a vaguely specified social revolution. It recognises that the choice between libertarian and authoritarian solutions occurs every day and in every way, and the extent to which we choose, or accept, or are fobbed off with, or lack the imagination and inventiveness to discover alternatives to, the authoritarian solutions to small problems is the extent to which we are their powerless victims in big affairs. We are powerless to change the course of events over the nuclear arms race, imperialism and so on, precisely *because* we have surrendered our power over everything else. Or, more accurately, I think that the unwritten handbook would interpret it in terms of the power-vacuum. The vacuum created by the organisational requirements of a society in a period of rapid population growth and industrialisation at a time when unrestricted exploitation had to yield to a growing extent to the demands of the exploited, has been filled by the State, because of the weakness, inadequacy or incompleteness of libertarian alternatives. Thus the State, in its role as a form of social organisation rather than in its basic function as an instrument of internal and external compulsion, is not so much the villain of the piece as the result of the inadequacy of the other answers to social needs.

This is the implication of Gustav Landauer's profound contribution to anarchist thought:

> The State is a condition, a certain relationship between human beings, a mode
> of human behaviour; we destroy it behaving differently.

The unwritten handbook, using the immense amount of study that has been made, in the last twenty years, on social groups of all kinds, examines these "other relationships". What has gone wrong with them? it asks. Why has the trade union movement got bogged down in the morass of reformist politics, demanding nothing more than better wages and conditions? Why has the producer co-operative movement failed to expand? Why has consumer co-operation, after such ambitious aspirations, become little more than a dowdy elder sister of the chain stores?

Why did the Friendly Societies and the voluntary hospital system fail to provide the comprehensive health service which the cumbersome and expensive machinery of the NHS had to be initiated to supply? Was the last word in the organisation of public education said by the Act of 1870, on which all subsequent elaborations have been based? Is nationalisation the only alternative to private capitalism in industrial organisation? Why is the local government system a byword for bumbledom and petty officialdom, and how does this affect anarchist notions of local autonomy?

It is because they attempt to answer some of these questions that some of the series that appear in FREEDOM, for instance, Geoffrey Ostergaard's study of "The Tradition of Workers' Control" and Gaston Gerard's current authoritative examination of the Independent Commission's report on the Co-operative Movement, are of such value for people who want to hammer out a social as well as an individual conception of anarchism, which is something more than slogans and shibboleths and which takes into account the actual experiences of industrial societies in this century. They are notes for the unwritten handbook.

# 7. PEOPLE AND IDEAS TAKES
# A LAST LOOK ROUND AT THE 50s

To look at history in terms of decades is usually misleading, and the epithets we apply to them are often partial. The gay nineties, the roaring twenties, the pink thirties, are not very complete or accurate adjectives for those days: only the hungry forties sums up the truth, whether in this century or the last. What are we going to say about the fifties?

Although there has been less actual warfare for a very long time, and although the word peace has been on everybody's lips, you could hardly call them the peaceful fifties. The last ten years began with the Korean War, and continued with warfare in Malaya, Indo-China and Algeria, Kenya and Cyprus, palace revolts in the Middle East, the Sinai and Suez invasions and the Chinese invasion of Tibet, the Hungarian revolution, and the usual punitive expeditions and police actions.

The most considerable movements against war and war preparation in this country have come right at the end of the decade, in the Aldermaston marches—a constitutional exercise for the troubled many, and the acts of obstruction at missile bases—symbolic acts of the determined few. To the imprisoned members of the Direct Action Committee Against Nuclear War, who will see the end of the year and the end of the decade in jail, goes the honour of introducing to this country the techniques of civil disobedience, which may develop to greater effect in the sixties.

The fifties which began in the period of post-war "austerity", and the fag-end of the Labour government, with rationing still in force and Lord Woolton crusading for "More Red Meat", end with the third Conservative electoral victory in succession and the Prime Minister's observation that we've never had it so good. These years have seen the rehabilitation of the prestige of big business, and they end with a burst of mergers and take-overs. At the beginning of the period the emphasis in industry was on re-tooling for the competition in export markets. Today the interest of a firm is in its potentiality as the subject of financial speculation. From "Britain Can Make It" to "Make Me An Offer" sums up the ten years. Present industrial prosperity is confined mainly to consumer goods, and, of course, to the armaments programme which absorbs up to a tenth of the national product. The British share of the world market has steadily declined since 1950 and production has been stagnant since 1955. In the trade union world the prospects for a

Originally printed in *Freedom* Volume 20, No. 52 (December 26, 1959).

movement agitating for workers' control are slighter than they were ten years ago. "People's Capitalism" on the American model offers more attractions.

Looking for the keynote of the fifties, a number of observers noted the 'swing to the right', the 'decline of ideologies', the neo-conservatism and increasing conformism of the intelligentsia, the preoccupation with trivialities—all the tedious social make-believe about 'U' and 'non-U', the cult of 'gracious living' and the fashionable concern over the subtler aspects of wining and dining. A few years ago Mr. Rayner Heppenstall described this "new Elizabethan age in its Edwardian décor" as "the commercial traveller's paradise with its rather sexy royalist mystique".

Then just as we were getting used to the idea, with an occasional outburst by the angry old men, along came an angry young man in the form of the heroes of the novels of Messrs. Wain and Amis, who blew a raspberry through the *House and Garden* dining rooms. Perhaps he was going to be the man of the decade; the welfare state baby with a provincial accent seeing through all the social humbug and staging a one-man battle with the 'establishment'. But he turned out to be another sensitive chap underneath his brash exterior and either got a job on commercial television with a cynical leer, or else, like the hero of Mr. Osborne's *Look Back in Anger*, nagging his missus because he couldn't find a cause to fight for. For a mercifully brief period he gave place to the Outsider, who quickly died of anemia.

Then in 1956 the real world broke through. Instead of the inward-looking contemplation of social niceties, and instead of identifying itself with the archetypes of current literature, the generation of the fifties found itself faced with Suez and Hungary. Mr. John Bevan wrote in the *Twentieth Century*: "The two crises have moved all of us deeply, even the apolitical young who had refused to get excited about two welfare parties with a common and static foreign policy. At the universities, I am told, it has been like the thirties all over again—but with Abyssinia and Spain happening in the same week ... some of the moral problems of 1935 and 1936 have been forced upon a generation which may have been able to evade them until these past few weeks."

With this belated discovery of the real climate of the fifties and the recognition that our own little bit of the sky doesn't cover the whole world, came a realisation of impotence. What could they do about Suez except write letters to the *Guardian*? What could they do about Hungary except support the Red Cross? And could anything else be expected? The intelligentsia were unable to prevent the incredible folly of the Suez adventure because, after careful cultivation of uncommittedness and detachment, they were in no position to become the mouthpiece or the conscience of the nation, while the people who actually *were* in a position to frustrate the government's policy, the servicemen engaged in it and the transport workers concerned with the shipment of war materials, couldn't care less about the uses to which their lives and labour were put. The tone of the nineteen-fifties had been set for them, and it was one of indifference and apathy.

One of the legacies of the Suez-Hungary period was the movement whose organs have just amalgamated to form the *New Left Review*, but, as our correspondent asked, writing of its inauguration last week: How new is the New Left? Abroad, the fifties have seen a few changes. America has been mercifully bereaved of Joe McCarthy and John Foster Dulles, and a resurrected Ike is doing the rounds. In Russia the great event of the fifties has *not* been Sputnik, Lunik, or the other side of the moon, but the death of Stalin. Undoubtedly life in the Soviet Union is happier today than it has been for generations. Every visitor reports on the change in the atmosphere. What is not yet clear is how long the change in the weather will last. Would it survive the slightest public manifestation of opposition to the régime? France slumbers under the eye of its Governess. Salazar and Franco remain. In China, the hundred flowers were ruthlessly cut down as soon as they appeared. A Polish joke about Mao Tse-Tung's government remarks "Thank God we have Russia in between as a buffer state". Ghana, achieving independence during the decade, moves steadily towards dictatorship.

Those tendencies in other countries with a particular interest for us do not seem to be advancing. The Bhoodan movement in India, one of the most hopeful trends of the fifties, appears to have reached a stalemate, with the discouragement of many of its workers, and the impending return to politics of some of its well-known adherents, because of the 'crisis' in Indian-Chinese relations. The Civil Disobedience campaign in South Africa, another feature of the decade, struggles with little success against racialism. The gap between the rich and the poor nations continues to widen. The 'under-developed' countries seek desperately to emulate the developed ones, and these copy the over-developed ones. They all want to be more like America. And the most trenchant and telling critics of American society and institutions continue to be Americans. The decade has seen David Riesman's *The Lonely Crowd* with its emphasis on the struggle for personal autonomy, William H. Whyte's *Organisation Man* with its message: "Fight the organisation", J.K. Galbraith's *Affluent Society*, with its call for the divorce of income from production, and C. Wright Mills' *Causes of World War Three* with its castigation of the American power elite. No such forceful and trenchant social criticism has come from the British or European equivalents of these writers.

The anarchist movement throughout the world can hardly be said to have increased its influence during the decade. In several countries it has been weakened by internal divisions. Yet the relevance of anarchist ideas was never so great. Anarchism suffers, as all minority movements suffer, from the fact that its numerical weakness inhibits its intellectual strength. This may not matter when you approach it as an individual attitude to life, but in its other rôle, as a social theory, as one of the possible approaches to the solution of the problems of social life, it is a very serious thing. It is precisely this lack which people have in mind when they complain that there have been no advances in anarchist theory since the days of Kropotkin. Ideas and not armies change the face of the world, and in the sphere of what we ambitiously call the social sciences, too few of the people with ideas couple them with anarchist attitudes.

For the anarchists the problem of the nineteen-sixties is simply that of how to put anarchism back into the intellectual bloodstream, into the field of ideas which are taken seriously.

# 8. ADVENTURE PLAYGROUND:
## A PARABLE OF ANARCHY

When we call ourselves anarchists, that is, people who advocate the principle of *autonomy* as opposed to *authority* in every field of personal and social life, we are constantly reminded of the apparent failure of anarchism to exercise any perceptible influence on the course of political events, and as a result we tend to overlook the unconscious adoption of anarchist ideas in a variety of other spheres of life. Some of these minor anarchies of everyday life provide analogies, some provide examples, and some, when you describe their operation, sound like veritable parables of anarchy.

All the problems of social life present a choice between libertarian and authoritarian solutions, and the ultimate claim we may make for the libertarian approach is that it is more efficient—it fulfils its function better. The adventure playground is an arresting example of this living anarchy, one which is valuable both in itself and as an experimental verification of a whole social approach. The need to provide children's playgrounds as such is a result of high-density urban living and fast-moving traffic. The authoritarian solution to this need is to provide an area of tarmac and some pieces of expensive ironmongery in the form of swings, see-saws and roundabouts, which provide a certain amount of fun (though because of their inflexibility children soon tire of them), but which call for no imaginative or constructive effort on the child's part and cannot be incorporated in any self-chosen activity. Swings and roundabouts can only be used in one way, they cater for no fantasies, for no developing skills, for no emulation of adult activities, they call for no mental effort and very little physical effort, and we are giving way to simpler and freer apparatus like climbing frames, log piles, 'jungle gyms', commando nets, or to play sculptures—abstract shapes to clamber through and over, or large constructions in the form of boats, traction engines, lorries or trains. But even these provide for a limited age-group and a limited range of activities, and it is not surprising that children find more continual interest in the street, the derelict building, the bombed site or the scrap heap.

For older boys, team-games are the officially approved activity, and as Patrick Geddes wrote before the first world war, "they are at most granted a cricket pitch, or lent a space between football goals, but otherwise are jealously watched, as potential savages, who on the least symptom of their natural activities of wigwam-

Originally printed in *Anarchy* No. 7 (September 1961): 193–201.

building, cave-digging, stream-damming, and so on—must be instantly chivvied away, and are lucky if not handed over to the police."

That there should be anything novel in simply providing facilities for the spontaneous, unorganised activities of childhood is an indication of how deeply rooted in our social behaviour is the urge to control, direct and limit the flow of life. But when they get the chance, in the country, or where there are large gardens, woods or bits of waste land, what are children doing? Enclosing space, making caves, tents, dens, from old bricks, bits of wood and corrugated iron. Finding some corner which the adult world has passed over and making it their own. But how can children find this kind of private world in towns, where, as Agnete Vestereg of the Copenhagen Junk Playground write:

> Every bit of land is put to industrial or commercial use, where every patch of grass is protected or enclosed, where streams and hollows are filled in, cultivated and built on?
>
> But more is done for children now than used to be done, it may be objected. Yes, but that is one of the chief faults—the things are *done*. Town children move about in a world full of the marvels of technical science. They may see and be impressed by things; but they long also to take possession of them, to have them in their hands, to make something themselves, to create and re-create.

The Emdrup playground was begun in 1943 by the Copenhagen Workers' Co-operative Housing Association after their landscape architect, Mr. C. T. Sorensen, who had laid out many orthodox playgrounds had observed that children seemed to get more pleasure when they stole into the building sites and played with the materials they found there. In spite of a daily average attendance of 200 children at Emdrup, and that 'difficult' children were specially catered for, it was found that "the noise, screams and fights found in dull playgrounds are absent, for the opportunities are so rich that the children do not need to fight."

The initial success at Copenhagen has led in the years since the war to a widespread diffusion of the idea and its variations, from 'Freetown' in Stockholm and 'The Yard' at Minneapolis, to the *Skrammelegeplads* or building playgrounds of Denmark and the Robinson Crusoe playgrounds of Switzerland, where children are provided with the raw materials and tools for building what they want and for making gardens and sculpture. In this country we have had at least a dozen adventure playgrounds, several of them temporary, since their sites were earmarked for rebuilding, but there has been enough experience and enough documentation of it, for us to gauge fairly well their successes and pitfalls.

These accounts—which should disabuse anyone who thinks it is easy to run an adventure playground, as well as anyone who thinks it a waste of time, include the following:

> *Adventure Playgrounds*, Lady Allen's pioneering pamphlet, which incorporates Agnete Vestereg's account of the Emdrup playground and John Lagemann's of The Yard.

*Adventure in Play* by John Barron Mays, describing the Rathbone Street Adventure Playground at Liverpool.

*Annual Reports of the Grimsby Adventure Playground Association*, by Joe Benjamin, the project leader until 1959, who has also written elsewhere on this playground.

*Lollard Adventure Playground*, a pamphlet by Mary Nicholson, and *Something Extraordinary*, by H. S. Turner, the warden at Lollard Street.

*Play Parks*, by Lady Allen of Hurtwood, an account of the Swedish play parks with suggestions for their adoption here.

*Adventure Playgrounds*, a progress report by the National Playing Fields Associations on the playgrounds at Lollard Street, Grimsby, Romford, Bristol, Liverpool and St. John's Wood, with facts and figures useful to people thinking of starting a playground.

When The Yard was opened at Minneapolis with the aim of giving the children "their own spot of earth and plenty of tools and materials for digging, building and creating as they see fit",

it was every child for himself. The initial stockpile of secondhand lumber disappeared like ice off a hot stove. Children helped themselves to all they could carry, sawed off long boards when short pieces would have done. Some hoarded tools and supplies in secret caches. Everybody wanted to build the biggest shack in the shortest time. The workmanship was shoddy.

Then came the bust. There wasn't a stick of lumber left. Hi-jacking raids were staged on half-finished shacks. Grumbling and bickering broke out. A few children packed up and left.

But on the second day of the great depression most of the youngsters banded together spontaneously for a salvage drive. Tools and nails came out of hiding. For over a week the youngsters made do with what they had. Rugged individualists who had insisted on building alone invited others to join in—and bring their supplies along. New ideas popped up for joint projects. By the time a fresh supply of lumber arrived a community had been born.

As in Copenhagen the prophesied casualties did not happen. "After a year of operation, injuries consisted of some bandaged thumbs and small cuts and bruises for the entire enrolment of over 200 children. No child has ever used a tool to hit another person."

This question of safety is so often raised when adventure playgrounds are discussed that it is worth citing the experience in this country (where the pernicious notion that whenever accidents happen someone must be sued has actually caused some local authorities to close their orthodox playgrounds—so that the kids can get run over instead). The insurance company was so impressed by the engrossed activity at the Clydesdale Road (Paddington) playground, with its complete lack of hooliganism that it quoted lower rates than for an ordinary playground. At Rathbone Street, Liverpool, the 'toughest' of the English playgrounds:

So many children crowded together with so many opportunities for muti-
lating one another were bound to produce a steady flow of abrasions, cuts
and bruises with the occasional more serious wound requiring stitching or
a fractured bone. Statistically, however, the slide appeared to be the highest risk while the permanent ironwork equipment generally produced more
accidents than the junk and scrap materials in the Adventure Playground
proper.

Reading Mr. Mays' account of the Liverpool playground, with its stories of
gang-warfare, sabotage, thieving scrap-metal merchants, hostility and indifference in the neighbourhood except for one street of immediate neighbours, sense-
less and wanton destruction, the reader may wonder how on earth it could keep
going. But the author, reminding us that the essence of an experiment is that it is
experimental, concludes that

> In spite of all its shortcomings, many of which were the result of hasty plan-
> ning and lack of solid financial support, in spite of mistakes made by its man-
> agement committee and the errors of its two appointed leaders, in spite of the
> roughness of the site, the endless brickbats, the noise, the dirt, the disorder,
> sufficient evidence has accrued to support the main thesis on which the play-
> ground was established—that given the tools, the materials, the adult inter-
> est, advice and support children will indulge in constructional play, they do
> derive satisfaction from using hand and eye in making and building, fetching,
> carrying, painting and digging.

The shortcomings, he points out, are no more inevitable than the community allows them to be. The Rathbone Street playground only seemed a failure from a
distance: those closest to it, as Mr. Mays says, "are much less gloomy about its
value", and it has already led to further adventuring in Liverpool.

On the other hand, the Lollard Playground which seemed from the outside
to be as the *Evening Standard* called it, "a heartwarming success story" gave rise
among its workers to the kind of feeling which Sheila Beskine describes in this
issue of ANARCHY, a "fantastic spontaneous lease of life" followed by a slow decline, so that its spirit had died *before* the LCC took over the site for building. But
permanence is not the criteria of success. As Lady Allen says, a good adventure
playground "is in a continual process of destruction and growth". The splendid
variety of activities which came and went at Lollard from vegetable-growing to
producing a magazine, plays, operettas, jiving and 'beauty sessions' were a measure
of its success. As at Emdrup, this playground kept the interest of older children
and young people up to the age of twenty thus enlarging the scope of possible projects. The older boys built and equipped a workshop and eagerly sought to serve the
community in which they lived, doing repairs and redecorations for old people
in the district, paying for the materials from a fund of their own. These were the
same young people who are such a "problem" to their elders. The difference is that
between the atmosphere of the irresponsible society, and that which was precari-

ously built at the playground. The place, said the warden "stands for far more than a mere playground", and the Chairman summed up

> This playground is different because it's a place where the children have an infinite choice of opportunities. They can handle basic things—earth, water plants, timber—and work with real tools; and they have an adult friend, a person they trust and respect. Here every child can develop a healthy sense of self-esteem, because there is always something at which they can excel. The wide age range, from two years to twenty-three, is perhaps unique in any playground. There can be progressive development through rich play opportunities, to a growing sense of responsibility to the playground, to younger children and, finally, to others outside the playground. Their willingness to help others is the sign of real maturity which is the object of all who work with young people.

The Grimsby playground, started in 1955, has a similar story. Its cycle of growth and renewal is annual. At the end of each summer the children saw up their shacks and shanties into firewood which they deliver in fantastic quantities to old age pensioners. When they begin building in the spring, "it's just a hole in the ground—and they crawl into it". Gradually the holes give way to two-storey huts. But they never pick up where they left off at the end of the previous summer. It's the same with fires. They begin by lighting them just for fun. Then they cook potatoes and by the end of the summer they're cooking eggs, bacon and beans.

Similarly with the notices above their dens. It begins with nailing up 'Keep Out' signs (just as in The Yard at Minneapolis). After this come more personal names like 'Bughole Cave' and 'Dead Man's Cave', but by the end of the summer they have communal names like 'Hospital' or 'Estate Agent'. There is an ever-changing range of activities "due entirely to the imagination and enterprise of the children themselves ... at no time are they expected to continue an activity which no longer holds an interest for them ... Care of tools is the responsibility of the children. At the end of 1958 they were still using the same tools purchased originally in 1955. Not one hammer or spade has been lost, and all repairs have been paid for out of the Nail Fund." Mr. Benjamin, the project leader for the first years at Grimsby has thought deeply on the implications and lessons of the adventure playground movement [and] answered sceptical critics in a memorable letter:

> By what criteria are adventure playgrounds to be judged? If it is by the disciplined activity of the uniformed organisations, then there is no doubt but we are a failure. If it is by the success of our football and table tennis teams then there is no doubt we are a flop. If it is by the enterprise and endurance called for by some of the national youth awards—then we must be ashamed.
> But these are the standards set by the club movement, in one form or another, for a particular type of child. They do not attract the so-called 'unclub-

bable', and worse—so we read regularly—nor do they hold those children at whom they are aimed.

May I suggest that we need to examine afresh the pattern taken by the young at play and then compare it with the needs of the growing child and the adolescent. We accept that it is natural for boys and girls below a certain age to play together, and think it equally natural for them to play at being grown up. We accept, in fact, their right to imitate the world around them. Yet as soon as a child is old enough to see through the pretence and demand the reality, we separate him from his sister and try to fob him off with games and activities which seem only to put off the day when he will enter the world proper.

The adventure playgrounds in this country, new though they are, are already providing a number of lessons which we would do well to study ... For three successive summers the children have built their dens and created Shanty Town, with its own hospital, fire station, shops, etc. As each den appeared, it became functional—and brought with it an appreciation of its nature and responsibility.

The pattern of adventure playgrounds is set by the needs of the children who use them; their 'toys' include woodwork benches and sewing machines. The play of the children is modelled closely on the world around them—and as such has a meaning that is understood easily by all types. We do not believe that children can be locked up in neat little parcels labelled by age and sex. Neither do we believe that education is the prerogative of the schools.

●●●

Apart from the kind of objection you will always get from people who resent anything pleasurable that doesn't make money, three kinds of objections are made to adventure playgrounds—danger, unsightliness, and expense of supervision. Happily the danger is more apparent than real, and the Secretary of the National Playing Fields Association has stated that the accident rate is lower than on orthodox playgrounds since hooliganism which results from boredom is absent. They *are* unsightly in the ordinary sense (and so is nine-tenths of our physical environment), for as Mr. Mays notes,

> Children like disorder or find some invisible order therein. Most adults hate it. Children do not in the least mind being dirty. Most adults abhor it. Children will find a source of enjoyment in the oddest and most unlikely play material: tin cans, milk bottle tops, broken slates, soil cinders, firewood. The adult mind thinks of these things in terms of refuse and rubbish ...

The solution of course is to use a solid fence instead of chicken wire, as is after all customary for adult building and demolition operations. (The Emdrup playground has a 6ft. high bank with a thicket hedge and fence on top, which also absorbs the high frequencies of children's voices.)

Certainly more skilled adult assistance is needed than in a conventional playground. Indeed everything depends upon having some thing different from a park-keeper saying 'Don't!' or a patronising leader saying 'Do!'. Against the cost of this can be set the lower capital costs than for a conventional playground and the fact that much public goodwill, assistance as gifts of materials can usually be counted on. (Many advocates of adventure playgrounds who see them as "saving children from delinquency" would set the cost of leaders' salaries against the enormous cost of putting children in remand homes, approved schools and so on.) On the question of such costs, local authorities are empowered under section 53 of the Education Act to grant aid to the cost of employing play leaders, and the adventure playgrounds in this country, mostly run by voluntary organisations, have in fact had financial help both from local councils and from the National Playing Fields Association and in some cases from philanthropic foundations.

Much could be said about the nature of adult help in an adventure playground. The NPFA report sees the person of the play leader as the over-riding factor in success besides which the other considerations fall into insignificance. (It is worth nothing that Stockholm with a population of 3/4 million has 84 play leaders and London with 8.5 million has eight or nine.) Yet as Mr. Turner in his book about Lollard shows, there is no specification for the ideal person, the most bizarre characters have been wildly successful. Discussing the early experience at Clydesdale Road, Lady Allen made the point that, although we use the word *leader* we want something different:

> it must be a grown-up who exerts the minimum authority and is willing to act rather as an older friend and councillor than as a leader ... It is these children, particularly, who so deeply enjoy the companionship of an older person who is willing to be understanding and very generous of his time. We cannot think of a good title for this individual: supervisor is wrong, connected in the children's minds with discipline; a play leader is trained for a different type of work, and for younger children, so we use the word 'leader' but it is not right.

The role of the 'leader' is catalytic, and it is apparent from the various accounts of adventure playgrounds that too few adults have had to fulfil too many roles— from social worker to begging letter writer and woodwork instructor. An informal and changing group of people, both full-time and voluntary, and including friendly neighbours and older children is evidently the happiest combination.

•••

Finally, in case it isn't obvious, why do we claim the adventure playground movement as an experiment in anarchy? Well, let us repeat yet again, Kropotkin's definition of an anarchist society as one which

> seeks the most complete development of individuality combined with the highest development of voluntary association in all its aspects, in all possible

degrees, for all imaginable aims; ever changing, ever modified associations which carry in themselves the elements of their durability and constantly assume new forms which answer best to the multiple aspirations of all. A society to which pre-established forms, crystallised by law, are repugnant; which looks for harmony in an ever-changing and fugitive equilibrium between a multitude of varied forces and influences of every kind, following their own course ...

Every one of these phrases is recognisably a description of the microcosmic society of the successful adventure playground, and it leads us to speculate on the wider applications of the idea which is in essence the old revolutionary notion of "free access to the means of production", in this instance to the means of every kind of creative and recreative activity. We think of course of the Peckham Experiment—a kind of adventure playground for people of all ages, or the kind of variations on work and leisure in freely chosen activity envisaged in Paul and Percival Goodman's *Communitas*. The adventure playground is a free society in miniature, with the same tensions and ever-changing harmonies, the same diversity and spontaneity, the same unforced growth of co-operation and release of individual qualities and communal sense, which lie dormant in a society devoted to competition and acquisitiveness.

# 9. FRINGE BENEFITS: COLIN WARD REAPPRAISES THE TITMUSS BOOK THAT GAVE NEW MEANING TO THE EXPRESSION "BLOOD BANK"

When Richard Titmuss, the insurance clerk who became our most acute analyst of social policy, produced his last book, *The Gift Relationship*, in 1970, I dismissed it as an elaborate and academic restatement of Kropotkin's *Mutual Aid*, filled with indigestible detail about the pale yellow fluid known as plasma and constituents like immunoglobulin. Happily, when I wanted to consult it recently, the county library had a copy in its reserve stock, stored, like plasma, for my needs, and I changed my view.

What set Titmuss off on his investigation must have been a 1968 publication from the Institute of Economic Affairs, *The Price of Blood*, which made an economic case against a monopoly of altruism in blood transfusion. So he embarked on a comparison of the commercial market in bought blood with the voluntary donation of blood.

He found that the dominant characteristic of the American blood-banking system was a redistribution of blood and blood products from the poor to the rich, since the sellers tended to be the unskilled, unemployed and other "low-income groups and categories of exploited people".

He found that when voluntary donors in Britain were asked about their motives, "the vividness, individuality, and diversity of their responses add life and a sense of community to the statistical generalities", but that 80 per cent of answers suggested feelings of social responsibility towards other members of society.

Titmuss concluded that on four testable, non-ethical criteria, the commercial trade in blood was bad: "In terms of economic efficiency, it is highly wasteful of blood; shortages, chronic and acute, characterise the demand and supply position and make illusory the concept of equilibrium. It is administratively inefficient and results in more bureaucratisation and much greater administrative, accounting and computer overheads. In terms of price per unit of blood to the patient (or consumer), it is a system which is five to 15 times more costly than the voluntary system in Britain. And finally, in terms of quality, commercial markets are much more likely to distribute contaminated blood."

He died in 1974 and consequently did not live to see the phenomenon that he called "the philistine resurrection of economic man in social policy." And al-

Originally printed in *New Statesman & Society* (8 March 1996): 35.

though he was to record that among cardiac surgery transfusions in the US, "in the commercial group the total hepatitis attack rate was 53 percent, in the voluntary group nil," neither he nor anyone else could have anticipated the Aids epidemic, and the disaster that befell haemophiliac patients, heavily dependent on blood products, as a result of the importation of contaminated commercial blood.

Not did he live to see the vast confidence trick we have witnessed since the 1970s where, as Brendan Lambon argued on the letters page (26 January), business studies and economics, as taught today, amount to "the most successful programme of political propaganda ever undertaken in the country". Economics has become simply market economics, and other concepts of social interaction are relegated to the public relations industry. ("If it's uneconomic, get the mugs to volunteer.")

Rereading Titmuss is a reminder of how rapidly the market ideology has been transferred from economic theory to social policy, with a pathetically weak dissenting voice. I'm now inclined to see his book as a parable. Blood, as the saying goes, is thicker than water, which is the fluid that holds it together. We can't survive without blood, but nor can we survive for more than a few days without water.

A century before Titmuss died, the Public Health Act required every household to have a water supply. Twenty years after his death, profitable, privatised water companies were depriving people of a water supply because of non-payment of bills.

# 10. ANARCHISM AS A THEORY
# OF ORGANIZATION

You may think in describing anarchism as a theory of organisation I am propounding a deliberate paradox: "anarchy" you may consider to be, by definition, the *opposite* of organisation. In fact, however, "anarchy" means the absence of government, the absence of *authority*. Can there be social organisation without authority, without government? The anarchists claim that there can be, and they also claim that it is desirable that there should be. They claim that, at the basis of our social problems is the principle of government. It is, after all, governments which prepare for war and wage war, even though you are obliged to fight in them and pay for them; the bombs you are worried about are not the bombs which cartoonists attribute to the anarchists, but the bombs which governments have perfected, at your expense. It is, after all, governments which make and enforce the laws which enable the 'haves' to retain control over social assets rather than share them with the 'have-nots'. It is, after all, the principle of authority which ensures that people will work for someone else for the greater part of their lives, not because they enjoy it or have any control over their work, but because they see it as their only means of livelihood.

I said that it is governments which make wars and prepare for wars, but obviously it is not governments alone—the power of a government, even the most absolute dictatorship, depends on the tacit assent of the governed. Why do people consent to be governed? It isn't only fear: what have millions of people to fear from a small group of politicians? It is because they subscribe to the same values as their governors. Rulers and ruled alike believe in the principle of authority, of hierarchy, of power. These are the characteristics of the *political principle*. The anarchists, who have always distinguished between the state and society, adhere to the *social principle*, which can be seen where-ever men link themselves in an association based on a common need or a common interest. "The State" said the German anarchist Gustav Landauer, "is not something which can be destroyed by a revolution, but is a condition, a certain relationship between human beings, a mode of human behaviour; we destroy it by contracting other relationships, by behaving differently."

Anyone can see that there are at least two kinds of organisation. There is the kind which is forced on you, the kind which is run from above, and there is the

Originally printed in *Anarchy* No. 52 (June 1966), 171–178.

kind which is run from below, which can't *force* you to do anything, and which you are free to join or free to leave alone. We could say that the anarchists are people who want to transform all kinds of human organisation into the kind of purely voluntary association where people can pull out and start one of their own if they don't like it. I once, in reviewing that frivolous but useful little book *Parkinson's Law*, attempted to enunciate four principles behind an anarchist theory of organisation: that they should be

(1) voluntary, (2) functional, (3) temporary, and (4) small.

They should be voluntary for obvious reasons. There is no point in our advocating individual freedom and responsibility if we are going to advocate organisations for which membership is mandatory.

They should be functional and temporary precisely because permanence is one of those factors which harden the arteries of an organisation, giving it a vested interest in its own survival, in serving the interests of office-holders rather than its function.

They should be small precisely because in small face-to-face groups, the bureaucratising and hierarchical tendencies inherent in organisations have least opportunity to develop. But it is from this final point that our difficulties arise. If we take it for granted that a small group can function anarchically, we are still faced with the problem of all those social functions for which organisation is necessary, but which require it on a much bigger scale. "Well," we might reply, as some anarchists have, "if big organisations are necessary, count us out. We will get by as well as we can without them." We can say this all right, but if we are propagating anarchism as a social philosophy we must take into account, and not evade, social facts. Better to say "Let us find ways in which the large-scale functions can be broken down into functions capable of being organised by small functional groups and then link these groups in a federal manner." The classical anarchist thinkers, envisaging the future organisation of society, thought in terms of two kinds of social institution: as the territorial unit, the commune, a French word which you might consider as the equivalent of the word 'parish' or the Russian word 'soviet' in its original meaning, but which also has overtones of the ancient village institutions for cultivating the land in common; and the syndicate, another French word from trade union terminology, the syndicate or workers' council as the unit of industrial organisation. Both were envisaged as small local units which would federate with each other for the larger affairs of life, while retaining their own autonomy, the one federating territorially and the other industrially.

The nearest thing in ordinary political experience, to the federative principle propounded by Proudhon and Kropotkin would be the Swiss, rather than the American, federal system. And without wishing to sing a song of praise for the Swiss political system, we can see that the 22 independent cantons of Switzerland are a successful federation. It is a federation of like units, of small cells, and the cantonal boundaries cut across linguistic and ethnic boundaries so that, unlike the many unsuccessful federations, the confederation is not dominated by one or a few powerful units. For the problem of federation, as Leopold Kohr puts it in *The Breakdown of Nations*, is one of division, not of union. Herbert Luethy writes of his country's political system:

> Every Sunday, the inhabitants of scores of communes go to the polling booths to elect their civil servants, ratify such and such an item of expenditure, or decide whether a road or a school should be built; after settling the business of the commune, they deal with cantonal elections and voting on cantonal issues; lastly ... come the decisions on federal issues. In some cantons, the sovereign people still meet in Rousseau-like fashion to discuss questions of common interest. It may be thought that this ancient form of assembly is no more than a pious tradition with a certain value as a tourist attraction. If so, it is worth looking at the results of local democracy.
>
> The simplest example is the Swiss railway system, which is the densest network in the world. At great cost and with great trouble, it has been made to serve the needs of the smallest localities and most remote valleys, not as a paying proposition but because such was the will of the people. It is the outcome of fierce political struggles. In the 19th century, the "democratic railway movement" brought the small Swiss communities into conflict with the big towns, which had plans for centralisation ... And if we compare the Swiss system with the French which, with admirable geometrical regularity, is entirely centred on Paris so that the prosperity or the decline, the life or death of whole regions has depended on the quality of the link with the capital, we see the difference between a centralised state and a federal alliance. The railway map is the easiest to read at a glance, but let us now superimpose on it another showing economic activity and the movement of population. The distribution of industrial activity all over Switzerland, even in the outlying areas, accounts for the strength and stability of the social structure of the country and prevented those horrible 19th century concentrations of industry, with their slums and rootless proletariat.

I quote all this, as I said, not to praise Swiss democracy, but to indicate that the federal principle which is at the heart of anarchist social theory, is worth much more attention than it is given in the textbooks on political science. Even in the context of ordinary political institutions its adoption has a far-reaching effect. Another anarchist theory of organisation is what we might call the theory of spontaneous order: that given a common need, a collection of people will, by trial and error, by improvisation and experiment, evolve order out of chaos—this order being more durable and more closely related to their needs than any kind of externally imposed order.

Kropotkin derived this theory from the observations of the history of human society and of social biology which led to his book *Mutual Aid*, and it has been observed in most revolutionary situations, in the *ad hoc* organisations which spring up after natural catastrophes, or in any activity where there is no existing organisational form or hierarchical authority. This concept was given the name *Social*

*Control* in the book of that title by Edward Allsworth Ross, who cited instances of "frontier" societies where, through unorganised or informal measures, order is effectively maintained without benefit of constituted authority: "Sympathy, sociability, the sense of justice and resentment are competent, under favourable circumstances, to work out by themselves a true, natural order, that is to say, an order without design or art."

An interesting example of the working-out of this theory was the Pioneer Health Centre at Peckham, London, started in the decade before the war by a group of physicians and biologists who wanted to study the nature of health and healthy behaviour instead of studying ill-health like the rest of their profession. They decided that the way to do this was to start a social club whose members joined as families and could use a variety of facilities including a swimming bath, theatre, nursery and cafeteria, in return for a family membership subscription and for agreeing to periodic medical examinations. Advice, but not treatment, was given. In order to be able to draw valid conclusions the Peckham biologists thought it necessary that they should be able to observe human beings who were free—free to act as they wished and to give expression to their desires. So there were no rules and no leaders. "I was the only person with authority," said Dr. Scott Williamson, the founder, "and I used it to stop anyone exerting any authority." For the first eight months there was chaos. "With the first member-families", says one observer, "there arrived a horde of undisciplined children who used the whole building as they might have used one vast London street. Screaming and running like hooligans through all the rooms, breaking equipment and furniture," they made life intolerable for everyone. Scott Williamson, however, "insisted that peace should be restored only by the response of the children to the variety of stimuli that was placed in their way," and, "in less than a year the chaos was reduced to an order in which groups of children could daily be seen swimming, skating, riding bicycles, using the gymnasium or playing some game, occasionally reading a book in the library ... the running and screaming were things of the past."

More dramatic examples of the same kind of phenomenon are reported by those people who have been brave enough, or confident enough to institute self-governing non-punitive communities of delinquents or maladjusted children: August Aichhorn and Homer Lane are examples. Aichhorn ran that famous institution in Vienna, described in his book *Wayward Youth*. Homer Lane was the man who, after experiments in America started in Britain a community of juvenile delinquents, boys and girls, called The Little Commonwealth. Lane used to declare that "Freedom cannot be given. It is taken by the child in discovery and invention." True to this principle, remarks Howard Jones, "he refused to impose upon the children a system of government copied from the institutions of the adult world. The self-governing structure of the Little Commonwealth was evolved by the children themselves, slowly and painfully to satisfy their own needs."

Anarchists believe in *leaderless groups*, and if this phrase is familiar to you it is because of the paradox that what was known as the leaderless group technique was adopted in the British and American armies during the war—as a means of selecting leaders. The military psychiatrists learned that leader or follower traits are not exhibited in isolation. They are, as one of them wrote, "relative to a specific social situation—leadership varied from situation to situation and from group to group." Or as the anarchist Michael Bakunin put it a hundred years ago, "I receive and I give such is human life. Each directs and is directed in his turn. Therefore there is no fixed and constant authority, but a continual exchange of mutual, temporary, and, above all, voluntary authority and subordination."

This point about leadership was well put in John Comerford's book, *Health the Unknown*, about the Peckham experiment:

> Accustomed as is this age to artificial leadership ... it is difficult for it to realise the truth that leaders require no training or appointing, but emerge spontaneously when conditions require them. Studying their members in the free-for-all of the Peckham Centre, the observing scientists saw over and over again how one member instinctively became, and was instinctively but not officially recognised as, leader to meet the needs of one particular moment. Such leaders appeared and disappeared as the flux of the Centre required. Because they were not consciously appointed, neither (when they had fulfilled their purpose) were they consciously overthrown. Nor was any particular gratitude shown by members to a leader either at the time of his services or after for services rendered. They followed his guidance just as long as his guidance was helpful and what they wanted. They melted away from him without regrets when some widening of experience beckoned them on to some fresh adventure, which would in turn throw up its spontaneous leader, or when their self confidence was such that any form of constrained leadership would have been a restraint to them. A society, therefore, if left to itself in suitable circumstances to express itself spontaneously works out its own salvation and achieves a harmony of action which superimposed leadership cannot emulate.

Don't be deceived by the sweet reasonableness of all this. This anarchist concept of leadership is quite revolutionary in its implications as you can see if you look around, for you see everywhere in operation the opposite concept: that of hierarchical, authoritarian, privileged and permanent leadership. There are very few comparative studies available of the effects of these two opposite approaches to the organisation of work. Two of them I will mention later; another, about the organisation of architects' offices was produced in 1962 for the Institute of British Architects under the title *The Architect and His Office*. The team which prepared this report found two different approaches to the design process, which gave rise to different ways of working and methods of organisation. One they categorised as centralised, which was characterised by autocratic forms of control, and the other they called dispersed, which promoted what they called "an informal atmosphere of free-flowing ideas." This is a very live issue among architects. Mr. W. D. Pile, who in an official capacity helped to sponsor the outstanding success of postwar British architecture, the school-building programme, specifies among the things he looks for in a member of the building team that: "He must have a belief in what I call the nonhierarchical organisation of the work. The work has got to be organised not on the star system, but on the repertory system. The team leader may often be junior to a team member. That will only be accepted if it is commonly accepted that primacy lies with the best idea and not with the senior man."

And one of our greatest architects, Walter Gropius, proclaims what he calls the technique of "collaboration among men, which would release the creative instincts of the individual instead of smothering them. The essence of such technique should be to emphasise individual freedom of initiative, instead of authoritarian direction by a boss ... synchronizing individual effort by a continuous give and take of its members ... "

This leads us to another corner-stone of anarchist theory, the idea of workers' control of industry. A great many people think that workers' control is an attractive idea, but one which is incapable of realisation (and consequently not worth fighting for) because of the scale and complexity of modern industry. How can we convince them otherwise? Apart from pointing out how changing sources of motive power make the geographical concentration of industry obsolete, and how changing methods of production make the concentration of vast numbers of people unnecessary, perhaps the best method of persuading people that workers' control is a feasible proposition in large-scale industry is through pointing to successful examples of what the guild socialists called "encroaching control." They are partial and limited in effect, as they are bound to be, since they operate within the conventional industrial structure, but they do indicate that workers have an organisational capacity on the shop floor, which most people deny that they possess.

Let me illustrate this from two recent instances in modern large-scale industry. The first, the gang system worked in Coventry, was described by an American professor of industrial and management engineering, Seymour Melman, in his book *Decision-Making and Productivity*. He sought, by a detailed comparison of the manufacture of a similar product, the Ferguson tractor, in Detroit and in Coventry, England, "to demonstrate that there are realistic alternatives to managerial rule over production." His account of the operation of the gang system was confirmed by a Coventry engineering worker, Reg Wright, in two articles in *Anarchy*.

Of Standard's tractor factory in the period up to 1956 when it was sold, Melman writes: "In this firm we will show that at the same time: thousands of workers operated virtually without supervision as conventionally understood, and at high productivity; the highest wage in British industry was paid; high quality products were produced at acceptable prices in extensively mechanised plants; the management conducted its affairs at unusually low costs; also, organised workers had a substantial role in production decision-making."

From the standpoint of the production workers, "the gang system leads to keeping track of goods instead of keeping track of people." Melman contrasts the "predatory competition" which characterises the managerial decision-making system with the workers' decision-making system in which "The most characteristic feature of the decision-formulating process is that of mutuality in decision-making with final authority residing in the hands of the grouped workers themselves." The gang system as he described it is very like the collective contract system advocated by G. D. H. Cole, who claimed that "The effect would be to link the members of the working group together in a common enterprise under their joint auspices and control, and to emancipate them from an externally imposed discipline in respect of their method of getting the work done."

My second example again derives from a comparative study of different methods of work organisation, made by the Tavistock Institute in the late 1950s, reported in E. L. Trist's *Organisational Choice*, and P. Herbst's *Autonomous Group Functioning*. Its importance can be seen from the opening words of the first of these: "This study concerns a group of miners who came together to evolve a new way of working together, planning the type of change they wanted to put through, and testing it in practice. The new type of work organisation which has come to be known in the industry as composite working, has in recent years emerged spontaneously in a number of different pits in the north-west Durham coal field. Its roots go back to an earlier tradition which had been almost completely displaced in the course of the last century by the introduction of work techniques based on task segmentation, differential status and payment, and extrinsic hierarchical control." The other report notes how the study showed "the ability of quite large primary work groups of 40–50 members to act as self-regulating, self-developing social organisms able to maintain themselves in a steady state of high productivity." The authors describe the system in a way which shows its relation to anarchist thought:

> The composite work organisation may be described as one in which the group takes over complete responsibility for the total cycle of operations involved in mining the coal-face. No member of the group has a fixed work role. Instead, the men deploy themselves, depending on the requirements of the on-going group task. Within the limits of technological and safety requirements they are free to evolve their own way of organising and carrying out their task. They are not subject to any external authority in this respect, nor is there within the group itself any member who takes over a formal directive leadership function. Whereas in conventional long-wall working the coal-getting task is split into four to eight separate work roles, carried out by different teams, each paid at a different rate, in the composite group members are no longer paid directly for any of the tasks carried out. The all-in wage agreement is, instead, based on the negotiated price per ton of coal produced by the team. The income obtained is divided equally among team members.

The works I have been quoting were written for specialists in productivity and industrial organisation, but their lessons are clear for people who are interested in the idea of workers' control. Faced with the objection that even though it can be shown that autonomous groups can organise themselves on a large scale and for complex tasks, it has not been shown that they can successfully co-ordinate, we resort once again to the federative principle. There is nothing outlandish about the idea that large numbers of autonomous industrial units can federate and co-ordinate their activities. If you travel across Europe you go over the lines of a dozen railway systems—capitalist and communist—co-ordinated by freely arrived at agreement between the various undertakings, with no central authority. You can post a letter to anywhere in the world, but there is no world postal authority—representatives of different postal authorities simply have a congress every five years or so.

There are trends, observable in these occasional experiments in industrial organisation, in new approaches to problems of delinquency and addiction, in education and community organisation, and in the "de-institutionalisation" of hospitals, asylums, children's homes and so on, which have much in common with each other, and which run counter to the generally accepted ideas about organisation, authority and government.

Cybernetic theory with its emphasis on self-organising systems, and speculation about the ultimate social effects of automation, leads in a similar revolutionary direction. George and Louise Crowley, for example, in their comments on the report of the Ad Hoc Committee on the Triple Revolution, (*Monthly Review*, Nov. 1964) remark that, "We find it no less reasonable to postulate a functioning society without authority than to postulate an orderly universe without a god. Therefore the word *anarchy* is not for us freighted with connotations of disorder, chaos, or confusion. For humane men, living in non-competitive conditions of freedom from toil and of universal affluence, anarchy is simply the appropriate state of society."

In Britain, Professor Richard Titmuss remarks that social ideas may well be as important in the next half-century as technical innovation. I believe that the social ideas of anarchism: autonomous groups, spontaneous order, workers' control, the federative principle, add up to a coherent theory of social organisation which is a valid and realistic alternative to the authoritarian, hierarchical and institutional social philosophy which we see in application all around us. Man will be compelled, Kropotkin declared, "to find new forms of organisation for the social functions which the State fulfils through the bureaucracy" and he insisted that "as long as this is not done nothing will be done." I think we have discovered what these new forms of organisation should be. We have now to make the opportunities for putting them into practice.

# Section Two

## Culture, Place and Housing

# 1. PLOTLANDS:
## THE UNAUTHORISED VERSION

... [Plotlands] is a shorthand description for those areas where, in the first 40 years of this century, farmland was divided into small plots and sold, often in unorthodox ways, to Londoners wanting to build their holiday home, country retreat or would-be smallholding. The word evokes a landscape consisting of a gridiron of grassy tracks, sparsely filled with bungalows constructed from army huts, railway coaches, shanties, sheds, shacks and chalets, which when left to evolve on its own, slowly becomes like any other ordinary suburban landscape, leaving only a few clues to its anarchic origins.

By 1939 this plotland landscape was to be found in pockets across the North Downs, along the Hampshire Plain, and in the Thames Valley at such riverside sites as Penton Hook, Marlow Bottom and Purley Park. It was interspersed among the established holiday towns on the East and West Sussex coast as places like Shoreham Beach, Pett Level and Camber Sands and, most notoriously, at Peacehaven. It crept up the East Coast, from Sheppey in Kent to Lincolnshire, by way of Canvey Island and Jaywick Sands, and it clustered inland all across South Essex.

The plotland phenomenon was not confined to the south-east of England. Every industrial conurbation in Britain once had these escape routes to the country, the river or the sea. For the West Midlands there was the Severn Valley, the Wye Valley and North Wales, for Liverpool and Manchester the North Welsh coast and the Wirral, for Glasgow the Ayrshire coast and even the bonny banks of Loch Lomond. Serving the industrial populations of the West Riding towns and cities were sites along the Yorkshire coast and the Humber estuary, and for those of Tyneside and Teesside there were the nearby coasts of Northumberland and Durham.

It was as though a proportion of the population was obeying a law of nature in seeking out a place where they could build for themselves. But it is certainly worth remembering that, when the plotland phenomenon began, most families in British cities and towns were only one or two generations away from rural life.

A series of factors made the plotlands. The first was the same economic fact that influenced Ebenezer Howard, the price of rural land. There is an old saying that land loses its value long before it loses its price. But agricultural decline as a re-

---

Originally printed in Peter Hall and Colin Ward, *Sociable Cities: The Legacy of Ebenezer Howard*. (Chichester: Wiley, 1998), 71–77.

sult of cheap imports, which had begun in the 1870s and continued (with a break during World War I because of submarine blockades) until 1939, encouraged the buying and selling of bankrupt farms at throwaway prices. In 1913 you could buy land in Kent at £10 an acre (£4/ha) with a £1 deposit, or a plot on Canvey Island in Essex for 11s.6d. (57.5p). The break-up of landed estates after the Liberal government's doubling of death duties, together with the slaughter-rate among sons and heirs of landowners in World War I, added to the pressure among sellers to seek a multitude of small buyers in the absence of a few large ones.

A second factor was the spread down the social scale of the holiday habit and the idea of the "week-end". The Holidays with Pay Act of 1938 affected 18.5 million employed workers (and consequently their dependents), nearly 11 million of whom were to receive holiday pay for the first time. Those who previously took a holiday paid for by savings, were likely to seek a cheap one, and a glance at *Dalton's Weekly* in the 1930s would show that, apart from a tent in a field, the cheapest holiday advertised was to rent someone else's plotland bungalow.

Another factor was the accessibility of cheap transport. There was the incredible ramification of railway branch lines, reaching places for which the station had become an unexpected link with the outside world, but also the pleasure boat industry, fighting back against railway competition in the holiday trade, not merely up the Thames, but also along the Essex and Kent coasts. A final, decisive factor was the gradual democratisation of private motoring.

The fourth factor is best summed up as the growth of the cult of the great outdoors. This had several aspects. One was belief in the health-giving qualities of fresh air, as a defence against such scourges of urban life as bronchitis and tuberculosis. Another aspect was the pursuit of popular riverside and seaside sports such as fishing, boating and sailing. Yet another aspect was the attraction to dwellers of "the simple life", whether in a country cottage with three acres and a cow, or as a long-distance commuter.

There was, finally, the idea of a property-owning democracy. At the end of the twentieth century, the major mode of tenure in Britain is the owner-occupied house. When the century began, 90 per cent of households, whether rich or poor, rented their dwellings,[1] and throughout the twentieth century the attraction of possessing a few square yards of England has had its appeal. Long before a minor Conservative politician coined the phrase about property-owning, one plotland entrepreneur, Frederick Francis Ramuz, twice mayor of Southend-on-Sea, who operated as The Land Company, was advertising in 1906 that "Land Nationalisation is Coming", meaning that the dominance of the absentee landlord would be replaced by every family owning its portion of our common birthright. Like the developer of Peacehaven, Mr Ramuz claimed that on his sites at Laindon "A real garden city without the aid of philanthropists and on a perfectly sound basis, is likely to be created."[2]

The plotland sites have several common characteristics. They are invariably on marginal land. The inland Essex sites are all south of an invisible line across the county separating the more easily worked soil from the heavy clay, known to farmers as three-horse land, which went out of cultivation earliest in the agricultural depression. Other plotlands grew up on vulnerable coastal sites, of which the best-known were Jaywick Sands and Canvey Island, or on riverside sites in the Thames Valley, also liable to inundation. Or they are on acid heathland or chalky uplands. Even Peacehaven was built on an area of the South Downs where the ancient sheep pasture had been replaced by a tough, wiry grass as a result of ploughing in the Napoleonic and subsequent wars, with the result that it was the earliest to be abandoned as grazing.

Another characteristic of all the plotland areas was that the holiday home remained in the same family and became the retirement home of the first generation. What seemed to the outside observer to be inconvenient, substandard and far from the shops, was for them loaded with memories of happy summer days when the children were small. A final common attribute was the tendency of the plotlands, unless deliberate obstacles were put in the way of the residents, to be the subject of a process of continuous upgrading over time. Extensions, the addition of bathrooms, partial or total rebuilding, the provision of mains services and the making-up of roads, are part of the continuous improvement process in any such settlement that has not been economically undermined or subjected to "Planners' blight".

The conservationist literature of the inter-war years reveals the intense horror that was felt by all "right-thinking" (i.e. privileged) people at the desecration of the landscape they saw as happening everywhere. Dean Inge, a celebrated publicist of the period, coined the phrase "Bungaloid growth", with its implication that some kind of cancer was creeping over the face of the home counties. Clough Williams-Ellis, who later built the holiday village of Portmerrion, was the author of *England and the Octopus* (1928) and editor of the compendium *Britain and the Beast* (1937), in which Howard Marshall declared that "a gimcrack civilisation crawls like a giant slug, across the country, leaving a foul trail of slime behind it". In retrospect, it is hard not to feel that part of this disgust was ordinary misanthropy. The wrong sort of people were getting a place in the sun.

The plotlands were, of all developments, the most vulnerable. They seldom complied with the building by-laws. They could be held to be a menace to public health since, like most of the homes of the rural poor at that time, they were not connected to sewerage systems. They provided very little income for local authorities, since their rateable value was very low, and their owners were not people with an influential voice in public affairs. They looked, when raw and new, more like boom towns, pioneering in the American West or the Australian bush, than like the expected pattern of urban growth in the south-east of England.

But there is an irony in the fact that the simple life and the rural weekend also attracted the liberal intelligentsia who were the backbone of the preservationist lobby. Reginald Bray was a progressive philanthropist and member, in succession, of the London School Board and the London County Council. In 1919 he left London to administer his father's estates based on Shere in Surrey. When Dr Peter Brandon studied the estate papers he found that Bray provided sites for many of the good and the great of the 1920s and 1930s, including a majority of members of the first Labour cabinet and several crusaders for the protection of the countryside. Clough Williams-Ellis was among them, while deploring the way in which

"the adventurous bungalow plants its foundations—a pink asbestos roof screaming its challenge—across a whole parish from some pleasant upland that it has
lightheartedly defaced".[3]

Another of the weekend residents was Bray's fellow Harrovian, the historian
G.M. Trevelyan, who lamented that "the State is Socialist enough to destroy by
taxation the classes that used to preserve rural amenity, but is still too Conservative to interfere in the purposes to which land is put by speculators to whom the
land is sold".[4]

Time and nature have changed the plotland sites, just as they change any raw
new settlement. For example, those offending salmon-pink asbestos-cement slates
have, besides proving themselves as durable as other roofing materials, attracted
moss and lichen so that their present appearance is like that of Cotswold stone.
At the end of the century we may smile at the way the shapers of policy took it for
granted that *they* were entitled to a rural retreat, while wanting to deny on aesthetic grounds the same opportunity to people further down the hierarchy of chance
and income. Patrick Abercrombie, in introducing his Greater London Plan, was
careful to stress this point: "It is possible to point with horror to the jumble of
shacks and bungalows on the Langdon Hill and at Pitsea. This is a narrow-minded
appreciation of what was as genuine a desire as created the group of lovely gardens
and houses at Frensham and Bramshott."[5] As so often, Abercrombie failed to go
with the flow of conventional opinion; he understood the aspirations of those he
was planning for, in a way that his counterparts almost never did.

The postwar planning legislation, and the fact that landowners were now
subsidised for upgrading marginal farmland, effectively put an end to plotland
development, and planning authorities have perceived the existing sites as among
the problems they are expected to solve. Sometimes the aim has been to eliminate
them totally and return the land, if not to agriculture, then to public recreational
use. In most places such policies have failed and have simply resulted in patches
of empty, scrubby wasteland between those plots still occupied by determined
people who fought planning decisions, with the result that local authorities were
overruled by central government.

In some other places the clearance policy has succeeded. At Havering Park in
Essex, the Greater London Council demolished all plotland dwellings to make
a country park. Nearby, in 1949, the New Town of Basildon was designated to
make some kind of urban entity out of Pitsea and Laindon, where, by the end of
World War II there was a settled population of about 25,000 on 75 miles (120
km) of grass-track roads, mostly unsewered and with standpipes for water supply.
More recently the Essex County Council eliminated another scattered plotland
area to make the new residential town of South Woodham Ferrers. In many other
parts of the South East, planning authorities have tried to freeze development by
refusing all applications for planning permission improvements, and upgrading,
refusals which have often been reversed on appeal.

Attitudes towards the plotlands have changed over the years. They began as a
blot on the landscape. Then they were seen as odd, curious and vaguely interesting or quaint. After that, inevitably, they were perceived as a precious aspect of

our heritage. At Basildon, one of the few remaining bungalows called The Haven at Dunton Hills became a plotland museum. At Dungeness in Kent, a plotland site was designated as a Conservation Area in order to preserve it from redevelopment. In the effort to save a plotland site in Swansea Bay from a bid to redevelop it, the local authority similarly designated it as a Conservation Area in 1990, on the grounds that the site was "arcadian". On other sites, even the antiquated railway carriages that the first settlers bought for £15 each, including delivery by horse-drawn transport to the site, have become precious for the railway antiquarians.

But the last word on the significance of the plotland era comes from Dr Anthony King, in his monumental, global history of the bungalow as a building type. He observes that:

> A combination of cheap land and transport, prefabricated materials, and the owners' labour and skills had given back, to the ordinary people of the land, the opportunity denied to them for over two hundred years, an opportunity which, at the time, was still available to almost half of the world's non-industrialised population: the freedom of a man to build his own house. It was a freedom that was to be very short-lived.[6]

How right he was.

# 2. THE PEOPLE ACT:
## THE POSTWAR SQUATTERS' MOVEMENT

*"In the last few weeks there has been organised squatting in empty mansions,
with enough public approval to force the government and the authorities into
more active requisitioning—a score for the anarchists ... "*
—F. J. Osborn, 26 July, 1945.

The politicians of the post-war Labour government, who were taken by surprise
by the squatters' movement which swept Britain (and other countries) in 1946,
showed, by their astonishment and unpreparedness, how far out of touch they were
with the desperateness of the housing situation, and with the mood of the people.
They were blind to the evidence provided by the earlier seizures of empty buildings by homeless returning servicemen which occurred in 1919, or by the Scottish
examples during the 1939–1945 war—the "Blitz Hotel" incident in Glasgow, and
the occupation of empty houses at Blantyre in the spring of 1945. Above all, they
ignored the lessons of the Vigilante campaign of the summer of 1945—that far-off
summer which saw the beginning of the "peace" and of the atomic age.

The picturesque, but perhaps ill-advised name of "Vigilantes" was adopted by
committees of, largely, ex-servicemen who, under cover of night, installed homeless families and their furniture in unoccupied houses—usually successfully,
since no action could be taken to evict them once they were in, until the usually absentee property-owners could initiate legal proceedings against them. This
campaign started, and was most active, in seaside towns, for example Southend,
Hastings and, most of all, Brighton, which has a rather unique place among the
South Coast resorts in that it has a large working-class population. The original
and outstanding grievance against which the Vigilante campaign was aimed, was
the way in which big seaside houses were being kept empty for most of the year in
order to be let at very high rents during the short holiday season.

Originally printed in Colin Ward, *Housing: An anarchist approach*, Second Edition.
    (London: Freedom Press, 1983), 19–27. NB: This is a compilation of reports on the
    squatters' campaign published in *Freedom*, 27 July, 10 August, 24 August, 7 Sep-
    tember, 21 September, 5 October, and 19 October 1946. Printed in this form in
    *Anarchy*, January 1963. Reprinted by the London Squatters in 1969. The quotation
    at the top comes from *The Letters of Lewis Mumford and Frederic J. Osborn*, ed. by
    Michael Hughes (Adams and Dart 1971).

From this, as the movement spread, it became an attack on the right of land-lords to keep property unoccupied for any reason. The success of the Vigilantes forced the government to grant wider powers to local authorities to requisition property for housing purposes, while the threat of further direct action ensured that the councils would use these powers. Thus the campaign began with the ef-fort to put right an obvious public scandal, it spread to become a challenge of the hitherto hardly disputed right of the landlord to do as he liked with his own property without reference to public needs, and it ended with the official sanction of this challenge.

The squatters' movement of the following year sprang from another of these scandalous anomalies—the emptiness of hundreds of army and air force camps during the worst housing shortage we have known. The first of the 1946 squat-ters was Mr. James Fielding, a cinema projectionist at Scunthorpe, Lincolnshire, who, desperate for somewhere to live, moved on May 8th with his family, into the former officers' mess of an unoccupied anti-aircraft camp. As soon as the news of their action got around the town, other young couples in a similar predicament moved into the other huts, and the first colony of squatters was born. Shortly after this two other camps in the same area were seized, and this was followed by the occupation of several camps around Sheffield. The Sheffield settlers formed a Squatters' Protection Society and quickly linked up with the pioneer squatters at Scunthorpe.

These events were rapidly followed by the seizure of hundreds of camps every-where in Britain. The authorities who at first disclaimed any responsibility for the squatters—passing the buck from one department to another—were forced into recognising the occupations, and local authorities were instructed to turn on wa-ter and electricity and to provide essential services. Later in the year the Ministry of Works, which had previously declared itself "not interested", found it possible to offer the Ministry of Health (which was then the government department re-sponsible for housing) 850 former service camps.

The government announced on the 11th October 1946 that 1,038 camps in England and Wales had been occupied by 39,535 people, and on 5th September it was stated that four thousand people had squatted in Scotland. Since the govern-ment could not destroy the movement, it tried to absorb it, and expressed itself confident that the settlers would "see reason" and "move out when the situation had been explained to them". A leading article in *The Observer* commented: "The Ministry piously hopes that squatters, after certain explanations, will 'return to the homes from which they have come'. What homes? Bits of caravans or crannies in the overcrowded lodgings or the premises of others from which they are desper-ately trying to escape? The fact that ex-soldiers who have had plenty of camp life in their time should now regard an army hut as a little bit of heaven is surely strong enough evidence of their misery and despair. Nor are they likely to be terrified by the talk of winter weather."

As the camps began to fill, the squatters turned to other empty buildings: houses, shops, mansions, disused school buildings, race tracks and a stadium, were among the places occupied, and on August 26th, two Aberdeen hotels and a hostel were taken, while on the 29th two big hotels in Glasgow were seized, though they had to be abandoned later.

The final and most spectacular phase of the campaign began in London on Sunday, 8th September, when the 148 luxury flats of Duchess of Bedford House, Kensington, another block in Weymouth Street, Marylebone, and houses in Holland Park and Camden Hill were invaded. On the following day three more houses in Beaumont Street, Marylebone were taken over, and on Tuesday 60 families entered Fountain Court, a block of flats in Victoria. On Wednesday the flats at Abbey Lodge, Regents Park and the 630-room Ivanhoe Hotel, Bloomsbury, were occupied.

The tactics adopted by the police in this final stage of the campaign varied from day to day. At first at the Duchess of Bedford House their human sympathy seems to have got the better of their role as protectors of the interests of the propertied classes, and, according to the press, "Police called to the scene made themselves helpful and an Inspector made arrangements for a WVS van to supply hot drinks." But on the Tuesday they were organising a watch on unoccupied property to prevent further squatting, and the Home Office instructed Scotland Yard to "enquire into the origin of the organisation behind the squatters" and to keep the government "fully informed of the activities of political agitators who ferment trouble". (Needless to say, the CID soon announced "secret documents".) On the Wednesday, after Abbey Lodge and the Ivanhoe Hotel had been seized, the police cordoned the buildings. Their refusal to allow any more than twenty-five blankets into Abbey Lodge for the children, caused a scene outside in which demonstrators lay down five deep in the road and held up traffic for a quarter of a mile. Later, food and blankets were allowed in.

There were similar scenes at the Ivanhoe Hotel. The state of siege was resumed during the night at the four main "squatters' fronts" and the blockade continued on the following day, while the police took more action to prevent people from entering or re-entering the buildings. The same scenes were repeated on the Thursday night, and mounted police were used to disperse the crowd at Abbey Lodge. On Friday there were rumours that they intended to use tear gas. Police leave was stopped, and the route to the Sunday meeting in Hyde Park was lined with mounted police. The first arrests, apart from the usual ones on charges of obstruction and insulting behaviour, were made on the Saturday, when five Communists were charged with "conspiring together with other persons to incite people to trespass on property". (They were subsequently found guilty and bound over.)

On the same day, the Minister of Health, the late Aneurin Bevan, who was just back from his holiday in Switzerland, instructed all local authorities to cut off gas and electricity supplies to all property under their control occupied by squatters. The Labour government advised all owners of empty buildings to ensure that all doors and windows were secured, but it did not ask them why, at a time when families were being prosecuted for sleeping in fields and ditches, their property remained empty.

The Communists, although they had a year earlier denounced the Vigilantes, were very active amongst the squatters in London. So much so that people who had to rely on newspapers for their information assumed, and have assumed since, that the whole thing was a Communist stunt. Diana Murray Hill, the only person to make a serious study at the time, of who the squatters were, and what kind of straits they had been in (*Pilot Papers*, November 1946), reported from Abbey Lodge that "as to the argument that the Communists gave them the idea of squatting, they said there was nothing to it. Many of them had been squatting of their own accord before the taking over of the flats. In some cases the huts they had been squatting in had been taken away from them". And, "finally the crowd of sympathisers outside, the majority of whom Mr. R. knew personally and could vouch for their not being Communists ... " And of the squatters themselves: "Again he knew many of them personally, and of the ones he knew none were Communists. The squatters formed their own committee". Or as we put it in *Freedom* (21 Sept., 1946):

> The fact is that the Communists wish to exploit the movement now that it has become widespread. One must recognise this fact even when one expresses sympathy with the arrested leaders, and solidarity with those rank and file Communists who have given genuine support to some squatters. Nevertheless the support of the Communists is a real danger to the movement. Legal action against the squatters was obviously very difficult; but the attempt of the CP to organise them has provided the government with just the handle they needed. The legal prosecutions will deflect attention from the real issue—the desperate plight of the homeless. It will lower the whole question to the level of political strife and opportunism. Perhaps most dangerous of all, the CP themselves will seek to turn the movement into legalistic channels. They have already formulated 'demands' of the government. Soon they will be urging the homeless to avoid further direct action and to 'do nothing to hamper the realisation of your demands'.

The truth of this evaluation was shown in the anti-climax of the "general evacuation" by the London squatters when the High Court injunction was granted. This was treated by the press as the end of the squatters, and the fact was concealed that the many thousands of camp settlers were not affected by the set-back, and had settled down until they could find something better, while many of the London squatters were eventually provided with accommodation of one sort or another by the LCC.

In October, Aneurin Bevan sought to turn public feeling against the camp squatters by suggesting that they were "jumping their place in the housing queue", when in fact they were jumping out of the housing queue by moving into buildings which would not otherwise have been used for housing purposes. It took most of them years in fact to get into the "housing queue". Over a hundred families who in 1946 occupied a camp known as Field Farm in Oxfordshire, stayed together and in 1958–9 were re-housed in the new village of Berinsfield on the same site.

•••

A notable feature of the whole campaign was the way in which, quite spontaneously and without disputes, the accommodation was divided among the would-be squatters in accordance with their needs, the size of their families, and so on. The best huts and buildings, usually the former Officers' Mess, needless to say, went to large families, while the ordinary Nissen huts were divided among the childless couples. Of one of the earliest squatters' camps it was reported on 24th July, 1946, . "The campers today discovered a 20,000-gallon water tank and have turned on the water. A youth appointed as water inspector, is carrying out hourly checks to ensure that taps are not left running. A camp committee has been elected and the camp is being run on communal lines. Tradesmen call with their vans."

In camps I visited in Hampshire I found everywhere that hopeful, adventurous spirit that springs from independence and spontaneous co-operation. Everywhere I saw attempts to make those bleak huts look "more like home". Communal cooking, laundering and nursery facilities sprang up. Fathers took turns to stoke the boilers, mothers took turns to do the settlement's shopping, and the children collected up the rubbish left by the army and made bonfires of it. For them at least, it was a real adventure. Squatters Protection Societies and Federations were formed to protect their mutual interest. Some memorable scenes of solidarity were seen during the seizures at London hotels, when, in the face of police opposition, complete strangers threw into the buildings blankets and parcels of food, without hope of recompense.

One of the remarkable features of the squatters' communities was that they were formed of people who had very little in common except their homelessness— tinkers and university dons were amongst them. A very revealing report on the squatters, in a series "How Are They Now?" appeared in the *News Chronicle* for January 14th, 1947. The correspondent describes a camp in Lancashire:

> ... There are two camps within the camp—the official squatters (that is, people who have been placed in the huts after the first invasion) and the unofficial squatters (the veterans who have been allowed to remain on sufferance). Both pay the same rent of 10s. a week—but there the similarity ends. Although one would have imagined that the acceptance of rent from both should accord them identical privileges, in fact it does not. Workmen have put up partitions in the huts of the official squatters—and have put in sinks and numerous other conveniences. These are the sheep; the goats have perforce to fend for themselves.
>
> An interesting commentary on the situation was made by one of the young welfare officers attached to the housing department. On her visit of inspection she found that the goats had set to work with a will, improvising partitions, running up curtains, distempering, painting and using initiative. The official squatters on the other hand, sat about glumly without using initiative or lifting a hand to help themselves and bemoaning their fate, even though they might have been removed from the most appalling slum property. Until the overworked corporation workmen got around to them they would not attempt to improve affairs themselves.

How much this story reveals, not only about the squatters, but about the difference between the state of mind that induces free independent action, and that of dependence and inertia; the difference between people who initiate things and act for themselves, and the people to whom things just happen.

•••

When the squatters movement is viewed against other historical examples of direct action applied to the housing problem in a non-revolutionary situation, four definite phases, common to them all, can be discerned. Firstly *Initiative*, the individual action that begins the campaign, the spark that starts the blaze; secondly *Consolidation*, when the movement spreads sufficiently to constitute a real threat to property rights and becomes big enough to avoid being simply snuffed out by the authorities. The third phase is that of *Success*, when the authorities have to concede to the movement what it has won; and the fourth phase is that of *Official Action*, usually undertaken unwillingly in order to placate the popular demand, and to avoid further attacks on the interests of the propertied class. For nothing succeeds like success, and governments usually realise that, as Kropotkin observes, "Once the principle of the 'Divine Right of Property' is shaken, no amount of theorising will prevent its overthrow."

The first phase was seen in Glasgow in 1915 when the Govan housewives refused to pay the rent increases demanded by rapacious landlords, while Partick women rough-handled the rent-collectors; it was seen in Vienna in 1921 when homeless ex-soldiers seized land in the ex-Emperor's hunting park, and began to build houses; it was to be seen again in 1938 when 250 tenants of Quinn Square, Bethnal Green refused to pay any more rent until repairs were done and rents reduced; it was seen in Brighton in June 1945, when ex-servicemen moved a homeless family into a house in Round Hill Street, and thus began the Vigilante campaign; and it was seen in May 1946, when the Fielding family initiated the Squatters by settling in the Scunthorpe camp.

The second phase was represented by the great demonstration of housewives in George Square during the Clydeside Rent Strikes, and the strike of the shipyard workers who passed a resolution that "unless the government took action to reduce rents to their pre-war level, a general strike on the Clyde would follow". In Vienna it was the formation of the Land Settlement Movement, whose banners were inscribed with the words: "Give us Land, Wood and Stone, and we will make Bread!" In the London Rent Strike Movement, this phase was apparent in the development of the Stepney Tenants' League and the spread of rent strikes all over the London area; in the Vigilante campaign it took the form of widespread occupation of empty apartments, and among the squatters it was still more noticeable in the seizure of service camps in every part of the country.

The third phase was implicit in the Glasgow Sheriff Court's decision in favour of eighteen workers summoned for non-payment of rent, after a deputation had pointed out to the Sheriff that "These men will only resume work in the event of your deciding against the factor: if you do not, it means that the workers on the lower reaches will stop work tomorrow and join them." It was seen in the Vienna Municipality's recognition of the Co-operative Building Clubs; and it took a very obvious form in the rent strikes before the last war when the landlord of Brady Street, Stepney, had to agree to big rent reduction, and to large-scale repairs. The official sanctioning of the first wave of camp squatters was the latest example of this phase.

In the final phase we see the complete justification of direct action as a means of forcing the authorities to take radical measures that they would not otherwise have considered. Fearing further big strikes on the Clyde in the First World War, a government completely representing the landlord class, was forced to pass the first Rent Restrictions Act, and, remembering this, and with the 1938–9 rent strikes fresh in mind, Chamberlain's government hastened to introduce the 1939 Rent Restrictions Act on the outbreak of the Second World War. The militant action of the Austrian workers made it necessary for the authorities, at a time of complete economic and financial collapse, to initiate the Vienna Municipal Housing and Town-Planning Scheme, one of the biggest and most comprehensive in Europe. In 1945 the Vigilantes coerced the government into granting local authorities wide requisitioning powers and the threat of further action made sure that they used them. In the same way the announcement that "Eight hundred and fifty former service camps are being offered by the Ministry of Works to Mr. Aneurin Bevan to help him in his emergency housing drive", was the measure of the success of the camp squatters. But for the opportunist intervention of the Communists, it seems likely that the seizure of hotels and luxury flats would have forced even more significant and spectacular concessions from the authorities.

●●●

Today, direct action is again overdue. Isn't it extraordinary that in a period when homelessness in London has been building up steadily, State House in Holborn, one of the vast new prestige office blocks should have stood empty for at least two years? In the new Solidarity pamphlet *Homelessness*, Sheila Jones of the Tenants' Association at one of the LCC's "half-way houses" says, "To some of us it is beginning to be clear that if we want anything done we will have to do it ourselves. The LCC tries to keep these places as terrible as possible to prevent others taking advantage of the 'facilities' provided. An imaginative and selective breaking of the artificial LCC rules might be an effective method of protest. What would happen for instance if a group of families got together and decided to bring in their own furniture to replace the LCC stuff? Would the LCC wardens call the police in against tenants whose only crime was that they had tried, at their own expense, to make living conditions more bearable for themselves and for their children?"

And another contributor, Ken Jones, points out that there are possibilities for the unfortunate occupants of the reception centres who have literally nothing to lose. He suggests for example that husbands should disobey the "curfew" so that if the authorities dare, they must use force to separate a man from his family.

But must the homeless and dispirited be left to fight their own battles?

# 3. THE DO-IT-YOURSELF NEW TOWN

The New Towns movement in Britain, sparked off at the turn of the century by Ebenezer Howard's book *Garden Cities of Tomorrow* and built into post-war planning legislation and policy, has had its successes and its failures. The successes are there for all to see, and as for the failures—well it always seems to me that the New Towns policy is criticised for the wrong reasons. One of the criticisms of the New Town ideology which has developed in the last few years is that the New Towns have won their success at the expense of the urban poor in the old inner city areas, and that they are consequently irrelevant to real important issues like social justice. It has been rather amusing to watch this notion spiralling round the academic chat-shows, getting cruder and more dogmatic all the while, since it was launched in 1972. It is already beginning to affect policy in the cities. It is a difficult argument to come to grips with because sometimes people say a lot of different and contradictory things at the same time. How often one hears the giant fringe housing estates like Thamesmead, or Chelmsley Wood, or Kirkby or Cantril Farm, described as New Towns, when of course they are not. If you point out that the New Towns have absorbed only a small proportion of the enormous outward movement from the cities (only 13 per cent of the movement from London), or if you take the example of Milton Keynes which has provided 16,000 jobs of which a little over a thousand came from London, while 12,000 people have moved there from London, then the critics say that the New Towns have become irrelevant. If you point out that the New Towns have provided homes and jobs for large numbers of working-class people who would not be enabled otherwise to get a more ample life out of the city in the way that middle class people take for granted, they reply that the New Towns have done nothing for the really under-privileged or deprived. Well, I'm delighted to see the pundits of planning emerging as the champions of the inner city poor. It makes a change when you consider what the planning orthodoxy of the last twenty years has done to inner city London, Glasgow, Liverpool or Cardiff.

Of course I recognise that there is a large element of social snobbishness in the deprecators of the New Towns. Some people can't stand the upward social mobility of the skilled worker. And then we have to carry like a cross the Marxist intelligen-

Lecture given at the Garden Cities/New Towns Forum at Welwyn Garden City on October 22nd 1975 and at the Institute of Contemporary Arts, London on 19th February 1976. Originally printed in Colin Ward, *Talking Houses: Ten Lectures By Colin Ward*. (London: Freedom Press, 1990), 15–35.

tsia who can't bear to think of the working class being lost to the class struggle and developing a taste for wall-to-wall carpeting. They are like the people who would *like* the poor to be starving in the slums so as to hasten the day of revolution. Apart from our moral distaste for such an outlook, life never happens that way.

What we are talking about is the missing half of Ebenezer Howard's formula. He wanted dispersal in order to make possible the humane redevelopment of the inner city. He thought, seventy years or more ago, that once the inner city had been "de-magnetised", once large numbers of people had been convinced that "they can better their condition in every way by migrating elsewhere" the bubble of the monopoly value of inner-city land would burst. "But let us notice," he wrote in his chapter on The Future of London, "how each person in migrating from London, while making the burden of ground-rents less heavy for those who remain, will (unless there is some change in the law), make the burden of rates on the rate-payers of London yet heavier". He thought that the change in the inner city would be effected "not at the expense of the ratepayers, but almost entirely at the expense of the landlord class".

Now of course it hasn't happened that way because of our continued failure to cope with the problem of land valuation. We can hope, if without much conviction, that the Community Land Act and the temporary collapse of the property boom will bring us closer to the situation that Howard envisaged.

Last year in Swindon, a town rescued from decay by the Town Development legislation, I was talking to a post office worker who told me of the conditions his wife and children had had to endure living in two rooms in Islington. The move out of London of the department of the post office in which he worked had dramatically improved the conditions of life for his family. Funnily enough, it is likely that the very house he moved out of has become part of the humane, low density redevelopment of the inner city through the process known as gentrification. Perhaps instead of four families sharing the same dilapidated house with one WC in the backyard, one family now lives there and the immaculately painted house has central heating and a bathroom while the backyard has changed its name to the patio and is full of grapevines and frisbies. The old WC houses a Moulton bicycle. The occupant is probably an ecologically-conscious planner who leads a busy and blameless life crusading for the urban poor. Space for decent living is something that money can buy.

A few years ago Sir Frederic Osborn was invited to attend a meeting of the Covent Garden Community in central London. "What should the Odhams Press site be used for?" he was asked. "Why, a public open space of course" he replied, and everybody laughed. Yet a few years later, thanks to the temporary collapse of property speculation in London, the Community itself has built a garden on that site—fantastically heavily used during the long hot summer last year. And interestingly enough, in the analogous district of Paris, Les Halles, where the vegetable market again has been moved to the suburbs, the President has decided that the site is to become a public open space.

All this is simply a necessary introduction to the approach to the idea of a New Town which I want to propound. Inner City and New Town are not rivals, they are two sides of the same policy or should be.

My real purpose is to look at the New Town movement through anarchist spectacles, defining anarchism as the social philosophy of a non-governmental society. The philosopher Martin Buber begins his essay *Society and the State* with an observation from the sociologist Robert MacIver that "to identify the social with the political is to be guilty of the grossest of all confusions, which completely bars any understanding of either society or the state". The political principle for Buber is characterised by power, authority, hierarchy, dominion. He sees the social principle wherever men link themselves in an association based on a common need or a common interest. The anarchist Peter Kropotkin (and you will see that his view is different from that of Marxism and of social democracy) believed that "The State organisation, having been the force to which the minorities resorted for establishing and organising their power over the masses, cannot be the force which will serve to destroy these privileges", and he declared that "the economic and political liberation of man will have to create new forms for its expression in life, instead of those established by the State". He thought it self-evident that "this new form will have to be more popular, more decentralised, and nearer to the folk-mote self-government than representative government can ever be", reiterating that we will be compelled to find new forms of organisation for the social functions that the state fulfills through the bureaucracy, and that "as long as this is not done, nothing will be done".

Now you may wonder why I have chosen to inflict on you this slice of anarchist theory and speculation. Well, if I asked you who were the founders of the town planning movement in this country, you would unquestionably reply Ebenezer Howard and Patrick Geddes. One of the interesting things about this pair of sages, since we have all been brainwashed into thinking of planning as a professional mystery or amalgamation of mysteries, is that neither of them would be accepted today as a member of the Royal Town Planning Institute. (Howard was a stenographer. A major preoccupation of his was the invention of a shorthand-typing machine. Geddes was a biologist.) Nor would they have been accepted into the academic world. Geddes was regarded with great suspicion in academic circles, failed to get any of the jobs he applied for and was finally made a professor because a philanthropist endowed a chair especially for him. As for Howard, his biographer remarks that his book did not "receive any recognition by those who specialised in political, economic or sociological matters. Those very factors which enabled him to see clearly with eyes unbiased by preconceptions, in particular his lack of academic background, kept him out of the charmed circle of the Establishment."

It is salutary to be reminded of these facts, but to me the most striking thing about both Howard and Geddes is something different. In the Osborn-Mumford correspondence, FJO remarks about Howard that "He had no belief in 'the State'". Does this mean he was an anarchist? No it doesn't. As Lewis Mumford remarked about him, "With his gift of sweet reasonableness Howard hoped to win Tory and Anarchist, single-taxer and socialist, individualist and collectivist, over to his experiment". But it does mean that Howard did not believe that the State was the only means, or the most desirable means with which to accomplish social ends.

The same thing is true of Geddes. His most recent biographer Paddy Kitchen in her book *A Most Unsettling Person* (Gollancz 1975) says, "Intellectually he was closest to anarchists such as Peter Kropotkin and Paul and Elisée Réclus, all of whom he knew well", while his earlier biographer Philip Mairet remarks that "an interesting book could be written about the scientific origins of the international anarchist movement, and if it were, the name of Geddes would not be absent". There were in fact innumerable cross-currents between the ideologists of planning and the ideologists of anarchism at that time. The Réclus family made several of the exhibits in Geddes' Outlook Tower in Edinburgh. Kropotkin's *Fields, Factories and Workshops* (to my mind a book full of significance for our contemporary dilemmas) came out at the same time as Howard's *Tomorrow: A Peaceful Path to Real Reform*. When Howard's, book was re-issued under its more familiar title of *Garden Cities of Tomorrow,* and when Kropotkin's book was re-issued in an enlarged edition, each paid tribute to the other's work. When Thomas Adams, the first secretary of the Garden Cities Association, and later the first secretary of the Town Planning Institute, wrote his book *Garden City and Agriculture* in 1905, he based it on Kropotkin's work. There are similar cross influences with Raymond Unwin, Lewis Mumford, right down to the astounding book *Communitas* by Paul and Percival Goodman, which after its publication by the University of Chicago in 1947, led a kind of underground existence until its re-appearance as a paperback in the '60s. It is on sale in this country and I would recommend it to you as the most significant book in our field since Howard's.

Well these are merely literary crosscurrents of course. But when First Garden City Limited was started it was not conceived as a forerunner of action by the governmental machine, it was conceived as the forerunner of what F. J. Osborn called, summarising Howard, "progressive experimentation in new forms of social enterprise". An ordinary company in its structure, it had the important feature of dividend limitation and the famous provision that "any balance of profit" was to be devoted "to the benefit directly or indirectly of the town or its inhabitants". In its planner it was fortunate to have Raymond Unwin with those great qualities that Nicholas Taylor summed up as "his acute practical sense of the complexity of everyday life, and also his political stress on co-operative management as the means of bringing the good life to the many". When Howard found that his working-model failed to inspire others, he embarked, at 69, on his second garden city, having succeeded in borrowing less than one-tenth of the purchase price of the site. Staggering foolhardiness. Can you imagine such an enterprise today?

Now we know from the recollections of people like C.B. Purdom and Frederic Osborn and from the anecdotes of early residents that there was a kind of gaiety and a sense of high adventure in the pioneering of Letchworth and Welwyn, that was absent from the early days of the postwar New Towns. Some people would deny this of course, and say that it is all a matter of the transforming power of time. FJO says that at Letchworth, the people who had been there from the start eight years before he arrived told him he'd missed the golden age. But listen to him reminiscing about Welwyn and the fantastically difficult balancing act of choreographing the arrival of people, basic services and jobs, on a shoestring and by himself. A task which would employ a vast staff in a modern New Town.

But behind the rosy reminiscence, isn't it true that the grumbles and the New Town Blues that we used to hear in the fifties, did not have their equivalents in the early years of the two garden cities, just because people were conscious of being pioneers and of having to do their own things if they wanted something done?

Now once the building of New Towns, after years of campaigning, had become a governmental enterprise, the mechanism of the Development Corporation followed the pattern set by Lord Reith (in the BBC) in the 1920s, or by Herbert Morrison (in the London Passenger Transport Board) in the 1930s, or by the boards of the nationalized industries set up at the same time in the 1940s. We know that the style of the Development Corporation has proved itself adaptable to many other circumstances than that of the original green-field New Towns. The trouble is that the style has not changed, even though our ideas about many other forms of social organisation are changing and are going to change still more in the future. Mr Tony Wedgwood Benn who ten years ago was using government funds to enforce shot-gun weddings among giant capitalist concerns to enable them to compete with the European giants, is by now an advocate of using government funds to enable workers' co-operatives to take over ailing capitalist enterprises. He embarrasses us all by conducting his education in public, but other people too are looking back to see where we went wrong in our theories of social organisation. At what stage in the evolution of our administrative ideology did we go wrong? Some people would say it was back in the thirties when the Labour Party opted for the vast public corporation as the vehicle for social enterprise. Other people would say, in connection with housing, that it was the time of the Tudor Walters report in 1918, which froze out all other forms of social housing in favour of direct municipal provision. Today, with public housing policy in collapse, we are suddenly discovering the virtues of co-operative housing—a notion dear to the heart of Howard and Unwin which has been neglected for sixty years, even though if you go to a country like Denmark where a third of housing is in the hands of tenant co-operatives they say to the English visitor, "We owe it all to your Rochdale Pioneers".

Today, when people are urging, in the name of democracy that New Town housing should be transferred to the local authorities, at least one Development Corporation Chairman was approached the Minister to ask whether he will make some stipulation about allocation procedures, since in his area the allocation of council, as opposed to development corporation housing has been delegated from the council meeting to the party meeting of the ruling party. He is interested in tenant control because he sees local democratic control as worse than the paternalism of his corporation.

I think that the watershed in the development of social and socialist ideology came much further back. It was possible for one of the earliest Fabian Tracts to declare in 1886 that "English Socialism is not yet Anarchist or Collectivist, not yet defined enough in point of policy to be classified. There is a mass of Socialistic feeling not yet conscious of itself as Socialism. But when the unconscious

Socialists of England discover their position, they also will probably fall into two parties: a Collectivist party supporting a strong central administration and a counterbalancing Anarchist party defending individual initiative against the administration." Well the Fabians rapidly found which side of the watershed was theirs, and the Labour Party long ago finally committed itself to that interpretation of socialism which identified it with the unlimited increase of the State's power and activity through it's chosen form: the giant managerially-controlled public corporation.

Now in putting forward the notion of a do-it-yourself New Town, I am not saying that, in our kind of society, the public authorities have no role. They have an indispensable role, which for short we call *site and services*. If you are familiar with the phrase it is because you have been watching the unfolding drama of housing in the cities of the Third World. For if the cities of the rich world lack the income to maintain their expensive infrastructure, it is not surprising that in the exploding cities of the poor world, transportation, water supply, sewerage and power supplies cannot cope, and still less can medical, educational or housing services. The European visitor is appalled by the miles and miles of shanty-towns which surround the capital, often not shown on the map or included in the population statistics, even though the unofficial inhabitants may outnumber the official population.

People with a historical sense are reminded of the mushroom growth of our own industrial cities in the early nineteenth century, but there is a significant difference. Here industrialisation preceded urbanisation: there the urbanization precedes industry. The anthropologist Lisa Peattie once told me of her puzzlement in Bogotá, where there was no economic base to sustain the exploding population, but where no one looked ill-nourished and everyone was shod. She realised eventually that beside the official economy that figured in the statistics there was an unofficial, invisible economy of tiny enterprises and service occupations which provided purchasing power for the unofficial population whose squatter settlements evolved over time into fully serviced suburbs.

There is a perceptible pattern of population movement: the peasant makes the break with his village firstly by moving to some intermediate town or city as his first staging post, then moves on to the inner city slums of the metropolis, usually to some quarter occupied by families with the same place of origin. Finally, wised-up in city ways, he moves on to a squatter settlement, usually on public land on the periphery of the city. In favourable circumstances, his straw shack develops over the years into a house: he has turned his labour into capital and has a modicum of security in the urban economy. This happens quickly in a city of rapid economic growth like Seoul. It does not happen in a city of negative economic growth like Calcutta, where people are born and die in the street.

This is why English architects like John Turner and Pat Crooke who have worked for years in the shanty-towns of Latin America see them as something quite different from the official view and that of the rich visitor which is as breeding-grounds of crime, disease, social and family disorganisation. *They* see them as a triumph of self-help and mutual aid among people who would gain nothing from the usual expensive official housing programme. They point out that what begins as a squatter settlement can become through its own efforts in fifteen years a fully functioning community of adequate, properly serviced households.

In their chapter contributed to the recent book *The Exploding Cities* they contrast two examples of evolving dweller-controlled housing, one in Barcelona and one in Dar-es-Salaam and conclude:

> These two superficially different cases show how ordinary people use resources and opportunities available to them with imagination and initiative—when they have access to the necessary resources, and when they are free to act for themselves. Anyone who can see beyond the surface differences between the many forms of dwelling places people build for themselves is bound to be struck by the often astonishing economy of housing built and managed locally, or from the bottom up, in comparison with the top-down, mass housing supplied by large organisations and central agencies. Contrary to what we have been brought up to believe, where labour is an economy's chief asset, large-scale production actually reduces productivity in low-income housing. The assumed "economies of scale" are obtained at the expense of reduced access to resources local owners and builders would otherwise use themselves, and of the inhibition of personal and community initiative.

If you have a lingering belief that this is simply romanticising other people's poverty, I ought to remind you that the poor of a poor country in an efficiently administered city like Lima have not been deprived of the last shred of personal autonomy and human dignity like the poor of a rich and competently administered city like London. They are *not* trapped in the culture of poverty.

Just imagine that we were a poor country. Suppose Dockland were Dar-es-Salaam, or Liverpool were Lusaka, and we adopted the policy of "aided squatting" which in some Third World cities has replaced the pointless and wicked governmental persecution of squatters. Following the advice of people like Turner and Crooke and D. J. Dwyer, the World Bank is ceasing to aid grandiose housing projects, though many governments are refusing to take this advice. They would rather pay large fees to Western planning consultants, for they cannot believe that what poor people do for themselves can be right. The World Bank is now sponsoring ten "site and services" programmes around the world. Wilsher and Righter report that these experimental projects "encompass a wide variety of space allocations, financial assistance, provision of utilities, types of tenure, construction standards, and participation of private enterprise, but its officials are already convinced that the approach holds out a good deal of promise" (*The Exploding Cities* 1975).

Now suppose we applied such a policy to some of the derelict inner city districts in the man-made wastelands. Provide roads and services and a service core: kitchen sink, bath, WC and ring-main connection, put up some party walls (to overcome the fire-risk objection) and you will have long queues of families anxious to build the rest of the house for themselves, or to employ one of our vast number of unemployed building workers to help, or to get their brother-in-law or some moonlighting tradesman or the Community Industry to help, within the party walls. Such a carnival of construction would have important spin-offs in other branches of the social problems industry: ad hoc jobs and training for unemployed teenagers, turning the local vandals into builders, and the children into back-yard horticulturalists. Why, it would be like those golden days at Letchworth!

Why, we already have experience of a do-it-yourself New Town on the site-and-service principle. If I announce that I am referring to Pitsea and Laindon: the precursor of Basildon New Town, people in the planning profession will groan and say, "Well, precisely, and we don't want that particular expensive muddle to mop up again!" But look at it in a different light and you will see why some-one with my point of view cherishes Basildon with particular affection. There the dwellers got their sites but had to wait many years for the services. If you don't know the Basildon epic (which I have already told at the ICA in the symposium on squatter settlements on 23 May 1972) let me re-tell it as briefly as I can.

The building of the London-Tilbury-Southend Railway in 1888 coincided with a period of agricultural depression, and several farmers around Pitsea and Laindon in Essex sold to an astute land agency which divided the land into plots for sale. They advertised these as holiday or retirement retreats and organised ex-cursion trains from West Ham and East Ham at the London end of the line, with great boozy jaunts to the country (large hotels were built at the stations), and in the course of the outings plots of lands were auctioned. Some people returned home without realising that they were now landowners and these remained unde-veloped, or perhaps were built on without title by someone else.

In the period up to the end of the nineteen-thirties other agents or the farm-ers themselves sold plots in the area, sometimes for as little as £3 for a 20-foot frontage. A lot of ex-servicemen dreaming of a good life on a place of their own sank their gratuities after the first world war in small-holdings (for which there could hardly be a less satisfactory soil than that around Pitsea) or in chicken farm-ing. Most of them soon failed: they lost their money but they had some kind of cabin on the site, and the return fare from Laindon to Fenchurch Street was 1s2d in 1930. The kind of structures people built ranged from the typical inter-war speculative builder's detached house or bungalow, to converted buses or railway coaches, with a range of army huts, beach huts and every kind of timber-framed shed, shack or shanty.

During the second world war with very heavy bombing in East London, espe-cially the dockland boroughs of East Ham and West Ham, many families evacu-ated themselves or were bombed out, and moved in permanently to whatever foot-hold they had in the Pitsea, Laindon and Vange districts, with the result that at the end of the war the area had a settled population of 25,000.

There were some 8,500 existing dwellings, over 6,000 of them unsewered. There were 75 miles of grass track roads, main water in built-up areas only with standpipes in the roads elsewhere. There was no surface water drainage apart from ditches and old agricultural drains. Only fifty per cent of dwellings had mains electricity. There were about 1,300 acres of completely waste land of which 50 per cent had no known owner. The average density was 6 persons to the acre. Of the 8,500 dwellings, 2,000 were of brick and tile construction to Housing Act standards, 1,000 were of light construction to the same standard, 5,000 were chalets and shacks and 500 were described as derelict, though probably occupied. The average rateable value was £5.

In 1946 the New Towns Act was passed and various places were designated by the government as sites for New Towns. In many cases there was intense local opposition, not only from residents and landowners but also from the local authorities. In the case of the place we are considering, and Basildon was unique among the New Towns in this, the Minister was petitioned by the Essex County Council and by the local council to designate the area as a New Town. They were joined by the County Borough Councils of West Ham and East Ham who saw the place as a natural overspill town for their boroughs—many of whose former citizens were now living there. The argument was that there was no other way of financing the infra-structure of essential municipal services. At the first round the application was turned down. Harlow was chosen as the first Essex New Town and there was talk of Ongar as the second. After a further delegation to the Minister, Basildon was accepted.

The New Town was planned to start from a nucleus at the village of Basildon itself, expanding eastwards and westwards to incorporate Laindon and Pitsea. The first general manager, Brigadier W. G. Knapton, set out his policy in 1953 thus: "Any solution which includes the wholesale demolition of sub-standard dwellings cannot be contemplated. However inadequate, every shack is somebody's home, probably purchased freehold with hard-earned savings, and as often as not the area of land within the curtilage is sufficient to provide garden produce and to house poultry, rabbits, and even pigs. To evict the occupier and to re-accommodate him and his family in a corporation house, even on such favourable terms as the Act may permit, will probably cause not only hardship, but bitter feelings. The old must be absorbed into the new with the least detriment to the former and the greatest advantage to the latter."

His successor, Mr Charles Boniface, adopted the same humane and sensible attitude. He remarked that "the planners' task here is like a jigsaw puzzle, with the new fitting into the old instead of being superimposed upon and obliterating it". This is in fact the policy which has been followed, and the grid-iron pattern of the grass-track roads has been incorporated into the fully-developed New Town plan. Mr Boniface has always maintained (against some opposition) that "existing residents and allotment owners have as many rights as incomers or the corporation itself".

Let us zoom in on one particular street in the Laindon end of Basildon. It probably has a greater variety of housing types than any street in Britain. It starts on the right with two late Victorian villas—a sawn-off bit of terrace housing stuck there hopefully when the railway was first built. On the left is a detached house with a porch embellished with Doric wooden columns, like something in the Deep South of the United States. Then there are some privately-built houses of the 1960s, and next a wooden cabin with an old lady leaning over the gate—a first world war army hut which grew. On the other side of the road is some neat Development Corporation housing: blue brick, concrete tilehanging and white trim. Here is a characteristic improved shanty with imitation stone quoins formed in cement rendering at the corners of the pebbledash. Most of the old houses have some feature in the garden exemplifying Habraken's remarks about the passion to create and embellish. This one has a fountain, working. This one has a windmill about five feet high painted black and white like the timber and asbestos house it adjoins. The sails are turning. Here's one with a pond full of goldfish.

And now we see an immaculate vegetable garden with an old gentleman hoeing his onions. He was a leather worker from Kennington, who bought the place 43 years ago for week-ends and then retired down here. No, he wasn't the first occupier, who was a carpenter from Canning Town who bought three 20-foot plots for £18 in 1916, giving a site 60ft by 140 ft. In the post-1918 period when, according to Mr Syrett, the present owner, the banks were changing their interiors from mahogany to oak, the carpenter brought down bits and pieces of joinery from Fenchurch Street and built his dream bungalow. After Mr Syrett had bought it, it was burnt down except for the present kitchen and Mr Syrett himself built the present timber-framed house. Later he had it rendered, and although he is now 85, he has been making improvements ever since. For example he has recently cut out the mullions of his 1930-type windows to make them more like the ones in the Development Corporation houses opposite.

I showed him a description of the area as a former "vast pastoral slum". He denied this of course, remarking that most people came down here precisely to get away from the slums. But what was it like before the road was made up? "Well, you had to order your coal in the summer as the lorry could never get down the road in wintertime." But there was a pavement. "People used to get together with their neighbours to buy cement and sand to make the pavement all the way along the road." Street lighting? No, there was none. "Old Granny Chapple used to take a hurricane lamp when she went to the Radiant Cinema in Laindon." Transport? "Well, a character called Old Tom used to run a bus from Laindon Station to the Fortune of War public house. And there were still horses and carts down here in those days. They used to hold steeplechases on the hill where the caravan site is now." In the same road lived Mr Budd, who died last year at 97. He was a bricklayer by trade and every time he had a new grandchild would add a room to his house.

Mr and Mrs Syrett's house is immaculate—large rooms with all the attributes of suburban comfort. The house was connected to the sewer and electricity mains in the 40s and got gas 15 years ago. The urban district council made up the road under the Private Street Works Act, charging £60 in road charges. The road was recently made up again to a higher standard by the Development Corporation. The rates are £12 a half year, and as old age pensioners they got a rate rebate.

They live happily within their pension, they assured me. No rent to pay, some fruit and vegetables from the garden and the greenhouse. It is a matter of pride for them that they are not obliged to apply for supplementary benefits which they regard as scrounging. It is quite obvious that Mr Syrett's real investment for his old age was this one-time substandard bungalow which today has all the same amenities and conveniences as the homes of his neighbours. The truth of this can be seen if you look in the estate agents' windows in Pitsea, where houses with the same kind of origin are advertised at prices similar to those asked for the spec builder's houses of the same period. The significant thing is that their original owners and builders would never have qualified as building society mortgagees in the inter-war years, any more than people with equivalent incomes would today. The integration of shacksville into new development has been outstandingly successful in Basildon but the same upgrading of dwellings and improvements in facilities happens in the course of time anywhere—further down the line at Canvey Island for example—without benefit of New Town finance. What the New Town mechanism *has* done of course is to draw the sporadic settlement together into an urban entity and provide non-commuting jobs through the planned introduction of industry. Pitsea and Laindon could be called do-it-yourself New Towns, later legitimised by official action.

But, the cheap, substandard unfinished kind of development that gives the underprivileged a place of their own has ceased to be available. In the 1930s, aesthetic critics deplored this kind of development as "bungaloid growth" and so on though the critics themselves had a great deal more freedom of manoeuvre in buying themselves a place in the sun. It is interesting that Sir Patrick Abercrombie in the Greater London Plan of 1944 said, "It is possible to point with horror to the jumble of shacks and bungalows on the Laindon Hills and Pitsea. This is a narrow-minded appreciation of what was as genuine a desire as created the group of lovely gardens and houses at Frensham and Bramshott". This may be obvious today, but it was unusually perceptive in the climate of opinion then.

What in fact those Pitsea-Laindon dwellers had was the ability to turn their labour into capital over time, just like the Latin American squatters. The poor in the third world cities—with some obvious exceptions—have a freedom that the poor in the rich world cities have lost: three freedoms, in John Turner's words: "the freedom of community self-selection; the freedom to budget one's own resources and the freedom to shape one's own environment". In the rich world the choices have been pre-empted by the power of the state, with its comprehensive law-enforcement agencies and its institutionalised welfare agencies. In the rich world as Habraken puts it, "man no longer houses himself: he is housed".

You might observe of course that some of the New Town and developing towns have—more than most local authorities have—provided sites and encouragement to self-build housing societies. But a self-build housing association has to provide a fully-finished product right from the start, otherwise no consent under the building regulations, no planning consent, no loan. No-one takes into account the growth and improvement and enlargement of the dwelling over time, so that people can invest out of income and out of their own time, in the structure.

Now when Howard wrote his book, the reason why it appealed to so many people was that the period was receptive. This was the period of Kropotkin's *Fields, Factories and Workshops*, of Blatchford's *Merrie England* and of H.G. Wells's *Anticipations*. Certain ideas were in the air.

Now we are once again in a period with a huge range of ideas in the air, especially among the young. There is the enormous interest in what has become known as alternative technology. There is, for obvious reasons, a sudden burst of interest in domestic food production, and there is an enormous new interest in alternative forms of housing, once again for obvious reasons: there are vast numbers of people whose faces or lifestyles don't fit in either the Director of Housing's office or the Building Society office, and who are consequently victims of the crude duopoly of housing which, without intending to, we have created.

There are large numbers of people interested in alternative ways of making a living: looking for labour-intensive low-capital industries, because capital-intensive industries have failed to provide them with an income. A Community Land Trust was set up last year (no connection with the Act of a similar name, though the Act may be the essential prerequisite in providing land for the site-and-services do-it-yourself New Town). A New Villages Association was set up recently.

I am continually amazed by the growth of interest in alternative energy sources, especially since I was writing on the themes of solar power and wind power exploitation in the anarchist paper *Freedom* twenty years ago. Nobody at all seemed to be interested in those days. ... One of the essentials of a do-it-yourself New Town would be a relaxation of building regulations to make it possible for people to experiment in alternative ways of building and servicing houses, and in permitting a dwelling to be occupied in a most rudimentary condition for gradual completion. This is virtually impossible at the moment and people here with an interest in that field will recall that Graham Caine and the Street-farmers had to dismantle their experimental house at Eltham last October because their temporary planning permission expired.

I ought to say something about the density of dwellings. Some advocates of more intelligent land-use policies advocate high densities rather than what they think of as suburban sprawl, in order to conserve those precious acres of agricultural land. A worthy motive but a wrong conclusion. The agricultural industry is interested in maximum productivity per man. But with limited land we ought to be interested in maximum productivity per acre. Sir Frederic Osborn always argued that the produce of the ordinary domestic garden, even though a small area of gardens is devoted to food production, more than equalled in value the produce of the land lost to commercial food production. Surveys conducted by the government and by university departments in the 1950s proved him right. Some people will remember the enormous contribution made to the nation's food supply by domestic gardens and allotments during the war years. (The facts of the argument were set out by Robin Best and J. T. Ward in the Wye College pamphlet *The Garden Controversy* in 1956.) I would simply say that low-density housing is the best way of conserving land. Perhaps I can make the point best, by going one stage further than the do-it-yourself New Town to Mr John Seymour's views on self-sufficiency. He says in the new edition of his book *The Fat of the Land*:

> There is a man I know of who farms ten thousand acres with three men (and the use of some contractors). Of course he can only grow one crop—barley, and of course his production *per acre* is very low and his consumption of imported fertiliser very high. He burns all his straw, puts no humus on the land (he boasts there isn't a four-footed animal on it—but I have seen a hare) and

he knows perfectly well his land will suffer in the end. He doesn't care—it will see him out. He is already a millionaire several times over. He is the prime example of that darling of the agricultural economist—the successful agri-businessman.

Well, I don't want to preserve his precious acres for him, and John paints a seductive alternative:

> Cut that land (exhausted as it is) up into a thousand plots of ten acres each, giving each plot to a family trained to use it, and within ten years the production coming from it would be enormous. It would make a really massive contribution to the balance of payments problem. The motorist with his *News of the World* wouldn't have the satisfaction of looking over a vast treeless, hedgeless prairie of indifferent barley—but he could get out of his car for a change and wander through a huge area of diverse countryside, orchards, young tree plantations, a myriad small plots of land growing a multiplicity of different crops, farm animals galore, and hundreds of happy and healthy children. Even the agricultural economist has convinced himself of one thing. He will tell you (if he is any good) that land farmed in big units has a low production of food per acre but a high production of food per man-hour, and that land farmed in small units has the opposite—a very poor production per man-hour but a high production per acre. He will then say that in a competitive world we must go for high production per man-hour and not per acre. I would disagree with him.

And so would I, and though I am arguing for an experimental town rather than an experiment in land settlement, his argument holds good. Self-sufficiency is not the aim, but an opportunity for people to work in small-scale horticulture as well as in small-scale industry is. I recently edited a new edition of Kropotkin's *Fields, Factories and Workshops* and found it extraordinarily relevant.

The late Richard Titmuss used to say that social ideas "may well be as important in Britain in the next half century as technical innovation". One of these ideas it seems to me is the rediscovery of Howard's garden city as a popular and populist notion.

It may *have* to happen. There may be *no other* way of rescuing inner Liverpool. There may be *no other* way of rescuing some of the Development Corporations faced with a diminishing rate of growth. Perhaps Milton Keynes is destined to become an agri-city, a dispersed city of intensive horticulturists. Perhaps the right idea to offer participants in the Letchworth competition is that the Letchworth Garden City Corporation should sponsor New Letchworth at Milton Keynes or in Central Lanes, to develop an area with waivers on the planning and building legislation. It should be possible to operate some kind of usufruct, some kind of leasehold with safeguards against purely cynical exploitations, which would enable people to house themselves and provide themselves with a means of livelihood, while not draining immense sums from central or local government.

Some people had the hope in the very earliest days of the New Towns that this kind of experimental freedom would apply there. Peter Shepheard, for whom it was my pleasure to work for ten years, worked in the one-time Ministry of Town and Country Planning on the early plans for Stevenage. He once recollected:

> I remember that when first working at Stevenage we felt it vital not only to get the New Town Corporation disconnected entirely from the treasury, but from the whole network of central government, by-laws and so on. The idea was to build in ten years, a new experimental town ... One of the early technicians at Stevenage actually proposed that we should write our own by-laws. The idea was to have no by-laws at all. (*AA Journal* May 1957)

Well some hopes he had, a quarter of a century ago or more ago, of developing an anarchist New Town. And after its stormy early years, you might say "Well, what's wrong with Stevenage. Some aspects of that town are the admiration of the whole world".

And a lot of people in the town-making business: chairmen, general managers, and all their hierarchy, have had a marvellous and fulfilling time, wheeler-dealing their babies into maturity. They have been the creators, the producers. The residents, the citizens, have been the consumers, the recipients of all that planning, architecture and housing: not to mention the jobs in the missile factory. Now we are twenty-five years or more older, wiser and humbler. A new generation is turning upside down all those cherished shibboleths about planning, architecture and housing, not to mention the ones about jobs. We have to change the role of the administration from providers to *enablers*. We have to change the role of the citizens from the recipients to *participants*, so that they too have an active part to play in what Lethaby called the great game of town building. What was it that old Ben Howard said to young Frederic Osborn? "My dear fellow, if you wait for the government to act, you'll be as old as Methusaleh before they start. The only way to get anything done is to do it yourself."

# 4. FICTION, NON-FICTION AND REFERENCE

The library of Central Milton Keynes is dominated by a vast mural, nine metres or 30 feet wide, which is illustrated in miniature on the cover of this book. It is the work of Fionnuala Boyd and Leslie Evans, who came to Milton Keynes in 1982 to be artists in residence for two years and have lived there ever since. It is called, in deference to its situation, 'Fiction, Non-fiction and Reference'. Visitors to the library relish its sidelong references to places and politics and its sly allusions to the work of other artists.

This work is a useful starting point in seeking out the lessons of the post-war British New Towns. It exemplifies an unexpected paradox. When the New Towns were conceived much use was made of concepts of environmental determinism. A clean, new, shiny environment would produce new, shiny people. And of course it was true that the frustrations and deprivations that resulted from bad, damp and overcrowded housing would be remedied by adequate housing and access to open space. But the miseries of life are not assuaged simply through a change of environment. As W. H. Auden put it, "Put the car away. When life fails/What is the use of going to Wales?"

If you were blindfolded and dropped in any housing, shopping, educational or sporting environment in Britain, apart from your attempts to identify the architecture as that of the 50s, 60s or 70s, how would you know whether you were in a New Town or in the suburban expansion or rebuilding of existing towns? Would the people around you, or the houses, shops or schools be any different? Would the grass be greener or the buses any more frequent?

The best clue might be the presence of public works of art. Friends of the New Towns would see it as an example of enlightened patronage, enemies would see it as characteristic extravagance, but the New Towns commissioned more works of art in public places from contemporary artists than any established town or city. And the artists have often risen magnificently to unexpected opportunities. In 1957, *The Times* observed that "Ideal sites abound among the maze of small houses, shopping areas and factories, public buildings, only waiting for a piece of sculpture to pull them all together in a brilliant way ... "[7] The reference was to Harlow New Town, which must be the only town in England to have a vast family group by Henry Moore, a magnificent work by Elizabeth Frink, and even Rodin's 'Eve' in public places, as well as many pieces of sculpture by later artists.

---

Originally printed in Colin Ward, *New Town, Home Town: The Lessons of Experience*. (London: Calouste Gulbenkian Foundation, 1993).

This aspect of the New Towns fails to touch our novelists and poets. Their New Town image is the rather stereotyped picture of brick boxes glittering in the sun, which our most-read modern poets John Betjeman and Philip Larkin deplore in passing. The only notable work of fiction set in a New Town is Angus Wilson's *Late Call*, published in 1964. The author died in 1991 and in 1992 Penguin Books re-issued the book with a comment that is rather more explicit than the text itself:

> Sylvia Calvert has had to give up her career as manageress of the Palmeira Court Hotel and move to the concrete jungle of Carshall New Town. 'Just think of The Sycamores as a hotel without the responsibilities,' her son Harold had said, surveying his ranch-style house with pride. For Sylvia it seems less a new life than a diary full of blank pages. For Angus Wilson it is an opportunity to deliver some of his sharpest observations on post-war England's visions of Utopia.[8]

I find this standardised superior dismissal of the New Town adventure by the privileged hard to take. For I well remember visiting Mrs Blake at Fishermead in Milton Keynes. She was older than Sylvia in Angus Wilson's novel, and she told me that she had lived for 40 years in Townmead Road, Fulham, a street I knew well, and had never had a WC of her own and no bathroom at all. It was marvellous, she said, not to have to make a weekly trip to the public baths. We met soon after some royal anniversary, and of course Mrs Blake had done the catering for a street party for the local children, just as she would have done in Townmead Road.

In 1946, Lord Reith, the chairman of the committee appointed by the government to advise on New Towns, declared that they would be "an essay in civilisation", which in Mrs Blake's case they were. Twenty years later, Leslie Lane, Director of the Civic Trust, saw the New Towns as "the greatest conscious programme of city building ever undertaken by any country in history".[9] But in 1992 the 25th anniversary of Milton Keynes and the demise of its development corporation were celebrated in a leading article in *The Times* under the heading 'Paradise Mislaid'.

*The Times* perceived the anniversary as "a memorial to a tradition of social engineering that must be seen as dead and buried. Hardly, however, to be mourned". It found that "An eagerness to force large numbers of people out of city centres, shared with authoritarians in less democratic societies, led to the desertion and dereliction of many of Britain's inner cities and the spoliation of millions of acres of countryside," and that "residents, many moved compulsorily and callously, found themselves in single-class towns with poor services and a lack of communal continuity vital to a humane neighbourhood". For the leader-writer, "Milton Keynes was the last desperate throw of a generation of British planners who were distasteful of the traditional British towns and cities and had the political power and public money to fashion the environment to their will ... The architect was god and history was the devil". And, of course, "from Crawley and Corby to Skelmersdale, Washington and Cumbernauld, new-town blues became a widespread syndrome".[10]

These opinions are important, not for their truth or falsehood, but because they express the perceptions of people with ample freedom of choice as to where they live, about the opportunities open to people with less choice. Readers with a greater grasp of social and geographical facts were quick to respond. David Hall of the Town and Country Planning Association pointed out, in connection with those despoiled millions of acres, that "the total development area of the 28 new towns of Great Britain is 255,487 acres (0.45 per cent of its total land area), and contains only 7.5 per cent of all the new housing built in Britain since 1951". And to the fiction that the New Towns were responsible for inner city dereliction, he countered the non-fiction that a GLC study in the early 1980s showed that in the case of London, "about 7 per cent only of the population that had moved elsewhere went to the new or expanded towns".[11]

It is hard to know how the leader-writer reached the conclusion that many residents were "moved compulsorily and callously" to New Towns, though this certainly happened in the efforts of some city authorities to re-house people within the cities.[12] The assumption must lie in the fact that a minority of residents had to move when their firms relocated there, like the move of *The Times* from Printing House Square to Wapping, or the Inland Revenue's shift of a major department to Cumbernauld, and the prospective transfer of its headquarters to Nottingham. David Hall's comment was that residents *chose*, "and were helped to move because of the prospect of better housing, better employment opportunities, better access to the countryside, and better futures for their children".[13] In the late 1970s I conducted a series of interviews with New Town dwellers and this was certainly the impression I gained.[14] In those days it was clear that the new and expanded towns were the one way in which house renters as opposed to house purchasers were able to share the general outward movement from the overcrowded pre-war city in search of ampler living space. Ebenezer Howard, grandfather of the New Towns, was more accurate than most other social and demographic observers, when he remarked in 1904 that "while the age we live in is the age of the closely compacted, overcrowded city, there are already signs, for those who can read them, of a coming change so great and so momentous that the twentieth century will be known as the period of the great exodus".[15] The real issue has been whether this exodus is to be absorbed in endless suburbs, or in the leap to towns and villages beyond the green belts, or whether planned provision should be made for it.

## THOSE NEW TOWN BLUES
The spectre of 'New Town Blues' was also revived for this valedictory comment. This was widely reported in the early post-war years, as a condition affecting people who found themselves in half-finished estates, far from the shops and from relations, not only in New Towns.

> A post-war survey by a team from the London School of Hygiene of the large Oxhey Housing Estate near Watford—to which Londoners were moved— showed anxiety neuroses running at twice the national figure. Cases of sleep disturbances and undue tiredness were four times, headaches three times, and duodenal ulcers two and a half times more frequent than the number expected from national experience.[16]

Some people move gladly and never look back, others take longer to adjust and spend a longer time 'grieving for a lost home'. There were other factors beyond the newness of the New Town, like the family's income and employment prospects. Significantly, among the places specifically mentioned by *The Times*, two are New Towns which suffered grievously from the unexpected closure of big employers. The most extensive examination of this field was made in Harlow in 1964 by two doctors who reported that:

> Our survey has shown that the creation of a new town with full social and economic planning results in an improvement in general health, both subjective and objective. About nine-tenths of the new population are satisfied with their environment and the one-tenth who are dissatisfied are for the most part constitutionally dissatisfied—that is to say, they would be dissatisfied wherever they were. Full satisfaction with environment is a product of time ... We have found no evidence of ... new town blues. Some people had indeed shown loneliness, boredom, discontent with environment and worries, particularly over money. It is easy enough for enterprising enquirers to find such people and to attribute these symptoms to the new town. But a similar group of similar size can be found in any community, new or old, if it is sought.[17]

On specific issues, the comment in *The Times* appears surprisingly ill-informed. On more imponderable matters it faithfully reflected a change in the climate. Large-scale government-funded enterprise was taken for granted in the 1940s. By the 1990s, after a decade of privatisation, the faith that market forces were more efficient and more responsive to public needs had spread far beyond the ideologists, and ventures like the New Town programme had become perceived as an aspect of the 'Nanny State'. The year 1951, when the first New Town tenants moved in, was the year of the Festival of Britain, an opportunity for the first generation of post-war architects to demonstrate that the Modern movement had a human face. There *was* an assumption that planners and architects were experts in their field, providing a value-free public service of social welfare. The New Towns provided them with a *tabula rasa* on which, at last, they could practise their skills. The concept of 'Public Participation in Planning' did not arise until the 1970s and has penetrated the official consciousness slowly and patchily. I well remember a seminar where the Chief Planner in the Department of the Environment, Sir Wilfred Burns, made a carefully-worded admission that the climate had changed:

> People have many different perspectives on their environment and on community life but only now are we beginning to see these articulated. It is not all that many years ago since people trusted local or central government to analyse their problems and prescribe the solutions. Those were the days when people accepted that new and exciting developments were bound to be better and when change seemed to be welcomed. We then moved into a period when unique and prescriptive solutions gave way to the presentation of alternatives so that the public could express views before final decisions were taken. Today

we face a different situation. Community groups, voluntary organisations of many kinds, and indeed individuals, now demand a say in the definition of problems and a role in determining and then implementing solutions. Even in the professional field that we normally think of as part of the establishment, there are various movements concerned with reinterpreting or changing the professionals' role. Self-help groups of many kinds have sprung up, sometimes around a professional, or at least, advised or guided by a professional. It is quite clear that a number of people believe that the traditional professionals are not able adequately to communicate with people in a way that will help them solve their problems or make their wishes known to those who make the decisions."[18]

It is easy to caricature or exaggerate the dictatorship of the professionals and managers of the New Towns. Their own task was constrained by strict Treasury control, by the cost yardsticks applied to all subsidised housing and by government-imposed standards which changed over time. The earliest New Town houses were built to the, in retrospect, generous space standards of the Dudley Report of 1944, many more to the severely-reduced standards of Harold Macmillan's *Houses 1952*, and the more recent to those of the Parker-Morris Report of 1961, which argued that, "changes in the way in which people want to live, the things which they own and use, and in their general level of prosperity ... make it timely to re-examine the kinds of homes that we ought to be building, to ensure that they will be adequate to meet the newly emerging needs of the future."[19]

Privately-built housing for sale was not subject to the government's standards. It had only to comply with the building regulations. In terms of space it was usually below the Parker-Morris provisions, but it was more highly-cherished by its occupants, though deprecated as "spec-builders' ticky-tacky" by the architectural profession.

The first major criticism of New Town architecture came from within the profession itself. In 1953, an issue of the *Architectural Review* on the 'Failure of the New Towns' criticised the "prairie planning" of streets of low-rise low-density housing, inhabited by "footsore housewives and cycle-weary workers", indistinguishable from any suburban estate anywhere, so that "what should have been a great adventure has come to nothing".[20] Defenders of the New Towns were quick to point to errors in the critics' assumptions and confusions about residential densities, and distinguished land economists conducted careful surveys which showed that "there are no low-density new towns"[21] and that the New Town approach was far less of an encroachment on the national stock of agricultural land, than the suburban expansion of the 1930s or that of the post-war years.[22]

Behind the polemics over densities was an issue that was neglected for years. Most people appreciate the charms of the town or village street, with its sense of enclosure and shop or pub on the corner, but the principal obstacle to its achievement in new housing, distinguished by wide roads with scarcely any traffic, its extravagant provision of turning circles for vehicles and its easy access for the largest of possible fire appliances and refuse collection lorries, was the highway engineer, imposing absurdly high road widths on every new residential district, everywhere. Slowly the issue was rethought, first in Essex, then in Cheshire, and then by new government guidance.[23] Meanwhile the Development Corporations resolved to be more architecturally varied, and to bring in more outside advice. The results have not always been what they intended. At Peterlee, for example, I visited tenants of the earliest housing from 1951, built to the standards of the Dudley Report with ample gardens where one ex-miner cultivated his prize leeks. "You wouldn't think so," he said, surveying surrounding neglect, "but when we first came here, everyone lived in this street, doctors, solicitors ... " The Development Corporation resolved that further developments should be more adventurous and engaged the painter Victor Passmore to advise on the development of the south-west of the town with long timber-clad terraces, lacking gardens, but looking beautiful across a lovingly-landscaped valley. The historian Arnold Whittick asked a key question about this architectural exercise of 1962:

> What will we think of the scheme in 20 years' time? Its authors have been very scornful of the earlier more traditional housing, one remarking rather despotically that 'we decided that we shall not tolerate the back garden mania of the new town'. But it is not improbable that in 20 years' time we shall realise that the earlier housing of Peterlee was nearer to human needs and wishes than this rather academic architectural exercise.[24]

He was proved right. Long before those 20 years were up, I talked to tenants at Sunny Blunts who complained, not about the landscape, but about the damp that spread everywhere, and that their distress was continually ignored by their landlord, the development corporation, whose response was to blame *them* for not opening more windows. The truth was best expressed by the *Northern Echo* journalist Brian Morris who found the houses "brave and imaginative in their general design" but "wretched and shabby in their details and practical execution".[25] Passmore himself designed the Pavilion nearby, which he described as "an architecture and sculpture of purely abstract form through which to walk, in which to linger and on which to play; a free and anonymous monument which, because of its independence, can lift the activity and psychology of an urban housing community onto a universal plane". This was not how it was seen in the locality. Covered in graffiti it was seen by neighbours as the venue for undesirable activities. According to Peterlee's managing director

> The result, in March 1982, was a lively meeting in which Passmore began by telling the large crowd who assembled that he thought the graffiti had improved the sculpture and had 'humanised and improved it more than I could ever have done'. It was the measure of his artistic integrity that he then told his audience that a far more desirable solution to the problem would be to dynamite the neighbouring houses rather than the Pavilion: it was equally the measure of his likeability and the Durham miners' weakness for a 'card' that the meeting ended in good humour and he emerged unscathed.[26]

I have encountered similar cautionary tales in most other New Towns. At Runcorn, in the central area of Southgate, the development corporation employed a world-famous architect, Jim Stirling, to design housing "grouped around formal squares and along streets to reflect the environment that is enjoyed in a Georgian city such as Bath".[27] It was unpopular with its tenants who disliked its grey, stained concrete panels and circular windows which were thought dangerous and were hideously expensive to maintain. Children told me that their school-mates made fun of them as they lived in a washing-machine. By the time you read these words the estate will have been demolished. On the other hand, and to prove the impossibility of generalising about New Towns, it was in Runcorn that I encountered the most attractive public housing I have ever seen. I knocked on a door, and the ex-Liverpudlian tenant said "It's my Utopia, living here". This was Halton Brow, designed by the development corporation's anonymous architectural staff.

Several key figures of the architectural and landscape team from Runcorn moved on to key offices at Milton Keynes, the last and most ambitious of the New Towns. There the architectural dominance as perceived by *The Times*, even though curtailed by government financial policy, was closest to achievement. Jeff Bishop explains that "In particular the corporation became the home for a group of young architects ... known in MK as 'the undertakers' because of their penchant for black suits ... For them, this new town was the classic sheet of blank paper ... They won out to the extent that each was 'given' a grid square to design and they did just that—starting from scratch as if nothing else would ever exist".[28] The corporation also employed the most currently-respected prestige-laden architects as consultants: Norman Foster, Richard MacCormac, Archigram and Edward Cullinan among many. But when Jeff Bishop was a member of a team employed to investigate resident reaction to the built environment of Milton Keynes on matters ranging from its overall "image" to the design of estates and the distribution of facilities, he found that the work of the most prestige-laden architects in housing at Milton Keynes was, with one significant exception, liked least, while the houses, whether publicly or privately built, that most resembled our traditional picture of house and home were liked most. The exception, in the work of famous architects was Eaglestone, designed by Ralph Erskine for a private developer, Bovis Homes. Bishop and his team had another thought-provoking finding. He noted that hundreds of environmental professionals from outside Britain visit Milton Keynes every year, "no doubt many more than those members of the general public tempted to turn off the motorway at Junction 13 for a quick look at 'that funny place you cannot even find when you are there'". He found that residents themselves very rapidly got used to the place. A couple who had lived there for less than six weeks commented that it was very easy to find your way around, and another said "I like the way MK is laid out—the grid squares help you to know people in the area. Each estate's separateness makes for local feeling." He tells us that "At the outset the research team were told that people find MK confusing and they get lost. This was patently not true of the residents so what was the source of this rumour? A chance encounter provided the answer: that those who get lost seem to be predominantly visiting architects and planners who come with a preconceived idea of what clues and landmarks a 'city' should offer ... and are then confused when such clues are not apparent. The residents of course have no such problems".[29]

They concluded that "MK *is* a success—to the extent that one might also add *despite* the planners," but also that their findings "did not just cast doubt on the specific approaches used thus far in MK, but on the whole ethos of the planning and architectural professions". Residents see themselves not as living in the new city of Milton Keynes but in Linford or Heelands, etc which they see as a series of *villages.* They conceive of MK "as somewhere only a little better than usual, a normal landscape dotted with villages which have managed to appear without spoiling the countryside, complete with bypasses". Shrewdly they note the way professional ideologies contain a set of perceptions of what is urban and what is rural, and that these are *threatened* by suburban and Garden City environments precisely because they are "symbols of individual aspirations rather than corporate ones".[30]

## CLASS AND STATUS

It would, consequently, be easy to agree with the castigation of the professionals by *The Times*, with the proviso that there is no reason to suppose that private developers as clients will be any more sensitive to popular aspirations than public corporations. But there is a further charge: that New Towns are "single-class towns", a view reinforced by the electoral analysts of 1992 who found Basildon to be "the capital of the C2s, where more than half of households read *The Sun*".[31]

Here we are touching on that most pervasive of British preoccupations: social class. Implicit in the recommendations of the Reith committee and of the promoters of the New Towns Act, were assumptions of social balance and an erosion of class differences. Thus Lewis Silkin declared in 1948 that he was "very concerned indeed, not merely to get different classes of the community, people of different occupations, living together in a community, but to get them actually mixing together".[32]

Frederic Osborn (who as we shall see, could be called the father of the New Towns, just as Ebenezer Howard was their grandfather) was always more sceptical about the use of architectural means to achieve social aims. He observed to Lewis Mumford that

> Community life in a new town is of the interest-group pattern, not the neighbour pattern—except in the very earliest days, when everybody is uprooted and willing to let the accident of being co-pioneers determine their associations with others. Very soon the interest-group pattern reasserts itself. The only 'community' you are then conscious of is the whole town, and that consciousness, though it diminishes with size, continues to some extent because the town is separated from other towns by a green belt of some width. I doubt if you can create in a town strong neighbourhood consciousness, though you can provide neighbourhood convenience, and that produces just a little such consciousness. People gravitate towards others of like social class and interest.[33]

The class composition of New Towns was originally dependent on the kind of work available there: old heavy industries, new light industries, high technology or office employment. But social class is a big factor in the way that New Towns are perceived. People rich enough to have freedom of choice live elsewhere. They may even value the New Towns as a means of corralling those elements in the outward movement of population with which they do not want to mix.

For the older the house we inhabit, the higher your social prestige, and the biggest of the huge imponderables since the 1940s has been that shift in perception that changed the British from a nation of neophiliacs, welcoming the new post-war society that would sweep away the shameful legacy of poverty and deprivation, mean streets and smoky skies into a nation of antiquarians, cherishing the past and an imaginary "Heritage". The architecture of the New Towns, both in houses and in public buildings from schools and hospitals to factories and shopping centres, is the utilitarian, and all too frequently, poorly maintained architecture of the 1950s and 1960s, and is consequently automatically despised.[34]

These intangible factors are probably the most powerful in shaping current attitudes towards the New Towns, but there are other significant social changes. The first, and saddest, of the lost assumptions of the 1950s is that of full employment, taken for granted in the post-war years. The second is the dramatic change in modes of tenure of housing. In 1947 the norm was renting and 26 per cent of households were owner-occupied. Today the figure is closer to 66 per cent, while government policy in the 1980s deliberately curtailed the provision of new rental housing, whether by local authorities or New Town corporations. The result was predictable. Every New Town has its homeless next-generation young adults. A third vast change has been in car-ownership. Universal motoring is in fact far from being universal, particularly in low-income areas. But it has profoundly affected the viability of public transport. A fourth change is the shift from shopping in the neighbourhood, first to the shopping centre in the middle of the town and then to the out-of-town hypermarket. Here again, access to the family car is a prerequisite.

The last and largest of the New Towns, Milton Keynes, was originally conceived around an efficient public transport network. This aim was abandoned in the Master Plan, in favour of a car-based city, intended to be flexible enough to meet the assumed needs of the next century. Had the original proposals been accepted, writes the historian of the town, "they would undoubtedly have given Milton Keynes better public transport, but at the cost of turning it into a glorified council estate".[35]

That we automatically assume that nothing could be worse than that fate is a final confirmation of the changes in public aspirations and perceptions since the New Towns became public policy.

# 5. SELF-HELP IN URBAN RENEWAL

In his introductory essay to the modern editions of Ebenezer Howard's book *Garden Cities of Tomorrow*—the book and the author responsible for the founding of the Town and Country Planning Association at the end of the last century—Lewis Mumford remarks that 'with his gift for sweet reasonableness Howard hoped to win Tory and Anarchist, single-taxer and socialist, individualist and collectivist, over to his experiment. And his hopes were not altogether discomfited; for in appealing to the English instinct for finding common ground he was utilising a solid political tradition.'

The Association itself, operating in a political world, has always had to win support from that small number of politicians in any party who are actually interested in planning issues, or to educate those who actually hold office, nationally and locally. This is a task which of course becomes more and more difficult with the apparent polarisation of politics and political attitudes.

I am notoriously a non-political person. I always aspire to attain Ebenezer Howard's gift of sweet reasonableness, and to win over people from both right and left. But, alas, I seem to have a knack of antagonising both sides. I don't do it to annoy because I know it teases, I am simply obliged to do it because I have a different view of the world. And if my subject is 'self-help in urban renewal', I have to begin by antagonising everyone.

Let me begin by antagonising the left, by saying that a major example of self-help in urban renewal has been the process stigmatised as 'gentrification'. We have a stereotype of young, pushing, upwardly mobile, middle-class trendies (or whatever adjective suits you best) driving old and poor working-class tenants out of their traditional habitat. We all used to have our horror-stories about Rachmanism, and we all had our ready-made sneers about the in-comers. What we mostly remained silent about was that the particular middle-class trendies driving out the traditional inhabitants were in fact the officers of the local authorities pursuing the then fashionable trends in urban renewal.

This is why Wilfred Burns, Newcastle's planning officer and subsequently the Government's chief planner, was able to say that 'when we are dealing with people who have no initiative or civic pride, the task, surely, is to break up such groupings

Originally printed in *The Raven* Anarchist Quarterly 2 (August 1987): 115– 120. A talk given on 27 January 1987 to the Town and Country Planning Association conference on 'Our Deteriorating Housing Stock: Financing and Managing New Solutions'.

even though the people seem to be satisfied with their miserable environment and seem to enjoy an extravert social life in their own locality' (*New Towns for Old: The Techniques of Urban Renewal*, 1963); and it explains why another Newcastle architect, Bruce Allsop, felt obliged to remark that 'it is astonishing with what savagery planners and architects are trying to obliterate working-class cultural and social patterns. Is it because many of them are first-generation middle-class technosnobs?' (*Towards a Humane Architecture*, 1974).

Nobody cared to listen in the 1950s and 1960s, and even in the 1970s, when the cash was still swilling about in the urban renewal bran-tub, to those who pointed to the grotesque paradox that a line drawn on a map in town halls and county hall selected one side of whole streets for demolition and redevelopment as unfit for human habitation, while on the other side of that line absolutely identical houses, blighted by the redevelopment process, were beginning their upward progress, aided by the merry whirr of Black and Decker, into the desirable residence end of the market. A comparison of the bizarre prices that the rescued houses fetch today with the sorry state of the estate opposite is interesting in pondering the conclusion reached a decade ago by Dr Graham Lomas (formerly deputy strategic planner for the Greater London Council) that in London more *fit* houses had been destroyed by public authorities than had been built since the war (*The Inner City*, 1975).

The orgy of publicly financed destruction and of slapping compulsory purchase orders on everything in sight (which eventually reached the pitch that really progressive authorities like the GLC were actually setting in motion the procedure of compulsory purchase on properties they already owned) was followed by what should have been the gentler, more creative climate of General Improvement Areas and Housing Action Areas. Once again the *official* gentrifiers from the town hall took command, and urban renewal took the form of cobbles and bollards, and planting in the street. Several people here must remember Susan Howard's tragi-comic account, at the TCPA's 1974 conference on Housing Action: the Opportunities and the Dangers, of the experience of the first General Improvement Area in Leicester. At that conference Jim Grove underlined the principle that 'sovereignty over decisions must lie with the inhabitants' and Lawrence Hansen of Waltham Forest made the very significant remark that 'house improvements have value only as perceived by the occupants'.

We were now in the era of Public Participation. All of us here must have had the experience of attending those meetings of citizens held in the name of participation to discover what residents actually wanted, where *invariably* residents wanted things that the special central government cash could not provide: an improvement of ordinary municipal services, the kind of things that councils actually existed to provide—things like street-paving, street-lighting, street-cleaning and refuse-collection. They were revealing an unmentionable fact: that there has always been a hierarchy of excellence in these services, based on who complains most. The presence of complaining gentrifiers in fact pushed up standards for everyone.

There was one General Improvement Area in the country which was proposed, implemented and subsequently managed by the residents themselves. It was also an example of the ironical crudity of official designations of places, for it moved in a few years from being a Clearance Area not worth saving to being a Conservation Area where every brick became part of our Priceless Architectural Heritage. That street was of course Black Road, Macclesfield, and it owed its transformation to the fact that in 1971 a young gentrifying architect moved in because it was cheap and had his application for an improvement grant turned down because his slum cottage was 'structurally unsound'. He, of course, spiralled up to becoming the next president of the Royal Institute of British Architects, and must often reflect on the truth of the remark of Samuel Smiles in his celebrated book *Self-Help* where the author remarks that 'the duty of helping one's self in the highest sense involves helping one's neighbours'.

Now what have these gentrifiers got, apart from an expanding asset in a milieu of dwindling assets? They have *dweller control*, which people like me always insist is the first principle of housing, more important than housing standards assessed from outside. And the other thing they have is *know-how*: that is, they know how to work the system. The whole thrust of the TCPA's innovations in the 1970s, with their planning aid service and their environmental education service, was towards expanding this kind of knowledge into something available for everyone.

I now have to antagonise the right by asserting that a further major example of self-help in urban renewal is the process stigmatised as squatting. We have a stereotype of vandals, junkies and dole scroungers jumping the housing queue, and we have all heard squatter horror-stories and have done for years. They are as untypical as the tales about the gentrifiers. We all know the reasons for the growth of organised squatting since the late 1960s. In the crude duopoly that emerged in postwar British housing in the period between owner-occupation and council tenancy, whole categories of people—notably the young, single and childless—were left out of account altogether, for housing policy was based upon the standard family of two parents and two-and-a-half children, even though by now this unit has been overtaken by demographic facts and is a tiny statistical minority of households. Sub-letting and taking in lodgers—the traditional way of getting a room for the mobile young—was usually specifically forbidden by mortgage agreements in one category and by tenancy agreements in the other. At the selfsame time, policies of accumulating huge sites for eventual comprehensive redevelopment left a vast number of houses either slowly rotting awaiting demolition, or similarly rotting awaiting eventual renovation. Policy itself, as Graham Lomas stressed, 'left great areas unoccupied and ripe targets for vandalism and squatting' (*The Inner City*).

Fortunately the squatters sometimes got there before the unofficial vandals. The response of the authorities was interesting. Central government changed the law on squatting for the first time since the fourteenth century—although squatting is neither criminal nor illegal, it is simply unlawful (see the *Squatters' Handbook*). Local government in many places distinguished itself by destroying its own property to keep squatters out—ripping out services, smashing sanitary fittings, and pouring wet concrete down drains. In others it employed so-called 'private investigators' as agents of the council to terrorise and intimidate squatting families (see Nick Wates and Christian Wolmar, *Squatting: The Real Story*, 1980). On several occasions councils actually blamed the squatters for damage to property done on their instructions by their own employees.

Just in case you, either in the past or today (when there are 50,000 squatters in London), believed the stories told about squatters, surveys showed that in Haringey 51 per cent were actually people with children, in Lambeth over 60 per cent, and in Cardiff 77 per cent. And what property did they squat? 'The Haringey survey found that of 122 squats, only three were required by the Council as part of its permanent housing stock (i.e. ready to let). Over half were privately owned and those owned by the council were either awaiting renovation or demolition. The squats had been empty, on average, for over six months. And a survey on squatters in council property commissioned by the Department of the Environment found that only one-sixth of the sample was in permanent stock, and that even much of this was regarded as "difficult to let". The reality is not that squatters jump the housing waiting list or deprive others of a home but rather that they opt out of the queue altogether and make use of houses that would otherwise be empty.' (*Squatting: The Real Story*)

The squatters' movement has been a most remarkable example of self-help in urban renewal, since it has operated against every kind of obstruction and opposition. So keen have they been on urban renewal that the Department of the Environment survey found that 71 per cent of squatters claimed to have made some kind of improvement to the property they occupied. One of them, Andy Ingham, wrote a *Self Help House Repairs Manual* specifically for squatters, published by Penguin in 1975 and continually reprinted. Of course the one thing most squatters most desire is legitimisation with a rent book, and the London Borough of Lewisham was the pioneer authority in 'licensed squats'.

Several of our most enterprising and successful housing co-operatives have grown out of the squatters' movement. In a forthcoming study of housing co-operatives, Dr Johnston Birchall of the Institute of Community Studies reminds us that some well-established co-ops, like Seymour Co-op in West London, grew out of squatters who 'took on the management of short-life property and then evolved as they gained experience and confidence, into the promotion of long-life co-ops' and that short-life housing in general 'originated out of the squatters' movement' (*Building Communities: The Co-operative Way*, 1988). Roof Housing Co-operative in Lambeth evolved from a squat by people who were convinced that housing allocation policy was discriminatory. (Surveys conducted by the Commission for Racial Equality showed that their conviction was correct.) Jheni Arboine, the secretary, told Shelter that 'the days when white middle-class people determined the needs of black people are over so far as we are concerned. Groups like ours are going some way towards destroying the "old boy network" that exists in housing, a network that until recently excluded anyone who was black.' She goes on to say that 'black people are now prepared to take on their own housing problems and we no longer want or need white missionary types to treat us like poor people with problems that we're not capable of solving ourselves' (*Roof*, November/December 1986). The squatters' movement, just like gentrification, is a great know-how builder: a lesson in the art of working the system. It's a lesson in dweller control.

And a consideration of the evolution of several groups from despised squatters to admired co-operators leads me to my last case-history of self-help in urban renewal, based once again on what has actually happened, rather than on what could happen, or what I would like to happen. Ideology may prevent you from learning from the gentrifiers on the one hand and the squatters on the other, but I want for my final example to evoke Ebenezer Howard's 'gift of sweet reasonableness' in 'appealing to the English instinct for finding common ground'.

Housing co-operatives, of which we had hardly any fifteen years ago, but of which we have several hundreds today, ought to appeal right across the political spectrum. They should win the support of the present Government—and in fact a clause in the Housing and Planning Act of 1986, which came into force in January 1987, allows local authorities to delegate the management of houses and flats to tenant co-operatives as well as giving tenants' groups the right to put such a proposition on the council's agenda'. They should win the support of the present Opposition, since the co-operative movement as a whole was part of that network of organs of working-class self-help and mutual aid which created the labour movement in the nineteenth century. And they should appeal to the various parties in between.

It was my privilege in November 1986 to chair a meeting which brought together the various people from up and down the country who are involved in monitoring the experience of co-operative housing. (It is precisely because this form of dweller-controlled self-help has been neglected for a century that we have had to gain experience and learn about the successes and failures in a hurry.) One of the striking things about the preliminary findings that we were told about concerned precisely the burning question of repairs and renovations—of urban renewal, in fact. For example, Peter Bolan of Bristol Polytechnic reported that, at Cloverhill Self-Management Co-operative at Rochdale, there was felt to be 'considerable improvement especially on smaller repairs'. David Clapham of Glasgow University reported on his research in the very interesting large-scale transfer of former council housing in Glasgow to tenant co-operatives. He found that among tenants it was thought immensely important that tenants themselves should be able to organise and carry out not only minor and major repairs, but also renovations and modernisation programmes, and that they and not the council should employ people for this purpose. It was Glasgow's Director of Housing who declared last year that 'our greatest resource is not our 171,000 council houses, but the tenants. The potential is there waiting to be released' (*Roof*, July/August 1986). And at that same meeting Anthea Tinker, giving a preliminary account of the Department of the Environment's current research on housing co-operatives, found 'a high degree of satisfaction. The speed and quality of repairs are valued more than anything else' (to be reported in *Housing Review*).

We have varieties of self-help in urban renewal to suit all tastes. What we need is not only a huge extension of access to finance, but a broadening of access to know-how and a simplification of procedures. We also need, as Ebenezer Howard insisted ninety years ago, to burst the bubble of urban land valuation.

# 6. FRINGE BENEFITS: SQUATTERS IN RURAL NORFOLK HAVE A MESSAGE ...

In retrospect, I belonged to the golden age of house-purchase. We both had regular jobs and the building societies were still non-profit-making, friendly societies with their origins in 19th-century working-class self-help. Foreclosure on mortgage debts was unknown. The societies would tumble over themselves to avoid it by reducing and extending repayments.

Market-worship has changed all that. It instigated a real-estate boom that turned every investor into a property-speculator, from the Church of England to the pension funds. Almost all the societies have joined the indecent rush to stop being friendly and become ruthless usurers.

Coupled with the deliberate casualisation of jobs in a flexible labour market, the collapse of property prices has brought misery to 300,000 households in the past five years alone. And, of course, we have auctioneers specialising in repossession jobs, knocking down the houses to the highest bidder at a fraction of the outstanding debt. Even then, some houses remain unsold and rot, at a time of acute housing distress, urban and rural.

There are, of course, possible solutions: like turning the failed home-owners into tenants, or adopting the "urban homesteading" approach favoured in the US 20 years ago, or setting up housing co-ops renting rooms to members of the young and dispossessed.

In East Anglia we have one marvellously creative solution. At Pulham St Mary, near Diss in Norfolk, there's a 20-room 16th-century manor house, a listed building, repossessed by the Leeds and Holbeck Building Society. It had been empty for years, during which thieves and vandals broke windows and ripped out five marble fireplaces, fountains, gates and lead from the roof.

Last October, six squatters, all from Norfolk, moved in as an alternative to sleeping rough, mended the leaky roof and windows, and set about making the place habitable. They were sued for repossession by the Leeds; but two of them, Paul Wessell and Matt Bevan, went to court with an Affirmation of their needs, supported by a petition from local residents and councillors arguing that the house ought to be inhabited and protected from further decay.

They succeeded and were granted a shorthold tenancy at £80 a week for six months. A building society spokesman told the *Eastern Daily Press*: "We are cur-

Originally printed in *New Statesman & Society* (June 9, 1995): 30.

rently finalising a formal agreement. It must be stressed, however, that this is a unique case ... and it is not the normal policy of the society to allow squatters to take over empty properties that are up for sale."

Some of us argue that it should be. And that the next step for the Pulham St Mary squatters is to form themselves into a Co-operative Housing Society and consolidate their position in the village. We also remember how, when some urban local authorities shifted from using thugs to drive out squatters to a policy of acceptance, some very durable housing co-ops were formed that flourish to this day.

Economists warn that the downturn in house prices is permanent, not temporary, and this is bad news for both families and mortgage-lenders left with a mountain of debt. But with an ounce of foresight we could transform it into good news for the next generation of the homeless. The Norfolk squatters have won a toehold to a future. Shouldn't the 250,000 borrowers owing six months or more of mortgage arrears, link with others in their own areas to become squatters in their own homes? And wouldn't the resulting housing co-ops reduce not only their own misery, but the actual financial debts of the mortgage-lenders?

Inevitable losses, resulting from the speculators' Thatcherite utopia, would be transformed into small aims: domestic security for those households that need it most, and a recovery of the tarnished reputation of the building societies, faced by the results of their improvidence.

# 7. THE LAND IS WHOSE?

*"Hardly noticed at first, 'Property is Theft' was to become one of the great phrases of the nineteenth century, bandied about between anarchists and conservatives, borrowed by socialists and communists, and suspended like a sensational placard above the popular image of its author. Ironically enough, Proudhon did not even mean literally what he said. His boldness of expression was intended for emphasis ... He was denouncing the property of the man who uses it to exploit the labour of others without any effort on his own part, the property that is distinguished by interest, usury and rent, by the impositions of the non-producer upon the producer. Towards property regarded as 'possession', the right of a man to control his dwelling and the land and tools he needed to work and live, Proudhon had no hostility; he regarded it as a necessary keystone of liberty, and his main criticism of the Communists was that they wished to destroy it."*

—George Woodcock, *Pierre-Joseph Proudhon: A Biography*[36]

In September 1969 we all cheered when Proudhon's phrase *Property is Theft* was placarded in letters three feet high on the walls of 144 Piccadilly in London, a former royal residence. The squatters were evicted and the slogan removed. And as the Crown and the royal family owns more of Britain than anyone else, Proudhon's slogan had an unqualified and unequivocal appropriateness, obvious to all.

But of course, there has always been a distinction between squatting as a political demonstration, from that of Winstanley and the Diggers at St George's Hill in Surrey in 1649 to that of *The Land is Ours* at Wandsworth in 1996, and squatting as a personal solution to a housing problem. In the first instance the intention is, for propagandist purposes, to be noticed. In the second, the hope is to be inconspicuous and to blend into the landscape. Given the public perception of the squatters' movement, it has always been a paradox that, just as the Herefordshire village squatters yearned to establish their children's rights in their wills, so the typical modern squatter actually hopes for the security of a rent book.

Theoretical revolutionaries may be disappointed by the gulf between rhetoric and daily life because of a curious inability to distinguish between the property of the landlord and that of the peasant. "No man," urged Winstanley, "shall have any more land than he can labour himself, or have others to labour with him in love,

Originally printed in Colin Ward, *Cotters and Squatters: Housing's Hidden History.* (Nottingham: Five Leaves, 2002), 167–176.

working together and eating bread together,"[37] and this is precisely the difference between the appropriation of land by squatters and that by enclosers.

Many cultures share the tradition that the land was once the common property of the people. "The landlord owns the peasants but the peasants own the land" was a Russian saying from the days when land-owners measured their wealth in 'souls'; and the peasant seizure of the land preceded the Bolshevik seizure of power in 1917. David Mitrany recorded how

> The collapse of the old regime had been like a break in a dam, through which first a small trickle and then a rushing stream of spontaneous revolutionary action poured. The peasants began at once to take over forcibly large estates and forests, the number rising with every month from 17 in March, 204 in April, 259 in May, 577 in June, to 1,122 in July. It was estimated that in the first two years the peasants in thirty-six departments had taken over 86 per cent of the large estates and 80 per cent of their farm equipment; this increased their holding from 80 to 96.8 per cent of all usable land.[38]

In retrospect, the 1920s were the golden age of the Soviet 20th century, when "it was possible to find arrangements allowing peasant households to form a co-operative and yet keep their land, housing and equipment separately from each other and to make their own separate profits".[39] But in his very next sentence, the historian Robert Service, observes that "The idea of peasants taking most of their own decisions was anathema to Stalin." From the end of the decade, mass collectivisation destroyed the Russian peasantry. "The price was awful. Probably four to five million people perished in 1932–3 from 'de-kulakization' and from grain seizures."[40]

As citizens of the Soviet Union and its subsequent satellites were not allowed to discuss this terrible lesson, alternative approaches to food production had to emerge in the gaps that were subsequently allowed to emerge within the official policies. Eventually peasants were allowed to cultivate "private plots" and these became the salvation of Russia's food supply:

> In 1963, private plots covered about 44,000 square kilometres or some 4 per cent of all the arable land of the collective farms. From this 'private' land, however, comes about half of all the vegetables produced in the USSR, while 40 per cent of the cows and 30 per cent of the pigs in the country are on them.[41]

There are parallels between Winstanley's insistence that the woes of the English people stemmed from the Norman conquest and the claim that all land belonged to the King, and the insistence by millions of Soviet citizens that they had a right to colonise some minute patch of the land that they were told had been won back by the people. In England, as Oliver Rackham put it,

> William the Conqueror introduced the un-English doctrine that all land ultimately belongs to the Crown. It was part of the King's new, supreme, status

that he had the right to keep deer on other people's land which lies at the heart of the Forest system.[42]

The same often-forgotten point was stressed by Simon Schama, noting that,

> Such 'forests' could be, and were, imposed on large areas of the English countryside, including the entire county of Essex, that were not wooded at all and which included tracts of pasture, meadow, cultivated farmland, and even towns.[43]

And just as the landless poor of mediaeval England sought out marginal patches of wasteland that they could colonise, so the economist Hugh Stretton reported from the Soviet Union in the 1970s that "Pathetically, Russian town dwellers go out and comb the countryside for patches of neglected land they can plant, visit, enjoy, 'make their own', however tenuously. Their masters, who own everything just as the masters did in Marx's day, discourage this petit-bourgeois practice."[44] But with the gradual collapse of the Soviet regime it was reported in 1985 that

> For the average Russian city dweller, it looks as if the first symbol of the Gorbachev era will be an allotment. The Politburo has authorised a series of measures designed to increase the number of private gardens—and these have already proved too few for the soaring demand ... Once the plot has been dug, planted and harvested, the owner is allowed to put up a garden shed and, with a little creative interpretation of the rules, a shed can become a small dacha ...[45]

All the countries of Eastern Europe provided variations on the Soviet experience. Western visitors to the cities of Poland, Czechoslovakia, Hungary, Romania, Bulgaria and Yugoslavia would notice the landscape of gardens and dweller-built chalets along the routes from the airport to the city centre. Ian Hamilton reported that

> The existence of peasant-owned land on the fringes of cities offers opportunities for piecemeal evolution—indeed 'overnight mushrooming' of 'wild settlements' as in Nowy Dwor and elsewhere outside Warsaw or in Kozarski Bok and Trnje on the margins of Zagreb ...[46]

Closer to home, the British planning system, built around the Town and Country Planning Acts passed by democratically elected parliaments and administered by democratically elected local authorities, has been far more effective in excluding the urban poor from the rural hinterland. The application of the legislation on planning, building and public health has ensured a bloodless elimination of any surviving peasantry from rural England. In Chapter 11 I quoted the industrial historian L.C.T. Rolt, who described in the 1970s the changes he had witnessed in the west of England, where cottagers became council house dwellers.[47]

The local gentry despised those raw new council houses, and made jokes about the inhabitants keeping coal in the bath. The tenants were thrilled to be offered not only a bathroom but a water-closet, and adequate damp-free rooms, offered by no previous village landlord. But under the Thatcher regime, not only were councils obliged to sell their houses, but they were prevented from spending the income on building more. This fact, together with the shift in attitudes which makes all new buildings (apart, thanks to the political influence of the agricultural lobby, from farm buildings) a blot on the landscape, has to be coupled with the fact that permission to build multiplies the value of a rural site tenfold. The result is that the adult children of local families have little chance of housing themselves, and rent rooms in the nearest town, while the new occupants of those picturesque cottages are in the forefront of the village preservation society, since as Professor Gerald Wibberley used to explain, they want their particular village to remain exactly as it was on the day before they decided to move there.

In one of several reports, Mark Shucksmith has described the way in which rural Britain has been transformed into an exclusive countryside where only well-off people can afford to live. He observes that,

> The studies suggest that progressive 'gentrification' of rural England will continue, as wealthier households outbid poorer groups for scarce housing, and 'social exclusion' thus becomes 'geographical exclusion'. Planning for and resourcing affordable housing provision is fundamental to sustaining rural communities and to the life-chances of many people.[48]

The effective challenge to the situation where only the affluent with their double garages and four-wheel-drive vehicles, can inhabit rural Britain has come, not from political movements, but from people with aspirations to feed themselves on a small patch of ground and warmly supporting the British government's commitment to sustainable development agreed at the Earth Summit at Rio in 1992. Simon Fairlie was one of a group of friends in the west of England who rented a house with a large garden on a country estate, but was evicted to make room for a golf course. After living in a van for two years, he joined another group and bought a smallholding with no house attached. They pitched seven tents and started cultivation. The result, he reported, was that "In the two years since we moved onto our land, we have been through almost the entire gamut of planning procedure: committee decision, enforcement order, stop notice, Article 4 application, Section 106 agreement, appeal, call in by the Secretary of State and statutory review in the High Court. All this for seven tents!"[49]

Eventually, he and his friends won the right to stay, and similar settlements, like the bender community of King's Hill, also battled with the planning legislation, and likewise won permission to stay. Fairlie's case is interesting, not only as a precedent, but because it led to his very significant involvement in the debate on planning. His purpose has not been to demonise the planning machinery. He believes in it because he knows that without it, speculative developers would have completed the destruction of the countryside, subsidised for years to destroy woodlands, wetlands, hedges and wildlife. At the Town and Country Planning Summer School at Lancaster in 1993, Sir Richard Body, a farmer and then a Conservative Member of Parliament, had revealed that "the intensification of agriculture in the last 25 years has gone ahead faster and more furiously in the United Kingdom than in any other member state of the EC." He read to the assembled planners what he called "the woeful litany of statistics of the damage inflicted on the rural environment by government subsidies to farmers." These included:

—130,000 miles (210,000 km) of hedgerows ripped up
—40 per cent of our ancient woodlands gone
—seven million acres (2.8 million ha) of pasture-land ploughed up
—over 95 per cent of our wetlands drained
—875 miles (1410 km) of stone wall destroyed
—95 per cent of the downlands of Southern England gone
—180,000 acres (73,000 ha) of moorland ploughed up

He went on to say that it infuriated participant observers like him, that having subsidised the owners of rural land to do all this damage in the name of increased food output, we are now "Paying the farmer to manage the countryside and thus protect the rural environment."[50]

In the last years of the last century changes in subsidy policy, arising from the embarrassment of European 'food mountains' reduced the incomes of rural land-owners, which had been inflated for decades, and brought the emergence of a 'rural lobby' claiming that the countryside was under threat from ignorant townsmen who failed to understand traditional rural ways. It was left to Peter Hall and the present writer to point to the evidence of official statistics that the quantity of land 'set aside' under European agricultural policy and handsomely subsidised for producing nothing, was three times the amount of land needed to accommodate all urban development predicted in Britain for the coming quarter century.[51]

The facts about rural Britain are a quiet testimony to the way in which the affluent, pleading the cause of countryside protection have sought to exclude the poor. The immense value of the campaigns associated with "The Land is Ours" has been that, virtually alone, they have re-opened discussion of the key issue of the right of all of us, just through having been born on this earth, to enjoy a right of access to our modest share of it. The Rural Planning Group of that campaign is known as 'Chapter 7'. This is because that section of the Agenda 21 agreement on 'Promoting sustainable human settlements' had a series of affirmations, the first of which explains that "the objective is to provide access to land for all households ... through environmentally sound planning."

Chapter 7A of that document, stressing social justice, urged that "all countries should, as appropriate, support the shelter efforts of the urban and rural poor by adopting and/or adapting existing codes and regulations to facilitate their access to land finance and low cost building materials."

Chapter 7G is a reminder of the aims of those of the Arts and Crafts movement of a century earlier, like William Richard Lethaby, who wanted rural housing that would 'rise like a lark from the furrows'. For Chapter 7G declares that

> All countries should ... strengthen the indigenous building materials indus-
> try, based, as much as possible, on inputs of locally available natural resources
> ... promote the increased use of energy efficient designs and technologies and
> sustainable use of natural resources ... promote the use of labour-intensive
> construction methods ... develop policies and practices to reach the informal
> sector and self-help builders ... discourage the use of construction materials
> and products that create pollution during their life cycle.[52]

The British government is committed to these aims through its predecessor's sig-
nature of the Rio Declaration of 1992, and this also involved commitment to the
concept (in Chapter 7C) of "access to land for all households ... through environmentally sound planning." There is little sign of the acceptance of these precepts
in the Planning Policy Guidance Notes that flow from government to local planning authorities. There are signs, however, not that planning authorities are abandoning the profligate policies of the past, but that, with the added incentive of the
incorporation into British law of the European Convention on Human Rights,
they will be obliged to accommodate the planning system to those people supported by Chapter 7—those "who sort out their own housing, in self-built houses,
mobile homes, trucks, benders or sheds at no cost to the taxpayer more or less in
defiance of the planning system."[53]

This recognition, when it comes, will be an ultimate gesture towards the centuries of cotters and squatters who housed themselves in the margins of history.

# 8. SELF-HELP AND MUTUAL AID:
# THE STOLEN VOCABULARY

*"Private faces in public places*
*Are wiser and nicer*
*Than public faces in private places"*
—W.H. Auden, "Marginalia"

The most depressing thing about the ideological mess we have made for ourselves in the field of housing is that whenever someone on a public platform eulogizes self-help and mutual aid, half the audience stop listening since they regard these words not merely as Conservative platitudes but as a smokescreen to conceal the abdication of governmental responsibilities. I cannot imagine how these phrases came to be dirty words for socialists since they refer to human attributes without which any conceivable socialist society would flounder.

Nor are they part of the official perception of housing policy. The Department of the Environment in its towers at Marsham Street has a vast library. You could, if you were admitted, go there and read the entire official literature of housing, from the 1880s to the 1970s, and you would not find either phrase. They have never been on the agenda in the language of government.

They are resonant phrases because both are the titles of famous books from the Victorian era. *Mutual Aid* by the Russian anarchist, Peter Kropotkin, was a celebration of the propensity to co-operate, whether among insects, animals or humans, intended as a rebuttal of the misinterpretations of Thomas Henry Huxley and Alfred Russell Wallace of the implications of Darwin's theory of natural selection.

*Self-Help* by Samuel Smiles was a much-reprinted volume which exhorted its readers to apply thrift and self-improvement to their lives so as to progress from rags to riches. Smiles himself was outraged that his book had been regarded as a manual on devil-take-the-hindmost individualism, declaring in the Preface to the second edition that this was 'the very opposite of what it really is ... Although its chief object unquestionably is to stimulate youths to rely upon their own efforts in life rather than depend upon the help of others, it will also be found ... that the duty of helping one's self in the highest sense involves the helping of one's neighbours.'

---

Originally printed in Colin Ward, *When We Build Again: Let's Have Housing that Works!*
(London: Pluto Press, 1985), 27–45.

Our ancestors were kept alive only by a combination of self-help and mutual aid, and this was the dominant characteristic of the emerging working-class organizations of the nineteenth century, whether we are thinking of the co-operative movement, the trade union movement, the friendly society movement or the adult education movement. It is ironical that the twentieth-century political heirs of these organizations have put their faith exclusively in the governmental bureaucracy and have not only ignored this heritage, but despise it.

Interestingly enough, until the revival of interest in the late 1960s in the application of mutual aid and self-help to housing, it was only among immigrant groups in Britain, whose whole experience of the role of government in their lives predisposes them towards non-governmental solutions, that you could find the modern equivalent of the very earliest building societies. Thus the Milner Holland Report on housing in London noted that,

> Particularly among Indians and Pakistanis, housing finance pools are found with a substantial membership—perhaps as many as 900—which meet periodically once a fortnight or once a month, and make calls of, say £10 on each member. Those who draw upon the fund thus created are subject thereafter to periodic calls until the whole amount drawn by them has been liquidated. Drawings under this system are substantial and may cover the whole purchase cost. Occasionally West Indians operate on similar but less ambitious lines ... Their pooling arrangements usually only provide for the initial deposits necessary for house purchase, thus enabling them to 'get off the ground'.

Of course, the whole owner-occupation sector in housing is, though it very unfashionable to say so except in Conservative circles, a triumphant example of self-help and mutual aid. Building societies originated as working-class organizations; they are by definition and by law non-profit-making bodies, even though the vain attempts by ordinary members to get elected to their boards may persuade us that they are ruled, like many other organizations with similar origins, by self-perpetuating oligarchies.

One could even make a case, historically, for the notion that the first building societies were formed when as a result of the enclosures, squatters or cottagers (two terms which were once synonymous) were no longer able to erect their dwellings on waste or common land. Not only in Britain, but in many parts of Europe, and hence in the New World, it became widely accepted that if a person succeeded in erecting a dwelling between sunset and sunrise and lighting a fire in it, he or she could not lawfully be dispossessed. There are innumerable variations of this formula—six months, a year and a day, twelve years—in which property might be occupied unchallenged to gain title, whether enshrined in folk law, common law or even statute law.

Observers noted how the hovels of the peasantry could develop over generations into a fully finished house. For William Cobbett, the cottager was a free and independent spirit saved from the craven property of the landless labourer. An account of the squatters of the New Forest stresses their prosperity and self-sufficiency, and their 'singular combination of reticence and self-possession, with good humour and friendliness.' To relate personality characteristics to the mode of tenure is a risky argument since so many factors quite outside the control of the individual shape our lives and life-chances. But such generalizations are still made. When Ferdynand Zweig asked people how they felt when they became house owners, 'the overwhelming majority felt deeply about it' and the words which came to their lips were 'satisfaction, self-confidence, freedom and independence.'

In his study of the history of working-class housing in Nottingham, Stanley Chapman notes that as late as 1785 just a few industrious artisans were to be found building their own cottages. He cites the case of William Felkin, a knitter in the hosiery trade, an abstemious man engaged on the highest-quality work, who was 38 before he was able to build his own cottage. He was granted a plot, 60 yards by 10 yards, by the squire of the village of Bramcote, and with the aid of his son, built his cottage of brick, stone, timber and thatch.

> The dwelling house, consisting of house place and weaving shop, scullery, pantry, and with two bedrooms above, was 32 feet long and 16 feet in width, and the height of the roof tree was 26 feet, the roof thatched or tiled. Adjoining was a building open to the roof, furnished with a large bread oven, copper and space for coal and firewood. Another lean-to was for a piggery and hen roost ... The garden space was 450 square yards.

For most working men this was a dream rather than a reality, but as enclosures and urbanizations created the industrial proletariat, various mutual aid institutions grew up among people who wanted to free themselves from landlords and rent. Chapman finds traces of the existence in Nottingham of working-class 'money clubs' for the raising of capital to enable builders to erect small houses for club members. Borrowing from these money clubs seems, he says, to represent a transition between the friendly society and the 'terminating' building society. In another paper he examines such institutions in Birmingham in the late eighteenth and early nineteenth centuries. Two kinds of societies were organized, from below, to serve as the mechanisms of both self-help and mutual aid in housing. The terminating building societies (so named to distinguish them from the permanent building societies which superseded them) were formed by groups of people who pooled their credit-worthiness to build a group of houses which, when completed were allocated to members of the group. Freehold land societies, with a similar aim, acquired land for subdivision into plots for their members. One of the motives of the Freehold Land Society in Birmingham in the mid-nineteenth century was also that of providing the property qualification for the parliamentary vote, and in the words of Chapman and Bartlett, it 'was quickly taken over by the artisan elite and small manufacturers.'

The incomes of the poor were so low and their insecurity so manifest, that the capacity for regular saving through any such societies did not apply to them. But between the appalling housing conditions of the 'submerged tenth' and the propensity for self-help and mutual aid of the highly skilled artisan class, there were families living in rented houses in the long terraces of the familiar 'by-law' streets built between, say 1875 and 1914. Our impression of such streets may very well be one of 'dirty brick or stonework, rusting metalwork, and unpainted timber', but Francis Jones reminds us that 'prior to 1914 the renting of a house was an economically sound policy, and maintenance, however it was organized, was essential to the landlord.' And the tenants' part in the process? Jones remarks that,

> In addition to the standard of landlord maintenance the tenants had common standards for the exterior of the house. This included sweeping the pavement and often even mopping it for the full width of the house. The window-sills were painted and polished, doorsteps were rubbed clean and colourwashed white or buff. Metal door furniture was either directly polished if brass or black-polished if cast-iron. The external woodwork, i.e. of door and lower windows, was washed and regularly polished. Through the windows clean curtains and shining metallic fittings would be visible. The general visual quality of the street was therefore bright, and even in streets consisting entirely of houses, uniformity did not necessarily mean a deadening monotony.

After the slow decline in the interwar years, accelerating in the post-war period, this tradition of tenant involvement in maintenance became eroded as landlords themselves were unable or unwilling to meet their own maintenance obligations. What was the point in polishing the front door when the roof leaked? Today, if we see a house in a terraced street of this kind, treated with the sort of loving care that Mr Jones describes, we know that it has been purchased freehold by the occupier (in spite of the discrimination of most of the building societies against loans for this kind of house), or has been taken over by a tenants' co-operative.

The little Buckinghamshire town of Wolverton exemplifies this point dramatically. It grew up in the railway boom of the last century, with the district called New Bradwell being built by the railway company to house the people employed in the railway workshops in streets of little terrace houses characteristic of any industrial town. By the 1950s the local council, dominated by retired railway workers, saw this housing as mean and obsolete, redolent of the bad old days of nineteenth-century capitalism. Several streets were demolished and on their sites were built blocks of three-storey municipal flats, neither better nor worse than those of any other local authority. By the 1970s it had become evident that many people actually preferred the old streets to the new blocks, and there was fierce local argument about the wisdom of demolition. Finally, thanks to the sympathetic attention of members of the staff of Milton Keynes Development Corporation, the very oldest of the railway cottages (by now, such is the capriciousness of the cycle of taste, regarded as a little gem of nineteenth-century industrial architecture) were rehabilitated for the Rainbow Housing Co-operative which leased them collectively from the Corporation. They are now seen as the most attractive and desirable houses in the whole town.

When I asked a co-operative member there what the adventure meant for him, he replied,

Well, we're in a position where we have more control over the houses that we're living in, how to decorate them, the way we'd like the house to look. There's more interest, more involvement and this provides a sort of common thread that runs through the street, and everybody knows everybody as a result through this common interest in running the place. It creates a very friendly atmosphere.

But so tortuously complex have we made the procedures for improvement grants and the establishment of co-operatives that this venture could never have got off the ground had it not been for the lucky accident that the Development Corporation staff's professional expertise was available. I say this not to praise the professionals, but to deplore the complexity of the legislation.

Another example of this deployment of self-help and mutual aid, which, however, was only brought about through the lucky accident of professional presence, is that of the Black Road, Macclesfield (a town in Cheshire which had played an important part in the early silk-weaving industry). The houses in this street, built around 1815, were originally scheduled for demolition in 1968. An architect, Rod Hackney, bought one of the houses towards the end of 1971 and applied for the standard improvement grant. The council turned down his application, as his 'structurally unsound' cottage was in the clearance area. When he wrote to the *Macclesfield Express* complaining of 'official vandalism' he found that many of his neighbours were in the same situation and of the same mind, and inevitably he became both their spokesperson and their architect. The rest of the story is very well-known in housing circles and made the architect's reputation.

Black Road has certain special features which make it the archetypical example of self-help and mutual aid in housing renovation. It became, for instance, the first general improvement area in the country to be proposed, implemented and subsequently managed by the residents themselves. It was also the first example of that supreme irony of the crudity of official designations of places: of a clearance area being transformed into a conservation area. From being worthless the houses became priceless.

The Black Road Action Group succeeded in winning over the council's officers so that the rules could be relaxed in a most sensible way. For example, the rules specify that self-help is penalized in the sense that the dweller's own labour cannot qualify for grant. The authorities would rather pay a firm of building contractors than pay you or recognize your contribution. At Black Road neighbours set up as contractors for each other, so that they might qualify for grant aid. Poor and elderly tenants were enabled to become owner-occupiers, again just to qualify, through what Hackney calls Robin Hood financial arrangements, and each tenant got the improvements actually wanted, rather than those which the regulations or the architect thought was good for them, so that no two houses are by now alike. This marvelously intimate approach to the creative adventure of house improvement is symbolized by the fact that the building workers left their plant on Friday night at the most convenient places for the residents to take it over at the weekends.

Once again, the sad truth is that just because of the mountain of legislation and regulations, and just because it was necessary to have someone to put the case convincingly to the holders of power and dispensers of funds—a power of life and death over a street—it was essential to have someone present with professional knowledge and a vested interest in the success of the project. This in no way diminishes the potential of self-help and mutual aid. It simply demonstrates the extent to which the procedures introduced by government to improve the housing situation have unwittingly complicated it and made it unresponsive to the aspirations of ordinary citizens. The habit of self-help and mutual aid have been deliberately repressed by inducing the habit of reliance on the bureaucratic organization of housing. To paraphrase Habraken again, people are no longer enabled to house themselves: they have to rely on being housed.

Not only that: they are expected to be grateful and to stay put. For one aspect of the demise of the private landlord which nobody ever mentions is the loss of the freedom to move. The public sector is the immobile sector, and owner-occupiers, with the millstone of mortgages round their necks are more mobile than council tenants, dependent upon the goodwill of the clerks in the housing department. Our views on the historical inevitability or political desirability of the decline of the private landlord have blinded us to an aspect of the housing situation of our grandparents. When private renting was the norm, given the lower standards of services in housing that we take for granted today, there was considerable freedom of choice in the housing market, even for very poor families, and this resulted in a degree of dweller satisfaction which is much rarer when a multiplicity of landlords has given way to the monopoly of the local authority.

This was impressed on me by listening to hours of tape recordings of interviews with old people made by primary school children. Time and again the old ladies would say, 'Of course, you wouldn't understand, my dear, but in those days it was easy to move.' Their recollection is confirmed in a dozen working-class autobiographies. 'In the thirties,' recalls Elizabeth Ring, 'there was no such thing as a housing shortage. For from five shillings to five pounds a week, there were rooms for all.' Jack Common says of his childhood in Newcastle, 'At that time, families were always moving. There were houses to let everywhere.' Arthur Newton says of Hackney in East London, 'To change houses was easy then.' Mollie Weir from Glasgow describes with relish the many moves of her childhood and her mother's fondness for 'flitting', which in her family's context did not imply a 'moonlight flit'. 'How different everything looked,' she says, 'even if we'd only moved to the next close, which my mother did twice, for we knew our houses so intimately that the slightest variation in a lobby or a window-frame, or the size of a fireplace, was of enormous significance. Everybody loved a flitting ... '

From a totally different background, the East End of London, A.S. Jasper in *A Hoxton Childhood*, describes a whole series of childhood environments, starting in August 1910 when 'We were living at number three Clinger Street, Hoxton, in a hovel on the ground floor. It comprised two rooms with a kitchen, with an outside lavatory, which also served the family upstairs.' By page 15 we are told,

It was agreed that Mother would try to find a bigger house. In those days it was easy; one had only to go to an agent, pay the first week's rent and move in. On more than one occasion my father came home late, drunk as usual, and was told by the next-door neighbour we 'didn't live there any more'. We had owed so much rent but the fact was that we had to have a larger house. My mother duly found and inspected a house in Salisbury Street, New North Road. It wasn't a bad area and I always remember it was the nicest house we ever had.

And he describes with gusto how they set about redecorating it: 'Wallpaper was about threepence a roll; a ball of whitening and boiled size made whitewash for the ceilings.' But bad times came again, and on page 39 we hear, 'Our new abode was Ebenezer Buildings, Rotherfield Street. What a dump it was after the nice little house we had just left!' Soon his mother and sister went house hunting again and decided on a house in Loanda Street, by the side of the Regents Canal near the bridge in Kingsland Road. But a little later, 'Everything was getting too much for Mum and she reckoned the house had a curse on it. The only way was to move again. This time she found a house in Scawfell Street. This wasn't far from Loanda Street. It certainly looked a road with some life in it, which was what we were used to. Loanda Street was a drab place of flat-fronted houses where everyone closed their doors. There wasn't the friendliness.' But by page 88, 'We were now in 1917 and we were on the move again. Why, I cannot remember. This time we moved to Shepherdess Walk, off City Road. It was a very large house let off in flats. We had a ground floor and basement flat consisting of five large rooms and a scullery ... ' Not many pages later, in September 1918, 'We now lived in a very nice place in the main road. The rooms were large and there was always something going on.' But in the following year, the man who owned the dairy downstairs 'shocked us by saying that he was going to sell the dairy and we would have to quit the flat. He told us he had a house at Walthamstow we could rent and he would pay all the expenses if we would move. In 1919 Walthamstow to us was like moving to the country. The whole family discussed the matter and it was agreed they would go and see the place ... ' So, a couple of pages later in his narrative, they moved. 'It was a small house just off the High Street. The rent was eight shillings a week. I was beginning to like our new surroundings. For a penny you could get to Epping Forest, and this was all so different to the slums of Hoxton and Bethnal Green ... '

Thus there were eight moves in Mr Jasper's childhood between the ages of four and fourteen. The moves were intimately related to shifts and changes in the family's minimal income and to the family size—whether his sister's husband was living with them or not, and so on. And the final move brought the family right out of the inner city and into the ampler opportunities of the leafy suburbs. With both Mr Jasper and Miss Weir, there glows through the pages what teachers are trained to call an 'affective relationship' between the family and its housing. This was the result of having, even among poor people, some degree of consumer choice. Changes in family circumstances as well as aesthetic preferences were reflected in the ability to move. Neither were they the families of skilled artisans.

Miss Weir's father died when she was a baby and Mr Jasper's father was a drunken casual labourer. Both were effectively one-parent families.

Today, when the population of Glasgow and of Inner London are both dramatically lower than could have been imagined in those days, the element of freedom of choice and the opportunity for self-help in housing that those families had has totally disappeared.

When Peter Hall was given an opportunity to discuss the enormous and, to the public purse, expensive expansion of the architectural profession after the Second World War, he asked, 'Didn't it, unbelievably, result in an environment much worse than the one we had before?' And he went on to say,

> It's chastening to ask what would have happened if we'd never trained the architects, but had spent all that slum clearance money quite differently. Suppose, in the Liverpool of 1955, we hadn't said: 'a problem of replacing 88,000 unfit houses', but rather: 'a problem of making 88,000 houses fit', we could have given very generous improvement grants, encouraged small builders, opened DIY shops. The whole environment would have been improved piecemeal. It wouldn't have been very efficient—small-scale work never is—and besides, a good deal of the basic infrastructure would have had to be renewed. But it would have involved ordinary people in fixing up their own houses and helping improve their own neighbourhoods. It wouldn't have caused the enormous disruption, physical and social, that gave us the Everton Piggeries and the vandalized streets of Kirkby.

By now most of us would agree with Peter Hall. I think myself that he understates the case. I am sure that piecemeal, dweller-controlled reconstruction would have been more efficient than anything that was actually inflicted on Liverpool, where enormous sums were paid out to the professionals, both inside the corporation and as outside consultants, from McKinseys and the most expensive urban planners down, for giving the worst possible advice. What did the ordinary tenant say, in a place like Cantrill Farm?—'I wish I was back in the Dingle.' I think that Hall was wrong to single out the architects as responsible for the disasters of policy in Liverpool. The whole coalition of politicians, experts and administrators had a vested interest in not enabling people to find their own solutions. Ivan Illich remarks that

> In 1968, for example, it was still quite easy to dismiss organized lay resistance to professional dominance as nothing more than a throwback to romantic, obscurantist or elitist fantasies. The grass roots, common-sense assessment of technological systems which I then outlined, seemed childish or retrograde to the political leaders of citizen activism, and to the 'radical' professionals who laid claim to the tutorship of the poor by means of their special knowledge. The reorganization of late industrial society around professionally defined needs, problems and solutions was still the commonly accepted value implicit in ideological, political, and juridical systems otherwise clearly and sometimes violently opposed to one another. Now the picture has changed ...

The picture has changed, even in Liverpool, as we shall see. But Liverpool was simply the most dramatic and poignant instance of the housing disasters of most British cities, including many London boroughs. This becomes clear whenever someone has taken the trouble to document the evolution and effect of housing policy in a particular place. One well-documented town in this respect is Sunderland, where Norman Dennis has described the workings of progressive housing policy in practice in two devastating books, *People and Planning* and *Public Participation and Planners Blight*. He shows with innumerable examples how, in the making of decisions affecting our environment, ordinary people's own perceptions of their housing and their own networks of self-help and mutual aid have been left entirely outside the calculation. (Where, in fact, in the days of vast public investment in housing, the life or death of a street could be made on a clip-board from the passenger seat of a moving council car.)

Norman Dennis talks about Millfield, a district of Sunderland, and the two ways of looking at the place. Within the first frame of reference, he says, 'Millfield, for example, is a collection of shabby, mean and dreary houses, derelict back lanes, shoddy-fronted shops and broken pavements, the whole unsightly mess mercifully ill-lit.'

A second frame of reference, that of, say, a 60-year-old woman living there gives a very different picture:

> Millfield is Bob Smith's which she thinks (probably correctly) is the best butcher's in the town; George McKeith's wet-fish shop and Peary's fried-fish shop about which she says the same with equal justification; Maw's hot pies and peas, prepared on the premises; the Willow Pond public house, in which her favourite nephew organizes the darts and dominoes team; the Salvation Army band in a nearby street every Sunday and waking her with carols on Christmas morning; her special claim to attention at the grocers because her niece worked there for several years; the spacious cottage in which she was born and brought up, which she now owns, has improved, and which has not in her memory had defects which have caused either her or her neighbours discernible inconvenience (but which has some damp patches which make it classifiable as a 'slum dwelling'); the short road to the cemetery where she cares for the graves of her mother, father and brother; her sister's cottage across the road—she knows that every weekday at 12.30 a hot dinner will be ready for her when she comes from work; the bus route which will take her to the town centre in a few minutes; the homes of neighbours who since her childhood have helped her and whom she has helped; church, club and workplace within five minutes' walk; and, in general (as is said) 'every acre sweetened by the memory of the men who made us'.

There is a terrible irony about the fact that public policy has frustrated both those people like A.S. Jasper's family who loved to be always on the move, and those, like the lady in Norman Dennis's account, who were ruthlessly uprooted from the social networks of self-help and mutual aid which sustained their lives, by the determination of local authorities to wipe out the past at the public expense. To me the description of Millfield evokes the way of life of many people I have known, as well as that of people I have casually interviewed in several British cities; others don't see it like that. Members of the audience at conferences about housing and planning to whom I've quoted this passage have seen it as just a sentimental evocation of the past.

The web of relationships, habits, associations and mutual obligations that formed the whole framework of that woman's life, was totally invisible to the politicians, the councillors, the Director of Housing, the Planning Officer and Director of Environment Services and the Medical Officer of Health. They reflected *her* history, not theirs. Professor A.H. Halsey has remarked on the radio that

> The movement which had invented the social forms of modern participatory democracy and practised it in union branch and co-op meeting was ironically fated to develop through its political party the bureaucratic corporate state ... And the supreme irony is that when a person like Norman Dennis protests against the emerging tyranny of government with the authentic voice of deeply rooted English socialism, he is heard with approval by Sir Keith Joseph and dismissed as a nuisance by the Labour establishment.

People who insist on the importance of ordinary dwellers' perception, who declare that the important thing about housing is not what it *is* but what it *does* in the lives of its inhabitants, are often misrepresented as saying that people *like* having substandard housing, damp walls or an outside lavatory. They are, rather, saying that people's preferences, perceptions and choices are not only, perhaps not mainly, concerned with officially perceived housing standards, and that in any case, there is a gulf between these standards and what people want. In the first place, there is the indisputable truth that defects in your housing are infinitely more tolerable if they are *your* responsibility than if they are someone else's. In the second, there is the fact that housing policy has been, from its inception, intended to 'improve' or change people's domestic habits. And in the third, it has been based on the erroneous assumption that we are so short of land that people should be housed in flats.

Every study of ordinary people's wants, complaints and satisfactions, not just in Norman Dennis's studies in Sunderland, but those of others everywhere else, indicate that there is a certain kind of housing which over 80 per cent of English people prefer (I can't speak for the Welsh with their much higher proportion of owner-occupation or for the Scots with their lower one, much modified by the aspirations of the young). Their preference is for the ordinary small house with a back garden, traditionally provided, not just in the suburbs but in the cities themselves. But the public authorities, with their virtual monopoly of the provision of housing for rent, decided than an increasing proportion of people should be housed in a way which denied all of their own desires.

Paralysed by a capitalist conception of land values, and aided by the lobby of the National Farmers' Union which urged that every last acre or hectare of unwanted wheat or barley would protect the country from urban infestation, it was felt that people should be protected from their own aspirations. And yet the housing that citizens actually yearn for is cheaper to build, infinitely cheaper to maintain and infinitely more adaptable to changing needs and demands.

Take one hilarious example: for generations, in municipal housing, the kitchen became smaller and smaller, in order to cure people of the reprehensible habit of eating in the kitchen. The result is that, up and down the land, you can meet families, squashed in a corner, taking turns at eating their meals on a table as big as a shelf. Meanwhile the socially conscious architect of the 'scheme' they have been obliged to inhabit, eats in his kitchen, surrounded by his family, off a scrubbed deal table, and his wife prides herself that their kitchen looks exactly like that of a Provençal peasant. There's a string of onions hanging from the beam of *her* kitchen ceiling in a house which is two miners' cottages joined together into one, in a Category D village to which Durham County Council has denied improvement grants.

The deliberate flouting of what people actually wanted didn't only happen in the North East. Ashley Bramall, a London Labour politician, remarks that the old County of London

> was mainly a city of small houses. Not only did the war scatter the population and destroy the homes, but it led to the rebuilding of London as a city of blocks of flats, of increasing height. This change has never been fully accepted by the population and there has been an increasing urge for movement to outer London and to the counties beyond, where the old pattern of street and house and garden could be recaptured.

He blames the war for the habit of giving people the kind of housing they didn't want, just as Peter Hall blames the architects. Nowadays, in our present chastened mood, we say, 'But nobody told us at the time.' It isn't true. For it wasn't in 1975 or in 1965 or 1955 but in 1945 that Frederick Osborn, said, just as he had been saying at all those wartime conferences on postwar housing,

> I don't think philanthropic housing people anywhere realize the irresistible strength of the impulse towards the family house and garden as prosperity increases: they think that the suburban trend can be reversed by large-scale multi-storey buildings in the down-town districts, which is not merely a pernicious belief from a human point of view, but a delusion. In a few years' time the multi-storey technique will prove unpopular and will peter out. Damage will be done to society by the trial, but probably all I can do is to hasten the date of disillusion. If I have underestimated the complacency of the urban masses, the damage may amount to a disaster.

What in fact he underestimated was the complacency of the politicians and their professional advisers. In his book, *Towards a Humane Architecture*, Bruce Allsop remarks, 'It is astonishing with what savagery planners and architects are trying to obliterate working-class cultural and social patterns. Is it because many of them are first-generation middle-class technosnobs?'

Long familiarity with the housing problems industry tells me he is right. If you are escaping from a history of poverty and deprivation, you will simply see our old industrial areas as a mean and cruel past, best expunged from the physical environment as well as from the human memory. It is the same with the councillors. If you have dedicated your lives to the fight against capitalism and exploitation, you will, in those areas of life like local government where you actually win control, resolve to eliminate the mean streets, the shared lavatories in the back yards and so on. And you will react with outrage and a feeling of betrayal when people like Norman Dennis conclude that *you*, the politician and the professional, are the enemy, ruthlessly uprooting people from familiar ways and familiar places. All those dedicated chairs of housing and planning committees and their professional employees weren't consciously conducting a battle against the weak and poor. They had simply absorbed the message of their times: firstly, that the only possible approach to housing was wholesale clearance and redevelopment in vast building contracts, and secondly, that people's own capacity for self-help and mutual aid was totally irrelevant to their housing.

# 9. HIGH DENSITY LIFE

*Over the next 20 years Britain will require millions of new homes. Where should they go? Should we favour high density inner city redevelopment, as Richard Rogers's urban task force does? Or is it better to expand the low density towns in the south east, where people actually want to live?*

I am one of the few people I know with an interest in cities who has not visited Barcelona. It's an accident of timing. For decades, I used to say that I would not go until I could sit at a café table on the Ramblas, arguing loudly about sex and freedom with my anarchist friends. By the time this had become possible, in 1975, we met at a café table in the Campo San Polo in Venice instead, laughing over their magazine *Bicicleta* and arguing about what should happen to the shanty towns on the fringe of Barcelona, housing rural immigrants. Should there be dweller-controlled upgrading on the Latin American model or new municipal estates on the north European pattern? There was nothing to say about downtown renovation, because, like the propped-up Venice which surrounded us, it was only for the benefit of us tourists.

These discussions came to mind when I read Michael Eaude's *TLS* review of two Barcelona novels by one of Spain's best-known writers, Manuel Vásquez Montalbán. "Montalbán," says Eaude, "is a strong critic of the message successfully sold by Barcelona's elite that their city is a haven of fine urban planning and good living." Barcelona is not the only city to sell itself well. Ten years ago, a procession of British government ministers filed through downtown Baltimore, the Barcelona of those days, and I followed in their footsteps. Kenneth Clarke was thrilled, as he remembered the place as "the ultimate rust-bucket dump." I was impressed, too, by the redevelopment of the inner harbour, with three new shopping pavilions on what used to be the waterfront. Grady Clay, an acute observer of the US urban scene, told me of the incredible sums from the federal treasury that had been pumped into Baltimore's Charles Centre and Inner Harbour redevelopments. Meanwhile, the inner city, from which the poor were being squeezed out, had at least 5,800 empty houses awaiting rehabilitation. Less than half a mile from the city's downtown miracle I met some of the hard-pressed people struggling to establish the rights of the poor majority to live decently in their own city.

Reading Montalbán on the tedious routines of getting by in Barcelona makes me wonder whether, just as Thatcher's ministers were seduced by downtown Bal-

---

Originally printed in *Prospect* (July 2000): 38–40.

timore, so Blair's advisers have been bought by a few delicious urban experiences at open-air Barcelona cafés. My suspicion is heightened by the news that in 1999 the RIBA gave its gold medal not to an architect, but to the city of Barcelona, and by the fact that *Towards an Urban Renaissance*, the report of the government's urban task force which reported one year ago, contains a foreword by the former mayor of Barcelona.

Now I know perfectly well that if I were at last to visit Barcelona I would fall in love with the place. And I could already list a dozen lessons for Britain from the few continental cities that I *do* know, such as Amsterdam, Zurich or Bologna, in particular the blessings of efficient, safe, cheap public transport. But the main lesson of Barcelona for architect Richard Rogers, chairman of the task force, is found in one sentence on page 59: "The most compact and vibrant European city, Barcelona, has an average density of about 400 dwellings per hectare." That is about twice as dense as central London. Government research suggests that, thanks to longevity, divorce and the growth in single person homes, we shall need some 3.8m additional households in England alone over the next generation. No wonder that partisans for urban ("brownfield") sites as opposed to rural ("greenfield") ones embrace the Barcelona story.

We have been here before; our great-grandparents had their own task forces to show for it. In 1891, Lord Rosebery, speaking as the Liberal chairman of the young London County Council, used language more forthright than anything we recently heard from the candidates for the office of mayor: "I am always haunted by the awfulness of London: by the great appalling fact of these millions cast down, as it would appear by hazard, on the banks of this noble stream, working each in their own groove and their own cell, without regard or knowledge of each other ... the heedless casualty of unnumbered thousands of men. Sixty years ago Cobbett called it a wen. If it was a wen then, what is it now? A tumour, an elephantiasis sucking into its gorged system half the life and the blood and the bone of the rural districts." Those rural districts were sunk in a depression lasting from the 1870s until the second world war.

Charles Booth's *Life and Labour of the People of London* (1889–1903) was a 17-volume urban task force report for the 1890s. The government also appointed the novelist Rider Haggard to serve as a one-man rural task force with his *Rural England* (1902). But the decade saw other independent *franc-tireurs* firing their own magic bullets at the linked horrors of city and country. There was Booth's namesake, General William Booth of the Salvation Army, who published *In Darkest England, and the Way Out* (1890) recommending rural colonies to prepare the urban unemployed for a new life on the land or in Britain's overseas possessions. William Morris's *News From Nowhere* described a post-industrial Britain, and Robert Blatchford's *Merrie England* (1893) explained the evils of monopoly landlordism in both city and country and advocated a revival of small-scale horticulture by ex-urbanites. His book sold almost 1m copies before the end of the century.

But the most influential of these testimonies was Ebenezer Howard's *Tomorrow! A Peaceful Path to Real Reform* (1898). A century ago the Garden Cities Association (now the TCPA) was founded to propagate his message. His book was reprinted in 1902 as *Garden Cities of To-morrow* and has been in print ever since. His home-made illustrations are the most famous planning diagrams in the world.

In spite of this, Howard is often misinterpreted. It is suggested that he wanted the suburbanisation of everywhere. In fact his concept of the Garden City, like the New Towns after the second world war, was an *alternative to* suburban expansion of existing cities. He had no connection with Hampstead Garden Suburb. Nor did he recommend low residential densities. With the typical family of five in 1898, his suggestions work out at 90–95 persons per acre; and with the family sizes of the period after the second world war it would be about 70 persons per acre.

Howard was convinced that once the inner city had been "demagnetised," once large numbers of people had been convinced that "they can better their condition in every way by migrating elsewhere," the bubble of the monopoly value of inner city land would burst. "But let us notice," he wrote on the future of London, "how each person in migrating from London, while making the burden of ground rents less heavy for those who remain, will make the burden of *rates* on the ratepayers of London yet heavier." He thought that the change to more humane urban densities would be effected "not at the expense of the ratepayers, but almost entirely at the expense of the landlord class." (Howard would have been shocked to learn that, a century later, we had failed to regain that "unearned increment" in site values that the community had created by clustering together. He would have been further saddened by the fact that we no longer even talk about this issue.)

The century which has passed since Howard asked the question "The People—Where Will They Go?" has seen the re-population of the countryside. By the 1960s, the map of population change was the reverse of the 1890s, with the areas then suffering the biggest population losses—in particular, East Anglia and the south west—becoming the areas with the biggest gains. But, 85 years after Howard foresaw the great exodus, John Prescott, deputy prime minister, tells us that the "exodus from inner cities" has been "driven by a lack of confidence in schools, fear of crime, an unhealthy environment, and poor housing." And he declares that, "This is bad for our people, bad for quality of life, bad for our economy, and bad for society."

This is taken from Prescott's preface to the urban task force report, while a few pages later, in the introduction, Richard Rogers explains that several essential issues—education, health, welfare and security—fall outside the remit of the report. This leaves only one of the factors listed by John Prescott: housing. And neither Prescott nor Rogers mention jobs—even though our cities were the product of the industrial revolution, and despite the fact that the pressure on housing in the south of England is partly the result of the loss of work opportunities elsewhere.

In *Victorian Cities*, Asa Briggs noted how in 1837 "England and Wales boasted only five provincial cities of more than 100,000 inhabitants: by 1891 there were 23 and they housed nearly a third of the nation." The late 20th century collapse of industry has reversed the mushroom expansion of the 19th century. Anne Power and Kathleen Mumford, in their report *The Slow Death of Great Cities? Urban Abandonment or Urban Renaissance* (Joseph Rowntree Foundation 1999), studied Manchester and Newcastle, which have lost a fifth of their population since 1961, and where "Good quality, modernised homes are being abandoned in some inner city neighbourhoods. House prices have fallen in some cases to zero, and some blocks and streets are being demolished.... Whole areas have virtually no demand for housing." Such places will only revive when they provide incomes. But regional job creation remains out of fashion, and enthusiasts for the new cyber-economy fail to migrate to Sunderland.

It used to be said that for a carpenter, all problems call for a nail and a hammer. Perhaps, for an architect, all issues are design issues. The task force led by Rogers tells us that "successful urban regeneration is design-led. Promoting sustainable lifestyles and social inclusion in our towns and cities depends on the design of the physical environment." This elevation of the role of the designer has been used to promote every new architectural ideology since 1945.

For decades after the war (under the slogan of comprehensive redevelopment) urban regeneration was design-led. It tore the cities apart. This is now well docu-mented. I myself wrote six books describing its terrible results. In London, the LCC's former chief strategic planner, Graham Lomas, found that in the post-war decades, as councils sought high-density solutions in system-built tower blocks, more fit housing was destroyed than was provided.

...

Giving the Rogers' report a cautious welcome in *Prospect* last year, Anatol Lieven said that "for the first time since 1945 a humane consensus of ecological, aesthetic and civic values" enjoy a powerful new voice among those working in the field. The date he gave was well-chosen, because from that moment on the mysteri-ous Hubert de Cronin Hastings, the owner of the *Architectural Review*, aided by the draughtsmanship of Gordon Cullen, was propagating the ideology of Town-scape. This ideology is illustrated in the Rogers' report by a drawing of "a mixed-use urban centre" and by a photograph of the streets north of the old market at Covent Garden and another of The Lanes at Brighton. All three illustrations bear that *imprimatur* of well-heeled urban hedonism, the open-air café table. I confess that I too have sat contentedly drinking at such tables, but a lifetime of hearing architectural propaganda tells me that the praise for all that bustling street life is always accompanied by the advocacy of high density living for *other* people.

In 1945, when postwar housing policy was taking shape, Frederic Osborn wrote to Lewis Mumford: "I don't think philanthropic housing people anywhere realise the strength of the impulse towards the family house and garden as pros-perity increases; they think the suburban trend can be reversed by large-scale multi-storey buildings in the downtown districts. This is not merely a pernicious belief from the human point of view but a delusion ... In a few years, the multi-storey method will prove unpopular and will peter out ... Damage will be done to society by the trial ... the damage may amount to a disaster."

The damage amounted to several disasters and hideous expense, but 50 years on, we find the Rogers' report telling us how some of the most lively inner city areas, such as Bloomsbury and Islington, can rise as high as 100–200 dwellings per hectare. Alongside this comment is a photograph of mansion flats near the Albert Hall, captioned "A different take on high rise living." In the early 1960s, I used to lecture to final year architecture students on human aspects of high densities, and always pointed to the arrogant folly of generalising from the lives of the affluent. "They are out of the house more, because they can afford to be. Mum isn't isolated at home with the babies, she is out shopping at Harrods. The children, when small, are taken to Kensington Gardens by Nanny. At the age of eight they go to a prep school, and at 13 to a public school, both of them residential. And during the holidays they are either away in the country, or winter-sporting, sailing and so on ... At any rate they are not hanging around on the landing or playing with the dustbin lids."

The reason for all this talk about densities is the search for an answer to the question Ebenezer Howard asked a century ago: "The People—Where Will They Go?" Both the present government and the last one have been blown by every wind in the political micro-climate in the game of deciding whether 40 per cent, 50 per cent or 60 per cent of the required new housing should be built on recycled urban land. Howard anticipated that the relief of the pressure on urban land through falling site values would enable the greening of the city. But of course some brown fields are browner than others, and it is cheaper to redevelop urban allotment sites and playing fields than industrial land. In the 1980s central government put great pressure on local government to release such sites for profitable development, and this can happen again.

And yet, notwithstanding its trendy disdain for the home-centred culture of the lower middle classes, the Rogers' report did raise some important issues. It rightly stressed the crucial importance of maintaining public spaces. The 1980s saw not only the return of mass unemployment, but also pressure from central government on local councils to spend less. To do this they cut many of the things that made inner city life civilised. One thing that is certain about mobile caretakers on housing estates is that they don't take care; similar observations can be made about street-cleaning and park-keeping. The work of Ken Worpole and Liz Greenhalgh, summed up in their report on *The Richness of Cities: Urban Policy in a New Landscape* (Comedia 1999), and in particular Worpole's paper *Nothing to Fear? Trust and Respect in Urban Communities*, go a long way towards explaining why people don't enjoy living in cities any more. One-person operated buses make bus travel even less attractive. Removal of the park keeper can be disastrous for parks. Parks, Worpole has argued, are still places where "the indeterminacy and inconclusiveness of daily life is suspended" and where "people's behaviour changes once they step into the park from the surrounding streets, becoming much more relaxed, gregarious and sociable." Similarly Worpole's study of public libraries, the urban facility used by a wider cross-section of the public than any other, shows how they can reinforce good citizenship. "In such settings most people do still subscribe to the values of respect for other users' interests and needs, waiting one's turn, not greedily dominating particular resources."

The task force would presumably endorse these observations, as Howard would have a century ago, but nowhere in the report is it spelled out that the insecurity that people associate with city life relates to the fact that our rulers think that it is bad business to have people standing around being helpful.

Twenty years ago, Stephen Holley, who was for years the general manager of Washington New Town in County Durham, and watched with growing exasperation the shifts in central government policy—expressed his feelings in a sharp little verse:

> Isn't it a pity about the Inner City?
> People leave who shouldn't ought
> And that affects the rate support.
> If only those who stayed behind
> had left instead, no one would mind.

Nowhere in the task force report do I find endorsement of those struggling initiatives of self-help and mutual aid which penetrate areas that other urban solvents fail to reach. I am thinking not only of successes against the odds, like Coin Street on the riverside in central London, but of housing co-ops like the Eldonians in Liverpool and those self-build housing groups such as See Saw and The Diggers at Brighton, which were enthused by the simple building method propagated by the Walter Segal Self-Build Trust. For me, nurturing these precious shoots is more important than the succession of old policies under new names in the task force report.

So where *should* the people go? The new households should go into new and expanded settlements along viable public transport corridors in the places where people want to live (or have to live, for their jobs). This is where they *are* going, mainly in the south east. Behind all the rhetoric and posturing about rural values, the planning authorities are working together to accommodate the new households around towns such as Milton Keynes and Ashford, or along the M11 corridor and the Thames Gateway extending to Southend. Many of these new growth zones cluster around New Towns like Milton Keynes, Corby, Harlow and Basildon. Indeed, one of the best-kept secrets of social policy is that the postwar New Towns, by comparison with suburban expansion or high-density inner city redevelopment, were a social and financial success and were far more economical in land use than any other form of urban expansion. Let us build on what has worked—not on the high density living which has not.

# Section Three

Design, Architecture and Creativity

# 1. THE FUTURE OF THE DESIGN PROFESSIONS

My name is Colin Ward. I am the author of half a dozen books on housing and planning and associated themes like environmental education and vandalism. For many years from the ages of 16 to that of 40, I worked on the drawing board for several well-known firms of architects and planners. By chance, my last architectural job, almost twenty years ago, was as Director of Research for the firm of architects responsible for the complex of buildings we are in today [the Barbican, London]. I thus have considerable experience of the way design decisions are made.

The evidence I want to give is on three aspects of design. The first is on the professionalisation of design, the second on the bureaucratisation of design and the third is on what I have chosen to call the narcissism of design.

## ABOUT PROFESSIONALISATION:

The most uncomfortable part of the design professions' legacy from the Arts and Crafts movement is the notion that everyone is a designer, or that, in the language that Eric Gill inherited from William Morris, the artist is not a special kind of person, each person is a special kind of artist. They looked to a past in which professional designers, in their opinion, did not exist. They were right to the extent that most of the physical environment that survives from the pre-Victorian past, and that people flock to admire, was never touched by professional designers, except to destroy it. Architects themselves, bored with the precepts of the modern movement which they imposed on the public for decades, are involved in what they call 'post-modernism', the major form of which is a style known as 'neo-vernacular', which is a back-handed compliment to the non-professional designers of the past.

Yet the restriction of the design professionals to the fact that we have, from experience, lost faith in them, has been to suggest that some improvement in their own education, a broader base, a higher standard of entry, a longer period of training, more research, more science, more computers, more knowledge, will put everything right. ... let me cite the particular case of architecture. To be accepted for professional training [in the UK] involves at the outset three O levels and two A levels, preferably in the approved subjects, followed by six years of professional

Evidence given in support of Mike Cooley at the Enquiry on the Future of the Design Professions, at the Barbican, London, 30th November 1983. Originally printed in Colin Ward, *Talking to Architects: Ten Lectures by Colin Ward*. (London: Freedom Press, 1996), 18–23.

training, after which the successful aspirants find themselves preparing, say, window and door schedules for some building in the design of which they have had no part. Now, within living memory—and I think you will probably agree that architectural standards were no lower aesthetically and slightly higher technically within the lifespan of some people still alive—it was totally different. Sir Clough Williams-Ellis confided to Sir Edwin Lutyens that he spent a term at the Architectural Association school learning his trade. "A term" said Lutyens, horrified. "My dear fellow, it took me three weeks." Well, I would ask people who flocked to the Lutyens Exhibition at the Hayward Gallery last year, or who are glued to the television to watch the re-runs of *The Prisoner* for the sake of its setting in Williams-Ellis's architectural joke at Portmerrion, whether those two were better or worse architects than the people who by a restrictive Act of Parliament are entitled to call themselves architects. I deliberately mention these architectural knights to indicate that I am not generalising from the experience of the riff-raff of the architectural profession, who all, no doubt, have been through the academic treadmill.

Professionalism *is* a conspiracy against laity, because the greater the expertise, the power and status of a profession, the smaller the opportunity for the citizen to make decisions. Ivan Illich, the most damaging of the new critics of the professionalisation of knowledge, remarks that:

> It makes people dependent in having their knowledge produced for them. It leads to a paralysis of the moral and political imagination. This cognitive disorder rests on the illusion that the knowledge of the individual citizen is of less value than the 'knowledge' of science. The former is the opinion of individuals. It is merely subjective and excluded from policies. The latter is 'objective'—defined by science and promulgated by expert spokesmen. This objective knowledge is viewed as a commodity which can be refined, constantly improved, accumulated and fed into a process, now called 'decision-making'. This new mythology of governance by the manipulation of knowledge-stock inevitably erodes reliance on government by people. ... Over-confidence in 'better decision making' first hampers people's ability to decide for themselves and then undermines their belief that they can decide.

## ABOUT BUREAUCRATISATION:

The comment I have just quoted is valuable because it links the process of professionalisation with that of bureaucratisation. For in the modern world professional design is a commodity which only the rich can afford, and this means whether business or government. In business the role of design is obvious to every consumer. It is that of inducing obsolescence by changing fashions of essentially the same produce by styling, and thus keeping the production lines rolling. The design ideology, inflating its role as usual, claims that it is concerned with the total product. The consumer knows that it's just a matter of changing the image, and has seen the streamlined-look, the rounded-corner-plastic-look, the rectilinear-teak-look, the two-tones-of-grey-look and the brushed-aluminium-look. Much more serious is the bureaucratisation of design in the public sector, where British firms of architects have felt competent to design everything from new cities in India to the organisation of hospitals in Canberra. Didn't their training and expertise make them world planners capable of planning anything in the world at the people's expense? They are also, of course, competent to design execution chambers for prisons in the gulf states. All part of the design brief.

In a highly centralised state like Britain, where design expertise has been put at the service of the bureaucracy, every error that would be trivial if it happened once, is multiplied a hundredfold when sanctified by the label 'design'. This is the lesson of the tower block fiasco in housing. It is the lesson of the various consortia for school design, and it is the lesson of our experience of hospital design....

William Tatton-Brown, who was the department's [Department of Health and Social Security] chief architect from 1959 to 1971, has concluded that the advice on hospital design, which his department pushed out for years, was misguided. He claims in fact that nearly half (i.e. £1,500 million) of the public investment in hospital building in the 1970s has been mis-spent. Yet there is no area of architectural design in which more expertise and research has been invested than in that of hospital design. Tatton-Brown's conclusion, after his retirement of course, is quite significant. "Delegate responsibility as low down as possible" he said. "Give it to the people nearest to the patients". ...

I will move to my third objection to the design lobby.

## THE NARCISSISM OF DESIGN:

The concentration of design in the hands of professional designers has meant that, inevitably, designers seek at all costs the approbation, not of their anonymous clients, but of their fellow designers and, in particular, that of those who are influential in the media of the profession. This is why it has become almost axiomatic that the kind of building that wins an award becomes one which is loathed by the people who live or work in it. They just call their school or office The Hothouse, or their block of flats Alcatraz or Casablanca because it reminds them of the vernacular architecture of penology or the forts of the French Foreign Legion. In the new city of Milton Keynes there is a quite measurable scale by which housing is assessed. At the most disliked end of the scale comes the housing by the most prestigious architects, the leaders of the profession. The most sought after is that which most resembled the traditional image of house-and-home, with a pitched roof and a chimney on top and a front porch with roses round the door. This, of course, is most despised by the design professions. The highest praise that any council tenant can give his home is the well-worn phrase 'it doesn't look like a council house'. This is why the design professionals have the utmost contempt for the people who are obliged to use their buildings.

There *are* alternative approaches to environmental design. I have walked down the street in British towns with architects who were greeted by everyone we met because they had been enablers and not dictators. They had helped people to make their own environment.

I am just like anyone else who has pondered for years on the failure of the design professionals to serve, beyond a trivial level, the needs of citizens. We need an

alternative theory, even one that denies that there *is* a future for the design professionals in the sense in which we have known them in the past. The best expression
I have ever found of an alternative approach was in a paper by Simon Nicholson,
which I published ten years ago in the *Bulletin of Environmental Education*. He
called it the Theory of Loose Parts, and he set it out thus:

> In an environment, both the degree of inventiveness and creativity and the
> possibility of discovery, are directly proportional to the number and kind of
> variables in it.

The argument he used to explain how he arrived at this principle is that the imposed environment, the one in which the citizen has a merely passive part to play,
results from cultural elitism. He says:

> Creativity is for the gifted few: the rest of us are compelled to live in environ-
> ments constructed by the gifted few. We listen to the gifted few's music, we
> use the gifted few's inventions and art, and read the poems, fantasies and plays
> by the gifted few. This is what our education and culture conditions us to be-
> lieve, and this is a culturally induced and perpetuated lie.
>
> Building upon this lie, the dominant cultural elite tell us that the plan-
> ning, design and building of any part of the environment is so difficult and so
> special that only the gifted few—those with degrees and certificates in plan-
> ning, engineering, architecture, art, education, behavioural psychology and
> so on—can properly solve environmental problems.
>
> The result is that the vast majority of people are not allowed (and worse—
> feel that they are incompetent) to experiment with the components of build-
> ing and construction. Whether in environmental studies, the abstract arts,
> literature or science, the creativity—the playing around with the components
> and variables of the world in order to make experiments and discover new
> things and form new concepts—has been explicitly stated as the domain of
> the creative few, and the rest of the community has been deprived of a crucial
> part of their lives and lifestyle.

We are groping both for a different aesthetic theory and for a different political
theory. The missing cultural element is the aesthetic of a variable, manipulable,
malleable environment: the aesthetic of loose parts. The missing political element is the politics of participation, of user control and of self-managing, self-
regulating communities.

## 2. FRINGE BENEFITS: COLIN WARD IS AMAZED AT GETTING OUT OF THE LABYRINTH

I've never been a wild enthusiast for mazes and labyrinths, though I've known plenty of people who seek out every chance to walk in one in stately homes, ancient sites and public gardens. And whether they are constructed with hedges or walls, or are simply a pattern of turf, stone or brick on the ground, you never know until you do it whether it is truly a labyrinth, like the one where Thesus slew the Minotaur, with a route that leads you inevitably to the centre, and sometimes out again, or whether it really is a maze, with teasing choices and dead ends.

It was when I was trying to disentangle history from legend in Chartres cathedral that I got entrapped in the labyrinthine scholarship of puzzle-building. The maze there is the largest decorative feature in the whole of that vast structure: 12 metres wide with a path of white stones separated by thinner blue ones, 294 metres long.

Several other French cathedrals of the 13th century had them set in the floor, but only three remain. The one at Amiens was removed, because the noise of children playing on it was distracting during services.

The Chartres maze was known as "The Road to Jerusalem", and I learned from its interpreter, Keith Critchlow, that this is also the name given in Germany to the children's game hopscotch, chalked on pavements and playgrounds.

There's now a project called Learning Through Landscapes, which urges that school grounds could be transformed from tarmac deserts into experiences for both learning and pleasure. One of its mentors, Wendy Titman, was telling me about her book *Special Places, Special People; the hidden curriculum of school grounds* ... , and the results of learning children's own preferences.

"Why do you think that the number of mazes open to the public has grown from 40 in 1980 to over 100 today, and why are they a playground priority for children?"

I was unable to provide a reason. "Computer games," she said triumphantly.

So I read another book *The British Maze Guide* by Adrian Fisher and Jeff Saward ... , and dared to chase up one of its authors, Adrian Fisher, billed as the world's most prolific maze designer ... Fisher is certainly the hot gospeller of the maze world and designs them everywhere in all materials.

---

Originally printed in *New Statesman & Society* (April 22, 1994): 30.

When I raised the computer game analogy, he said: "Yes, it's true, but our colour mazes are a much more rewarding experience than the usual solitary situation of children, on their own, working through an over-structured programme. We give a starting set of rules, but our colour mazes demand creative and cooperative play by being deliberately deficient in formal rules."

London visitors will be familiar with the visual pun on the word "Warren", in Crosby Fletcher Forbes' ceramic tile mazes on the platform walls of Warren Street underground station, and may even have surfaced to see John Burrell's medieval-style brick maze on the pavement of the Warren Street Playground nearby.

But Fisher insists that the greatest play-value of mazes arises when children abandon the rules and invent new games. "This is very creative: inventing new rules, playing with them to see how they work and modifying them in the light of experience. This process requires a high degree of communication, persuasion, social skills, interactions and cooperation."

Inevitably, I saw his conclusion as a social parable. We can take a solitary pilgrim's progress on the road to Jerusalem. Or we can change the rules through negotiation with other travellers, and take a different route, not into, but out of, the labyrinth, evading all those dead ends on the way.

# 3. ALTERNATIVES IN ARCHITECTURE

Now that the modern movement in architecture has spent its force, we can see that its ideological foundations were elitist or crudely mechanistic, that it ignored in the first place the environmental preferences of ordinary people, and in the second, the fact that modern bureaucratic systems, whether of the Western or the Eastern kind, would inevitably subvert the humane aspirations of architects, turning the professional either into computers producing packages or prima donnas producing jewellery. Yet there are, and always have been, alternatives.

The first is the vernacular alternative. Most of the world's buildings were not the result of the work of the professional architect. Everywhere, people built for themselves, using such locally available materials as were available to them. A decade ago Bernard Rudofsky's exhibition of *Architecture Without Architects* dazzled the visitor with its demonstration of the sheer perfection of the many forms that vernacular building had developed all round the globe, yet he told me last year that in the United States (it is less true of Britain) the teaching of architecture leaves no room for the study of unpedigreed, undated buildings. The monstrous growths, from Babylon to Brasilia, as Rudofsky put it, are all documented, what is left out is the ordinary, which is like restricting the science of botany to lilies and roses. Vernacular architecture has never been homogenised, it can never be an international language, for it is rooted in places and their indigenous materials and patterns of life. Its most disturbing feature for the businessman is its longevity, and its builders, Rudofsky emphasised, never thought of themselves as professional problem-solvers.

But it would be a mistake to suppose that it was produced by people who were naively unaware of the elements of design. J. M. Synge wrote of the Kerry peasantry that they "would discuss for hours the proportions of a new building—how high a house should be if it was a certain length, with so many rafters in order that it might look well ... "

In the West today, for an architect to design a vernacular building would (and does) simply result in Disneyland, but there are many countries where, just at the time when *we* are discovering the virtues of the still-extant vernacular tradition, considerations of prestige and status are leading to the adoption of Western-style high-technology building, using expensively imported ma-

Lecture at Sheffield University Architectural Society, 11ᵗʰ February 1976. Originally printed in Colin Ward, *Talking to Architects: Ten Lectures by Colin Ward*. (London: Freedom Press, 1996), 11–17.

terials and often providing a climatically unsuitable result. In Egypt, Hassan Fathy made heroic efforts to recreate the vernacular tradition, and produced structures which were cheap, efficient and beautiful, but could find no one in the ruling elite to support his activities. Indian architects like Charles Correa have had a similar experience. They want to use their understanding of traditional techniques for the poor, but only the rich can pay for it.

The vernacular is dead in the developed countries, though tribute is paid to it in neo-vernacular—or what Rudofsky would call volks-vernacular—buildings: the ranch-style house, etc. What may lead to the development of a new kind of vernacular tradition is the crisis of energy and resources.

So my second alternative is that of the ecological impulse. Contemporary building is distinguished by an extravagant energy input, because of the use of synthetic and highly-processed materials, because of the heavy use of power-plant on the site, and in terms of the continuous high level of power consumption in the working life of the building: permanent artificial lighting, heating and air-conditioning and mechanical services. The rising cost of energy and of raw materials will increasingly suggest the positive advantages of buildings which make fewer demands, especially in running energy costs.

This is a new factor in architectural thinking, although it would have been so obvious to our ancestors that they would not have needed to spell it out, and its implications are being studied at several levels. At one end of the scale is the study developed by Alex Gordon when he was president of the Royal Institute of British Architects, of Low Energy / Long Life / Loose Fit, and at the other are innumerable individual experiments in 'autonomous' housing using such devices as solar water-heaters, solar walls, wind generators, methane digesters, heat pumps, use of subsoil and other on-site materials. The research of this kind in the Department of Architecture in Cambridge (England) has as its objective "to devise a house with an integrated services system which is self-sufficient, making no demands on the centralised network system but at the same time providing a level of amenity similar to that currently enjoyed by the average householder".

On a wider scale is the attempt to devise an ecologically sound pattern of urban settlements as a whole. At either level the rediscovery of *constructional* methods of controlling the internal environment of buildings (for example, the 'bad-gir' or windscoop as a method of air-conditioning from Hyderabad) and the avoidance of materials whose original cost or processing cost would make their use prohibitive in the future, will lead to a new kind of architecture, as will the adaptation of existing structures.

And this leads me to my third, adaptive, alternative. Vernacular buildings waste nothing: they hate to destroy a structure, and will adapt the most unlikely buildings for new purposes. It is only a very few years since the orthodoxies of architecture encouraged the idea of throw-away buildings because most existing buildings had outlived their original uses. But this idea itself is by now more obsolete than the buildings to which it referred. Adaptability—which again was taken for granted by our ancestors—is an important criterion for an alternative architecture.

But an adaptable or malleable environment is important in another sense. The fully-finished *objet d'art* which was the aim of the great names of the modern movement (the environment designed to the last teaspoon and curtain by an architectural genius) relegates the occupier of the building to the role of caretaker. There is a school of thought among architects (for example, N.J. Habraken and Herman Hertzberger in the Netherlands) that seeks an architecture of alternative uses, which can be called in Ivan Illich's language *convivial*, because they give each person "the greatest opportunity to enrich the environment with the fruits of his or her vision" as opposed to those environments which deny this possibility to the user, and, as Illich says, "allow their designers to determine the meaning and expectations of others".

A fourth way of looking at alternative architectures can be called the counter-cultural alternative. The official culture prescribes certain architectural forms: the individual one-family per house or apartment: the office beehive (luxury accommodation for the queen-bees, standard cells for the worker-bees); the giant factory complex (different entrances, canteens and lavatories for separate levels of hierarchy); the huge educational institution; agro-industry on a vast scale, and so on.

The counter-culture postulates quite different building types: the multi-family house or commune; the reintegration of agriculture and industry and of brain work and manual work (in, for example, Kropotkin's *Fields, Factories and Workshops*, and the reflections on 'The New Commune' in Paul and Percy Goodman's *Communitas*); or the free school or college, which might be totally de-institutionalised, using the whole environment as an educational resource. Not only would the alternative culture prescribe quite different building forms, it would also combine them in quite different ways: the school which is also a workshop, the market-garden which is also an academy of music ...

For a fifth approach to alternatives, I have to turn to the populism of Simon Nicholson of the Open University, and his Theory of Loose Parts, to embrace the idea of an environment that can be shaped and re-shaped by its users. His Theory of Loose Parts claims that "In any environment, both the degree of inventiveness and creativity, and the possibilities of discovery, are directly proportional to the number and kinds of variables in it". This insight is closely linked to a sixth aspect of alternatives, the question of who is in control. We are fortunate that, once again, the principle has been very clearly stated, this time by the architect John Turner who, after years of experience in unofficial settlements in Latin America, set out precisely the concept of dweller control in the book he edited with Robert Fitcher, on *Freedom to Build* (Macmillan, 1972). As the publishers say on the cover of that book, "from their worldwide experience the authors show that where dwellers are in control, their homes are better and cheaper than those built through government programmes or large corporations". But their aim is not merely to save government money. They are concerned with personal and family fulfilment. Nor are they suggesting that their formula necessarily implies the owner-built house. But it does imply freedom from the exploitative or neglectful landlord. In new building, it does imply that, individually or collectively, the dweller should be his or her own general contractor. Nor does it necessarily mean doing without an architect. For example, one much-respected architect, Walter Segal, has, over the last ten years, been unlearning his previous assumptions and designing houses which achieve great economies by a meticulous use of stress-graded timber and of standard building components without any cutting to waste on the site. They are usually built by one or two carpenters who have become firm friends of his, with the help of the clients themselves. Current American experiences of 'sweat equity' and 'urban homesteading' are also relevant here.

And the reference to the particular skills of the building trades takes me to another nuance of the spectrum of alternatives, that I would call the syndicalist alternative. Bertolt Brecht asked one of the great questions of history in the poem that begins "Who built Thebes with its Seven Gates?" and goes on to wonder where the workers went when they knocked off for the day on the Great Wall of China.

Most of the monumental constructions of history were built by armies of slaves, and while the notion that the cathedrals of the Middle Ages were the product of dedicated bands of autonomous craftsmen is now regarded as a romantic myth (they were paid the current rate for a day's work), the very existence of this myth tells us how attractive is the idea of building as a communal activity, a cooperative enterprise in which the gap between designer and executant is closed, and in which the individual has pride of craft, skill and responsibility in the product.

Is it possible to create the kind of situation where this myth becomes true? And what effect would it have on actual buildings? There have been various attempts to change working relationships in the building industry itself. One example is that of the Building Guilds which had a brief life in England after the First World War, or the *sindicats de bâtiment* which exist to this day in France.

But from all these nuances of alternative approaches, I have to turn to the changing roles of architects themselves. The ethos behind their education and the assumptions behind the constitutions of their professional organisations is that the ethos of the architect is that of an independent professional. Actually a minority of architects, usually in small personal practices, rarely function in this way. Most are employed workers, either for other architects or for public authorities or private businesses. The majority of architects cannot be described as independent professional people, and the claims for specialised wisdom, judgement or expertise for the architect as 'leader of the building team' rest on assumptions that cannot be sustained.

Furthermore, the shift in the twentieth century in architectural training from pupilage of apprenticeship to university degree courses has been a matter of ensuring social status rather than of handing on professional wisdom. For example, John Turner asked 50–60 fourth and fifth year architectural students at the University of Morales in Mexico how many thought they would be earning a living as architects five years after graduating. None of them thought it likely, knowing that there was no effective demand for their services, nor for those of the 6,000 students of architecture in Mexico City alone.

At one time the architect's skill was considered to rest on his ability to manipulate the 'orders' or classical architecture, or the vocabulary of styles in general, or in the massing of volumes and spaces. These skills are irrelevant to all but a minute proportion of the designers of contemporary buildings. At one time, too, the architect was considered to be a 'master builder', but today is content to devote constructional and technical wisdom to specialists and technicians. If architects have a professional future at all, it is, in the phrase of Geoffrey Vickers, as "skilled understanders enabling people to work out their problems". This is not a matter for regret. I know several happy and fulfilled people who work in just this way, at the service of local community groups. Their reward is the friendship of everyone in the locality. Their problem is that of finding a free evening to pursue their own interests.

And if you ask them, they will tell you that the experience has transformed their lives. This is something that cannot be claimed through earning a living on the design of yet another new and unwanted speculative office block.

# 4. WALTER SEGAL — COMMUNITY ARCHITECT

The name of the late Walter Segal is now synonymous with self build housing. Whenever people meet to discuss what they could do to house themselves, someone mentions the Segal system of quickly-built, timber-framed dwellings which are environmentally friendly, and seem to generate friendship among the self build groups that have succeeded in housing themselves this way. The attraction increases when we learn that they include men and women with every kind of background, and they often say that the experience changed their lives.

The heartbreaks and delays that self builders experience are not to do with the process of building itself, but, as Walter Segal used to observe, are the result of the inflated price of land, the rigidities of planning and building controls, and the difficulty of getting mortgage loans for anything out of the ordinary. They are all made worse by the assumption of both regulatory authorities and providers of finance, that a house should be a full-finished product right from the start, rather than a simple basic structure that grows over time as needs grow and as labour and income can be spared. Segal's achievement was to devise a way of simplifying the process of building so that it could be undertaken by anyone, cheaply and quickly. He insisted that his was an approach, not a system, and he made no claims for originality or patents.

The Segal approach was essentially that of the medieval English house, or the American frame-house, or the Japanese house, but with the timber frame calculated and based on modular dimensions to avoid waste and to facilitate alterations and enlargements. He sought to eliminate or reduce the 'wet trades' of concreting, bricklaying and plastering, by reducing the sheer weight of the building and by using cladding, insulating and lining materials in their standard sizes. In his life, as well as his work, he tried to pare away the superfluous and concentrate on the important. My purpose is not to describe the Segal method, but to recount the effect on his life and personality of growing up in an anarchist commune, and his evolution late in life, as the architect, friend and advisor of community self builders.

Walter's parents were Jewish Romanians who met in Berlin, where his father, an expressionist painter, was taking part in an exhibition of the group called the New Secession. Walter was born in 1907 and in 1914 the family moved to the hills above Ascona in the Swiss canton of Ticino. Close by, in 1900, a colony had been started, trying, as Walter explained, "to find a new meaning in life," and was

Originally printed in Colin Ward, *Diggers and Dreamers: A Directory of Alternative Living*. (London: Freedom Press, 1989).

called Monte Verita, the Mountain of Truth. Like the aspirations of, say, Edward Carpenter's hopes of new communities around Sheffield, it was a revolt against the appalling stuffiness, in clothing, diet and means of livelihood of the atmosphere of the late-nineteenth century. Monte Verita was founded by Henri Odenkoven, a Fleming from Antwerp, and Karl Gruser, from the German minority in Hungary, whose younger brother Gustav, wandering through Germany "with long hair, sandals and bare legs" was met by the writer Herman Hesse, who followed him down to the colony and spent most of his life there. It figures in the lives of many subsequently famous writers, painters and revolutionaries.

Segal recalled that: "The colonists abhorred private property, practised a rigid code of morality, strict vegetarianism and nudism. They rejected convention in marriage and dress, party politics and dogmas: they were tolerantly intolerant." He reflected that "To have spent childhood and adolescence in an environment of artists, writers, life-reformers, thinkers and truth seekers, ideologues and mystics, charlatans and cranks, many of whom have left their mark upon our time— and unfortunately perhaps, continue to do so—was in a way a singular piece of good luck; but there were moments when I longed for ordinariness and went to seek it."

He found it among the village children, untrammelled by seriousness. "So I had playmates in both camps which meant that I was affected by the lives of both the Bohemians and the ordinary philistines. And I have since found myself all the time moving from one camp to the other, never really able to adjust to one world only." He was an outdoor child and realised early in life that his work was to be in building. "So I gradually slid into an understanding of how buildings are put up, and it was clear to me by the age of fourteen that I was going to be an architect." And he was fortunate in picking up an American house-carpenter's manual on the ordinary American tradition of 'balloon-frame' building of houses and barns.

The family were living in poverty, but suddenly a patron appeared for the painter Arthur Segal in the form of a rich anarchist sympathiser, Bernhard Mayer, and Walter was enabled to study architecture among the pioneers of the Modern Movement in Delft, Berlin. In Berlin, learning from engineers, he resolved that "every building I was going to make, I would calculate" and he won a scholarship to finish his education at the Technische Hochschule in Berlin.

In 1932 he was commissioned by the same Bernhard Mayer to build a little wooden holiday cabin, La Casa Piccola, at Ascona. It is still standing and has many of the characteristics of the Segal-style houses that self build cooperatives are putting up around the United Kingdom today. "I went back to Ascona to build," Segal recalled. "It became clear to me that one can have a small path and tread it alone." He was undoubtedly shaped by shaped by the free-thinking influences of his childhood ... The architectural critic Peter Blundell Jones was right in saying that "At Monte Verita, Walter saw enough artistic self-indulgence to last a lifetime," but he was also right in perceiving that "Walter was already steeped in far too rich and broad a culture and had become too much of a lone wolf ever to join any pack. He had to find his own way in everything, and confessed that he could never submit to authority."

## HARD TIMES AND A HAPPY ACCIDENT

Walter came to London in 1936, teamed up with Eva Bradt, a student from the Architectural Association School, and scraped a living on the fringe of the architectural world, during and after the second world war, writing prolifically in the trade journals and teaching at the Architectural Association School. As housing was bound to be a key post-war issue, he wrote a massive book *Home and Environment* (Leonard Hill 1948, 1953) and another on an issue which is more topical today than it was then, *Planning and Transport: Their Effects on Industry and Residence* (Dent, for the Cooperative Permanent Building Society, 1945). Books bring prestige but not an income and the post-war building boom passed him by. A handful of well connected left-wing architects had a huge output of housing and schools. They would not have taken seriously the small jobs that came to Walter: little buildings in Hackney for the Premium Pickle Company or a small office for Tretol Ltd and a few self-generated housing projects. Professional rejection meant nothing to him. He had a happy family life, was incredibly well read in several European languages and was a familiar figure in the architecture schools. I first met him when I went to talk at one of them and found a knot of students towering over a small, round, twinkling man pouring out a stream of paradoxes in a very soft voice. And his subsequent fame came by accident. Eva died in 1950 and a decade later Walter and a new partner, Moran Scott, with six children between them, decided to demolish and rebuild their home at Highgate and to put up a temporary house at the bottom of the garden to live in meanwhile. The lightweight timber structure, with no foundations other than paving slabs, and using standard cladding materials and linings in market sizes (enabling their reuse) took two weeks to build and cost £800.

It is there to this day, snug as ever. I remember sleeping in it when I was only 20 years old, with deep snow all around. Visitors to the Segals were more interested in the little house in the garden than in their new house on the street front. It led to a series of commissions around the country for houses built on the same principle, with Walter refining and improving the method every time. A carpenter, Fred Wade, followed him from site to site, and everywhere the clients were able to do more and more of the building themselves, varying the plans to suit their needs and make additions.

By the mid-1970s, as the crisis of confidence in local authority housing deepened, Walter was yearning to find one council that would sponsor a build-it-yourself experiment of this kind for people on its housing waiting or transfer list. Eventually, by one vote, the London Borough of Lewisham decided to do so, on pockets of land too small, awkward or sloping, to fit its own building programme. There were two and a half years of agonising delay, simply because the proposal didn't fit the standard ways of financing, providing or controlling buildings, but in the end it happened. Everyone involved was delighted. Ken Atkins of the Lewisham Self Build Housing Association reflected on what he called the "indescribable feeling that you finally have control over what you are doing." And Segal himself, in the context of the universal gloom hanging over housing in Britain was overjoyed to have helped to prove in the most convincing way imaginable "that there is among the people that live in this country such a wealth of talent." He found it unbeliev-able that this creativity would continue to be denied an outlet.

## THE SEGAL LEGACY

Walter died, aged 78, in October 1985. Within the architectural world his role had shifted from that of a loner and outsider to that of a moral force both inside and outside the profession. He is the only contemporary architect to have two roads named after him: Segal Close and Walter's Way, tokens of the affection he inspired among self builders. When I last talked to him a few weeks before his death, he was bubbling with enthusiasm about a demonstration structure at the Centre for Alternative Technology at Machynlleth in Wales, and about a build-ing his stepson was putting up on his smallholding, with three big frames, erected, like an American barn-raising, by emptying the local pub one weekend lunch-time. His friends and the people who had changed their lives by building Walter's Way set up the Walter Segal Self Build Trust to propagate the message and slowly, around Britain, examples of his approach to house building could be found. They are among the few bright lights in the dismal housing climate of the 1990s. Just as he hoped, his successors have continually adapted his approach to meet their own needs, and to changing assessments of environmentally-friendly materials and standards of construction.

# 5. PREFACE TO JOHN F.C. TURNER'S
## *HOUSING BY PEOPLE*

The moment that housing, a universal human activity, becomes defined as a problem, a housing problems industry is born, with an army of experts, bureaucrats and researchers, whose existence is a guarantee that the problem won't go away. John F.C. Turner is something much rarer than a housing expert: he is a philosopher of housing, seeking answers to questions which are so fundamental that they seldom get asked.

He is one of a group of thinkers who, working in different fields, often unknown to each other, have brought from the poor countries of the world lessons which are universal. For many years after the second world war it was assumed that the rich countries had an immense contribution of technical and organizational wisdom to bestow on the 'under-developed' or 'developing' nations: a one-way trip of know-how and high technology. Aid became a cold-war weapon and a vehicle of economic and ideological imperialism. Then, slowly, voices emerged which stated the issues in an entirely different way.

When E.F. Schumacher and his colleagues started the Intermediate Technology Development Group, to locate or design machines and tools that would help countries with a superfluity of labour and a shortage of capital, they were concerned with the real needs of the poor countries, but they gradually realized the importance of the principles they evolved for the poor areas of the rich world, and finally they came to see that they had formulated principles of universal application: intermediate technology became alternative technology. Paulo Freire and Ivan Illich, attempting to come to grips with the educational needs of Latin American countries, stumbled on truths which have changed the nature of the continuing debate on education throughout the world.

John Turner absorbed in Peru the lessons offered by illegal squatter settlements: that far from being the threatening symptoms of social malaise, they were a triumph of self-help which, overcoming the culture of poverty, evolved over time into fully serviced suburbs, giving their occupants a foothold in the urban economy. More perhaps than anyone else, he has changed the way we perceive such settlements. It was his paper at the 1966 United Nations seminar on Uncontrolled Urban Settlements that was most influential in setting in motion governmental

Originally printed in John F.C. Turner, *Housing By People: Towards Autonomy in Building Environments*. (London: Marion Boyars, 1976), 4–10.

'site-and-services' housing programmes—policies about which he himself has reservations. He evolved an ideology of housing applicable to the exploding cities of the Third World. But when he moved from South to North America, having been invited to the Joint Center for Urban Studies of the Massachusetts Institute of Technology and Harvard University, he found that the ideas he had formulated in Peru were also true of the richest nation in the world, and when he returned to England after seventeen years abroad, he found that the housing situation in Britain too fitted his formulation. He was, perhaps to his surprise, expressing universal truths about housing.

Turner is not a great believer in the value of books (the present work was wrung out of him by Ivan Illich's admonition that he was burying his ideas under a lot of Peruvian mud bricks), but out of his past writings and speeches I have, without any authorization from him, distilled Turner's three laws of housing. Turner's Second Law says that the important thing about housing is not what it *is*, but what it *does* in people's lives, in other words that dweller satisfaction is not necessarily related to the imposition of standards. Turner's Third Law says that deficiencies and imperfections in *your* housing are infinitely more tolerable if they are your responsibility than if they are *somebody else's*. But beyond the psychological truths of the second and third laws, are the social and economic truths of Turner's First Law, which I take from the book *Freedom to Build*:

> When dwellers control the major decisions and are free to make their own contribution to the design, construction or management of their housing, both the process and the environment produced stimulate individual and social well-being. When people have no control over, nor responsibility for key decisions in the housing process, on the other hand, dwelling environments may instead become a barrier to personal fulfilment and a burden on the economy.[1]

This is a carefully-worded statement that says no more and no less than it means. Notice that he says 'design, construction *or* management'. He is not implying, as critics sometimes suggest, that the poor of the world should become do-it-yourself housebuilders, though of course in practice they very often have to be. He *is* implying that they should be in control. It is sometimes said of his approach to housing that it represents a kind of Victorian idealization of self-help, relieving governments of their responsibilities so far as housing is concerned, and that it is therefore what Marxists would no doubt describe as objectively reactionary. But that is not his position. He lives in the real world, and however much he, like me, would enjoy living in an anarchist society, he knows that in our world resources are in the control of governmental or propertied elites. Consequently he concludes that 'while control over necessarily diverse personal and local goods and services—such as housing—is essential, local control depends on personal and local access to resources which only central government can guarantee'.

And even when governments make no such guarantees, it is clear that the poor in some (though by no means all) of the exploding cities of the Third World, often have a freedom of manoeuvre which has been totally lost by the poor of the decaying cities of the rich world, who are deprived of the last shred of personal autonomy and human dignity, because they have nothing they can depend on apart from the machinery of welfare. In London, Glasgow, New York or Detroit, in spite of an enormous investment in mass housing, the poor are trapped in the culture of poverty. But in the unofficial, informal sector of the economy of 'the cities the poor build' in Africa or Latin America, what Turner calls the 'lateral information and decision networks' enable them to draw on resources that the rich nations have forgotten about. Governments put their faith not in popular involvement, but in the vertical and hierarchical organization of large-scale works and services, but 'when these centralized systems are used to house the poor, their scale and the limitations of management rule out the essential variety and flexibility of housing options; even if the planners were sensitive to and could have access to the fine-grain information on which local housing decisions are made, it would be administratively impossible to use it'.

One irony is that when John Turner or his colleague Patrick Crooke, are commissioned by international agencies to report on housing strategies for particular 'developing countries' they urge governments to increase people's access to resources rather than grandiose housing projects, but find that while the agencies generally accept this advice, many governments reject it. They cannot believe that what poor people do for themselves can be right and proper.

People with a political or professional vested interest in the housing problems industry find it difficult to place Turner's message on the ideological spectrum. As he says, 'the common debate is between the conventional left which condemns capitalism and the conventional right which condemns personal dependency on state institutions. I agree with both, so nobody committed to either side can agree with me'. But his return to Britain in 1973 was well-timed. For in Britain this was the year that saw the lowest level of house-building for decades (just as in the United States it was the year that saw the withdrawal of Federal aid for housing). Housing policy in Britain rests on a very crude duopoly: owner occupation financed by mortgage loans (53%) and publicly rented housing (33%) with a dwindling private landlord sector, usually of sub-standard housing. This paucity of choice leaves a large section of the population with no way of getting housed— hence the rise and the legitimacy of the squatter's movement. In the public sector there is a crisis of finance, of maintenance and of management. Provided at great expense it fails to give commensurate satisfaction for its occupants who have been rigidly excluded from decision-making and control. ...

Some readers will perceive that the approach to housing outlined here, from a very rich fund of examples and case-histories, fits into a general framework of ideas. They are right. I have known the author intermittently for a quarter of a century, and I can see that it was inevitable that he should emerge as the most authoritative and persuasive advocate of housing by people. In the 1970s his analysis fits like a finger in a glove the climate of opinion moulded by such writers as Paul Goodman, Ivan Illich and Fritz Schumacher. We hardly need to ask what the author's opinions are on industry, work, leisure, agriculture or education. But the shaping of a mind which is actually receptive to the experience of poor families in far-away countries, their own struggles and aspirations, has deeper roots. I think there is a background to Turner's receptivity. As a schoolboy he was given the task of summarizing a chapter from Lewis Mumford's *The Culture of Cities*. This encounter led him to the work of Mumford's mentor, Patrick Geddes, whose book *Cities in Evolution*, written in the years leading up to the first world war, is really a handbook on the involvement of the citizen in environmental decision-making. Decades ago John Turner contributed to an appendix to the 1949 reprint of Geddes' book. He was then a student at the Architectural Association School of Architecture in London, having been seduced from military service by the anarchist newspaper *Freedom*, whose founder, Peter Kropotkin is another of the formative ideological influences in Turner's life. In 1948 I translated for *Freedom* an article from the Italian anarchist journal *Volonta* by the architect Giancarlo de Carlo, which attempted to formulate an anarchist approach to housing. I am happy that he was one of our readers, and when Turner, de Carlo, Pat Crooke and I first met in Venice in 1952, we discussed the crucial issue of 'who provides and who decides?' in housing and planning. In our different ways and in totally different circumstances, we have all been faithful to this anarchist approach to the fundamental issue of housing, and just in case anyone should suggest that John Turner's book is simply a reaction to the total bankruptcy of housing policy in all countries, rich or poor, I am glad to testify that it is the result of a lifetime of involvement in issues which are central to the hopes and happiness of ordinary people everywhere.

# 6. CHARTRES: THE MAKING OF A MIRACLE

Today, when we no longer believe in miracles, the medieval cathedrals of Europe, from the Baltic to the Mediterranean and from the Aegean to the Atlantic are still visited by a certain procession of people, in numbers far great than those of the age of faith. They are the most heavily trodden of all our monuments from the past. Indeed, at Canterbury, with up to two million visitors annually, the floor of the nave has had to be replaced and 'the noise reaches intolerable levels at times'. Chartres has as many and possibly more, and what strikes us is not divine intervention, but the fact that such an exquisite building, on a breath taking scale (Joris-Karl Huysmans calculated that it can hold almost 18,000 people), with its overpowering plenitude of sculpture and its vast collection of wonderful windows, could exist at all, seems to us a miracle. That the present building was put up in less than thirty five years and has survived almost intact, compared with the fate of most of the other great cathedrals of northern France, seems to us more incredible than any of the recorded miracles. When the north spire was added in 1507 to Bishop Geoffroy's north tower, the building brought together not only the magical spring, but also the flamboyant autumn of the Gothic period. But almost everything we see today was seen by the townsfolk and the pilgrims of the thirteenth century ... The English sculptor Eric Gill who....continually returned to Chartres as it was the fountainhead of his own work, spoke of the 'thrill and tremble of the heart' that he felt on his first close glimpse of the cathedral through an alley between the houses of the medieval town. It still has that power to move today....

> Medieval architecture attained its grandeur—not only because it was a natural development of handicraft; not only because each building, each architectural decoration, had been devised by men who knew through the experience of their own hands what artistic effects can be obtained from stone, iron, bronze or even from simple logs and mortar; not only because each monument was a result of collective experience, accumulated in each "mystery" or craft—it was grand because it was born out of a grand ideal. Like Greek art, it sprang out of a conception of brotherhood and unity fostered by the city. A cathedral or a communal house symbolized the grandeur of an organism of which every mason and stone cutter was the builder, and a medieval building appears—not as a solitary effort to which thousands of slaves would have

Originally printed in Colin Ward, *Chartres: The Making of a Miracle*. (London: The Folio Society, 1986), 16, 19–28.

contributed the share assigned to them by one man's imagination; all the city contributed to it. The lofty bell tower rose upon a structure, grand in itself, in which the life of the city was throbbing ...

Peter Kropotkin, *Mutual Aid*

The building that rose over Fuller's crypt was one of a dozen huge churches that was build in northern France at the same time: Sens, Saint-Denis, Notre Dame in Paris, Noyon, Soissons, Laon, Bourges, Rheims, Amiens and Beauvais. In both the twelfth and thirteenth centuries in France seven hundred churches were built, seven a year for two hundred years. And the cumulative number in England and in the other nations of western Europe must have been comparable.

Then the great building fever died away. Many of the great cathedrals took centuries, rather than decades, to complete, and some were never completed at all. Chartres was unique in the speed of its construction and in its good fortune in surviving, almost intact. It escaped from both the improvers and the restorers, just because it was so well-built, and it had the great good fortune to slip, for centuries, out of history. Happy the land that has no history, since as the most recent and most illuminating of the chroniclers of the cathedral, John James, explains, after the age of religious enthusiasm and of pilgrimages had passed, 'the region was by-passed by history and by war, as well as by prosperity. The good wines which came from the Beauce in the thirteenth century declined in quality. The cloth-weavers who had done well on the pilgrim trade found themselves too far from the new markets to the north and east of Paris, and without the climatic advantages of other regions. Gradually Chartres receded into a rural backwater, while the great events that excited the rest of France happily left it alone. The region remained a relatively prosperous one, with its rich wheat fields and silver mines, but, lacking both merchant princes and aristocratic grandees, there was neither the money nor the stimulation to change the cathedral. How fortunate for us.'

John James is an architect from Australia who came to Chartres on the inevitable visit and has stayed, on and off, for years, examining every visible stone of the cathedral to learn what it could tell us about the builders, the stages in which it was built and the intentions of the series of master masons. One of the minor tasks he set himself was that of attempting to put a building cost on the cathedral as if it were being built in the twentieth century. We shall see some of the implications of his figures. But he concluded that the greater part of the money raised was spent, not on the decoration, the glass and sculpture, but on the labour of building.

Probably the biggest single labour item in the making of Chartres was the cost of cartage. 'The slow lumbering wagons drawn by teams of local oxen would have taken a full day to draw a load from the quarry to the cathedral twelve kilometres away. A young boy could have helped his father cart the first load after the fire, grown up watching the outline of the new work rise slowly above the walls of the town, and retired as the speed of building declined after the vaults had been finished. It was truly the work of a lifetime!'

If cartage was the biggest single cost, we can see in a quite different light the stories of the cult of the carts, as well as the later efforts of citizens in the first three years after the great fire. Another recent historian, George Henderson, speculates that 'the speed with which the work got under way may have been due in part to there being a large quantity of building stone' ready to hand. The city of Chartres owed its stone pavements and a portion of its walls to the generosity of a recent Bishop of Chartres, Peter de Celles (1178–82). Fine dressed stone ... originally destined for or actually used in the city walls, may have been handed back to the cathedral authorities.'

But John James has other surprises in his attempt to sub-divide the cost of building Chartres. The glass, covering nearly an acre of window area, cost only ten per cent of the total, while 'the sculpture which so enthrals and moves us cost less than three per cent'. He believes that even this figure is over-generous, for he reached it by asking sculptors the time they would take to carve a figure and then doubling it, and by similarly doubling the normal contemporary labour rate for a skilled man. 'Yet we know from medieval accounts that sculptors were paid little more than other skilled carvers. They were not a race apart as they are today. The Middle Ages had no concept of the artist as a special sort of man, as we do. The post-Renaissance belief in individual genius had not entered their minds. They were paid well, but in proportion. Our exaggerated claims for artistic effort were happily unknown.'

The point he makes about the sculptors raises a more fundamental issue about the cathedrals of the Middle Ages. Who were the architects, how did they work and where are their plans? John Harvey, a scholar who has spent a lifetime identifying the architects of the great buildings of the Middle Ages complains that 'much nonsense has been written on the subject of medieval art, and several baseless ideas have gained wide currency. Among these have been the notion that all art was produced by the clergy and more especially by monks; that it was produced spontaneously by anybody, untrained but with some instinctive capacity for design and construction and that great architecture was produced entirely without drawings.'

These misconceptions arose though several kinds of misunderstanding. One of them arose from the contempt that was felt after the Renaissance for medieval buildings. The very term Gothic began as a term of dismissal for the rude artifacts of barbarian tribes. Put this attitude into reverse and you get the notion that anyone can do it. When the attitude was in fact reversed in the nineteenth century, and when it became assured that Gothic building was the only Christian architecture, the cathedrals were seen romantically through a haze of mystical religiosity.

But the most easily forgiven of these misunderstandings arises from an understandable over-simplification of the rediscovery of the medieval craftsman by the Arts and Crafts movement. The designers of the Gothic cathedrals, Eric Gill contended, were the working builders. "The Architect (unlike his modern bourgeois counterpart) rose from the scaffold and did not come down from the university. There was as little self consciousness among them as 'artists', as there is today among engineers. The only difference between a modern engineer and a medieval builder is that the latter controlled gangs of human labourers most of whom shared his enthusiasms and understood his theory (for he had risen from their own ranks) and none of whom was entirely deprived of intellectual responsibility, whereas the former is not a practical workman but a mathematical calculator and his buildings, (however grand and useful), are the work of men reduced to a subhuman condition of intellectual slavery.

Gill was echoing the opinions of the great nineteenth-century critic John Ruskin, who wrote an essay (it is embedded in the second volume of his book *The Stones of Venice*) on 'The nature of Gothic'. William Morris thought it 'one of the very few necessary and inevitable utterances of the century'. Ruskin exalted Gothic architecture for the very characteristics for which Renaissance taste-makers despised it: for its savageness.

This is a strange word to use about the buildings we now see amongst the finest triumphs of Western civilization but Ruskin explained it by claiming that the decoration of buildings 'might be divided into three: 1. Servile ornament, in which the execution or power of the inferior workmen is entirely subject to the intellect of the higher; 2. Constitutional ornament, in which the executive inferior power is, to a certain point, emancipated and independent, having a will of its own, yet confessing its inferiority and rendering obedience to higher powers; and 3. Revolutionary ornament, in which non executive inferiority is admitted at all.'

For Ruskin classical architecture was an approach to building in which the Greek master-worker and those for whom he worked could not endure 'the appearance of imperfection in anything' so that 'what ornament he appointed to be done by those beneath him was composed of mere line and rule, and were as perfect in their way, when completed, as his own figure sculpture'. In the renaissance too, 'the whole building becomes a wearisome exhibition of well educated imbecility'. But the extortions of the Gothic architect, he claimed were quite different. 'Do what you can and confess frankly what you are unable to do; neither let your effort be shortened for fear of failure, nor your confession silenced for fear of shame.'

'Understand this clearly', thundered Ruskin, 'you can teach a man to draw a straight line, and to cut one; to strike a curved line, and to carve it; and to copy and carve and number of given lines or form, with admirable speed and precise perfection; and you can find his work perfect of its kind; but if you ask him to think about any of those forms, to consider if he cannot find anything bettering his won head, he stops; his execution becomes hesitating; he thinks, and ten to one he thinks wrong; ten to one he makes a mistake in the first touch he gives to his work as a thinking being. But you have made a man of him for all that. He was only a machine before, an animated tool. And observe, you are put to stern choice in this matter. You must either make a tool of the creature, or a man of him. You cannot make both. Men were not intended to work with the accuracy of tools, to be precise and perfect in their actions ... '

We can, if we choose, readily refute Ruskin's dismissal of the place of the worker in industrial civilisation, since we, like him, are the beneficiaries of the kind of technology he despised. But Chartres confirms his analysis of the nature of Gothic. John James, with the authority of a man who has examined the actual structure of the building more closely than any historian since Jean-Baptiste Las-sus measured it a century and a half ago, finds that 'messiness can be a virtue', which is another way of phrasing Ruskin's praise of 'savagery'.

He says, and he is talking not about the 'ornamentation' of the building in sculpture and glass, but about the structure itself, that 'when you examine the cathedral closely, you discover to your immense surprise that the design is not a well controlled and harmonious entity, but a mess. We tend to think of a great work of art like Chartres as having been thought through to the end before it was begun. But Chartres is not like this, not at all. Our vision has been conditioned by the homogenising eye of the camera, but when we look carefully we see that there are few things at one end of the building that match those at the other. Windows and piers and buttresses change, as do hidden elements such as walls and footings, and of course all the details. The closer we look the messier it becomes: there is no other word for it'.

James demonstrates that if we really look at the side elevations of the building, rather than merely absorbing it as a unified forest of purple-grey limestone, we perceive a whole series of mis-matches. None of the details of the nave matches those of the sanctuary. The flying buttresses of the nave and the choir, the first so immensely solid, the second so light and elegant, belong to quite different ap-proaches to construction. The vast buttresses between the chapel windows in the apse at the east end sit, not on equivalent masonry in the wall of the crypt, but on arched openings, in a way that offends every layman's notion of the way a building should look. 'The nave is massive, and seems eternal, while the choir is so light it seems to vibrate. The stolid and the elegant. What a contrast within the one build-ing, or are we so habituated to differences that it makes no impact on us?' The confusion continues when we compare the north and south transepts and their great porches and windows. To the most casual observer these differ. The southern facade and its towers on either side of its rose window seem a much later work than the 'squat, plainer masonry' of the north, yet the more advanced window is that of the northern porch. 'How could this older window come to be placed within the newer tower, and vice versa? We cannot argue ourselves out of the realities of these situations. Either the building is a total confusion, in which case our feeling for what is great in art is remiss, or our concepts about architectural order are not those of the Middle Ages.'

Chartres lends itself to the stone-by-stone study that James undertook because its working masonry is uncovered and uncluttered, and he had access to the series of spiral staircases the builders made for their own use and to the galleries over the aisle roofs behind the triforium arcade. Through examining the way the stones are cut, the moulding of ornaments and the geometry that was used to set them out, as well as the mason's marks where they occur, he was able to tease out the sequence of the 'campaigns' of building. Dozens of scholars in the past century have tried to establish, on stylistic evidence, the sequence of building, frequently concluding, because the differences are obvious, that the choir was built later than the nave.

But what the stones tell us is that there were thirty campaigns involving nine different teams of masons, several of them returning several times to take up the work. Throughout the length of the building, they started at the bottom and worked upwards, though the transepts and choir lagged behind the nave. In view of the complete absence of written evidence, James has chosen to identify the master masons by colours: Scarlet, Bronze, Rose, Olive and so on, and he finds that some were more meticulous than others, and some imposed a greater degree of conformity on their craftsmen than others, in putting their own unconscious trade-mark on their portion of the work.

He is applying the same approach to the other great cathedrals of Northern France that were being built at the same time, Soissons, Rheims and Laon, and believes that he will find that several of the same contracting gangs can be identified there. Other scholars of twentieth century Gothic architecture have been anxious to stress, in rebutting sentimental notions that the cathedrals grew by inspiration, the importance of the emerging professional architects, much sought after by the clerical authorities and able to command high fees and great honour. No one denies this, but John James concludes from the Labour of love he has given to Chartres that 'the Cathedral of Chartres was not designed by three, nor even five or six architects. In the modern sense there was no architect only builders directed by men with a deep knowledge of the subtle aspects of their art. The stones tell us that 'we can be as deeply moved by a work created by many hands as we can by one created by a single genius'.

This is all the more remarkable because when we are standing in the nave of the cathedral we are aware of a powerful and unified consistency of design. Far from being conscious of 'savagery' we feel the presence of a supreme triumph of human intelligence and skill, even wit and a delight in the sheer virtuosity of the way the line of the ribs of the vaulting high above us is carried down from the very apex of the roof through the shafts on the columns to their very bases at our feet. The stones themselves seem to cry out 'look, we've done it', rejoicing in the visual excitement of the design.

Technically this was achieved by simplifying the vaulting (from the 'sexpartite' square bay of the early Gothic buildings to 'quadripartite' oblong bays of vaulting and columns) and by abandoning the four-storey internal elevations used at Noyon, Laon and Paris. These churches had high, wide galleries at an upper floor level, so that the effect as you looked down the nave was horizontal. At Chartres, above the tall arcade there was simply a band of arches, forming the vertical side of the triangle of the roofs over the aisles, and above that the tall clerestory windows.

The result is not only to give an immensely powerful and soaring vertical effect, but at the same time to pull the eye towards the eastern apse of the church, for the piers with their clusters of shafts accompany one on one's way down the nave and the aisles, in Nikolaus Pevsner's words, 'as closely set and as rapidly appearing and disappearing as telegraph poles along a railway line'.

These innovations set the pattern for the other high Gothic cathedrals: Rheims, Amiens, Beauvais and Tours. The same dazzling expertise is to be seen at the east end of the church. Above the crypt, Bishop Fulbert's choir ended with three narrow deep chapels with radiating rounded apses. The Gothic builders, by shortening the side walls of these chapels were able to achieve the double ambulatory around the new choir and to form further rounded projections between and on either side of the apsidal chapels. The result is the rippling wall of windows between buttresses that continually change in appearance as we follow the chancel screen around the ambulatory. The remarkable ingenuity of the arrangement is concealed. We simply experience the result.

# 7. HOW THE CHILD SEES THE CITY

*"Is it the mindlessness of childhood that opens up the world? Today nothing happens in a gas station. I'm eager to leave, to get where I'm going, and the station, like some huge paper cutout, or a Hollywood set, is simply a facade. But at thirteen, sitting with my back against the wall, it was a marvellous place to be. The delicious smell of gasoline, the cars coming and going, the fresh air hose, the half-heard voices buzzing in the background—these things hung musically in the air, filling me with a sense of well being. In ten minutes my psyche would be topped up like the tanks of the automobiles."*

—Frank Conroy

This account from Frank Conroy's autobiographical novel *Stop-time* describing the experience of idling at the gas station is used by Yi-Fu Tuan to illustrate the way in which 'unburdened by worldly cares, unfettered by learning, free of ingrained habit, negligent of time, the child is open to the world'. This capacity for vivid sensory experience, commonplace among children, is an aspect of the world that the adult has lost, not just because the senses are dulled by familiarity, but because there is an actual measurable physical decline in sensitivity to taste, to smells, to colour and to sound.

What meaning has the structure of the city for the child citizen? Any reader searching among his early recollections will recall how his own perception of his physical surroundings expanded from the floor, walls and furniture of the room in the house or apartment in which he grew up, its links with other rooms, the steps, stairs, yard, garden, front door, street, shops and public park. He probably does not remember how he put them together into some concept of the home and its relationship with the outside world, nor what gaps remained for years in his mental map of the city.

Further recollection will lead him to reflect that the environmental experience of the child *must be* different simply because of the difference of scale. Obviously, the younger the child the closer his eye-level is to the ground, and this is one of the reasons why the floorscape—the texture and subdivisions of flooring and paving, as well as changes of level in steps and curves (small enough to step over for an adult, big enough to sit on for a child)—is very much more significant for the young. Kevin Lynch and A.K. Lukashok asked adults what they remembered

---

Originally printed in Colin Ward, *The Child in the City*, Second Edition. (London: Bedford Square Press, 1990), 21–31.

from their city childhood and they named particularly the floor of their environment, the tactile rather than the visual qualities of their surroundings. When he
was teaching architecture at Nottingham, Paul Ritter got his students to mock-up
a room two-and-a-half times actual size, just to remind us what a child's eye-view
was really like. Erected in the Co-op Education Centre there, it brought gasps of
astonishment from the visitors. Because we grow so slowly, we have completely
forgotten—even though we see our own children doing it—how we used, without
any fuss, to move around stools, boxes or upturned buckets just to be able to reach
the light-switch, the door latch, shelves, cupboards or window sills.

At a less obvious level, the child, in his perception of the world, has a more
varied experience, just because it is not focused through the lens of existing mental
associations, just because it is indiscriminate. As Yi-Fu Tuan puts it, in adult life
'the gain is subtlety, the loss is richness'. He suggests that, growing older, we substitute appreciation for direct sensory experience, the most important element of appreciation being remembrance. But the child has little to remember: 'Because the
child's world is so full of miracles, the word miracle can have no precise meaning
for him.' Moreover, lacking social awareness, his perception of the environment
is not 'tainted' by social considerations. He has not acquired that selective vision
that distinguishes the beauty of the flowers from that of the weeds. Yi-Fu Tuan
stresses again in his book *Topophilia* that 'a child, from about seven or eight years
old to his early teens, live in this vivid world much of the time'. We might ask,
since ordinary observation suggests that for much of the time many children seem
oblivious to their surroundings, being involved in some personal or social activity which is even more absorbing, what the child actually does with this wealth
of vivid environmental impressions. How does he assemble it into an image of
the city? Paul Shephard, thinking of what he calls 'the halcyon acme of juvenile
fulfilment—the idyllic and practical age of ten' remarks that 'space in juvenile life
is structured differently than at later ages; it is much more critically defined. It
is intensely concerned with paths and boundaries, with hiding places and other
special places for particular things'.

Such experimental insights as we have about the child's perception of the built
environment come—as so often happens in creative research—from the mutual
accommodation of ideas from quite separate theoretical approaches. There is a
thriving academic industry in environmental psychology and the study of our
perceptions of the environment, which brings together two traditions of investigation: firstly, the *cognitive mappers*, exemplified by Kevin Lynch and, secondly,
the *developmentalists*, exemplified by Jean Piaget.

It was Lynch who, in his book *The Image of the City*, introduced us to the notion that we structure our personal concept of the city around certain elements.
These were:

(1) *Paths*, which are 'the channels along which the observer customarily, occasionally, or potentially moves ... People observe the city while moving through it
and along these paths the other environmental elements are arranged and related ...'

(2) *Edges*, which are 'the linear elements not used or considered as paths by the
observer ... such edges may be barriers, more or less penetrable, which close one

region off from another; or they may be seams, lines along which two regions are related and jointed together ... '

(3) *Districts*, which are 'medium-to-large sections of the city, conceived of as having two-dimensional extent, which the observer mentally enters "inside of" and which are recognisable as having some common identifying character ... '

(4) *Nodes*, which are 'the strategic spots in a city into which an observer can enter, and which are the intensive foci to and from which he is travelling ... The concept of node is related to the concept of path, since functions are typically the convergence of paths, events on a journey ... '

(5) *Landmarks*, which are 'another type of point reference but, in this case, the observer does not enter within them, they are external. They are usually a rather simply defined physical object: building, sign, store or mountain.'

It was Piaget, the Swiss psychologist who has greatly influenced educational theory, who in a series of books set out a developmental theory of the child's conception of space. In the first stage, roughly between the ages of five and nine, the child grasps what are known as 'topological' relationships which are those of (1) proximity or nearness, (2) separation, (3) order or spatial succession, (4) enclosure or surrounding, and (5) continuity. This is the *pre-operational* stage, and it implies that the child 'may be able to negotiate successfully sequences or routes, but cannot reverse these, hypothesise about them or add to them in any major way'. In the second stage, around the ages of nine to thirteen, the child comprehends 'projective space' and, as Jeff Bishop interprets it in environmental terms, 'the child now understands and is able to operate successfully amongst a series of known relationships and sequences of objects and situations. He therefore can now reverse his route to school while standing in school and can successfully negotiate alternatives, combinations and extensions of his route provided that they involve reshuffling of known sequences, rather than the deduction of new ones or large gaps between existing ones. At this stage the child can successfully represent correctly the sequence of events on a given familiar route, e.g. home to school, with a good level of scale and directional accuracy.' This is known as the *concrete operational* stage.

The final stage in Piaget's terms is reached round about the age of thirteen and is known as the *formal operational* stage, when the child can comprehend Euclidean space, when the child can conceive of spatial relationships in the abstract, and can hypothesise about them by reference not to a series of bits, but to an overall abstract grid. For Piaget, 'At the outset, the co-ordinates of Euclidean space are no more than a vast network embracing all objects and consist merely of relations of order applied simultaneously to all three dimensions; left-right, above-below and before-behind, applied to each object simultaneously, thus linking them in three directions, along straight lines parallel to each other in one dimension and intersecting those belonging to the other two dimensions at right-angles.'

The young lions of environmental perception, who have over the last decade enlarged our understanding of the way children see the city, are iconoclastic about the old masters who laid the foundations for their work. They point out that the original American research into the nature of the cognitive maps of the environment, which we are all said to carry around in our heads, was done with populations who were adult, middle-class, articulate and car-driving. They point out that Lynch's original work, while drawing upon what Kenneth Boulding calls the 'spatial image' and the 'relational image', ignores those components of our picture of the city which he calls the 'value image' and 'the emotional image'. They point out that Piaget's studies of children's perception were done indoors, in a classroom, without the stimulus or imaginative interest of work in the environment itself. They point out that the 'level of abstraction' children can cope with at different ages ignores the potentialities of imaginative teaching designed to make these abstractions comprehensible. Educational orthodoxy used to hold, for example, that there was some age before which it was pointless to teach the use of maps because children would not have made the leap from visual to symbolic representation of the environment. Roger Hart told me of the work he did in this field with children in the third grade (seven- to eight-year-olds) in an inner city district of Worcester, Massachusetts. Using low-altitude vertical aerial photographs in A4–sized sheets (Ozalid prints of which could be made for a few cents each) Hart and the class built up the map of the city on the classroom floor. He asked the children to bring in their matchbox-toy model cars which are made on an appropriate scale for the maps. Then everyone set out on the map to find the way to the city centre. This led them to difficulties of traffic congestion and of finding a place to park. It also resulted in crashes and in the need to get an ambulance through the traffic and back to St Vincent's Hospital.

Brian Goodey and his former colleagues at the Centre for Urban and Regional Studies at Birmingham have carried out some equally simple and pleasurable work in a British context using sketch-maps drawn by both adults and children. With the co-operation of a local newspaper, they inserted in a weekend edition a map of central Birmingham with the middle left out, so that respondents, who were assessed by age, sex, occupation and mode of travel, could fill in their mental maps of the missing bit. The maps established the very simple and fundamental truth that people's conception of the central city differed according to their age, social status and life-style. You might regard this as so obvious as to need no proving, but if you look at the redevelopment of central Birmingham, or of virtually any other British city, you can see that the unspoken assumption has been made that the city exists for one particular kind of citizen: the adult, male, white-collar, out-of-town car-user.

In an inner city district of the same city, David Spencer and John Lloyd applied a variety of techniques to gain 'a child's eye view of Small Heath', working with infant (age five to seven), junior (age seven to eleven) and secondary (age eleven to eighteen) schools. The technique used with the nine- to ten-year-olds and with thirteen- to fifteen-year-olds was that of obtaining from them free-recall sketch-maps of the route from home to school. Several hundred of such maps were aggregated to provide composite maps, the elements shown on which were classified as housing, shops, entertainments, public services, open spaces, industries, cars and roadside objects. In the drawings and written work obtained from the infants, much attention was given to people, animals, birds, vegetation and natural phenomena. Buildings, roads and roadside objects were seen by the infants especially in relation to human activities, particularly pupils' own homes, friends' and neighbours' houses and 'people waiting to cross the road assisted by wardens'. The experimenters concluded that young children see the environment primarily in human and natural terms since the human and natural elements appeared only occasionally in the work of the juniors and very rarely in that of the seniors.

The American investigators Robert Maurer and James C. Baxter characterise the 'impressive differences' between children's environmental imagery and that of adults as 'a quality of intricacy and attention to detail ... the individuality of individual houses, interest in animals, the unnerving confrontation with huge streets and bothersome trains'. They used mapping techniques to gauge the perceptions of neighbourhood and city of black, Mexican and 'Anglo' American children, and concluded that the Anglo children had a more complex imagery and life-style than the others. Their maps of their neighbourhood showed more unique features, their concept of the neighbourhood was wider, showing familiarity with a greater area, their maps of the whole city were closer to reality, they listed a greater variety of play preferences. Maurer and Baxter attributed this to greater mobility of the Anglo children through access to more varied transport, to the fact that their mothers were more likely to be at home during the day, giving more parental stimulation, to the fact that their friends were scattered more widely, giving motives for travel and awareness of a greater segment of the city.

Working with architectural students from Kingston Polytechnic, Jeff Bishop analysed, both for content and mapping style, the maps drawn by 180 children between the ages of nine and sixteen in the east coast port of Harwich. Their findings were similar to those obtained in American cities. Walkers, needless to say, provided more detail than bus riders or those who habitually travelled in their parents' cars. They found a remarkably sudden shift in the mapping style at the age of eleven, and, indeed, a difference between that of the eleven-year-olds who were in their final primary school year and those who were in their first year at the secondary school. The only explanation for this was that the secondary school children had begun to have formal geography lessons and had been taught to change to a more sophisticated style of representation. When Eileen Adams asked eleven-year-olds at Pimlico School in inner London to draw maps of the journey to school, she found that children living on estates of blocks of flats drew more detailed and more accurate maps than those who lived in streets of houses. She was puzzled by this, since she assumed that the flat-dwelling child would have a less intimate familiarity with the external environment. Discussing the maps with the class, the explanation emerged. Each estate had a large painted map at its entrance, showing the names and dispositions of the blocks and their relationship with the surrounding streets.

But the most significant thing to come out of Jeff Bishop's work in Harwich was the comparison of the children's maps with those of adults. In the middle of the port there is a lighthouse which featured as a significant landmark in all the maps drawn by adults. But none of the Harwich children showed the lighthouse on their maps, though many showed the public lavatory which stands at its base. Things which were important to them included kiosks, hoardings and other bits of unconsidered clutter in the street. One item that frequently recurred in their maps (and was totally ignored in those of adults) was a telephone connection box—a large metal object on the footpath with a fluted base. Obviously, as a feature for hiding behind or climbing on, this kind of obstruction has a value for children in their use of the street. What planners call 'non-conforming users', or places which the adult eye just does not see, have importance in the children's maps too. There was, for example, the council refuse depot, noted by many of the children as the place where they wash down the dustmen's lorries.

The building of the Kingston Polytechnic where Jeff Bishop used to work stands between the river and the road. Walking past the place 'where Daddy works' with his five-year-old son, he found to his surprise that the boy could identify the window of his room on the seventh floor, through remembering the view from the window. Now how could this be true of a child in Piaget's pre-operational stage? Well, of course, Bishop explains, Piaget was working with children in a room, and drew conclusions about three-dimensional ability from two-dimensional tasks. Furthermore, these tasks were not meaningful to the children performing them: they were not related to the real, actual environment of the child. Bruner has stressed the importance of the amount of interaction between the child and his environment, and another American researcher, Gary Moore, has developed an interactionist theory, emphasising that interaction and familiarity with the environment are the crucial factors in a child's progress along Piaget's stages. Age, sex and class he finds less important.

David Stea, also in the United States, has worked on toy-modelling techniques with children of three years upwards. The models were capable of being arranged to form a community, with houses, streets, shops, a fire-station and so on and, with these, three-year-olds have demonstrated their ability to understand linear systems in correct sequence, while of course if Piaget were to be interpreted in the age-specific way in which his theories are taught in the teachers' colleges, an eight-year-old could not find his way home from school.

But how often, Bishop asks, do we give children an opportunity to show us what they know about the space in which they move around? How often do we let them lead us home from school instead of us leading them? During the building of a new stand at Chelsea Football Club's ground at Stamford Bridge, he seized the opportunity to garner cognitive maps of the streets around the club, in terms of whether the mapper was a resident supporter of Chelsea, or a resident non-supporter, a non-resident supporter, or a non-resident non-supporter. From this study of the maps they produced, he reached the conclusion that motivation is an important factor in the perception of the environment, which may also depend on the circumstances of involvement, which he suggests may not be the same for the attender at a regular game as for the boy who plays truant on a Wednesday afternoon to see the reserves play. He also concludes that not everybody—of any age—actually reaches the final stage of Piaget's developmental sequence. Nothing in all this work, he thinks, actually refutes Piaget's stages, but it does indicate that they can be reached much earlier or much later than the age-related categories of his interpreters suggest.

There is also evidence that spatial ability can be well ahead of visual and graphic ability. (Trevor Higginbottom, director of the Schools Council Project on Geography for the Young School Leaver, told me that the work it includes on cognitive mapping—one of the first examples of the techniques of the environmental psychologists reaching the regular curriculum—produces remarkable work from those children considered to be the least able.) It is part of the orthodoxy of child development that girls are abler than boys of the same age in verbal ability, while boys' spatial ability is far greater than that of girls. The work of the cognitive mappers is cited to confirm this. John Brierley, reporting tests which involve proficiency in the manipulation of spatial relationships indicating the greater average ability of boys even from the age of two, argues that it is very likely that visuo-spatial proficiency is under the control of the sex chromosome-hormone machinery and has its roots in the right hemisphere development of the brain. His conclusion is that 'for practical purposes at school these findings strengthen the importance of systematic exposure of girls to early experience with toys, sand, water and boxes, which introduce numerical and spatial relationships, for doing so might well improve mathematical ability later on'.

Experiments with children in several different cultures, the best known of which are those reported by Erik Erikson, indicate that given a selection of wooden blocks, boys tend to build towers whereas girls build enclosed spaces. Boys produce streets, walls and façades with movement *outside* the buildings. Girls produce furniture arrangements with people in a static situation inside buildings. Erikson, with his psycho-analytical approach, concludes that 'the dominance of genital modes over the modalities of spatial organisation reflects a profound difference in the sense of space in the two sexes ... ' The kind of experimental evidence on which this statement is based can be repeated in any home or any classroom containing boys and girls. Often the results are too true to be good: they tend to be such an over-confirmation of the psychologists' findings that teachers are embarrassed in presenting them. But if we are convinced by the idea of innate differences, we have to admit that they are powerfully reinforced by the different assumptions made in the upbringing of boys and girls, and by the evidence of Bishop and others that spatial ability, as tested, relates strongly to motivation and to familiarity. The significance of this is discussed in a later chapter.

The most ambitious attempt to evaluate the relationship between children and the urban environment was undertaken in the early 1970s in a project directed by Kevin Lynch for UNESCO. This was concerned with children of eleven to fourteen years in the city of Salta in Argentina ... ; in the western suburbs of Melbourne, Australia; in Toluca, a provincial capital in Mexico and in Ecatepec, a largely dweller-built settlement on the northern fringe of Mexico City; in two contrasted neighbourhoods in Warsaw, and two similarly contrasted neighbourhoods of another Polish city, Cracow.

Some interesting contrasts emerged from the maps of their neighbourhood and city that the children produced. In the case of the Polish housing projects, the focus of the maps was on the outdoor play spaces used by the children between 'the blank ranges of apartments', and adult features were largely ignored. Their maps of the whole city showed islands of activity linked by 'bridges' of public transport, but the central city children of the two cities in Poland, 'produced much more systematic and accurate maps, based on rather elaborate street networks, and full of shops, institutions, places of entertainment, and historical memorials. They are more diverse in the area they cover and the elements they contain.' The investigators in Poland describe the 'hunger' for activity and stimulus of the children in the outlying estates, while the children of the central districts 'who are quite aware of their advantageous access to city excitements are hungry for outdoor space'.

In the case of the Colonia San Augustin at Ecatepec, Mexico, 'one group (mostly boys) represent the environment as a map of streets and blocks, schematic and lacking sensuous detail, a key to the location of activities, a down-to-earth image of a highly repetitive environment. The other group (mostly girls) make pictorial representations, showing shops, parks and green areas, full of details embellished with textures, ornaments and splashes of colour.'

What is very clear from the UNESCO study of these older children is that their picture of the city and their own part of it is conditioned by the esteem in which it is held by their elders. The Melbourne children, for example, were certainly the most affluent in this international sample. They were 'tall, well dressed, almost mature, apparently full of vitality' but they see themselves as the bottom of society, and 'if these Australians have hopes for themselves or their children, it is to be somebody else, and to get away'. The Argentinian children, on the other hand, are quite obviously conscious of being members of a community with 'features which make it amenable to change at their scale of possibility'. Only three of the interviewed children there thought that they would leave the area in the future. Only three of the Melbourne children thought that they would remain.

Alone in the UNESCO survey, the children of Ecatepec, the dweller-built settlement outside Mexico City 'consistently named their school as a favourite place, and gave it a loving emphasis on their maps'. The suggestions which they made to the interviewers 'reflect a genuine concern for their families, as well as their own future, and an empathy for fellow residents of the colonia'. They were the poorest children in the survey, and to the adult researchers their environment was harsh, bleak and monotonous, and it is obvious from their report that they were puzzled by the unique affection for their school displayed in the maps, drawings and interviews of the children of Ecatepec. 'This must be a tribute to the public education in that place', they surmise. No such tribute would be offered by the children of an equivalently poor district in Detroit, Boston, London or Manchester, though it might have been made there many years ago.

To know better how the child sees the city, it would have helped if the UNESCO project had contained some similar investigations in several of the exploding cities of Asia and Africa. I think it likely that this would have underlined the comparison between the social environment in a mature city like Melbourne and in the emergent urban areas like Ecatepec. The parents of the children of the Colonia San Augustin are poor rural migrants who have made the leap from rural hopelessness into the inner city slums, the *vecindades*, of Mexico City. Once they had got used to the urban system, they moved to a squatter settlement on the fringe of the city. In many such Latin American settlements, the parents have built their own school and hired their own teachers. For their children, life is visibly improving, 'there is less dust now, houses that used to be shanties are fully constructed, one does not have to go outside the colonia for certain services ... ' The parents in the working-class outskirts of western Melbourne, with an infinitely higher standard of living, are conscious that they haven't quite made it. The stigmatisation of the district where they live communicates itself to the children. In this place where 'football clubs and schools have two-metre-high wire mesh fence around the periphery topped with barbed wire' and where parks are 'flat featureless tracts of haphazardly grassed unused land', the local authorities believe that 'space for organised team sport is what is most urgently needed, despite the lack of use of what already exists'.

It is hard, no doubt, for those who have devoted themselves to campaigning for physical space for the young in the city, a claim which is certainly self-justifying, to accustom themselves to the idea that, very early in life, another, more urgent, and more difficult to meet, demand arises, for *social* space—the demand of the city's children to be a part of the city's life.

# 8. ANTIQUARIANS, EXPLORERS, NEOPHILIACS

*"'The kids don't notice.' What does a bit of dirt matter to children? Or a broken floorboard, damp in the walls? Or sharing a bed with their brothers and sisters? Or nowhere to wash? Children never look so happy as when they're in some kind of mess. And aren't children adaptable? Would it bother a child moving to another house or flat? Time and again, people will tell you how resilient children are. 'The kids don't notice.' They're great survivors. But the kids* do *notice ... "*
— Michael Locke and Moira Constable

One of our myths about urbanisation is the idea that rural poverty is more tolerable than poverty in the city. If it were true, the rural poor all over the world would not be flocking to the cities. 'The touching picture of country people leaving neat and pretty thatched cottages for the sins and slums of the city is easily dispelled by a closer look at the pretty cottages', remarks Enid Gauldie, examining the history of working-class housing in Britain and concluding that our rural slums were of a horror unsurpassed by the rookeries of London. The rural hovels of our ancestors were for sleeping in and little less. Boswell, in Hebrides, noted that 'the good people here had no notion that a man could have any occasion but for a mere sleeping place'. Life was lived outside. For exactly the same reason, the urban poor lived in the street. Many years ago, the Newcastle writer Jack Common pointed out, as of course Mayhew had done in the last century, that it was the use of the street that made working-class life tolerable:

> You can usually deduce your fellow-Briton's class status from the way he regards the street. To some it is merely a communication between one spot and another, a channel or runway to guide your feet or your wheels when you are going places. To others it's where you live. The average working-class house is a small and inconvenient place. Nobody wants to put up with the noise of children in it more than they have to—but they go, then, into the street. Similarly, a man can't do any casual entertaining there, not so as to suit him. If his pals call, they all go out together—down the street, that is, to the boozer. Even the women find it a pleasanter change if they want company to go and stand on the doorstep. Add these up and you get a most characteristic working-class scene: crowds of kids flying here and there across the road; boys and youths

---

Originally printed in Colin Ward, *The Child in the City*, Second Edition. (London: Bedford Square Press, 1990), 32–42.

by the shop-windows and the corner-ends; men strolling the pavements or sitting shirt-sleeved by the doors; and the women in their aprons taking a breather in a bit of gossip 'next-door'. These people live in the street.

It is a pattern of street-use which the architecture of municipal rehousing has done its best to destroy, but for children it still exists, and not only for poor children. An extensive and long-term study of urban childhood by John and Elizabeth Newson, of the Children Development Research Unit at Nottingham University, notes that it is not only working-class children for whom the street is a vital resource, 'a majority of middle-class children, almost all of whom have gardens, choose and are allowed to play in the street some of the time'. They conclude, however, that 'at the lower end of the class scale parents expect the child to pursue the busy and active part of his life *outside* the home, and then come in to relax; whereas at the upper end he is expected to "let off steam" physically for relaxation outside, and then come in and get on with something more serious and creative'.

The Newson study is intended to follow a representative sample of children in a typical British city from infancy to late adolescence and, apart from its value as an anatomy of the process of child-rearing, it provides innumerable vignettes of the way in which this is affected by the physical influence of the city home. The three volumes issued so far give a picture of 700 Nottingham children through interviews with their mothers, at the ages of one, four and seven. The families involved are divided, according to parental occupation, into five social classes, from 'professional' to 'unskilled', and into three housing types, 'central area', 'council estate' and 'suburban'. Not surprisingly, in class I and II 80 per cent of the families of four-year-olds were found in the suburbs and 6 per cent in the central area, while in class V (unskilled) only 17 per cent were in suburban housing, while 45 per cent were in the central area. Looking at their material from the point of view of the environmental psychologist, Charles Mercer has extracted a series of seven propositions from the data on working-class four-year-olds, none of which applies to the middle-class four-year-olds:

1) The working-class child lives in a more crowded environment—more siblings and less space.
2) The play of the working-class child must perforce take place in the streets or other communal areas and *not* on the home territory.
3) The working-class child is therefore more likely to come into contact with all sorts and a greater number of children.
4) The working-class child's choice of friends is not guided by the parents, as all children play on communal areas.
5) For the same reason, the play of the working-class child is not generally supervised by adults.
6) The working-class parent is reluctant to interfere in children's play, because this may lead to conflict with out parents who are also neighbours.
7) Conflict with neighbours is less easily tolerated in the working-class environment because of the greater propinquity of families and the fact that

working-class parents could not help but come into contact with the offended neighbours and, meanwhile, the children would have made it up anyway.

By the time the Newson children had reached the age of seven, they had made the transition from being relatively homebound to being school-children spending much of the day in an environment away from home. Seven-year-olds, the Newsons remark, 'have many interests which tempt them to the next street and beyond, with the adventurousness to follow such temptations. The fact that they go to and from school each day familiarises them with short journeys, and widens the circle of children they know by sight, who in turn act as lures away from their home territory.' The question they asked the 700 mothers concerning the children's use of the external environment was the very simple one: 'Would you call him an indoor child or an outdoor child?' The answers revealed both class and sex differences: 'Sixty per cent of children overall are described as outdoor children, but this rises to 71 per cent in class V and drops to 44 per cent in class I and II ... Overall, more boys than girls are said to be outdoor (67 per cent against 52 per cent).' They add that

> ... a further class weighting is given by the material circumstances of the family, which we noted as being relevant to how far the child was likely to be physically 'off out' among the peer group, or retained within the family circle. Descending the social scale, the accommodation dwindles while the family size increases, so that the mother is less able to tolerate children playing indoors and it quite simple becomes necessary to regard the street as overspill space. Furthermore, as one moves up the scale, the child is much more likely to have some place in the house which belongs to him, where he can keep his own things; this immediately means that indoor play is both more positively encouraged and more inherently attractive for the child further up the class scale.

It is when you think about the implications of the Newson findings that you begin to understand the impact of housing policy upon the poor who in the past have 'won space' from the dominant culture ... , but who have systematically been deprived of control over their living space, even though space standards and sanitary standards are higher in the new housing *project* (US) or *scheme* (UK). The relatively affluent, with the freedom of choice that money can buy, select the suburban street, where their children can be, at will, indoor or outdoor kids. The poor of the inner city, who over generations have evolved a code of practice which seeks to make life tolerable for themselves or their offspring, have been the victims of the decisions of others whose values do not include a consideration of the psychic damage they inflict. When the rich live in the city, they have that space that enables their children to choose their personal balance between indoors and outdoors, and they have the network of contacts, the chequebooks and the know-how with which to enrich the environmental experience of their children.

In Albert Street, Canton, Cardiff, I knocked at the door of one of the few houses which still had curtains in the windows—one which still had windows, in fact, and met Mr and Mrs Simms and their 13-year-old son, the last inhabitants. 'I was born in this street', Mr Simms said. 'We all were. My grand-parents lived here, and my parents were born here too. We children were in and out of each other's houses, and you can't imagine the fun we had, looking at the place now.' In his back-yard, beyond the dahlias and rhubarb, he opened a hutch and brought out his ferret, draping the creature round his neck and reassuring me, 'She won't bite you while I'm here. When I was a kid, it wasn't only ferrets. We had rabbits and chickens. It was like living in the country.'

He reminisced about the former occupants of the deserted houses all around. This one, whose pigeon house with its fretted decoration still stood, that one whose pear trees cropped so heavily and would again this year, with no one left to eat them ('Many's the pear I nicked from that tree when I was a boy'); that other one who had always organised street parties with tables, benches and bunting all down the street on occasions of national rejoicing. 'We were like one big family', he said, but now, of course, those neighbours were scattered to the winds in the new estates outside the city.

His own children had grown up in dereliction and decay, and in his view the Corporation had waged a war of attrition against a whole neighbourhood, steadily depriving it of its amenities. Pubs and chip shops had closed, street lights were not maintained, the pavement was unsafe. Vandals and petty thieves were looting the adjoining houses and had frequently broken into his. His neighbours used to be his childhood friends. Now the only neighbours were rats, winos, vagrants and lead thieves. 'And can you tell me one single way in which my boy's life will be better out on the estate than it would have been here?'

The same story is told in every British city. The traditional culture of the street is recalled in innumerable recollections from an earlier generation than that of Mr Simms. As history, they have to be treated with caution. Robert Roberts remarks that when he talked during the 1930s and 1940s with people who were already mature by 1914, 'they criticised the then fairly recent past, faculties alert, with what seemed like objectivity'. But by the 1960s 'myths had developed, prejudices about the present had set hard; these same critics, in ripe old age, now saw the Edwardian era through a golden haze'. Nevertheless, one factual theme emerged, as much from the recordings made by school children interviewing old inhabitants about the past of their district, as from innumerable published autobiographies. This was the freedom to move. Our views on the historical inevitability or political desirability of the decline of the private landlord in Britain have blinded us to an aspect of the housing situation of our grandparents, which profoundly affected the environmental experiences of children. When private renting was the norm, there was a considerable freedom of choice in the housing market, even for very poor families, and this resulted in a degree of dweller satisfaction which is much rarer when a multiplicity of landlords has given way to the local authority.

'In the thirties', recalls Elizabeth Ring, 'there was no such thing as a housing storage. For from five shillings to five pounds a week there were rooms for all.' Jack Common says of his childhood in Newcastle, 'At that time, families were always moving. There were houses to let everywhere.' Arthur Newton says of Hackney in East London, 'To change houses was easy then.' Mollie Weir from Glasgow describes with relish the many moves of her childhood and her mother's fondness of 'flitting', which in her family's context did not imply a 'moonlight flit'. 'How different everything looked', she says, 'even if we'd only moved to the next close, which my mother did twice, for we knew our houses so intimately that the slightest variation in a lobby or a window-frame, or the size of a fireplace, was of enormous significance. Everybody loves a flitting ... '

From a totally different background, the East End of London, A.S. Jasper in *A Hoxton Childhood* describes a whole series of childhood environments, starting in August 1910 when 'We were living at number three Clinger Street, Hoxton, in a hovel on the ground floor. It comprised two rooms with a kitchen, with an outside lavatory, which also served the family upstairs.' By page 15 "It was agreed that Mother would try to find a bigger house. In those days it was easy; one had only to go to an agent, pay the first week's rent and move in. On more than one occasion my father came home late, drunk as usual, and was told by the next-door neighbour we "didn't live there anymore". We had owed so much rent but the fact was that we had to have a larger house. My mother duly found and inspected a house in Salisbury Street, New North Road. It wasn't a bad area and I always remember it was the nicest house we ever had.' And he describes with gusto how they set about redecorating it: 'Wallpaper was about threepence a roll; a ball of whitening and boiled size made whitewash for the ceilings.' But bad times came again, and on page 39 'Our new abode was Ebenezer Buildings, Rotherfield Street. What a dump it was after the nice little house we had just left!' Soon his mother and sister went house-hunting again and decided on a house in Loanda Street, by the side of the Regents Canal near the bridge in Kingsland Road. But a little later 'Everything was getting too much for Mum and she reckoned the house had a curse on it. The only way out was to move again. This time she found a house in Scawfell Street. This wasn't far from Loanda Street. It certainly looked a road with some life in it which was what we were used to. Loanda Street was a drab place of flat-fronted houses where everyone closed their doors. There wasn't the friendliness.' By page 88 'We were now in 1917 and we were on the move again. Why, I cannot remember. This time we moved to Shepherdess Walk, off City Road. It was a very large house let off in flats. We had a ground floor and a basement flat consisting of five large rooms and a scullery ... '
Not many pages later, in September 1918 'We now lived in a very nice place in the main road. The rooms were large and there was always something going on.' But in the following year, the man who owned the dairy downstairs 'shocked us by saying he was going to sell the dairy and we would have to quit the flat. He told us he had a house at Walthamstow we could rent and he would pay all the expenses if we would move. In 1919 Walthamstow to us was like moving to the country. The whole family discussed the matter and it was agreed they would go and see the place ... ' So a couple of pages later they moved. 'It was a small house just off the High Street. The rent was eight shillings a week. I was beginning to like our new surroundings. For a penny you could get to Epping Forest, and this was all so different to the slums of Hoxton and Bethnal Green. My friend Dave would come some weekends and we have some good times together in the forest.'

Thus there were eight moves in Mr Jasper's childhood between the ages of four and fourteen. The moves were intimately related to shifts and changes in the family's minimal income and to the family size—whether his sister's husband was living with them or not, and so on. And the final move had brought the family right out of the inner city and into the ampler opportunities provided by the leafy suburbs. In both these instances there glows through the pages what teachers are trained to call an 'affective relationship' between the family and its housing. This was not the result of staying in one house or street for a lifetime as was the case with Mr Simms (for both families I have taken as examples seem to have been quite extravagantly fond of moving); it was the result of having, even among the very poor, some degree of consumer choice. Changes in family circumstances as well as aesthetic preferences were reflected in a move which was, for the children at least, a family adventure. Neither were they the families of skilled artisans. Miss Weir's father died when she was a baby and Mr Jasper's father was a drunken casual labourer. Both were effectively one-parent families.

Today, when the population of Glasgow or of inner London is dramatically lower than it was in their childhood, the element of freedom of choice in housing that their families had has totally disappeared. They would either be stuck in one particular bit of run-down accommodation in the fast-dwindling private landlord sector or, if they were lucky, they would be equally immobile in the flat which the council had provided (as suitable for unsatisfactory tenants) waiting years for a transfer. If they were unlucky, they would be parked, as happens in some London boroughs, in low-grade 'bed-and-breakfast' hotels which have to be vacated during the daytime, so that in the school holidays, for example, the children would be wandering, rather than exploring, the streets from morning to night. Incredibly, some children alleged to be in the 'care' of the local authority *in loco parentis* are dumped in overnight hotels in this way, through lack of anywhere else to put them.

Perhaps children and adults, too, might be divided between the *antiquarians*, who cherish an environment precisely because of its associations with continuity and familiarity, like Mr Simms; *explorers* like Miss Weir and Mr Jasper, who though they are very far from the migratory élite of the professional classes, positively enjoy and savour the change from one home to another in a known habitat; and the *neophiliacs* for whom the past smelt of decay and deprivation, while the new present promises hope and a more expansive life. Just as there is a consolation in being the most recent of many generations to occupy a building, so there is a promise in being the first to experience its newness, and this promise is strengthened and confirmed when the new environment is ampler and more spacious than the old. A post office worker, who moved from Islington in inner London (where his family of four lived insecurely in two rooms with shared facilities) to the expanding town of Swindon, told me of the difference in his children's lives that a self-contained house with a garden had made. 'They used to be frightened to use the toilet on the landing', he said, 'because they never knew what they would find there. It wasn't that people were dirty, it was just that so many people went there.' His remark illustrated the medical conclusion that constipation is a working-class disease, environmental in its origins.

Space, and the luxury of a room of one's own, are the positive advantages of the new or rebuilt environment, beautifully caught by Hazel Robbins, aged seven, who moved from inner to outer Birmingham.

> I like my house I am liveing in now better than my old house because it is nicer and I have three bedrooms and in my garden I have lots of flower and I have a liveingroom and a kitchen has well and I have a bathroom and a toilet to and I like it very much to and in my livingroom I have a fireplace and a book case to and a stereo recordplayer and two tables to and in my kitchen I have a gas stove and a fridge and some cubs to and in my bathroom I have a bath and a sink has well and I like my house because it is big and the bigis room are the liveing room and the kitchen and they are both and my curtains and the small bedroom is my bedroom.

Hazel's pleasure in the new environment leaps out of the page and, for her, all the new domestic equipment (the 'cubs' she refers to must be the ice cubes in the new refrigerator) is part of the new life-style that accompanies the move to the ampler life of the suburb. It is doubtful whether in later life she will recollect with fond nostalgia the days before the move. It is tempting to read some significance in her use of 'I' and 'my', where many English children would refer to 'us' and 'our' in these circumstances. (Many an only child will refer to 'our mum' or 'our dad', thinking of the family as a unit rather than of the individual's possessiveness.) Consequently, Hazel is unable to give any special significance to her own curtains and her own bedroom. She is just at the age when, according to the environmental psychologists, having a room of one's own becomes important, a need which accelerates as time goes by.

Hazel is a neophiliac. She rejoices in the new. When the UNESCO investigators A.M. Battro and E. J. Ellis walked around the Argentine city of Salta with Raul, aged twelve, and Patricia, aged thirteen, the children's comments, on what to antiquarian eyes was the most picturesque part of the city, expressed a clear preference for newness, neatness, and tidiness. 'A beautiful street must be a street with wide sidewalks, well-painted facades, clean and with modern houses. Everything that looks untidy, such as wires, rickety doors, worn steps, deteriorating signs, old adobe houses, must be eliminated.' This does not mean, the observers comment, 'that the child does not know the aesthetic value of the ancient convent, he would even "like to live there" if it were a private house, but what most attracts his attention is the recent coat of paint that distinguishes it from other antique houses semi-abandoned or converted into cheap grocery stores'.

For the explorer, apart from the excitement of change and the new experience it brings, the personal satisfactions to be won from an environment include the extent to which it can be used and manipulated, and the extent to which it contains usable rubbish, the detritus of packing-cases, crates, bits of rope and old timber, off-cuts and old wheels, that used to accumulate when there was a shop on every corner and a small factory or workshop down the bottom of the alley. In Bute Town, Cardiff—another district of the same city where Mr Simms and

his son championed the values of the traditional culture, which were being eliminated before their eyes by the city authorities—a devoted primary school teacher
had evolved a programme of local studies to ensure that her class, equipped with
cameras, were thoroughly familiar with their neighbourhood. Her ten-year-olds
took the visiting specialist in environmental education around the locality with
their Instamatics clicking. They stopped at the community centre, two mosques
and the geriatric hospital (housed in the old Seaman's Mission from the days
when Cardiff was a living port) snapping away where the visitor would have been
abashed to intrude.

'This is the factory where my Mam works.' Click went the camera as Mam
emerged to greet them. 'Look, there's my Dad', and click went the camera again as
the child's father came round the corner in his lorry. The educator was delighted.
Wasn't this an area where the working lives of the parents were accessible to the
educative lives of the children, and wasn't this something unique and precious in
modern urban life? He was quite right. It is rare for the mother to be able to leave
her workbench when summoned to greet her child and her classmates, and it is
rare for the father, high up in his cab, to be delighted by the appearance of his own
child in the group standing on the corner. But, in this instance, the educator's contact with the environment as experienced by the children went further. Because
once the class had taken him round their route of the recorded environment they
said goodbye. 'But where are you going now?' he asked. 'Where we always go', they
replied. 'Can't I come too?'

So, more gratified than shy, they took him into their unofficial play-spaces.
There was an almost mischievous glee among the children as they took him into
the scarey area of town, through alleys, ginnels and tunnels into the district which
had no longer an official existence. The council had here spent one-and-a-half day's
labour by three men in bricking up the doors and windows of each of the abandoned houses, but they still sustained a population, the inebriates, the junkies and
some bewildered homeless people who, along with the bloated dead domestic animals, provided the setting for the use the children made of these abandoned streets.
It was here, and here alone, that they were able to *use* the environment in a kind of
caricature of the way an earlier generation had used their streets. Here, and here
alone, they were able to indulge their appetite for either building or destroying.
Their human encounters in this sector of the city were those which the educator
would have most wished to spare them. But just because the adult users of this no-
man's-land were unofficial inhabitants too, they were not a threat to the children's
determined use of the area as an adventure playground, a place where anything
might be discovered—decomposed furniture and old gas ovens, timber for bonfires
and bricks for improvised buildings. It is here that tiles and slates can be ripped off
roofs, panels hammered out of cold doors, bushes ripped out of old backyards. For
the interloping educator, apart from its present squalor, the area was full of the pathetic mementoes of human occupation, the remaining hints that generations had
been born, lived and died here. For the children, it was a place of eerie encounters,
forbidden games, and for the acting out of destructive passions.

# 9. THE ANARCHIST HOUSE

I have to begin with problems of definition. We have no problem with the word *house*. We have few problems with the associated word *home* which adds an emotional significance to the first word. We have a *house* and we make it into a *home*.

My difficulties arise with the word *anarchist*. The hero of Vladimir Nabokov's novel *Pnin* is asked "Are you an anarchist?" And, very unwisely, he replies with a question for his interrogator: "First, what do we understand under *anarchism*? Anarchism practical, metaphysical, theoretical, mystical, abstractional, individual, social?" It did him no good. He spent two weeks on Ellis Island, before he was allowed to enter the USA.

I have a similar problem. I want to be open to every possible definition of anarchism, but I have to exclude plenty of interpretations simply to say something useful.

The first item of ballast that I have to throw overboard is the idea that there is an anarchist aesthetic, in opposition to bourgeois aesthetics. For a century in all the arts, visual, literary or aural, it has been assumed that the task of revolutionary artists is to stupefy the bourgeoisie. Having been stupefied for many decades, during which real life has been far more shocking than the arts, it is still the bourgeoisie who are the only effective customers for all that revolutionary art. Apart, that is, from the State.

In the visual arts, for example, the most obvious allies for the anarchists were the Surrealists, but with notable exceptions, the closest political links *they* sought were with the Communist Party. In Britain, the most celebrated artist with links to the anarchist movement was an academic painter of bohemian habits, whose reputation probably did not travel. This was Augustus John (1878–1961) who is remembered, not as an anarchist, but as the last of the great classical draughtsmen. And the most famous of all anarchist artists, Camille Pissarro (1831–1903), closely linked with the anarchist movement of his day, steadfastly declined to specify the content of an anarchist aesthetic. His letters ignore syntax and grammar and are absorbing human documents. The closest he gets to defining an anarchist aesthetic is in Volume III of his collected correspondence, where he says:

> Y a-t-il un art anarchiste? quoi décidément ils ne comprennent pas. Tous les arts sont anarchistes quand c'est beau et bien![2]

Originally printed in Colin Ward, *Talking to Architects: Ten Lectures by Colin Ward*. (London: Freedom Press, 1996), 99–110. Originally a lecture at the conference on Libertarian Culture, Grenoble, March 1996.

When we consider the art of architecture, the assumption that there is a specifically anarchist aesthetic becomes even more questionable. Many of us will remember a side-show in fair-grounds or amusement parks called 'The Crazy House'. We paid our pennies to experience a simulated house where the floors and ceilings were not parallel and where the walls, doors and windows were not rectilinear.

Much more recently, this kind of Crazy House architecture has been built seriously in real life. For example, at Montréal, Canada, for the World's Fair in the 1970s, Moshe Safdie designed the Habitat apartments where each flat is dropped apparently at random in an accidental-looking pile of containers. In practise, of course, every aspect of this chance arrangement was carefully calculated by structural engineers. Similarly in the Oude Haven (Old Harbour) area of Rotterdam you can visit a cloister of tilted houses designed by the architect Piet Blom, which are a solid reminder of the Crazy House structure in the Fun Fair.

If you imagine yourself as a building worker, living in a cramped apartment in a block of flats, and employed on the building of one of those architectural fantasies, you will readily agree that fantasy architecture is not anarchist architecture. It provides no liberation for the people involved in building it, and the joke of disobeying aesthetic assumptions probably gets stale rapidly for the people who live in it. The issue is not a matter of design, but is a question of *control*, a far more important aspect of the anarchist spectrum.

For me, the first principle of housing in any society, quite apart from the ideal for an anarchist society, is dweller control. We are fortunate that this principle has been very carefully enunciated by an anarchist architect, John Turner. He spent many years in the 1950s and 1960s assisting self-builders in squatter settlements in Latin America. He then moved to the United States and learned that the ideas he had formulated in the poor world were true of the richest nation in the world. And when he finally returned to Britain he found that the housing situation in his own country also fitted his formulation.[3] Turner's key insight is this:

> When dwellers control the major decisions and are free to make their own contribution to the design, construction or management of their housing, both the process, and the environment produced, stimulate individual and social well-being. When people have no control over, nor responsibility for, key decisions in the housing process, on the other hand, dwelling environments may instead become a barrier to personal fulfilment and a burden on the economy.[4]

This is a carefully-worded statement that says no more and no less than it means. Notice that Turner refers to "design, construction or management". He is not implying that we should all become *bricoleurs* or do-it-yourself house-builders, although of course, in practice, this is what people often have to be. He is stating as a principle that *they* should be in control.

I would like you to notice particularly his last sentence about dwelling environments which become "a barrier to personal fulfilment and a burden on the economy". Is this not the experience of huge, expensive housing projects undertaken by central and local governments, both in the United States and all around Western Europe? The only solution to the problems of these projects is to develop systems of dweller control through the various forms of housing co-operatives. Sometimes, in those vast housing projects on the outskirts of European and American cities as a legacy of bureaucratic managerial socialism, tenant control is adopted as a last desperate measure in the face of dereliction and decay. There is a well-known architect, Lucien Kroll of the *Atelier d'Urbanisme et d'Architecture* at Bruxelles. He is often asked to advise on the exercise of making habitable big, neglected municipal housing projects in France, Germany and the Netherlands.

The results are often described as anarchist architecture. Lucien Kroll insists, on the other hand, that it is dweller-controlled architecture. He told me that the *first* task, not the last, is to present residents with a budget for *them* to decide the priorities in expenditure. Do they want money spent first on improving the insulation in wells, or on making the building too publicly visible to be infiltrated by drug traffickers?

One general priority is to reduce the scale of buildings by removing a few storeys (*étages*) from the top and to have more building at ground level in the spaces between blocks. Another is the issue of 'traffic calming'. Would it be sensible to use the concrete rubble from the reduction of height of blocks to build a little hill on a road roundabout, planted with bushes and trees as an inescapable vehicle-hazard that kept traffic out? How about digging up the municipal grass to make playgrounds and allotments (*jardins potager*), and building an accretion of workshops and cafes as lean-to (*appentis*) extensions around the base of the towers? The results may not be anarchist architecture, but they are certainly *post-authoritarian* architecture.

Although Britain is seen as the country of origin of the co-operative movement, housing co-operatives are much more recent there than in many other countries. In the 1970s there were only two or three. Today there are about a thousand. This is a pathetically small number, and this indicates how far we are from separating control from ownership, since in Britain the preferred mode of tenure is owner-occupation (66%). But its composition is interesting. Some started through the legitimisation of squatter occupation of empty buildings. Some originated in 'short-life housing' (buildings awaiting demolition). Under conditions of dweller-control this short-life housing has had a very long life, simply because of the incentives the occupants have to improve it. Some, in Liverpool and London, are newly-built housing, where the architect worked to the instructions of poor people who, for the first time in their lives were able to employ expertise.[5]

But the most interesting are in the dweller-built sector. All through history, throughout the world, poor people have constructed their own homes, which were improved and expanded over decades and centuries, as families turned their labour into capital. The evidence can be seen in traditional peasant farmhouses in most parts of Europe. In the twentieth century this simple and natural way of building has become increasingly difficult for a variety of reasons.

The first is the key issue of access to land. In Britain the process known as 'Enclosure' ensured that land which was once described as common or 'waste', now has a legal owner. The second is in the nature of building materials. Once the self-builder would automatically use stone, clay, timber and straw from the locality, so that the house, as an English poet said, would "rise like a lark from the furrows". Twentieth century houses are constructed from materials which, whether they are natural or synthetic, have to be bought in the market. The third reason is of course, that we have surrounded the process of building with a pile of legislation and regulations which is incomprehensible to the citizen without professional help.

One English architect (of German origin) who surmounted these obstacles was Walter Segal (1907–1985). He, incidentally, was reared in an anarchist commune in Ticino, Switzerland.[6] Late in life he developed a method of lightweight timber-framed construction, using standard building components in standard sizes, and eliminating the 'wet' trades of concreting, brick-laying and plastering. It was eminently suited to the amateur builder. He was yearning for it to be made available to people in need of housing, and one London municipality decided to provide an opportunity, on plots of land too small or too sloping to be used by the council itself.[7]

The result was a triumph of dweller satisfaction. Members of the group described the experience as the event which changed their lives and felt that they were in control. And it was the happiest event in the life of their veteran architect. Segal recalled that:

> Help was to be provided mutually and voluntarily—there were no particular constraints on that, which did mean that the good will of people could find its way through. The less you tried to control them the more you forced the element of good will—this was astonishingly clear. Children were of course expected and allowed to play on the site. And the older ones also helped if they wished to help. That way one avoided all forms of friction. Each family were to build at their own speed and within their own capacity. We had quite a number of young people, but some who were sixty and over, who also managed to build their own houses ... They were told that I would not interfere with their internal arrangements. I let them make their own decisions; therefore we had no difficulties.[8]

He noted with pleasure, rather than with irritation, the "countless small variations and innovations and additions" that the self-builders made. His conclusion was that "It is astonishing that there is among the people that live in this country such a wealth of talent." Since this architect's death, the Walter Segal Self-Build Trust has successfully promoted his approach among a whole series of disadvantaged groups in the bleak political climate of the 1990s.[9] It always takes far longer to overcome the obstacles of finance and permissions and the planning and building legislation, than it does for the self-builders to construct and occupy their homes.

I have described the anarchist house in terms of real experiences among ordinary citizens in the world of today. But in view of the varieties of definitions of the word anarchism, I should explore a few other aspects. Some of us try very hard to bridge the gap between real life and anarchist theory over day-to-day issues like housing. Among the well-known theorists, Kropotkin is full of interest. His chapter on 'Dwellings' in his book on *The Conquest of Bread* (in French 1892, in English 1906) was, essentially, his manual on what should happen in a revolutionary society: an equitable share-out of existing housing according to needs.

Most of us do not live in revolutionary situations but still need to house our families and get by in whatever kind of society we chance to inhabit. Here, I think, another classical anarchist is a better guide. This was, of course, Pierre-Joseph Proudhon, who in a famous, but unreadable, book *What is Property?* (1840), coined the slogan that "Property is Theft". I'm like anyone else. I rejoiced on that day in September 1969, when the squatters at a former royal residence at 144 Piccadilly in London suspended a banner with Proudhon's slogan in metre-high letters.

But one of the ironies noted by Proudhon's critics was the fact that he also coined the slogan "Property is Freedom". It ought not to be necessary to explain that the first Slogan was directed at the absentee landowner, defined by George Woodcock as "the man who uses it to exploit the labour of others without any effort on his own part, property distinguished by interest and rent, by the impositions of the non-producer on the producer". The other kind of property, he explained, was that of the owner-occupier or peasant cultivator, and 'possession', or the right to control the dwelling and the land and tools needed to live was seen by Proudhon as "the corner stone of liberty", while "his main criticism of the Communists was that they wished to destroy it".[10]

The seventy-year history of the Union of Socialist Soviet Republics and the shorter life of the regimes it enforced upon eastern Europe provide a basis for examining Kropotkin's and Proudhon's opinions in the light of experience. There was a share-out of existing housing according to need. Most observers recorded that the needs of the Party hierarchy were more urgent than those of ordinary citizens, as of course was their need for a *dacha* in the country. Stalin's enforced collectivisation of agriculture literally liquidated the peasantry, resulting in millions of deaths and in famine. Meanwhile in the cities housing policy was an extreme version of the planners' infatuation with tower blocks that we also experienced in the West.

Slowly and subversively, Proudhonian popular attitudes began to reassert themselves. As Proudhon would have prophesied, the peasants' personal plots around their houses were the salvation of the ordinary Russian's food supply many Years before *perestroika*:

> In 1963, private plots covered about 44,000 square kilometres or some 4% of all the arable land of the collective farms. From this 'private' land, however, comes about half of all the vegetables produced in the USSR, while 40% of the cows and 30% of the pigs in the country are on them.[11]

Similarly, in the 1970s the economist Hugh Stretton was reporting that: "Pathetically, Russian town dwellers go out and comb the countryside for patches of neglected land they can plant, visit, enjoy, 'make their own', however tenuously".[12]

Their Marxist rulers, of course, had their *dachas*, but throughout Czechoslovakia, Hungary, Rumania and Yugoslavia, city dwellers were building their real life around what were called 'wild settlements' outside the city. Thus in 1979, a geographer was explaining that:

> The existence of peasant-owned land on the fringes of cities offers opportunities for piecemeal evolution—indeed 'overnight mushrooming' of 'wild settlements' as in Nowy Dwòr and elsewhere outside Warsaw or in Kozarski Bok and Trnje on the margins of Zagreb. Such communities are not encouraged, yet they are tolerated and even provided with utilities and welfare since they relieve some of the pressures on city housing and budgets.[13]

Observations like these, from the days when it was still assumed that the Communist regimes of Eastern Europe were expected to have a future, are a reminder to revolutionaries of every kind, of the importance of Proudhon's careful distinction between property as exploitation and property as possession.

Communism, enforced by terror, has brought an inevitable individualist reaction, and has tarnished every variety of socialist aspiration. But there has always been a quieter, gentler, libertarian advocacy of communal living. Together with other ideologists, both secular and religious, many anarchists have been critical of the nuclear family and of the one-family dwelling that is the universal provision for it. Like other critics, they have seen the individual house as a prison for its inhabitants and have sought a wider social unit. Thus Kropotkin declared:

> Today we live too isolated. Private property has led us to an egotistic individualism in all our mutual relations. We know one another only slightly; our points of contact are too rare. But we have seen in history examples of a communal life which is more intimately bound together—the 'composite family' in China, the agrarian communes, for example. There people really know one another. By force of circumstances they must aid one another materially and morally.
>
> Family life, based on the original community, has disappeared. A new family, based on community of aspirations, will take its place. In this family people will be obliged to know one another for moral support on every occasion ... [14]

Kropotkin, like Tolstoy, was the inspiration for a long series of communal ventures aiming to combine living with intensive horticulture, and their mostly short life-spans have been intensely studied in retrospect.[15] They offer us little illumination of the nature of the anarchist house, since their initiators were poor and had to make use of whatever buildings were available. But one of these failed ventures in Britain did evoke a very significant comment from Kropotkin. This was the Clousdon Hill Free Communist and Co-operative Colony, established on a twenty-acre (8 hectare) farm near Newcastle-upon-Tyne in 1895. Its founders wrote to him for advice, and the advice he gave was interesting. He warned the colonists to avoid isolation from the surrounding community, he urged that "barrack-like living conditions should be avoided in favour of combined efforts by independent families" and he wrote very sensibly about the situation of women. It was important, he wrote, to:

> ... do all possible for reducing household work to the lowest minimum ... In most communities this point was awfully neglected. The women and the girls remained in the new society as they were in the old—slaves of the community. Arrangements to reduce as much as possible the incredible amount of work which women uselessly spend in the rearing-up of children, as well as in the household work, are, in my opinion, as essential to the success of the community as the proper arrangements of the fields, the greenhouses, and the agricultural machinery. Even more. But while every community dreams of having the most perfect agricultural or industrial machinery, it seldom pays attention to the squandering of the forces of the house slave, the women.[16]

To my mind, this is one of Kropotkin's least-known, but most significant statements of an anarchist approach. And it has enormous relevance to any attempt to define the anarchist house. Consider classical house plans: Palladian villas, Italian *palazzi*, the English Georgian town house. They, unlike much modern architecture, were and are infinitely adaptable to innumerable uses, because they did not depend upon the endless variety of technical services—water, gas, electricity, heating systems and telecommunications—that we take for granted today. (As Le Corbusier remarked, "Heureux pour Ledoux: pas des tubes"). Instead, all these facilities were provided by human means: slaves, servants, housemaids, washerwomen, messenger boys. You have only to watch *The Marriage of Figaro* to be reminded of the way in which servants were part of the architecture: the mortar that really held it together.

As personal service declined, the designers of buildings continued to give priority to what were know as 'reception rooms' and the significantly named 'master bedroom' but squeezed key service areas—the kitchen, the bathroom, the laundry room—into smaller and smaller areas. The point is well made by the American experimenter Stewart Brand. Readers may remember him as the instigator in the 1960s and 1970s of *The Whole Earth Catalog* and its imitators in many countries. He has recently re-emerged as the author of a book *How Buildings Learn: What happens after they're built*, which in many ways can be seen as a manual on the anarchist house. Here he embraces the architectural philosophy of "Long life, loose fit, low energy", demanding that every building should, from the day it is begun, have the capacity to be endlessly adapted to meet the needs of its users. Many years ago the anarchist architect Giancarlo De Carlo declared that building users have to *attack* the building to make it their own, and the phrase that Brand adopts to define his kind of anarchy is "wholesome chaos".

In an important observation on the way in which this attitude changes our approach to houses, Brand explains that:

> One way to institutionalise wholesome chaos is to disperse significant design power to the individual users of a building while they're using the place.

Notice the difference between kitchens designed to be used by powerless servants—they are usually dark, cramped pits—and kitchens used by the heads of a family—bright, spacious, centrally located, crammed with conveniences. A building 'learns' much faster than whole organisations. This suggests a 'bottom-up' rather than 'top-down' approach in the building's human hierarchy ... What would a building look like and act like if it was designed for easy servicing by the users themselves? Once people are comfortable doing their own maintenance and repair, re-shaping comes naturally because they have a hands-on relationship with their space, and they know how to improve it ... [17]

There are several reasons for anticipating that, while anarchist houses are marginal in the housing economy of the rich world in the twentieth century, they will become more significant in the twenty-first century. I have several reasons for this forecast. The first is the expensive failure of official housing policy in the Western countries. It was constructed around a political notion of nuclear family households. But in Britain, the United States and France, most households today do not fit the statistical norm. The system is not designed for their needs. Alternative communal households are bound to develop.

The second reason is the lesson of the poor world and the poor segments of the rich world. The unofficial population of the poor world cities is larger that that of the official city. Whenever poor people can gain access to land and materials, they build dweller-controlled housing which grows and adapts according to need and opportunity.[18]

The third reason is the impact of feminism upon housing design. As Kropotkin indicated, half the population has always been excluded from housing decisions, but as Dolores Heyden insists, there has always been an alternative approach, hidden from history.[19]

My final reason is the impact of the Green movement and of considerations of ecological sustainability. Today, every individual family house has a huge investment in energy-wasting services and equipment with an in-built short life. Rational use of power demands durable, energy-saving, and shared equipment.[20]

The technical criterion for the anarchist house is "Long life, loose fit, low energy", but the political demand is the principle of Dweller Control.

# Section Four

## Work, Leisure, Education and Play

# 1. THE FACTORY WE NEVER HAD

As the decades roll by, it becomes more and more evident that the truly creative socialist thinker of the nineteenth century was not Karl Marx, but William Morris. His most eminent Marxist biographer, the late E.P. Thompson, virtually admitted this when he came to revise his massive volume *William Morris: Romantic to Revolutionary*. When it first appeared in 1955 critics complained that it was a great Stalinist steam-roller, flattening Morris into a cardboard cut-out of a card-carrying Communist Party member.

Maybe it was that, but it was a great deal more beside, and in his postscript to the later version, Thompson explained that "Morris, by 1955, had claimed me. My book was by then, I suppose, already a work of muffled 'revisionism'. The Morris/ Marx argument has worked inside me ever since. When in 1956, my disagreements with orthodox Marxism became fully articulate, I fell back on modes of perception which I'd learned in those years of close company with Morris, and I found, perhaps the will to go on arguing from the pressure of Morris behind me."

It was a namesake of his, Paul Thompson, who wrote the best of all accounts of Morris, *The Work of William Morris*, first published in 1967 and reprinted several times since then. What does it matter, he asks, whether Morris was a romantic, an anarchist, a Marxist, or even a crypto-Fabian? The important thing is that he had a world view of extraordinary richness, which again and again foreshadows our own preoccupations: "the destruction by the international economy not just of ancient cultures, but of the natural resources and ecology of the earth itself; the crippling of local independence by spreading centralization and bureaucracy, the stifling of natural creativity and zest for learning of children by institutionalized schooling; the cramming of working people into barrack-like housing … "

But beyond this relevance, for Paul Thompson there is a special reason for Morris's importance for us: his remarkable anticipation of the problems posed to socialists within a late-twentieth century consumer society: "Socialism was originally the product of the age of the factory, and it bears that mark in its primary focus on work. This is a major reason why socialism has always had a more direct appeal to men than to women, and equally why, with the growth of leisure and a home-centred way of life, its significance to ordinary life has become less and less obvious. But Morris stands alone among major socialist thinkers in being as concerned with housework and the home as with work in the factory. The transfor-

From William Morris and Colin Ward, *The Factory As It Might Be / The Factory We Never Had*. (Nottingham: Five Leaves Publishing, 1995), 21–29.

mation of both factory and home was equally necessary for the future fulfilment of men and women. Morris wanted everyday life as a whole to become the basic form of creativity, of art: 'For a socialist, a house, a knife, a cup, a steam engine, must be either a work of art, or a denial of art'".

Morris's account of *A Factory as it Might Be* comes from 1884, one of the busiest years of an endlessly busy life. He was writing, week by week in *Justice*, the organ of the Social-Democratic Federation, founded in January of that year, and in December had resigned, with a majority of the Executive, to form the Socialist League. But all through that year he was also lecturing in English and Scottish cities and towns with a series of topics, some of which became famous. E.P. Thompson records that the main themes he was offering at this time were "Useful Work versus Useless Toil", "Art and Labour", "Misery and the Way Out", and "How We Live and How We Might Live." He explains that "These lectures, with great variety of illustration and vigour of expression, followed a similar pattern. First Morris examined in some fresh and striking manner, the reality of life and labour in capitalist society. Next, he presented by contrast the vision of true society, creative and responsive to beauty, and called his listeners to action in the struggle to achieve this vision."

The factory of his vision is a handsome group of buildings, surrounded by gardens, cultivated co-operatively "for beauty's sake, which beauty would by no means exclude the raising of useful produce for the sake of livelihood." And he notes that "the Notting ham factory hands could give many a hint to professional gardeners."

...

Morris's factory would combine work and leisure with technical education, would have its nursery, school, restaurant and concert hall. It would be adorned with painting and sculpture. It would be a neighbourhood's social centre and the place where children learned by doing. His account of the factory also refutes those critics who, a century after his death, still dismiss Morris as a medievalist dreamer, and anachronism in the machine age, for he argues that "machines of the most ingenious and best-approved kinds will be used when necessary, but will be used simply to save human labour", so that the working hours will be reduced to about four hours a day.

As for the tedium of repetitive work, he observes that "the machine tending ought not to require a very long apprenticeship, therefore in no case should any one person be set to run up and down after a machine through all his working hours every day" since, apart from the reduction of work time, "whatever is burdensome about the factory would be taken turn in turn about, and so distributed, would cease to be a burden—would be, in fact, a kind of rest from the more exciting or artistic work."

Here Morris is anticipating the findings of highly-paid industrial psychologists a century later. Plenty of us find a repetitive task restful, provided that everyone else shares it and provided that it occupies a short amount of our working day. The whole tragedy of monotonous jobs on the assembly line, whether it is actually a line or a draughty shed where women gut chickens all day for the food-processing industry, is that the more hours they can get, the happier they are, simply for the sake of a pathetically small pay-packet.

So what became of Morris's factory vision? Several industrialists set about creating "model" factories. Eleven years after Morris's essay, George Cadbury moved his chocolate factory to Bournville outside Birmingham, where, the historian Gillian Darley explains, "The factory was surrounded by gardens, where the white-gowned workers could idle by the rose bushes in their lunch breaks; another palliative for the tedium of assembly-line work." And even earlier, in 1888, when William Hesketh Lever moved his factory to Port Sunlight, he explained that he wanted his workers to "learn that there is more enjoyment in life than the mere going to and returning from work and looking forward to Saturday night to draw their wages." But Gillian Darley quotes a trade unionist's comment that "no man of an independent turn of mind could breathe for long in the atmosphere of Port Sunlight."

The tradition of the model factory persisted. Studying the lives of two tragic sisters, Alexandra Artley found that their happiest days were the ten years they worked for Courthaulds Red Scar rayon works outside Preston from 1970 to 1980. "Going to Courthaulds was like a holiday camp to us." In her book *Murder in the Heart* (Hamish Hamilton, 1993) Alexandra Artley drew upon their Morris-like recollections of breakfast at Courthaulds; " ... here, from the largesse of a good employer, they could choose and choose and eat and eat the most delicious hot subsidized things they were denied at home ... the warmth of the vast room with windows steamy against a frosty northern day, committed cooks in absolutely spotless white aprons and caps, and the long, under-heated chrome counters, subtly lighting trays of crisply fried bacon, big round sausages, glistening fried eggs, kidneys, golden triangles of fried bread, hot buttery toast, well-grilled tomatoes so sweetly squidgy in the middle, and gallons and gallons of hot, sweet tea. 'Oh,' said June, looking back on the vast hungers of youth, 'the breakfasts at Courthaulds were *lovely!*'"

This sensual account is a reminder that what made factory work acceptable to millions, apart from the pay-packet, were incidentals, like the company of fellow workers, not a concern for the product. But if you travel in Morris's footsteps through industrial Britain in the 1990s you are overwhelmed by dereliction. Statistically, through the shift of manufacture from Europe and North America to the countries of the Pacific Rim or Latin America, where labour costs are cheaper, the owners of capital have shifted production, while automation and a change in the materials used, have made the factory itself obsolete. Capital has achieved its object which was to eliminate labour. ...

A handful of socially-conscious capitalists may have taken notice of Morris's industrial ideal, but have gradually abandoned it because industrial welfare added to the cost of production, by comparison with that of poor countries. And yet another of Morris's demands has been completely lost. He thought that "the factory could supply another educational want by showing the general public how its goods are made." This comment anticipated the principle that, generations later, the American anarchist Paul Goodman called the 'transparency of operation', the idea that we should all be able to understand the functioning of the industrial products we use every day. But every item of electronic equipment in our homes has a label that warns 'No user serviceable parts inside.'

It was Morris's contemporary and friend Peter Kropotkin who added some thoroughly modern contributions to his comments on industrial production. In his study of *Fields, Factories and Workshops* of 1899, he gathered a mass of statistical evidence to show that ideologists of both right and left had exaggerated the scale of factory production. Most of our ordinary daily needs were produced in a small-workshop economy. And he anticipated the changes in sources of motive power that in the 20th and 21st centuries would make the large factory obsolete. We see this in the obsolescence all around us today.

This does not mean that Morris's vision of a factory as it might be has no significance for the future. It simply means that we have failed to achieve the humanisation of work that was at the heart of his life's ambition to separate useful work from useless toil.

# 2. IN THE SANDBOX OF THE CITY

*"A sandbox is a place where adults park their children in order to converse, play or work with a minimum of interference. The adults, having found a distraction for the children, can get on with the serious things of life. There is some reward for the children in all this. The sandbox is given to them as their own turf. Occasionally, fresh sand or toys are put in the sandbox along with an implicit admonition that these things are furnished to minimize the level of noise and nuisance. If the children do become noisy and distract their parents, fresh toys may be brought. If the occupants of the sandbox choose up sides and start bashing each other over the head, the adults will come running, smack the juniors more or less indiscriminately, calm things down and then, perhaps in an act of semi-contrition, bring fresh sand and fresh toys, pat the occupants of the sandbox on the head, and disappear once again into their adult involvement and pursuits."*

—George Sternlieb

Nearly sixty years ago Berthold Brecht wrote a play *In the Jungle of the City*, set in the fantastically exotic dream-America which was his image of capitalist society. The metaphor gained currency and we have by now become over-familiar with phrases like the asphalt jungle or the concrete jungle as images of the city. Today they are deceptive. It would be closer to the truth to see the city as a wasteland. "Glasgow", declared *New Society*, "could well become the first city to be classified as industrial waste." The economic centre of gravity and the demographic focus have moved, permanently, from the inner city. George Sternlieb's mordant analogy of the city as sandbox gives a more illuminating picture of the place of the inner city in national preoccupations. Increasingly the inhabitants of the inner city are superfluous people, a drag on the national economy. This is more evident in the United States than in Britain, though there are British cities too which grew at an enormous pace in the nineteenth century, whose whole economic *raison-d'être* has collapsed, and which can never recover either the industry or the population they sustained, after a fashion, in those days. Government programmes with a bewildering series of initials follow each other in rapid succession, as fresh sops to, or fresh toys for, the inner city.

Originally printed in *Town and Country Planning* Volume 46, No. 1 (January 1977): 36–38.

Ebenezer Howard was convinced that the biggest single factor that stood in the way of the humane redevelopment of the inner city was the price of urban land, and that once the city has been "demagnetized" by outward migration, the monopoly value of inner city land would burst. For a number of reasons it hasn't happened that way. Roger Starr, the housing administrator for New York, told me of his mystification at the way land retained its price long after it had lost its value. In Britain there is what can only be called a capitalist plot, to which the Government is a party, to keep up the price of urban land, simply because in the speculative paradise of the property boom in the 1960s institutional investors, like the great insurance and pension funds, invested so heavily in property shares. What has this to do with the environmental education of the urban child? Simply that it is only when the thousands of acres of derelict inner city land in every British city are valued as the derelict land that they really are, that ordinary people's aspirations for housing at humane densities, for domestic and public open space, for low-rent premises for small businesses, and for all those activities which are the very essence of urban civilization but show a low rate of return on capital invested, can be realized.

The extent of the wastelands of the cities is demonstrated in a new and well-illustrated report from the Civic Trust. The potential of just a little of this land which is too "valuable" to be used, is indicated in *Make Waste Space Play Space*, a new action handbook issued by the Fair Play for Children Campaign.

Most of the environmental policies which would improve the lives of children in our cities would benefit adults too. In particular everything that would make the city a more tolerable place for the old, would make it more enjoyable for the young. The German writer Alexander Mitscherlich remarks that "The anthropologist cannot get over the fact that the commercially-oriented planning of our cities is clearly aimed at one age group only—working adults—and even then inadequately enough. How a child is to become a working adult seems to be a negligible factor. The world of the child is a sphere of the socially weak, and is ruthlessly manipulated." His comment points to an important distinction. Do we want to provide for the child as a special kind of person or as someone who is becoming an adult? There is a pendulum in the philosophy of child-rearing that swings between these two views. There are cities in the world with a terrifying absence of the reverence we feel we owe to the child, but there are also cities where we make it incredibly difficult for the child to enter a world of adult freedom and responsibility. In the cities of the West we get in some ways the worst of both worlds. We no longer cow our children into submission, in fact we indulge them as consumers, with the powerful aid of the advertising industry, but we fail to induct them into a world of adult decision-making, perhaps just because as adults we have delegated to others the habit of deciding.

Watch the scrimmage at the bus stop when the city child comes out of school, interview tenants on a housing estate terrorized by its children, learn that the annual cost of vandalism in England, Scotland and Wales is, at a minimum estimate, well over £114 million, and you will be in no doubt that the city has failed its children. It fails to awaken their loyalty and pride. It fails to offer legitimate adventures. Jane Addams, an astute urban reformer of seventy years ago, observed the "inveterate demand of youth that life shall offer a large measure of excitement" and she asked whether we oughtn't to assume that "this love of excitement, this desire for adventure is basic and will be evinced by each generation of city boys as a challenge to their elders?" It is certainly a challenge in the form of the manufactured excitements to which they respond and which they themselves, when interviewed by earnest students of sociology, usually attribute to boredom.

The modern city, in Jane Addams' view, failed to cater for "the insatiable desire for play, whereas the classical city had promoted play with careful solicitude and the medieval city held tourneys, pageants, dances and festivals". To advocate more circuses really is to recognize the city's function as a sandbox but for the young, if the whole city is not their playground, what else is it? There is an urgent need for a modern equivalent of the rituals of a calendar of excitement provided in the cities of traditional society. But the very fact that, looking for a means of providing excitement and adventure, we have to settle for ideas about carnivals and festivals, is a measure of the extent to which we have drained both these characteristics out of ordinary urban life.

In the United States the playground enthusiasts, environmental educators, and landscape architects with a concern for the needs of the urban child, keep up with each other through a valuable newsletter called *Childhood City* and it is tempting to adopt the words as a campaigning slogan. But we don't want a childhood city so much as a city where children live in the real world. If we seek a shared city, rather than a city where unwanted patches are set aside to contain children and their activities, our priorities are not quite the same as those of the crusaders for the child. We already have enormous expertise and a mountain of research on the appropriate provision of parks and play-spaces for use by children of different ages, but the ultimate truth is that children play anywhere and everywhere. Because some bit of the city is designated as a play space on a plan, there is no guarantee that it will he used as such, nor that other areas will not be. If the claim of children to share the city is admitted, the whole environment has to be designed and shaped with their needs in mind, just as we are beginning to accept that the needs of the disabled should be accepted as a design factor. I can think of no city that admits the claim of children, though I can think of many which seem deliberately designed to exclude them. How can a child *use*, for example, central Birmingham? Every step the city takes to reduce the dominance of motor traffic makes the city more accessible to the child. It also makes life more tolerable for every other citizen.

At what particular age do we cease to think of our city children as cute and begin to think of them as a social menace? Most people's recollections of childhood include some moment in some context when their pride and self-esteem were lifted by the fact that they were being treated as though they were not children. They rose to the occasion. Rather than throw in a few playthings, shouldn't we help them climb out of the sandbox and into the city?

# 3. PIONEER CAMPS

... It is just enough to mention the subject of holiday camps to bring on a know-ing grin. Like the seaside landlady, the saucy postcard and the garish kiosks along the front, holiday camps are part of a rich and colourful folklore of the seaside holiday ... But is there anything more to holiday camps than this? ... We have ... been drawn to the subject because we believe there is a wider story to tell. The era of the holiday camp, dating from the end of the last century, is also an era of radi-cal social change. Looking back on this era we may find that holiday camps tell us something of these broader changes.

Four themes in particular have interested us. The first is that in terms of their enduring popularity in the twentieth century, holiday camps merit attention as an institution in their own right. Since the turn of the century, literary millions have poured through the camp gates for a week or two of communal living....This annual process is itself a story worth telling ... A second theme is to probe the mo-tives for providing holiday camps in the first place. These motives are interesting in themselves but also reveal some of the wider conflicts of interest that character-ize the present century. Inevitably, commercial motives loom large and modern camps catering for thousands of visitors at any one time are linked exclusively with the profit making side of the leisure industry. Commercialism, however, of-fers only a partial explanation of camps in general. Educational ideas, trade unions and welfare considerations, the cult of the outdoor life, and political utopianism have all played their part ... Another source of interest lies in the planning and design of holiday camps. What we find is that this process is entangled within the wider concerns of an environmental lobby and of an emergent planning system. Camps were seen to pose both a threat and an opportunity. They were a threat in the sense that here was yet another source of development in a coast or countryside setting that was already under immense pressure. And yet, there was also a sense of opportunity, for no matter what went on within the camp compounds, the fact was that it could all be contained. Perhaps, too, the new buildings could even be well-designed. As such, the evolution of holiday camps is part of a broader history of planning and architectural control ...

## THE PIONEER CAMPS

... Well before the large commercial camps arrived on the scene in the 1930s

Originally printed in Colin Ward and Dennis Hardy, *Goodnight Campers! The History of the British Holiday Camp*. (London: Mansell Publishing, 1986), vii–viii, 23–53.

there was already a generation of holiday camps with a headstart. These were, in the words of their devotees, the *genuine* holiday camps or as they were also known, the *pioneer* camps.

In the latter half of the 1930s commercial camps and pioneer camps lived side by side, each drawing on their own sectors of an expanding holiday market, yet beyond sharing common classification as holiday camps the two types of venture were worlds apart. The new commercial camps were on an altogether different scale, catering for thousands rather than hundreds. Investment and organization reflected a corporate pursuit of profits, capitalizing on the fact that each year more people were taking holidays away from home. Huge white-painted concrete buildings with bright neon lights and tropical blue-lined swimming pools offered excitement and glamour for thousands who had been seduced by Hollywood on the screen and who had seen pictures of high living on the luxury trans-Atlantic liners, but for whom Skegness and Clacton marked the practical limits of their journeys into fantasy. For these the new camps hit just the right note. And over time it was the commercial camps (or *mass camps* as they were sometimes known) which wrested the initiative from their forerunners to set the pace and image for post-1945 developments.

Yet the original holiday camps were not to give ground easily. Theirs was a world that sought to turn away from the trappings of mass commercialism in search of the simpler qualities of fresh air, wholesome cooking and good, clean fun. It was an ideal that was closer to the more general pursuit of camping under canvas than to that of new developments in holiday camps.

For a couple of years (immediately before the outbreak of the Second World War ended the pursuit of innocent pleasures) the pioneers had their own magazine, *Holiday Camp Review*.[1] It was a cheerful, optimistic magazine, rooted in the belief that 'the Holiday Camp movement has come to stay ... [and] is destined to spread its influence far wider and even more rapidly than it has done during the past few years.'[2] In its columns it expressed the spirit of what had by the end of the 1930s become something of a cult in itself—an offshoot of earlier, more broadly-based movements in pursuit of the simple life, a return to the land and co-operation rather than competition. The whole emphasis was on community rather than commerce.

These were broad principles, subscribed to by varied sources. Pioneer camps were sometimes simply family ventures, modest in scale and offering plenty of fun at reasonable charges. In other instances, camps were sponsored by organizations for their members. They, too, were offering relaxing holidays in convivial surroundings, though sometimes with a dose of education and self-improvement to enrichen the experience. Local authorities, co-operative societies, trade unions and special interest groups shared a common interest in the holiday camp as a new and challenging dimension to their activities.

All the signs are that the pioneer camps were popular places. Each year more people spent their holiday in a camp. Fresh investments were made throughout the 1930s, and campers themselves were keen to tell the world of the wonders of a holiday in camp.

But, in a growing market for holidays, the early camps—generally small-scale and often run as family businesses—came under increasing competition from the much larger, 'mass' camps. The pioneers responded, not by trying to emulate the newcomers, but by championing their own special qualities. Above all, the 'true camp spirit' was something they claimed was theirs alone. The larger enterprises had appropriated the name 'holiday camp' but there the similarity ended. They were, in reality, nothing less than 'holiday towns masquerading as holiday camps.'[3]

At times the criticism of the new camps became quite vitriolic. 'Concentration Camps' was the heading of one diatribe, which then went on to describe them as the negation of everything that holiday camps have hitherto stood for. More, they are a definite menace to the future of genuine camps.... High-powered publicity allied to a Woolworth technique may temporarily add enormously to the population of mass camps. In the long run it must pervert the principles of holiday camps and destroy the camp spirit.'[4]

Visitors to the new camps were measured in thousands—5,000 weekly at Skegness for instance—but the pioneer campers were less than impressed. Some looked back nostalgically (albeit over no more than a decade) to the real pioneering days of tents and oil-lamps. Those who liked the pioneer camps invariably spurned the regimentation that went with the larger numbers. Typical was the comment of one camper who spent 'fifty-one weeks working in a factory. During the remaining week I like to escape from a factory, even though it is by the seashore.'[5]

In *Holiday Camp Review* the case for the pioneer camps was put by a group of journalists who 'have tasted the joys of camp holidays and ... want others to do the same.' Write to us, they asked, 'not as impersonal scribes in distant Fleet Street, but as, say, Jimmy, Harry or Bill, Peggy, Dorothy or Grace of Hut 16, 60 or 90.' Their aims were to keep holiday campers in touch with one another and also to widen the circle and generally to spread the benefits of 'the true camp spirit.'[6] They were also at pains to respond to critics of the movement—some (like seaside landladies) who saw their own holiday businesses under threat from the growing popularity of the camps, and others who tarred the movement with accusations of widespread immorality and sub-standard conditions that were a threat to public health.

As well as the campers' own magazine there was also a formal organization, the National Federation of Permanent Holiday Camps, to further the cause.[7] The Federation had its roots in an association of holiday camps in Norfolk and Suffolk that was formed in 1933. Two years later, in 1935, the National Federation (with representatives of the great majority of existing holiday camps) was established with the aim of guaranteeing basic standards of food, comfort, accommodation, conduct and amenities in its camps. In an attempt to shake off an image of primitive camps (with likenesses drawn even to the rough conditions of military encampments experienced on overseas campaigns), eligibility to join the Federation depended on meeting certain requirements. Most of the accommodation had to be permanent (as opposed to tents), with an acceptable water supply and sanitary system, dining and dance halls had to be large enough for the size of the camp, kitchens were required to be open to inspection, and unseemly conduct by visitors

was not to be tolerated. The day of simplicity for its own sake was already over.
Pioneer camps were coming of age.

## THE REAL PIONEERS
> What shall it profit a camper if he gain the service of a Grand Hotel and lose
> the easy camaraderie which made a holiday camp so refreshingly different
> from anywhere else?
> —View of correspondent to *Holiday Camp Review*, Vol. 2, No. 1, May 1939

Pride of place for the first holiday camp goes to the Cunningham Camp on the
Isle of Man from as early as 1894—starting life in tented accommodation and
remaining throughout an all-male camp. Mixed and family camps emerged some
ten years later, amongst the first of these being Harsent's Camp at Pensarn in
North Wales and the camp at Otley Chevin on the Yorkshire Moors. These were
the real pioneering days, when a rough wooden hut served as the common room
for the campers who lived in tents and did most of the camp work themselves:

> We prepared vegetables, laid tables, served meals, did the washing up, and
> looked after our tents and their contents. Chores were meticulously shared
> out. First business on arrival was to appoint the daily committees. Each camp-

er, young or old, served one day on the 'committee' and helped in practically all the essential work on the camp apart from cooking ... For the evening concert or camp sing-song a swinging oil lamp provided dim illumination in the common room. We stepped up one when the tents were given boarded floors; the advance from camp beds to regular bedsteads made us marvel at our good fortune; and when the first huts were introduced we could scarcely believe that such 'magnificence' was possible for the money we paid.[8]

Also in the early years of this century J. Fletcher Dodd opened a holiday camp at Caister-on-Sea, on the East Coast a few miles north of Great Yarmouth. In its later advertisements the Caister camp was to claim that it was the oldest established camp and also that it was the only camp with its own railway station. It was followed, especially after the First World War, with a succession of new camps, starting in 1920 with Potter's camp at Hemsby in Norfolk.

These were invariably small-scale family ventures and 'Pa' Potter's camp was typical. Inspired by visits to Caister, Potter set about raising capital through competitions in newspapers. With £950 from that source he joined with his brother on demobilization to start his first camp at Hemsby. From there he moved down the coast to a new site at Hopton-on-Sea in 1925 and then, eight years later, in 1933 opened nearby his famous 'Potter's Hopton Beach Camp' complete with all 'mod. cons.'. 'Gone are the days of candlelit huts. They have given place to brick verandah chalets with electric light and modern toilet conveniences.' In spite of the obvious improvements in the material well-being of the camp, Potter retained happy memories of the real camp spirit which abounded in the pioneer days. He was looking back nostalgically to the days when 'white American cloth was considered a luxury table cover and the few camps then in existence did a roaring trade on Saturday evenings with their penny candles which lit the sleeping quarters. Loud cheers used to proclaim my arrival with the pressure oil lamp which cast a dim religious light over the bare tables of the common room after supper had been served.'

Typically, the pioneer proprietors liked to be seen as 'characters'. As well as Fletcher Dodd and 'Pa' Potter, there was 'Maddy' Maddieson of Hemsby and Littlestone, and the jovial 'G.A.' (G. A. Price) of Bramble Chines. Invariably they took an active part in the life of their camp—organizing games and competitions, getting to know their visitors, and generally keeping a watchful eye on what went on. It was a paternalistic role with utilitarian aims, 'pulling together in a spirit of co-operation and goodwill, to the one common end so that the greatest number of campers can get the maximum amount of happiness.'[9]

Still in operation today, and typical of the cheap and simple holiday camps of the inter-war years, is Golden Sands, at Voryd, Rhyl. It was started in 1933 by Arthur Jones, formerly of the merchant navy, who had a timber yard in the town. It had both one-room chalets and tents as well as a vast pavilion, built entirely of wood, for dining and entertainments. The 20-acre site, bought from a local farmer, was by the sea, 'Right on the Beach' as its slogans proclaimed. So that the name could be seen from the road, it was carried on letters 6 feet high held by 60-

foot poles, and Mr. Jones, the founder was able to climb to the top of these poles without aids of any kind—a skill he had learned as a cadet in sailing ships.'

The camp was immediately successful, and in 1937 the Golden Sands Chorus, written by two campers from Birmingham and Sheffield was broadcast by the BBC and relayed 'to the Empire'. The words (to the tune of *Back to Those Happy Days*) were,

> Back to the Golden Sands
> Campers have congregated.
> Back to the Golden Sands
> Well worth the year we've waited,
> There's lots of Girls and Boys,
> The skies are always sunny;
> We are right on the beach,
> Rhyl is within our reach,
> Back to the *Golden* Golden Sands.

By 1939, when Mr. Jones's business was 'on its feet' the war brought an end to the annual holiday. The pavilion was used as a factory for making anti-gas capes, but the camp itself was not requisitioned for military use as the drains were not considered capable of coping, so it continued to be used to provide short breaks for people from Liverpool. A communal cook-house was equipped with rows of gas rings.

After the war, the founder was joined by his son-in-law, Victor Dodd, who has seen generations of the same families returning year after year. The Golden Sands publicity is disarmingly honest: 'Our chalets continue to be very well booked year after year. We ourselves feel they are somewhat dated, but they are well maintained and easy on the pocket.'

Another aspect of Golden Sands links the holiday camp with the caravan sites that proliferate on the North Wales coast. In the 1930s, plots on the site were rented to people who wanted a seaside caravan but who also wanted to use the facilities of the holiday camp. At the same time, a camp was developed on the other side of Rhyl, on a seaside site of 34 acres on the road to Prestatyn. The owner was a Mr. Hargreaves from Nottingham who began by renting bell-tents, and then employing out-of-work men from Liverpool to build three-room chalets, as well as renting caravan plots. The Robin Hood Camp (with its Maid Marion Store and its former Friar Tuck Café) now belongs to Golden Sands. All its chalets and caravans are privately owned, and all bookings arranged between the owners and campers, as with the caravans at Golden Sands itself.

The Rhyl Urban District Council obtained a private Act of Parliament to control camps, which are licenced from Easter to October. Standards of accommodation and the rules for lettings are closely supervised by the camp proprietors: 'Any owner who does not look after your interests doesn't last long at Robin Hood!', they claim in their advice to campers.[10]

Just as it was difficult in the 1930s to make a hard-and-fast distinction between holiday camps and caravan sites, so it was not easy to distinguish between organized holiday camps and colonies of individually-owned holiday chalets, like the 'bungalow town' of Shoreham Beach in Sussex, or like Jaywick Sands on the Essex coast, which we have described elsewhere, with its 'permanent carnival atmosphere'.[11] Colley's Camp at Withernsea on Humberside is typical of many such seaside plotlands. Mr. Colley senior started the camp in 1932, using unemployed joiners from Hull to build thirty-five chalets of timber, clad with match-boarding, asbestos-cement sheeting on timber framing. The price of a chalet was £75. An adjoining site with twenty-five plots, called Kenwood's Camp was bought by the present Mr. Colley in 1966. The Public Health Act of 1936 was used to prevent permanent occupation by limiting the period of use to the period between 1st March and 31st October each year. Most of the owners come from the Sheffield and Doncaster areas. A recent visitor concluded that 'even on a rainy day the place has a delightful atmosphere and the feeling of a backwater is emphasised by its concealed entrance. The bright colours, neat gardens and painted fences make a gentle and poetic image in stark contrast to the alien atmosphere of the nearby modern chalet and caravan camps with rows of identical and impersonal units.'[12]

Most of the early camps were on the coast, offering a popular blend of sea air and camp jollities. A few, however, took advantage of an inland site, like the Robinson Crusoe Club and Holiday Camp in Berkshire which used its woodland setting to create an image as 'the camp that is different'. Chalets were built in the trees and, as well as the usual range of camp activities 'in the happy company of campers', Robinson Crusoe offered the unusual quality of solitude and an opportunity 'to retire to bed to the song of the nightingale.'

As well as the private entrepreneurs the Holiday Fellowship also made its mark in developing the early camps. A non-profit-making organization formed in 1913 'to provide healthy holidays, and to encourage love of the open air', the Fellowship promoted holiday centres as well as camps. Of the latter, holiday camps were initially seen as a way of offering cheap holidays for parties of children, though later there were camps for families as well.....

Family camps later in the 1930s could boast superior accommodation for those who could afford it. At Kessingland in 1938 a family could be housed in wooden blocks of bedrooms for 43/6d each. There was also an option of cheaper garden huts and sheds, for which 'great delight has been expressed by families'. In the true spirit of camping, guests were expected to keep their bedrooms and tents tidy and to take their turn at waiting at table.

The prospect of cheap, healthy holidays encouraged other organizations to launch their own schemes. Towards the end of the 1930s the National Fitness Campaign was active in spreading the word about holiday camps and also had plans of its own. In 1938 a scheme was announced in which the Campaign was to sponsor a camp on the Lincolnshire coast, with the work to be carried out by Mablethorpe Council. The intention was to subdivide the 60-acre site into eight sections, each of which would receive 'poorer people' from eight counties in the Midlands and East Anglia. It was one of a number of plans that was foiled by the start of the Second World War, after which the holiday camp movement was to take a decidedly different direction.

## CHILDREN IN CAMP

Summer camp is a hallowed North American tradition. For close to 125 years large numbers of young Americans between the ages of six and 18 have set off each summer for their annual rest from tiresome parents. Parents over the years have had their own reasons for forking out the camp fees; this year, between June and August, some four million young Americans are expected to sign in at more than 10,000 summer camps across the country.
—*The Economist*, June 30, 1984

Since the very first British holiday camp grew out of the effort to provide a summer camp for poor Liverpool boys, and since bodies like the Scouts and the Boys' Brigade were pioneers of organized camping, it is very surprising that children's camps on the American pattern have not developed here on anything like the trans-Atlantic scale. There, summer camps are part of the folklore of growing up in America. They have inspired several minor literary classics, (and it is interesting to learn that the Camp Keyumah of Herman Wouk's *The City Boy* is the very same institution as the Camp Katonah of Paul Goodman's *The Break-up of our Camp*. They have inspired dozens of collections of 'camp-fire songs' which must be engraved on the American heart, though they probably don't include satires like *Hello mudder, hello fader*, or even an unofficial camp song that runs

No more days of vacation!
Off to the railroad station!
Back to civilisation!

In France the *colonies de vacances* were flourishing by 1920, but it was not until much later that organizations like the Forest School Camps and Colony Holidays were started in England. PGL, the largest British company providing children's adventure holidays (55,000 boys and girls at fifty centres by 1984) was founded as recently as 1957, when its founder, Peter Gordon Lawrence, first took canoe-camping expeditions down the River Wye in Herefordshire. Like its even more recent imitators running computer camps, it depends heavily on using preparatory and public schools during the summer holidays.

All these initiatives have catered for middle-class children at middle-class prices, but there have always been those who, true to the origins of the holiday camp movement, have pressed for an extension of their use for poor urban children. Apart from the work of the Holiday Fellowship and the pioneer work of the uniformed youth organizations, the propagandists for children's holiday camps earlier in the century frequently turned to the progressive example of the Scandinavian countries.

In an article in 1927, 'For England's Sake and the Children's', the author pointed to the growth of holiday camps in Denmark for children from the towns. Initiated in 1903—with the support of municipal corporations, trade unions, newspaper appeals for funds, and the State Railway which carried the children free to the camps—the system had grown to the extent of accommodating some

6,000 children in the year of the article. The camp system itself grew out of a longer tradition of sending children into the country, not simply to fill their lungs with fresh air but also to absorb some of the solid qualities and uncomplicated values of peasant life. Health and patriotism were intertwined and that, claimed the author, was why a comparable system of holiday camps was essential. 'England has no use for "little old men and women" ... while of sturdy, hardy boys and girls she can never have too many. And the great majority of our little East Enders might be turned into staunch patriots, in time, if only they were caught early enough, and enough trouble was taken.'[13]

By the end of the 1930s, some progress had been made in providing camps for children but the system was by no means as widespread nor as well-organized as it had already become in North America and Northern Europe. In addition to Denmark, the examples of Sweden, Germany and Poland were often cited. Reminiscing in the House of Commons, Philip Noel-Baker recalled how one of his most vivid memories remained that of going to the Stockholm Olympics in 1912 and being taken to a school camp in a forest outside the capital. It was something in which he regarded that Britain had been far outstripped.

Apart from limited examples of therapeutic camps, the main thrust in Britain had come from welfare organizations and education authorities which had established school camps for their children. Where this had been done the record was encouraging, and initiatives date back in most cases to the beginning of the 1930s, and in some cases even before.

The Education Department of Glasgow Corporation, for instance, set up a Necessitous Children's Holiday Camp Fund and made fifteen films for fund-raising purposes to be shown in Scottish cinemas, illustrating the benefits that camp life gave to poor city children. In 1928 it provided holidays for 6,000 Glasgow children in ten locations by the sea and in the country.

Of the welfare organizations, the National Council of Social Service made an important contribution. Through grants from the Commissioner for the Special Areas, the Council had been involved with setting up and maintaining sixteen school camps in the North of England and South Wales. Between 1935 and 1939 over 141,000 children spent a fortnight's holiday in one of these camps.

Reviewing the role of education authorities in 1939, the Chief Education Officer for Birmingham, for instance, used the evidence of 25,000 elementary school children to exhort councillors to extend the practice. He pointed to a discernible gain in health and physique amongst children from the city who consumed the regular meals, fresh air and sleep with voracious appetites. For many of the children a stay in a camp was their first visit to the country, and although at first 'the children were inclined to be undisciplined, and sometimes even frightened by the loneliness of the countryside after the busy hustle of town life ... they quickly settled down and were really happy.'[14] ...

By 1939 there were some twenty school camps in England and Wales provided by education authorities. About half the camps catered for under nourished and weakly children at no charge to their parents. The other camps were intended for use by children with no particular problems, who were simply offered the chance of doing their normal school work for a week or two in healthy surroundings. Parents contributed to costs according to their means, the average payment being between 2s.6d and 7s. weekly.

The success of school camps encouraged the view that the children of every education authority should enjoy this type of facility. At an exhibition at the Housing Centre in 1939 the planning and provision of school camps was one of the topics on display. Amidst talk of mass evacuations and impending war, the idea of school camps was couched in terms of the very health of the nation. Indeed, it was argued, not only would it contribute to a healthier population but children would grow up with a better attitude to life in general and with a more responsible approach to the countryside in particular.

## CAMPS FOR THE WORKERS

The development of large-scale holiday services by private enterprise has been rapid and successful during recent years, and more particularly during the last two years. Our members and their families have made this development possible: it is their savings that are pouring into the pockets of the owners of the modern luxury camps and similar services.

The members of the co-operative movement and their families represent one-half of the population, and, if one may assume a similar proportion of holiday makers and holiday makers to be, one can see at once the tremendous possibilities of co-operative holiday catering. There is no reason to believe that, properly undertaken, the movement within a very short time could not capture 30 per cent of the present holiday camp business ...

—John Corina (Director, Royal Arsenal Co-operative Society), 26 May 1938

A key element in the development of pioneer holiday camps is the contribution of workers' organizations—set up specifically for the purpose of promoting holiday camps or, more generally, as part of the co-operative and trade union movement. The attraction of holiday camps to this type of movement is twofold—serving both welfare objectives (in the sense of enhancing the quality of life for working people) and, at the same time, encouraging communal activity and a spirit of camaraderie.

The first co-operative holiday camp was started by the United Co-operative Baking Society at Roseland, on Canada Hill, overlooking Rothesay Bay, and lasted from 1911 to 1974. The Society had begun a holiday club in 1899 and in 1908 had sent twenty-five young people to the YMCA camp at Ardgoil. John Dewar, president of the Renfrewshire Co-operative Conference Association was keen on camping because of his annual experience with the Volunteers (a precursor of the territorial army) and his propaganda for a co-op camp was supported by another Renfrew co-operator, John Patori, who had been converted through a visit to the Cunningham Camp at Douglas.

SPEND YOUR HOLIDAY AT ROTHESAY IN
# "ROSELAND" SUMMER CAMP
### OPEN MAY TILL SEPTEMBER

*On the Breezy Upland of Canada Hill, Rothesay*
*The most attractive Holiday Resort in Scotland*

THE Camp adjoins the Golf Course and overlooks the Bay—the Bay th
Poet sings of—
> "When the mist creeps o'er the Cumbraes,
>     And Arran peaks are grey ;
>     And the great black hills like sleeping kings
>         Sit gran' roun' Rothesay Bay."

The accommodation is all that could be desired ; the company is good ;
the menu liberal.

### TERMS AND OTHER PARTICULARS FROM—
## " CAMP "
## UNITED CO-OPERATIVE BAKING SOCIETY Ltd.
### 12, McNEIL STREET, GLASGOW, C. 5

A site was found on the Ayrshire coast but the tenant farmer's landlord stepped in to veto the proposal. Then the little farm of Rosedale came on the market. The committee thought that to purchase it was 'too bold a step' and decided to lease the site for six months only. The staff were accommodated in the farmhouse, the campers in bell-tents with their meals served in a large marquee. They were 'unanimous in their praise of the beautiful situation, privacy and perfect catering' and the farm was bought for £600. The following summer showed that the water supply was inadequate in dry weather but also that in wet weather 'something more impervious to rain than a marquee was desirable for the gatherings of campers'. To put both defects right, the Committee sought a loan of £1,000 on the security of the property and before opening in 1913 had erected both a water tank and a dining hall to cater for several hundred campers. At the same time they urged the Baking Society to take it over as a going concern. 'They explained to the directors of the Baking Society that they were not taking this step because they disbelieved in its success, but solely on the ground that they considered dual control was not good for discipline and did not make for good management.'

After the First World War (when the camp was requisitioned for military purposes) improvements were made, and chalets built. It held 400 people and was very popular among Scottish co-op members for decades. The Baking Society was finally merged with the Scottish Co-operative Wholesale Society and, in turn, in 1973 with the Co-operative Wholesale Society. It was this latter body which decided to close the camp at the end of the 1974 season, to the regret of those veterans who remembered the days when the seven-acre hillside site, next to Rothesay golf course, was 'covered in the summer and autumn months with picturesque pyramids of white canvas.'

It has always been one of the principles of the co-operative movement that a certain proportion of trading surpluses should be set aside for education, and it was the education committees of co-operative societies that sought to promote holidays for members. In 1893 a Congregational minister in Colne, Lancashire started the Co-operative Holidays Association, of which the Holiday Fellowship was an eventual offshoot. Around the period of the First World War the Co-operative Wholesale Society ran an inland holiday camp on one of its farms outside Manchester, and various retail societies, in their long history, sought to follow the example of the Scots in venturing into the field of holiday camps. ...

Apart from the Roseland Camp, the most durable co-operative camp was the one established by the Coventry Co-operative Society at Voryd, Kinmel Bay, near Rhyl. It had its origins in 1929, when a small party of co-operators spent their Whitsun under canvas in the Peak District. One of the campers, Tom Snowdon, urged the society's education secretary to find a permanent site for annual camps, and part of a field near the seashore was rented. The equipment for the first camp in 1930 consisted of six sleeping huts, an old railway coach and an ex-army hut, two dozen square tents and some old bell tents. In July it was announced that 'no accommodation is available for the last week in July and the first two weeks in August. The bookings for these periods have passed our expectations, and only go to prove that the education committee was fully justified in its experiment.'[15]

In Coventry, as in most of the country, the last week in July was 'holiday week', so that the August Bank Holiday (then the first Monday) could be tacked on. People queued in February outside the Coventry Co-op offices to win a place in the ballot for that week. The immense popularity of the camp enabled the education committee to persuade the management committee to buy the whole of the field and to build about sixty chalets as well as providing space for campers to pitch their tents. Campers made their own meals with primus stoves, pans and crockery provided. The Rhyl Co-operative Society operated a shop with the dividend credited to the sports and entertainment fund. The camp was run on a non-profit basis from the education committee's share of trading surpluses in Coventry and its education grant from the Co-operative Wholesale Society.

Harold Worthington, who took over as manager in 1948 when the last of the evacuees had finally left, recalls how the weekly charge of two pounds ten shillings a week for a chalet for four left nothing for maintenance and improvement. 'I remember, after a lengthy discussion, getting permission to line with hardboard about a dozen chalets, which internally were simply the rough unfinished side of the external lap-boarding, with the 3"x 2" framework showing inside. I did this, then realised that because of the uneven floorboards (no lino or carpets) a skirting board was necessary. Not forthcoming, so I finished off the job by using the crates in which the hardboard had been delivered.'

Even the primus stoves remained until the 1950s. 'This entailed me selling paraffin by the pint in ex-lemonade bottles, and methylated spirit to get the wretched things going. I was hauled over the coals by (I think) a local inspector of the Board of Trade for selling meths, obtained in 'six-penn'orths' from the local chemist, without a licence, so we stopped. Instead we sold small sticks of formaldehyde at a penny a time.'[16] Services were later improved, and as late as 1966 when a quarter of a million people had stayed there, 'queues form outside the Education Department Offices in King Street at least 24 hours before the first day of booking.' But the stage was reached when only a wholesale rebuilding, beyond the budget of the education department, could bring it up to modern public expectations. The chalets were bulldozed in the late-1970s and the site remains empty as the right buyer has not been found.

But its beginnings in the 1930s had been full of promise: that of cheap holidays for the workers without the taint of charity or patronage. It seemed to many to be the way forward. At every co-operative conference in the late-1930s there were voices urging that the movement was 'missing the bus' in meeting the challenges both of the forthcoming legislation for holidays with pay and of the new commercial holiday camps. Finally, a new joint organization, Travco Ltd, sponsored equally by the Co-operative Wholesale Society and the Workers' Travel Association was formed. The Workers' Travel Association had been founded in 1922 and by the Second World War had become the second largest holiday organization in Britain. The new non-profit company was intended to make 'a practical contribution towards the holiday problem of the family as well as individual workers of limited means', and it sought to ensure that its camps would be as modern as possible in ideas, while at the same time in keeping with the best camp traditions.

Rogerson Hall at Corton, just north of Lowestoft in Suffolk (now a Holimarine Holiday Centre) was the first of these new-style camps intended to provide a 'luxury' holiday for lower-paid workers, drawn from the co-operative movement, the trade unions and workers' organizations generally. Rates to stay there were competitive, though a scheme was introduced in which deserving cases were nominated each week for a free place. Opened in August 1938 the camp took 200 campers a week in its first season, with early plans for 360 weekly and an ultimate ceiling of 500. It offered a full range of accommodation, communal facilities and gardens, though certain features attracted their critics. Single and double accommodation, for instance, was not segregated in separate blocks (which was common practice), and huts were linked in continuous terraces. 'Arrangement of the huts in long continuous rows is surely a mistake,' wrote the editor of *Holiday Camp Review* 'but the architect may have been more influenced by town planning than camp planning.'[17]

*The Architectural Review*, needless to say, saw this as a virtue: 'The fact that the architect has organized its chalets into unified blocks alone represents a great advance on the rows of individual shacks found in most speculative holiday camps.'[18] It was planned to follow Rogerson Hall with five more camps—on coastal sites in the South, the South West, South Wales, the North West and the North East. Although this particular strategy was not to materialize, other schemes in the 1930s certainly did.

A variety of welfare organizations showed an interest in the holiday camp idea. Along the Yorkshire coast, for instance, there was a Co-operative Holiday Association camp at Whitby, and at Hornsea a private firm (Needlers the chocolate-makers of Hull) had established their own camp for employees. In the 1930s the unemployed were not forgotten, but (in the workhouse tradition) strictly one sex at a time. It was women and children only at the Yorkshire Unemployment Advisory Council's camps at Cloughton and Filey. Unemployed men could stay at the Redcar School Camp in August but only in the weeks when no women were booked in.

In contrast to holidays on sufferance, a more progressive scheme was that of the Derbyshire miners. After a lengthy campaign for holidays with pay ('could anything be more absurd ... ?' was the view of one colliery owner in the 1920s) an agreement was reached shortly before the advent of national legislation. This, combined with a Holiday Savings scheme organized by the Derbyshire Mining Association, provided the basis for the miners' own holiday camp by the sea (at Skegness, only a short distance from the first Butlin camp).

Opened in 1939 (and still in business) the Derbyshire Miners Holiday Centre catered at the outset for nearly a thousand visitors a week. A capital sum of £40,000 had been raised by the Miners' Welfare Fund and by contributions from colliery owners. Miners and their families arrived with £4 per week (£3 for single men) from the savings scheme, and the weekly charges were very low. A miner and his wife could enjoy a week's holiday for 33s., with an extra 8s. 6d. for each child, and they also benefited from a special rate negotiated with the railway companies to take them on Sundays to and from Derbyshire and Skegness.

Families lived in chalets ('in a general colour scheme which will be expressive of the holiday spirit') and single visitors were accommodated in what were termed 'cubicles'. Apart from the expansive beach on the doorstep, camp life revolved around the dining-hall (with seating for 500) with its well-regarded cuisine and, when meals were not being served, the nightly concerts and dances. A week at the camp meant good food and fresh air for workers who knew only dust and darkness for most of the year, and a real holiday for their wives who could leave behind their usual tasks and whose 'day of rest and enjoyment [at the centre] begins when she rises.' In its first year, some 15,000 visitors took advantage of what must have been one of the most successful schemes of its kind, and Sir Frederick Sykes (Chairman of the Miners' Welfare Central Committee) was probably right when he claimed that there was nothing comparable and that it was a pioneer venture that was being watched with close interest.

The popularity of these various initiatives in the 1930s, and the continuing demand for cheap holidays encouraged the Trade Union Congress to take a more global look at the potential for more camps. A proposal was considered by the General Council for funds to be invested in a company to be formed jointly by the T.U.C. and the Workers' Travel Association to promote the building of a network of holiday camps and guest-houses throughout the country.

Although the Second World War was to intervene before plans could be implemented, the prospect of the T.U.C. (whose members and their families comprise a quarter of the population, and whose assets numbered millions of pounds) investing in the holiday industry encouraged fierce protests from traditional holiday interests. The plight of the seaside landlady was invoked in a cry of 'unfair competition'. But by 1939 the holiday camp had its own lobby and the legendary landladies, for years the butt of music-hall jokes, were given short shrift....

By 1939 it was estimated that a million and a half people spent their holidays under canvas and in camps of all kinds. But compare this with the figures claimed by the traditional resorts. Blackpool estimated that it had 7 millions a year (including day trippers), Southend 5.5 million, Hastings nearly 3 million, Bournemouth and Southport, 2 million each. All the same, the holiday industry felt that change was coming. Putting publicity claims aside, the resorts were uncomfortably aware that the number of summer visitors was declining year by year. At a meeting in January 1939 of the Chamber of Commerce in Lowestoft, one hotelier declared, 'It is time we faced up to the simple truth. We have got to recognise the competition of holiday camps, continental tours, cruises and motor tours at home. We have arrived at a period of great change and we have got to consider the new methods of taking holidays.'

## PEN-PUSHERS AT PLAY

> When the Gods look down and see the bronzed body of the young labourer they smile. When they see the pale-faced clerk crouched over his desk, they drop tears of sorrow.
> —*The Clerk*, quoted by David Lockwood in *The Blackcoated Worker*, 1958

The envy of the clerkly classes for the physical well-being of the manual labourer was founded on a fallacy. Statistical surveys in the interwar years showed without any doubt that unskilled workers had a lower life-expectation and a higher mortality rate than office workers. But, following the principle that a change is as good as a rest, it was the lower middle-class holidaymakers who most exploited the new opportunities for an active holiday in the sun, housed in tent, hut, cabin, chalet or sun-trap bungalow.

When the Industrial Welfare Society held a conference on Workers' Holidays in 1938, the Society reported that 'Holiday camps, private camping and visiting relations appeared to account for very few. The commercial holiday camp seemed to be hardly used at all by the average worker. Very few go abroad or to the country; fewer still take holidays through organizations such as the Holiday Fellowship, Co-operative Holidays Association, and the Workers' Travel Association.' The proprietors of commercial holiday camps similarly found that their visitors were not drawn from the factory floor but consisted mainly of the smaller salaried people, the black-coated worker and his family.' Even the new Rogerson Hall Holiday Camp, started specifically to extend holiday opportunities to working-class families, was booked up long in advance by school teachers, minor CMI Servants, etc, and the people for whom it was designed were crowded out.

And when Elizabeth Brunner compiled her remarkably informative survey of trends in holidaymaking at the end of the war, the secretary of the Workers' Travel Association told her sadly that 'It does seem to me that one of the disadvantages of present arrangements is that we cannot provide the working man and his wife with a holiday cheap enough to attract them, under decent conditions, and we fill our guest houses with middle-class people. If the WTA had to give a summary of genuine manual workers who went to their holiday centres, I do not think it would amount to 10 per cent.'[19] Two of the large unions of white-collar public employees were the pioneers of trade union holiday camps.

It was W. J. Brown, for many decades the ebullient general secretary of the Civil Service Clerical Association, the largest of the clerical unions, who claimed to have 'quite by chance set going what is now a very big and flourishing industry in Britain—the modern Holiday Camp industry.' He had found, as a parent, that to be at a seaside boarding house in wet weather with young children was 'purgatory', and at the same time he had recollections of the Caister Holiday Camp. He had spent a holiday there as a young man, in a bell tent, which was 'full of discomfort. One had to walk a hundred yards to get water for washing. The only light at night was candlelight; and the food was very poor, and the countryside bleak.'[20]

The idea that occurred to him in the early 1920s was, 'Suppose that instead of a bleak field we could have wooden chalets, with running water and electric light. Suppose we could have a recreation hall for dancing, concerts and the rest. Suppose we could have a place where, wet or fine, the children could make all the noise they liked, in circumstances where they wouldn't upset the adults who wanted quiet? Surely this would be a vast improvement on the seaside boarding house.'

He obtained the approval of his Executive Committee and found a site of wooded gardens by the sea at Corton, which had been laid out with loving care by the mustard magnate Jeremiah Colman. Brown wanted the camp to be a co-operative enterprise, run by his Association on non-profit lines. But then both his Executive and the Branches of the union got cold feet and found the enterprise too risky. 'Very well, I'd do it myself one way or another. I got together a few of my friends, and each of us contributed what we could, a few hundred pounds in all. Then I invited the members to take up shares at £1 a piece at 5 per cent. This raised the derisory figure of about £240. So, my friends having failed me, I went to the "enemy".' By this he meant the chiefs of various government departments, who lent £50 apiece. 'By one means and another we raised enough to justify us in placing an order for the erection of the camp, borrowing the balance from the bank as building got under way, and we had some security to offer. Altogether we spent many thousands of pounds, and we awaited the upshot of the venture with great anxiety.'

The company Brown formed, 'Civil Service Holiday Camps Limited' opened Corton Camp on 7 June 1924, though in the May issue of *Red Tape* he was still urging members to take up shares, which they were not doing 'anything like as rapidly as we hoped they would do.' On the other hand the accommodation was very quickly booked for the summer. The terms were £2.2s a week, with children under 12 at half price. Members were delighted, one of them writing, 'when I heard Brown say during a speech on the camp at Conference, "Corton is as near an earthly paradise as I ever hope to see," I thought he was being carried away by his enthusiasm. After a week at Corton my chief impression is that Brown understated this case. Corton is not "nearly an earthly paradise"—it *is* earthly paradise.'[21]

In the following year, would-be campers were having to be turned away, and it was announced that 'the time has arrived to consider the formation of a further camp on the South or West coasts.' A second site was bought, the Orchard Lease

Estate at Hayling Island, and opened in 1930. It was announced that between 170 and 200 people would be 'very adequately accommodated' and that 'profiting by the results of experiments at Corton, the huts will be built on the detached principle, each from its fellows, and their distribution will be artistically arranged to overcome that feeling of sameness which tends to result from rows of huts.'

The columnist of the Association's journal *Red Tape* glowed over the luxuriousness of the new camp, which he felt had secured 'the absolute maximum of comfort for everyone consistent with not destroying the essential feeling that one is a camper and not a mere resident in a hotel or boarding house.' By now annual reunions of campers were being held in London, and civil servants who booked for Corton in the 1930s found that the original camp could hardly be recognized, so much improved was it. In 1936 it was enlarged to take 200 campers. Prices scarcely rose from their 1920s level all through the decade.

Brown was triumphant, and when the Association's annual conferences were held at Corton, would silence criticism on other issues, by reminding delegates of their lack of faith in the holiday camp venture when he first mooted it. Was he tempted to give up the hectic life of a union boss and become a full-time camp entrepreneur? 'I suppose I should,' he mused, 'have set to work to do, what could easily have been done and has, in fact, been done by others—the building of a chain of such camps. But I confess that a life devoted to the making of money strikes me as the dullest kind of life of all.' He felt that Butlin had imitated his success, but commented that 'in my opinion, (*pace* my friend Bill Butlin) no camp should accommodate more than 500 people. Up to this number a very rich and full corporate life can be achieved. Beyond this number it cannot, and one of the best features of camp life disappears.'

The other union which to this day still operates the first of its holiday centres is NALGO, now the National and Local Government Officers Association. Like W. J. Brown in the CSCA (now CPSA) the officers of the association 'were men of exceptional business flair to which the restricted field of local government gave little scope,' but who were anxious to put it at the service of the union. They were aware that it was the multitude of ancillary services that the union gave to its members that drew potential members to the union and which held them there. Consequently, when at the 1930 conference of NALGO there was a call from the Manchester branch for the union to build a holiday camp for its members, this was both endorsed and eagerly accepted by the National Executive and the honorary treasurer, 'Billy' Lloyd, the borough treasurer of Hampstead. They appointed a committee to look for sites on the south and west coasts. They did not have to look far for the committee chairman W. G. Auger, a sanitary inspector from St. Pancras, had found the 'ideal spot' at Croyde Bay, North Devon, a newly built commercial holiday camp where he had spent his own holiday that year.

> It was perfectly sited on the edge of a deserted, surf-washed beach.
> Sheltered from the north by the whale-backed mass of Baggy Point, from the east by the foothills of Exmoor, from the sea by low sand-dunes, it lay trapped in sunshine and rural peace. It had ninety-five asbestos huts, a recre-

ation room and dining hall, a tennis court and putting green, a garage, and its own electricity plant and artesian well. Auger asked the owners if they were prepared to sell. They were, asking £13,000. NALGO offered £12,000 and the owners accepted the offer, plus £428 for stock. The former manager and assistant manager were taken over, and the camp was opened to members on 2 April 1931.[22]

Fired by this success the NEC itself went to the 1932 Conference seeking authority to acquire a second holiday camp in the north. This was readily given. Within two months, after inspecting ten sites, the Council's 'special activities' committee had agreed to buy one of 94 acres at the top of a wooded cliff at Cayton Bay, south of Scarborough. Before the year ended, plans had been prepared and building begun—for this camp was to be NALGO's own, to its own design. It comprised 124 wooden bungalows, housing 252 guests, plus dining hall, recreation room, billiards room, card room, bowling green, children's playground, and a separate bungalow on the beach below. The camp cost £25,000 and was opened in July 1933.

Croyde Bay was instantly popular, even though for half its pre-war years it had a financial deficit. Almost every post-war year has shown a surplus. Cayton Bay was always less popular and in most years resulted in a deficit. Some members began to criticize the association for concentrating on the 'frills' and not on the bread-and-butter issues of trade unionism. Our informants who as children saw the earliest days of Croyde Bay remember the 'spartan' accommodation but the beautiful surroundings, but in 1937 the wood-and-asbestos huts were replaced by brick bungalows with heating and hot water, and the recreation room by a concert hall with stage and dance-floor. The association's executive committee declared it to be 'several years ahead of any other holiday centre in the country,' for NALGO was one of the first camp operators to change from the title 'camp' to that of 'centre'. In the post-war decades Croyde Bay continued to be popular and profitable, but at Cayton Bay it remained 'difficult to attract a sufficient number of members for profitable operation' and the problem was made worse by a landslip in 1969 which necessitated the removal of eighteen chalets to new positions. The association's Council reported in 1970 that 'Between 1959 and 1979 the substantial profits produced by the Croyde Bay centre have been applied largely to offset losses at Cayton Bay. This has been frustrating to the management of the centre who have clearly demonstrated the ability to operate the centre successfully and profitably but have been unable to utilise the profits for the benefit of the centre.'[23] Already in 1959 the Council had recommended to the annual conference that Cayton Bay should be sold, but a strong lobby of local supporters led the conference to decide that it should be retained and improved.

The issue brought arguments year after year. 'Some members thought it was not a union's role to run holiday centres and wanted to dispose of them. Most members favoured the facilities provided the centres were self-supporting financially. A small core of seasoned campers wanted the centres maintained and enlarged regardless of the cost to the union funds. Such was their enthusiasm for the camps that they fought tenaciously whenever necessary to preserve them.'[24]

A Save Cayton Group was formed, and NALGO members throughout the country were urged to lend their support. An independent site survey and financial appraisal were commissioned, and details were circulated to show that the image of Cayton slipping into the sea, along with the association's money, was quite false. With modest changes in management and refurbishment, an attractive and viable recreational and educational centre could be created. But the campaign failed, and at the end of 1976 the centre was sold for about £100,000.

In spite of its chequered history, the centre is still remembered with affection by former visitors. Alan McDonald was taken as a child to Cayton Bay every year in the 1950s. The children were organized into teams by 'Skipper', and known as Yorkshire Lads or Lancashire Lasses. Each wore a badge with a nickname. As he belonged to the Yorkshire Cricketers, his was Freddie Trueman. He remembers the long walk down to the sea on the winding path through the woods, and he remembers the weekly camp-fire sing-songs which ended, inevitably, with the lugubrious *Goodnight Campers*, a parody of Jack Buchanan's song from the 1930s, *Goodnight Sweetheart*. Croyde Bay remains, completely modernized and rebuilt, as a monument to trade union involvement in the holiday camp adventure.

## CAMPS ON THE RATES

> In the past camps have mainly been provided by voluntary bodies, and public authorities have only been concerned under recent legislation to exercise some measure of supervision. But the camps provided by voluntary agencies by no means meet the great needs of the urban population today, particularly the London population ...
> —Secretary of the Area Committee for National Fitness, 24 May, 1938

Some of the more progressive local authorities also began to look to the holiday camp as a way of bringing relief to people living in unhealthy surroundings. Lambeth Borough Council, for instance, was a pioneering authority in this respect. In 1938 plans were announced for a municipal camp that could offer a week's holiday at a maintenance cost of not more than 45 shillings for adults and less for children. Councillors were told that after the initial costs the camp could be expected to pay for itself and would not be a burden on the ratepayers. As well as being of general social benefit it would also have an important welfare function, with health visitors alerted to identify families in need of a good holiday by the sea.

There was some discussion as to whether a local authority could lawfully involve itself in this form of activity. Reference was made, however, to the Physical Recreation and Training Act, 1937, as a source of intervention and it was also established that the Board of Education could contribute to capital costs. Thus empowered, negotiations were opened for a 50-acre site at Hillborough, Herne Bay and the architects Max Lock and Judith Ledeboer were commissioned to prepare plans. It was envisaged that the site could accommodate up to 500 campers, 400 in chalets and 100 in tents. The huts were to be constructed in timber, using prefabricated sections. As the social focus for the camp, there was to be a community block with facilities for games, recreation and children's play as well as rest rooms.

It was a progressive plan and there was optimism in the air. Lambeth's Alderman Wilmot expressed a common view amongst his fellow councillors when he said he was sure that the municipal camp idea was the beginning of a great development. The London Area Committee of the National Fitness Council promptly called a conference to discuss possible cooperation between all those councils intending to follow the Lambeth example. It was argued that camps so far provided by voluntary agencies fell short of the growing demands of the urban population, particularly in London. Areas of cooperation included ways of preventing competition in acquiring sites, reducing construction costs through placing bulk orders, and achieving a rational distribution of sites.

More than forty local authorities subsequently attended a conference on the theme of Camps for the Nation. Some authorities, like Chesterfield Borough Council, were already making similar plans to those of Lambeth. The focus of concern at the conference was for the 70 per cent of the population who were earning £3 a week or less and who were unable to afford traditional forms of holiday. It was argued that there was little point in legislating for 'holidays with pay' if most people could still not afford to go away for a week. To redress this had become nothing short of a 'national responsibility'.

For local authorities in areas of high unemployment the attraction of holiday camps was especially strong. In this context the Commissioner for the Special Areas in 1938 recommended the building of camps for the mutual assistance of the workers, their children and the unemployed in the distressed areas. Apart from the end product in the form of healthy holidays, the very process of construction could bring relief to the unemployed.

There was certainly, by the end of the 1930s, no shortage of ideas and enthusiasm for camps in one form or another. Undoubtedly, various local authorities would soon have established their own outposts by the sea. In the event, however, the outbreak of war dashed so many of these plans, including that of Lambeth.


## CAMPS FOR THE NATION

> It is all very well for the Hon. Member, in kind and soothing terms to say that if we had these State camps they would do good by advertising holidays. In another sphere he reminded me very much of Hitler. When he walked into Czechoslovakia and took over the country and put its people into concentration camps, he said it was all for their good. When the Government walk in and set up state competition to the holiday industry the Hon. Member says that it is very good for us.
> —Mr. Robinson, in debate on Camps Bill, House of Commons,
> 29 March, 1939

Preparations for war and thoughts of mass evacuation from the cities brought a new and more serious meaning to the idea of the planned camp. In debates on civil defence in 1938 and 1939 the question was addressed as to how and where to relocate children especially from urban areas in the event of a threat of enemy bombing. It was always expected that the great majority of children would be billeted in private homes away from congested areas. At the same time, purpose-built camps were considered as a partial solution, offering the dual benefit of being useful in peacetime as well as in the eventuality of war. To fulfil their implementation the Camps Act was passed in 1939 and the National Camps Corporation Ltd. was established by Parliament.

The very idea of government-sponsored camps was of obvious interest to existing holiday camp operators. Their interest was twofold. As the acknowledged experts in the business of building and managing camps they had a part to play in the government programme. There was also the question of what would happen to the new camps in peacetime, and whether or not the existing operators would find themselves in competition with the State. In Parliamentary debates on the issue there were certainly those on the Opposition benches who welcomed the possibility of a degree of national planning to enable the entire population (including the unemployed and lower-paid) to enjoy a holiday away from home. Others welcomed the possibility of the emergency camps being used for holidays in peacetime, but did not envisage the continuing involvement of the State. It was probably a fair reflection of opinion at that time to claim that 'in this country there is strong and healthy opposition to bureaucratic incursions into the spare time activities of the individual.'[25]

In itself, the idea of planning a network of camps on a national basis attracted support on both sides of the House. Arrangements for evacuation had been found wanting and camps seemed a sensible answer. Criticism was more about the inadequacy of finance to provide a sufficient number of camps to a suitable standard, and about details of design, rather than about whether to have them at all. The pioneer camp lobby welcomed the spread of camps but was opposed in principle to any that were too large. 'Mass camps are not a desirable development in times of peace. In the event of war they would provide targets for enemy action far more vulnerable than any town.' A few politicians, representing seaside towns, also raised a note of dissent. What they feared was the use of government money to create what might become unfair competition with the landladies and small hoteliers in their towns.

This possible growth in State investment was, of course, precisely what others were to welcome. Labour politicians regarded the camps as an overdue measure in social progress although it could at best, as it stood, be regarded only as a small experiment. More camps were needed and in peacetime they should be open to adults as well as for use by schools. The belief was that the need and demand for well-planned holiday camps was well in excess of what the government had indicated.

A month before the outbreak of the Second World War the Minister of Health reported on progress to date. At that time there were plans for between thirty and forty camps in England and Wales, each to be built at a cost of £20,000. One hundred and fifty-five sites had been investigated and thirty had been found suitable. For strategic reasons they were all in the countryside rather than along the coast. There had been some discussion about the ideal size of camps (with early plans for as many as 10,000 in a single camp) but a maximum of about 350 in each case was the general target.

Design and construction was standardized through the National Camps Corporation. Swedish-style timber hutments were favoured, using Canadian cedar with cedar shingle roofs. The units were standardized and contracts were shared between four firms.

In spite of a call to see the camps used for family holidays in peacetime, the National Camps Corporation was required to give first preference to education authorities who could use them as school camps. Politicians spoke euphorically of the prospect of giving every child a holiday in the country. It was regarded as a social experiment, and there were ' ... substantial hopes that these camps would be the means of building up a fit race; fit not only in body, but fit as citizens.'[26]

By the end of the 1930s, then, the potential moral and social contribution of camps to the life of the nation (which had always been a part of the debate surrounding their origins) had acquired a new meaning. The imminence of war created its own priorities, and camp planning could no longer be left to the mere whim of individuals and voluntary organizations. Inevitably, the State was itself drawn into the business of what had previously seemed a marginal issue. In 1939 there seemed little likelihood that in peace time the State would wish to retain a major interest. Yet the fact was already noted that camps, of all forms of holiday provision, lend themselves to an overall system of planning. And, in the ensuing years, when State planning became more widely understood and accepted, the possibility of a continuing role in this field became distinctly less remote. Though anathema to some, the idea of State holiday camps appealed to others as a practical means to bring the rhetoric of holidays for all into the realms of reality.

## HAPPY CAMPERS

> Old campers, I am sure all agree that the real camp spirit, which counts for more than anything else, cannot be found in the 'Town' Camps. The smaller camps will continue to maintain and strengthen their hold on the real camper, who, once a camper, is always a camper.
> —Camp pioneer, H. E. Potter, in *Holiday Camp Review*, May, 1939

The pioneer camps, then, had come a long way in the 1930s. In 1938 the Labour politician George Lansbury could rightly claim that 'holiday camps are now part of our national life.' As a socialist, though, he added a note of reservation, observing that it was not like other parts of Europe where 'Governments organize this and other social efforts'.[27]

Before the 1930s examples had been few, and with their rudimentary conditions some were more akin to army camps than holiday centres. By the end of the decade there were more camps, the range was more diverse and the standards had improved enormously. Each year more people visited a holiday camp (the figure was some 30,000 for all types of commercial camp in 1939) and although it was still a minority form of holidaymaking the trend was clear.

National Camps Corporation sites, 1939

Various factors had contributed to their growth in this period. Throughout the 1930s (with the help of the 1938 Holidays with Pay Act) more people were taking a holiday away from home. Although manual workers suffered long periods of unemployment, for artisans and white-collar workers it was a time of rising incomes—enough, at least, to pay for a week if not a fortnight at a camp.

Getting away to the sea with its 'bracing air' and open skies was also a fashionable and enviable thing to do. 'Wishing you were here' had real meaning for those left behind in the dreary, smoke-laden environment of the industrial cities. The omnibus also played its part in carrying families with their luggage from the railway station to the holiday camp that would invariably be away from established centres.

And, finally, the pioneer camps also benefited from the growing involvement and investments by the labour movement and local authorities in welfare issues.

More, though, than simply profiting from external circumstances the pioneer camps were nourished on a reputation of their own. Happy campers returned from one year to the next, and word spread that this was the way to spend a holiday. 'It is something good in life and needs to be exercised to the full ... The Holiday Camp ministers to every rational need of entertainment and healthful recreation at a cost which is well within the means of millions of people.'

In fact, the cost claim was true in one sense but it was also true that many with lower incomes were still excluded. Particularly as facilities were improved weekly rates were raised to a level that was beyond the reach of many working people. At a time when the average wage was about £3 weekly, holiday camp charges of about 50 shillings each made it very difficult to take a family. In the 1930s holiday campers were more likely to be clerks and skilled workers than dock labourers and factory hands. Another problem in terms of securing the best use of the camps was that of the people who could afford to pay many took the cheaper accommodation. While the problem was not easily soluble there was agreement that a means test would be objectionable while, in any case, the segregation of poorer holidaymakers was undesirable.

For the lucky ones, though, it seemed like fun all the way. The story of 'T.S.' a 23-year old clerk, printed under the heading 'First Time at a camp but Going Back for More' is typical:

> I am a clerk, 23 years of age, of good health and hearty appetite. Last year I went to a holiday camp for the first time ...
>
> I arrived on a Saturday evening after a sticky and crowded train journey (I found afterwards that I could have gone by coach but it never occurred to me).
>
> I won't say that the management brought out the red carpet and brass band because they didn't, but I was met immediately by a very pleasant manager chap who saw that I got a good meal right away. Then I was shown to my hut, a roomy enough place with running water.
>
> I found that I was in time for the regular evening dance and after a quick change I beetled in to survey my fellow campers.
>
> There were two or three hundred dancing. You know how it is when you walk right in among a crowd of strangers? Fortunately no one tried to introduce me to anyone—because I hate that sort of gushiness. Makes you feel a fool.
>
> It wasn't long before I was dancing and the company looked pretty good.
>
> At breakfast next morning I got to know a decent crowd of chaps who were sitting at my table. We quickly arranged a foursome at tennis and by the time I had met a lot of others swimming and sun-bathing on the beach I felt thoroughly at home.
>
> I've rambled on like this just to show that there's nothing like a holiday camp for good companionship. It's easy to get to know people, everybody's friendly and there's plenty of social life.

The campers elected a committee to organize all sorts of events and the management helped in every possible way. We had physical jerks before breakfast for the energetic early-risers, sports, tennis and ping-pong tournaments, beach games, rambles, cricket matches, sing-songs, whist drives and concerts. In fact there was something doing every minute of the day and the beauty of it was that if you wanted to be alone there was plenty of room to do it in—if you know what I mean.

We got up to all sorts of stunts—we found moonlight rambles and moonlight bathing highly popular and with the help of a BBC artist and a group of amateur actors we put on a revue that would have made Cochran himself sit up.

I stayed for two weeks and was pretty fed up at having to go back to work. The whole holiday cost me not a penny more than ten pounds. There was £2 10s. a week for the camp, about 30/- railway fares and the rest on personal expenses. There were absolutely no extras at the camp—all games and sports were free, although we sometimes subscribed sixpence each for our tournaments.

And £10 for a fortnight's holiday, living right on the edge of the sea and feeding like fighting-cocks is, I submit, pretty good value for money.

That's why I shall be going again this year. I'll be seeing you![28]

Different advocates cited more specific advantages of holiday camps. 'C.J.' was a doctor in Manchester who each year not only prescribed the restorative qualities of a week at a camp but like many other doctors he knew, took his own medicine to spend his own holidays in this way. In medical terms, camps were the perfect antidote to urban life—offering the means for rest, fresh air and a wholesome diet. For many of his patients—'the victims of bad housing, poor food, and indifferent factory conditions'—a stay in a camp would have been of more value than any medicine he could prescribe. But 'as it is, the majority are too poor to pay even the modest charges of a camp. I have, however, been instrumental in inducing scores of better-placed patients to visit camps. They all came back to thank me ... '[29]

, ....Another interesting claim for holiday camps was that they offered a fair deal for women. Pamela Frith of Putney was a typist, 'not a rabid feminist' but someone who found it 'annoying to have so many men admiring the hat that I have on my head instead of appreciating the thoughts inside my head.' In camps (like Peter Howarth said about classes) everyone was treated equally. 'At a camp alone a woman gains that pleasing sense of equality. The girl of 8, the maiden of 18, the grandma of 80 rank with the boy, youth and grandpa without any sort of distinction. They are campers first, last and all the time. Age and sex do not matter.

# 4. IMAGES OF CHILDHOOD IN OLD POSTCARDS

For about forty years the postcard served the same purpose that the telephone does today. It was a cheap, very convenient and incredibly quick way of sending a message. Plain cards were first issued as a Post Office monopoly. Picture cards were legalized in Britain in 1894, more than twenty years after their first use in continental Europe. The earliest pictures were small, with the message on the same side and the address and stamp on the reverse. In 1902 the 'divided back' was allowed and the golden age of the picture postcard began.

Available everywhere, usually for one old halfpenny, or at most twopence for 'real photographic cards', until 1918 they cost only a ha'penny to send. That year the doubling of the cost of the stamp, combined with the end of the First World War, halved the number of postcards sent. But the outstanding fact about the postcard years is the unbelievable speed of delivery. There were several collections and deliveries each day.

A card could be sent to the butcher in the morning requesting that a shoulder of lamb or a pound of sausages to be delivered for supper the same night; or one could ask to be met at the station from the 6.15 p.m. train. If you went on journey you could instantly announce your safe arrival.

Naturally an industry arose to serve this boom in instant communication. National firms produced cards for sale everywhere. Local photographers, printers and artists, found a ready market for both 'real' photographs in the days when newspapers were not yet able to reproduce them, and, as printing techniques advanced, for lithographic and half-tone reproductions of their work. They bought ready-printed photographic cards and almost as a matter of course produced family photographs and local events in postcard form.

The picture postcard became *the* popular means of recording any scene or news from fires and railway accidents to church outings and school parties, as well as the vehicle for universal sentiments and greetings.

Beyond these, what should the subject be? Obviously the first choice was topographical. Here we are at Beachy Head, or this is the High Street of Barrow-in-Furness. 'X' marks our room in the boarding-house at Rhyl. They went further. In the days before any new building development anywhere was seen as environmental disaster, the local photographer was busy recording each new street or shopping parade. Plenty of prints would be bought by the new residents or shopkeepers. ...

Very early on in postcard history, however, came cards with universal themes:

---

Originally printed in Colin Ward and Tim Ward, *Images of Childhood in Old Postcards*. (Stroud: Alan Sutton Publishing, 1991).

flowers, animals, motherhood and, above all, childhood. The comic postcard also made an early appearance: the joke to be shared between the sender and the recipient. ... Even today, seventy-five years after the postcard's heyday, on the wall of any workplace you can see a collection of current postcards from colleagues on holiday. The picture postcard survives as a way of saying 'Yes, I'm still thinking of you'. ...

Children were everywhere in the street scene of Edwardian Britain, partly because families were larger and secondly because the years of schooling were shorter. Until the end of the First World War most children left school by the age of thirteen out of economic necessity; their income was vital for the family budget. Girls would join the army of domestic servants, boys would become errand or delivery lads, always visible in the streets, or 'learners' (as opposed to apprentices) in industry or retail trade, to be sacked at the moment when they became entitled to an adult wage.

Postcards accidentally revealed another reason for the presence of children on the streets: it was a time when everyone enjoyed the freedom of the street. Before the surrender of the highway to the private motorist it was natural to pause for a conversation in the middle of the road, stepping out of the way of horse-drawn traffic and trams, and it was equally natural for children to play skipping games, hopscotch, football or cricket in the street, only grudgingly steeping aside to let the traffic through. Today few urban parents are happy at the thought of their children playing in the street, and most children with access to a bicycle are told by their parents not to use it in the street. It is a freedom that has had to be surrendered because of the revolution in transport.

There is a fourth reason why old postcards are full of children. Poor people, even as late as the Second World War, lived at population densities which now seem beyond belief. There were areas of Paddington with 400 people to the acre and in Glasgow with as many as 900 inhabitants to the acre. Children were doing the whole family a service by spending most of their waking hours outside the home. Whether the photographer wanted them or not, they were there.

In the years before radio and television, when even the cinema was in its infancy, the street itself was a theatre of drama and excitement. It was populated with peddlers, traders and hawkers. ...

Most people associate the postcard with the seaside. It is from here that many were posted. Even day-trippers, before the institution of holidays with pay, never failed to send cards to relations. Apart from comic cards with saucy jokes, there were instant pictures from the photographer on the promenade, and booths where the family poked their head through a painted scene of boats, beaches, bi-planes or the Ghost Train. There were also ready-made themes, like shells, buckets-and-spades, sand-castles, bathing machines and Punch and Judy shows. Children were seen as natural subjects of the seaside postcard. ...

Historians became interested in postcards as direct evidence of the past. And images of childhood gradually emerged as one of the most significant aspects of this historical legacy. As children are seldom free to make their own decisions, they reveal the way our predecessors expected children to behave, how they were dressed or undressed, their place in the economy, their education, their leisure

both as arranged for them and as they made it themselves. All this evidence is filtered through the market that local or national postcard producers operated. But
charitable organisations were there to present another side of childhood in order
to arouse sympathy and support. ...

## BIG DAYS AND FESTIVALS
In the days before the mass media and the family car, every city, town and village had
a series of big events, all eagerly awaited by children. There was the fair, sometimes
several throughout the seasons, like the Martinmas hirings, where farm servants,
including children were engaged for the year, and celebrations like Plough Monday,
when children blacked their faces with soot and demanded pennies, and festivals
like Easter and Whitsun. All over Lancashire there was a Walking Day with huge
processions of Sunday school children, dressed in white clothes and carrying banners and flowers, led by brass bands. Pamela Horn records how: "Varying from parish to parish, other dates were kept for events of considerable *local* significance, like
the Shrove Tuesday orange throwing at Oving in Buckinghamshire or the rather
tougher fun enjoyed by youngsters in Somerset, Devon and Dorset on that day ...
Here it was the custom for the children to go about after dusk, and throw stones
against people's doors, by what was considered by them an indefeasible right," and
she tells how, during the Harvest Festival season one village schoolmaster wrote
with gentle irony in the school log book, "This is the fifth thanksgiving the children
have left school to attend. Truly we are a thankful people."

There were enormous celebrations in the cities, like the annual fair on the
Town Moor in Newcastle, or the Nottingham Goose Fair, which until 1927 was
held in the Market Square in the city centre. Travelling circuses toured the country, as did amusement fairs with helter-skelters, roundabouts with fairground organs, the big dipper and endless sideshows. It was actually Billy Butlin who introduced the dodgem car to Britain in 1928.

Ancient festivals like May Day, with the crowning of a May Queen, also became Labour festivals with big processions led by the elaborate trade union banners, which were paraded at huge events like the Durham Miners' Gala. Secular
feasts like the annual roasting of an ox or Bonfire Night were intertwined with
religious occasions involving children: first communions or the installation of a
boy bishop.

Royal celebrations like coronations and jubilees provided excuses for firework
displays, demonstrations of loyalty and street parties. Empire Day gave an opportunity for a school holiday and parades by every uniformed organisation in the
town, juvenile or adult. It was as though there was a hunger for events in a drab
world. They were all accompanied by music in the days when few homes had a
gramophone and none had a radio.

Children had a big part in all these pageants, parades and festivals. Parents
saved and scraped to ensure that there were new dresses or new boots for the big
occasions. Girls and boys were at the centre of the stage in the carnival float, the
gymnastic display or the annual sports day. Even if they were only spectators they
were pushed to the front of the crowd to get a better view.

The postcard photographers seized the opportunities provided by high days and holidays. Their cards were on sale before any picture could appear in the local paper, and if your particular contribution was recorded, or if your children could be identified in the picture, you would certainly buy copies to post to everyone. Winning teams, prize-winners and little local champions were rounded up by the photographer to be immortalized for posterity.

# 5. WHOSE ENVIRONMENT?

*"I do not know whether all my readers will see whither this suggested inquiry will lead us; but this I do know, if Émile returns from his travels begun and continued with this end in view, without a full knowledge of questions of government, public morality, and political philosophy of every kind, we are greatly lacking, he in intelligence and I in judgement."*

—Jean-Jacques Rousseau, *Émile*

There is no school subject known as 'environmental education' in the sense that there is a subject called 'physical education' and one called 'religious education'. There is in some schools a subject called environmental studies, heavily biased in most instances to what used to be called rural studies. A variety of examination syllabuses are in use or in prospect, all with an emphasis on the 'bio-physical' as opposed to the 'socio-industrial' aspects of the environment. The widening scope of the subject involves taking elements from several existing subject areas, and drawing on the services of several specialist teachers, when they are available.

But environmental education has a much wider connotation and the truth is that any school subject can be taught in an academic way, without reference to the human habitat, or it can be taught in a way which seeks to enhance the pupils' understanding of, and concern for, their environment: geography, history, chemistry, physics, biology, art, music, English, maths, religious education; all can contribute. Whether they do or not depends on the personal priorities, understanding and ingenuity of the teacher. Like most observers of the English educational scene I am convinced that the best environmental work is being done in the primary schools, mercifully free from the vested interests of subject sub-division. I am delighted when one of my children brings home from the local primary school evidence of its environmentally-based work. I am appalled when another brings from his secondary school (one of the famous London comprehensives) R.E. homework based on Old Testament mumbo-jumbo (what do the Hindu and Muslim children get, I wonder?) when I would expect that at this stage of educational sophistication, that period would be used to explore the principle of Reverence for Life, the basis of environmental education, however it is defined.

What you expect a school to be able to provide in the way of environmental education depends on the nature of your own concern with the environment. If

Originally printed in Colin Ward and Anthony Fyson, *Streetwork: The Exploding School.* (London: Routledge & Kegan Paul, 1973).

you are a supporter of the Society for the Preservation of Rural England, you will want people to be educated to regard as their highest priority the visual aspects of the countryside. If you are a supporter of the Civic Trust you will want them to be taught to cherish the visual aspects of the urban scene. If you are a member of the Conservation Society you will want them to learn to oppose tin mining in Cornwall, reservoirs on Dartmoor and to remember that *Overpopulation is YOUR Baby*. If you are one of the Friends of the Earth you will want to persuade them that an ecological catastrophe is round the corner unless we change our habits and cease to exploit and pollute our planet. If you are a bird lover you will want them to protect birds. If you belong to Keep Britain Tidy you will want them to learn to do just that.

Whatever emphasis is given to environmental education, some of us are going to be disappointed. Perhaps, to get our aims in perspective, we should see the situation in historical terms. It is a hundred years and more since elementary education became free, compulsory and universal and we celebrated the anniversary by inventing a new word: de-schooling. A hundred years ago we made none of these inflated demands on education. It was a matter of teaching them to read, write and figure, and to praise God. Government was in the hands of the governing classes, land-use was a matter for landlords, local administration was in the hands of local bigwigs and their subservient officers. There was no question of public participation in planning—market forces were regarded as the ultimate arbiter. There was no question of the over-use of the national parks. The great unwashed did not drive out in their motor cars to picnic in beauty spots—a rather vulgar concept which had only recently been invented by Wordsworth and had not yet filtered down to the wrong people. Only people of approved sensibility went there (usually to slaughter the birds) apart from the local peasants, who were itching to move to an industrial slum and earn a living wage. Neither did their beastly bungalows disfigure the sea-coast, nor were their dustbins filled forty per cent with discarded packaging material. People stayed at home in their overcrowded rookeries, walked to work, and made few demands on their environment.

A hundred years later, everything is different. We have a mass society where everyone has the expectation of going everywhere and doing everything. (The expectation is unfulfilled of course, and is unfulfillable on this planet, but it is there.)

But the old paternalistic attitudes are there too. The aristocrats have interbred with the technocrats, and we are still in a world where one lot of people make the decisions and another lot abide by them, or sabotage them. What should our aim be in environmental education? To educate for mastery of the environment: nothing less than that. We are in the early stages of moving from a formal democracy to a participatory democracy, in which people cherish their environment because it is *theirs*.

The organisations of teachers concerned with environmental education are inevitably preoccupied with the definition of their subject-matter. One widely-accepted definition (the 'Nevada declaration') is that:

> Environmental Education is the process of recognising values and clarifying concepts in order to develop skills and attitudes necessary to understand and

appreciate the interrelatedness among man, his culture and his biophysical surroundings. Environmental Education also entails practice in decision-making, and self-formulation of a code of behaviour about issues concerning environmental quality.[30]

This is a good definition, even though it may seem a little remote from the daily concerns of the urban teacher or pupil. There is one basic distinction of course between those who see the environment as an object of study in its own right, and those who see it as a medium for the study of the standard subjects of the school curriculum. At a more analytical level, D. G. Watts, in his valuable survey of the claims made for environmental studies, distinguishes at least five overlapping but different possible definitions, 'the whole experience of the child; the character of the school features of the classroom and the school used in active learning; the physical and social characteristics of the child's home, neighbourhood, and wider world; and features of the neighbourhood and natural surroundings used in teaching.'[31]

This book is concerned with the last two of Mr Watts's definitions, but as the title implies, it confines itself to the urban environment. No apology is needed for this. Well over eighty per cent of our children live in urban surroundings and well over ninety per cent are taught in urban schools. And yet most environmental teaching ignores the built environment. There is a perfectly reasonable argument of course that education on rural matters is doubly important for the town child. As Rousseau (who expressed most of our educational thoughts two hundred years ago) remarked, 'Two schoolboys from the town will do more damage in the country than all the children of the village.' But we are concerned here with the education of active *citizens*, and where can this be undertaken if not in the city?

Formulators of ideal environments, from Thomas More to Paul Goodman, have been quite specific about the rural education of the urban child: they saw the town children spending the summer months *working* on the farm—the educative effect was an incidental accompaniment. The nearest thing in real life when I was a boy was the annual migration of families from East and South-East London to the hop fields of Kent: three weeks of sun and air and merriment in a holiday which paid for itself and 'set you up for the winter.' Mechanisation and affluence have put an end to that, but what is the rural education of the hoppers' grandchildren? A trip to a 'stately home', to wander, like moujiks shuffling beneath the painted ceilings of the Winter Palace, through some fully certificated bit of 'our architectural heritage', followed by a fleeting glimpse of the lions in the paddock. It has as much to do with environmental education as a visit to Snow White's palace in Disneyland. Fortunately the journey there and back might provide a few thrills.

Arthur Razzell, in his book *Juniors*, has caught beautifully in an urban context the difference between the environmental education that is intended, and the incidental education that actually happens. He is describing a visit to the Tower of London by a party of ten-year-olds from a 'deprived' area in London:

> For the children it was quite clearly an 'outing', in all the wonderful cockney meanings of the word. Everyone, right back to grandmother, knew what an

outing involved, and the children were ready to extract the maximum amount of pleasure from it. The teacher, on the other hand, had planned an 'educational visit' with great care, and it was to form part of the work that the class was doing on castles. She had carefully duplicated some excellent quiz sheets, on the lines of the 'I-Spy' books, and each child had a copy to complete on arrival at the Tower.

What the children enjoyed most was the Underground, with the thrill of the moving staircase. In their writing which followed the visit, they recorded at great length, the journey to and from the Tower, with every smallest detail described and dwelt upon—the warm rushing wind that preceded the arrival of the train, the automatic doors, the distinctive smell, the fear they felt at the rush of the train into the station, the smallness of the tube into which the train fitted, the signal cables that appeared to wobble up and down as the train sped past them, the automatic ticket machines, described as being 'worth four pence just to hear them whirr and the ticket poke out.' This list could be continued, but I query whether any other age-group in the human race could observe so vividly or so passionately the variety of things which those children saw and recorded. 'Cor, I'm going to save up a million pounds to buy one of them machines to have in my home!'

The teacher was mature enough not to feel despondent; the Bloody Tower would keep. The children had absorbed from the visit the things which were meaningful and had interest to them at that particular stage of their development. They were not inattentive during their time at the Tower, and they did all that was expected of them. However, when invited to write and talk about their experiences they selected those things which seemed significant to them, and they wrote with fluency, involvement and enthusiasm. However much the teacher may have desired them to attend to the details of Norman castle construction, she was wise enough to work 'with eyes unclouded by longing', and she took and built upon the interests of her children. The study of London's Underground service lasted on and off for several weeks, and the teacher herself now claims to be something of an authority on the subject.[32]

Mr Razzell's little anecdote has all the profundity of Tolstoy's educational fables from the school at Yasnaya Polyana.

The child is *right*. He extracts from the educational visit an education in *city sense*: the transport system and how to manipulate it, something more intrinsically interesting than the excesses of dead kings and castle builders.

The Council for Environmental Education in its report to the 'Countryside in 1970' Conference referred to schools 'exploding into the environment'.[33] In this book they explore some of the implications of this idea in an urban setting. There was never a more apposite moment for such an explosion. For there is not only a crisis of confidence in the school system; there is also a crisis of confidence in the wisdom of the decision-makers who shape our urban environment. Ideas are in the air today which could transform our whole conception of the school and of its place in the community.

I am referring of course to the *de-schoolers*, a catchword to describe a number of educational theorists who, thinking both locally and globally, have attacked the very idea of the school, some key works in this movement being those by Paul Goodman, Ivan Illich, Everett Reimer and Keith Paton.[34] Nothing could be more mistaken than the tendency to dismiss the ideas they represent as a passing fad. They have raised questions which may change the whole course of the continuing debate on education. The deschoolers make a number of radical criticisms of the school system which has evolved in all countries, rich and poor, seeing the institutionalisation of education as a means of preventing people from educating themselves. They decry schools as special and expensive structures for containing education, and teachers as special people licensed to accomplish this process. We have all met pretentious aldermen who announce at speech days that they were educated in the School of Life: they have now found unexpected allies who have turned their autobiography into ideology.

Our concern here is with their impact on environmental education, where they have already provided us with a fund of experiences and ideas. The Parkway Education Program in the city of Philadelphia[35] has been in operation for three years, supported and funded by the local education authority. Students are not handpicked but are chosen by lottery from a waiting list of applicants from the eight geographically-determined school board districts of the city, who are in grades nine to twelve (i.e. ages 14–18) regardless of academic or behavioural background. There is no school building. Each of the eight units or 'communities' (which operate independently) has a headquarters with office space for staff and lockers for students. All teaching takes place within the community: the search for facilities is considered to be part of the process of education: 'The city offers an incredible variety of learning labs: art students study at the Art Museum, biology students meet at the Zoo; business and vocational courses meet at on-the-job sites such as journalism at a newspaper, or mechanics at a garage .... The Program pays for none of its facilities, but instead looks for "wasted space", space which is maintained twenty-four hours a day, but is in use perhaps less than five or six of those hours. Students, then, in going from class to class, will travel around the city (normally on foot). There is a student-teacher ratio of 16:1 and for every teacher a "university intern" is added to the staff.' The Parkway Program claims that:

> Although schools are supposed to prepare students for a life in the community, most schools so isolate students from the community that a functional understanding of how it works is impossible. Few urban educators now deny that large numbers of students are graduating from our urban secondary schools unprepared for any kind of useful role in society. Since society suffers as much as the students from the failures of the educational system, it did not seem unreasonable to ask the community to assume some responsibility for the education of its children.

The Parkway Program, directed by John Bremer (formerly of Leicester University Department of Education), was followed a year later by Chicago's Metro

High School (Chicago Public High School for Metropolitan Study) which operates from:

> Three leased floors of an old office building in a decayed commercial area on the south edge of 'The Loop,' Chicago's central business district. Metro has also been given the use of one or two rooms in each of several office buildings and two churches scattered around the Loop. Buses and trains (underground and elevated) provide good access between the Loop and most other parts of Chicago....Metro's students are selected from among applicants by a lottery, taking an equal number from each school district in Chicago and, overall, an equal number of boys and girls. The resulting student body is a cross-section of the city's youth—from black slum and public housing residents to affluent whites—except that all are motivated to try this new school. For some the motivation is positive: they think Metro will be more fun, more interesting and rewarding than the conventional high schools they would otherwise attend. For many, the motivation is negative: to escape from bad schools, neighbourhoods dominated by violent gangs, personal problems etc. Metro offers a full-length (four-year) high school program and has the same requirements for graduation as any other Chicago high school ... but within each of these categories there is considerably more freedom of choice than in normal high schools.[36]

A similar project. Métro Éducation Montréal seeks to use that city's underground railway as the central corridor for the same kind of activity—since it is not used to capacity and gives rapid access to a variety of under-used facilities throughout the city centre. People have been approached to give an hour a week to teaching the young about their work. All the necessary equipment for an education system already exists: cinemas are empty all morning, there is vacant office-space, under-used computer centres, restaurants, libraries, clinics and laboratories.[37]

Lucky Montreal, to have an under-used Metro! One could hardly recommend the use of the London Underground for this purpose, in spite of Arthur Razzell's story of its educative function, although he has reminded us in *Teachers' World* that 'when the London County Council was responsible for both education and the operation of the London tramways, schools were issued with books of vouchers enabling children and teachers to travel freely on the trams during the period of normal schooling.' Well, although the trams have long since gone (and we are beginning on daring experiments with bus lanes) London Transport is now under the control, at last, of the Greater London Council, from which the Inner London Education Authority is not entirely divorced. Mr Razzell remarks that although the railways have been nationalised for almost three decades, we have still not learned to regard them as People's Trains. 'As a result, our railways have never been seriously considered as an available national resource capable of being more fully utilised in the cause of education, despite the fact that the taxpayer who pays for education is also the taxpayer who owns the railways.' Just to indicate how narrow our definition is of educational resources, he remarks that a recent major research project on resources for learning thought almost exclusively in terms of resources which were capable of being *introduced into the classroom*! Ought we not, he asks, to be planning for a major proportion of every child's education to take place beyond the confines of a school building?

These reflections lead us to another fruitful idea which is fashionable now: that of the community school. (None of these notions is new of course—the community school was the whole basis of Henry Morris's educational philosophy, and was put into practice fifty years ago in the most unpromising of circumstances by the remarkable head of a Lancashire elementary school, Edward O'Neil of Prestolee.) We talk a lot today of the idea that the school premises and facilities represent a community resource that should be available for other people besides those within the statutory age range, and that others besides teachers have an educative function in it. But there is an important corollary to this eminently sensible point of view. Just as the school should be open to the community, so should the community be open to the school. The argument is well put in the description I have quoted of the Parkway Project. All the resources of the community are educational resources. It ought to be taken for granted that the school has a claim on the factories, warehouses, offices, transport depots, municipal departments, supermarkets and sewage plants of the town. As it is of course, so hermetically sealed are our educational institutions that schools seldom have recourse to the specialist facilities of other schools controlled by the same authority. One primary school, embarking on an environmental project, a study of the effect of herbicides on roadside verges, was baulked by a lack of chemical expertise and apparatus—which it eventually found was readily available in the neighbouring secondary school. But how often does the secondary school have access to the facilities of the technical college, the polytechnic or the university? Open schools in an open city is the logical slogan for the community school.

Another contemporary trend which leads us to consider the potentialities of the exploding school is the crisis of community consciousness. The last few years have seen a fantastic flowering of locally-based bodies, amenity societies, community action groups, tenants' and residents' associations. Their newspapers and newsletters proliferate, and their activism is in striking contrast to the general level of apathy towards and disillusionment with the 'official' structure of local politics. The school, apart from hiring out its hall for meetings, is aloof from these stirrings of citizenship, even though its catchment area often provides the physical delineation of the neighbourhood, and even though much of our contact with neighbours arises from our common situation of parenthood. Shouldn't the school become the Enquiring School, and its students the local researchers who service the community with information on rents, traffic densities, current planning proposals, employment prospects, and so on? One of the discussion panels at the York Conference on Social Deprivation and Change in Education recommended that 'pupils ought, through problem-oriented community projects, to become involved in the actual problems of the local community. The results could be passed on to adults for appropriate action.'[38]

All these current tides of thought about the role of the school in its immediate neighbourhood are significant for the expectations we have of environmental education, its subject matter, its methods, and the kind of exploration which the school makes of the environment. They are important above all for what we have learned to call the *affective domain* of education where we are concerned with the attitudes and values which our students adopt. What do we want them to discover, think and feel about the built environment? Why does it matter? 'Civic education' says Bernard Crick, in an important paper quoted in the next chapter, 'must be aimed at creating citizens. If we want a passive population, leave well alone.'

# 6. THE ANARCHISTS AND SCHOOLS

My political attitude is that of anarchism, which in the definition written for the *Encyclopaedia Britannica* by its best-known spokesman, Peter Kropotkin, is "the name given to a principle or theory of life and conduct under which society is conceived without government—harmony in such a society being obtained, not by submission to law, or by obedience to any authority, but by free agreements concluded between the various groups, territorial and professional, freely constituted for the sake of production and consumption, as also for the satisfaction of the infinite variety of needs and aspirations of a civilised being".[39]

Such an ideology is bound to have implications for anarchist attitudes to schools and schooling, and indeed the editors of one of the many recent anthologies of anarchist writings remark that from the school prospectus issued by William Godwin in 1783 to Paul Goodman's book of 1964 *Compulsory Miseducation*, "anarchism has persistently regarded itself as having distinctive and revolutionary implications for education. Indeed, no other movement whatever has assigned to educational principles, concepts, experiments and practices a more significant place in its writings and activities".[40] This remark is amply justified, yet when I was first asked to talk on this topic at the Institute of Education, there was hardly anything in its vast library to which I could refer my listeners for a quick conspectus of anarchist opinions on schools and schooling. But while the educational climate has worsened, the range of accessible literature on anarchist views and experiences has widened, and this is why I'm handing out a booklist of half a dozen recent books in the hope that you will seek them out.

To my mind the most impressive anarchist philosopher of education was the earliest: William Godwin (1756–1836), who is best known as the husband of Mary Wollstonecraft and the father of Mary Shelley. When I trained as a teacher in the 1960s, I resolved to write my dissertation on his educational ideas, and quickly found that the then standard textbooks like *Doctrines of the Great Educators* made no mention of him and that, apart from his *Enquiry Concerning Political Justice*, now a Penguin Classic, it was dauntingly hard to get a sight of facsimiles or photocopies of his specifically educational writings.[41] Happily, his best recent biographer, Peter Marshall, has included a good selection of them in his book of extracts from Godwin.[42] His critics described him as "cold as ice" but

Originally printed in Colin Ward, *Talking Schools*. (London: Freedom Press, 1995), 9–20. Based on a lecture at the Institute of Education, University of London, May 1975, updated in 1994.

his educational proposals reveal him to be as passionately "on the side of the child" as Mary Wollstonecraft, and I have suggested that someone who enjoys that kind of research might analyse the influences on each other of these remarkable propagandists for the freedom of children.[43]

Godwin's first educational tract was published in 1783 as *An account of the seminary that will be opened on Monday the Fourth Day of August, at Epsom in Surrey, for the Instruction of Twelve Pupils*. It failed to convince enough parents and the school never opened. In this pamphlet he declared that "modern education not only corrupts the heart of our youth, by the rigid slavery to which it condemns them, it also undermines their reason by the unintelligible jargon with which they are overwhelmed in the first instance, and the little attention that is given to accommodating their pursuits to their capacities in the second". And he added that "there is not in the world a truer object of pity than a child terrified at every glance and watching with anxious uncertainty the caprices of a pedagogue".

He did not believe in a solitary education at home, nor did he want large schools. If he had lived 200 years later he would be a supporter of the National Association for the Support of Small Schools. He wanted the advantages of a social community, not in order to arouse the spirit of competition but because of the importance of *socialisation* in childhood: "I would wish to see the connection of pupils consisting only of pleasure and generosity. They should learn to love and not to hate each other."

Godwin's book *The Enquirer* of 1797 contains, as Peter Marshall rightly says, "some of the most remarkable and advanced ideas on education ever written". Its first words are the splendid affirmation that "the true object of education, like that of every other moral process, is the generation of happiness". And it goes on to assert the rights of the child against the automatic assumptions of authority of the adult world. I could quote his eighteenth-century rhetoric all night, but will content myself with one observation:

> Children, it is said, are free from the cares of the world. Are they without their cares? Of all cares, those that bring with them the greatest consolation are the cares of independence. There is no more certain source of exultation than the consciousness that I am of some importance in the world. A child usually feels that he is nobody. Parents, in the abundance of their providence, take good care to administer to them this bitter recollection. How suddenly does a child rise to an enviable degree of happiness, who feels that he has the honour to be trusted and consulted by his superiors?[44]

Between these two resounding manifestos came Godwin's most famous book, his *Enquiry Concerning Political Justice* in 1793. In the course of this book he diverged sharply from progressive opinion in Britain and from the Enlightenment philosophers Rousseau, Helvetius, Diderot and Condorcet, all of whom put forward schemes for national systems of schooling, postulating an ideal state, which in Godwin's view was a contradiction in terms. He had three cogent objections, which I will condense as far as I can:

The injuries that result from a system of national education are, in the first place, that all public establishments include in them the idea of permanence ... public education has always expended its energies in the support of prejudice ... This feature runs through every species of public establishment; and even in the petty institutions of Sunday schools, the chief lessons to be taught are a superstitious veneration for the Church of England, and to bow to every man in a handsome coat ...

Secondly, the idea of national education is founded in an inattention to the nature of mind. Whatever each man does for himself is done well; whatever his neighbours or his country undertake to do for him is done ill. It is our wisdom to incite men to act for themselves, not to retain them in a state of perpetual pupillage ... Thirdly, the project of a national education ought uniformly to be discouraged on account of its obvious alliance with national government. This is an alliance of a more formidable nature than the old and much contested alliance of church and state. Before we put so powerful a machine under the direction of so ambitious an agent, it behoves us to consider well what we do. Government will not fail to employ it to strengthen its hand and perpetuate its institutions ... Their views as instigators of a system of education will not fail to be analogous to their views in their political capacity ... (Even) in the countries where liberty chiefly prevails, it is reasonably to be assumed that there are important errors, and a national system has the most direct tendency to perpetuate those errors and to form all minds on one model.[45]

Now I've known admirers of Godwin's thought who are embarrassed by this rejection of 'progressive' opinion and who recollect the hard struggle to achieve free, universal, compulsory education for all under the Education Act of 1870, much delayed by silly disputes between the lobbies of the Church of England and the non-conformist factions, and not actually made effective until years later. A centenary publication from the National Union of Teachers explained that "apart from religious and charitable schools, 'dame' or common schools were operated by the private enterprise of people who were often barely literate", and it explained the widespread working-class hostility to the School Boards with the remark that "parents were not always quick to appreciate the advantages of full-time schooling against the loss of extra wages".[46]

But more recent historians have shown the resistance to state schooling in a quite different light. Stephen Humphries found that working-class private schools (as opposed to what we mean today by private schools) were, by the 1860s, providing an alternative education to that of the charitable, 'National' or 'British' schools, for approximately one-third of all working-class children, and he suggests that:

The enormous demand for private as opposed to public education is perhaps best illustrated by the fact that working-class parents in a number of major cities responded to the introduction of compulsory attendance regulations not by sending their children to provided state schools, as government inspectors had predicted, but by extending the length of their children's education in private schools. Parents favoured these schools for a number of reasons: they were small and close to home and were consequently more personal and more convenient than most publicly provided schools; they were informal and tolerant of irregular attendance and unpunctuality; no attendance registers were kept; they were not segregated according to age and sex; they used individual as opposed to authoritarian teaching methods; and, most important, they belonged to and were controlled by the local community rather than being imposed on the neighbourhood by an alien authority.[47]

I find this observation very significant and it was reinforced by a mass of contemporary statistical evidence exhumed by Philip Gardner in his book on *The Lost Elementary Schools of Victorian England*.[48] The author concluded that working-class schools, set up by working-class people in working-class neighbourhoods, "achieved just what the customer wanted: quick results in basic skills like reading, writing and arithmetic, wasted no time on religious studies and moral uplift, and represented a genuinely alternative approach to childhood learning to that prescribed by the education experts". In the view of the historian Paul Thompson, the price of eliminating these schools through the imposition of the national education system was "the suppression in countless working-class children of the appetite for education and ability to learn independently which contemporary progressive education seeks to rekindle".[49]

It is certainly ironical that the centenary of state education in Britain was accompanied by a chorus of Marxist sociologists explaining that the function of the public education system has been to Learn to Labour: to slot working-class children into working-class jobs, now that these traditional jobs have disappeared. I am anxious to learn whether the History of Education courses for teachers in training include the recent findings which support Godwin's warnings. But I must turn to later anarchist educational insights.

Historians of anarchist ideas tend, rightly or wrongly, to work their way through a series of Big Thinkers, chronologically through William Godwin, Pierre-Joseph Proudhon, Michael Bakunin and Peter Kropotkin. The more thorough of them also examine the German advocate of 'conscious egoism', Max Stirner (who was a teacher by profession), the educational ideas of Leo Tolstoy and his observations of the school he started at Yasnaya Polyana, and the Spanish teacher and founder of the 'Modern School' movement, Francisco Ferrer.[50]

It is certainly remarkable how an anarchist approach led a variety of anarchist thinkers to offer educational opinions in anticipation of the progressive opinion of a century later. For example, Bakunin, in a mere footnote to a polemic about something else, envisaged the school as a lifelong educational resource: "They will be schools no longer; they will be popular academies, in which neither pupil nor masters will be known, where the people will come freely to get, if they need it, free instructions, and in which, rich in their own experience, they will teach in their turn many things to the professors who shall bring them knowledge that they lack. This then will be a mutual instruction, an act of intellectual fraternity".[51]

He was writing in 1870 and if this argument about the future of schooling is familiar to you it is precisely because identical aspirations were expressed a century later by people like Ivan Illich and Paul Goodman, or in this country and in this building by people like Michael Young and Professor Harry Rée, who told an audience of young teachers that "I think we are going to see in your lifetime the end of schools as we know them. Instead there will be a community centre with the doors open twelve hours a day, seven days a week, where anybody can wander in and out of the library, workshops, sports centre, self-service store and bar. In a hundred years time the compulsory attendance laws for children to go to school may have gone the same way as the compulsory laws for attendance at church".[52]

I suspect, however, that for many people the actual practice of anarchist ideas in education is more interesting than the theories. For most of us, the most influential and longest-lasting of 'progressive' schooling in Britain is Summerhill School, and its founder A.S. Neill. Neill was suspicious of the embrace of the anarchist movement, though friendly and welcoming to individual anarchists like me. I would advise you to read Jonathan Croall's two excellent books on Neill.[53]

But if you want to read just a couple of general surveys of the anarchists and schools, I have just two to press on you, as both of them are concerned with both theory and experience in and out of the official education system. The first is Michael Smith's *The Libertarians and Education*.[54] When this book appeared I was asked to review it for a teachers' journal. I responded eagerly, anxious to publicise it, but my review was rejected, which left me downcast, not on my account but on Smith's. He reminds us that when A.S. Neill's first book, *A Dominie's Log* was published in 1915, one reviewer was scandalised by the fact that the author seemed totally ignorant of a tradition in progressive education, and offered him, as teacher-trainers are wont to do and just as I am doing today, a reading list. It consisted of names like Rousseau, Pestalozzi, Froebel, Montessori and Dewey.

Michael Smith suggests that a more appropriate reading list for a teacher of Neill's turn of mind would have been Godwin, Proudhon, Tolstoy, Robin and Ferrer. This is interesting, firstly because most teachers would not, then or now, have heard of most of these alternative gurus and those they did know would not be thought about in an educational context, and secondly because Smith is one of the very few to make a distinction between the liberal/progressive educators and the libertarian/anarchist ones.

The handful of people who have sought to put their ideas of 'free' education into practice have always been so beleaguered by the amused hostility of the institutionalised education system on the one hand and by the popular press on the other (with its photographers anxious to get shots of the children smoking, dancing naked in the dew or knocking nails into the grand piano) that they have tended to close ranks and minimise their differences. Neill just couldn't stand the high-minded and manipulative progressives. By the 1930s he was writing to Dora Russell of Beacon Hill School that she and he were "the only educators". As one of his mentors, Homer Lane, put it: "'Give the child freedom' is the insistent cry of the New Educators, but then its exponents usually devise a 'system' which, although based on the soundest of principles, limits that freedom and contradicts the principle."

Lane was echoing the opinion of William Godwin in *The Enquirer*, where he found that Rousseau, even though the world was indebted to him "for the irresistible energy of his writings, and the magnitude of his speculations", had fallen into the common error of manipulating the child. "His whole system of education is a series of tricks, a puppet-show exhibition, of which the master holds the wires, and the scholar is never to suspect in what manner they are moved".

Dr Smith's survey of anarchist approaches to education distinguishes between the libertarian *position* and the libertarian *movement*. He shares my enthusiasm for Godwin and before moving on to the concept of Integral Education developed by the French anarchists, he visits Harmony, the utopian community envisaged by Charles Fourier, whose educational ideals were directed, naturally, towards social harmony and the minimisation of the exercise of authority. What endears Fourier to me is his proposal that in the primary years education should be arranged around cooking and opera, these being activities which developed all the human arts and skills and which did not rely on booklearning. They would also be fun. In the secondary years the unruly impulses of children were to be channelled into socially valuable work. "Fourier envisaged two main independent child societies: the Little Hordes and the Little Bands. The Little Hordes would reflect children's taste for dirt and excitement. They would keep Harmony clean, repair roads, kill poisonous snakes, feed the animals and so on. Their highly necessary tasks were menial in themselves, but precisely because they were seen as nasty by the adult world and because they were performed for the community, the Little Hordes would be highly honoured. They would have special dress and badges of distinction, they would ride horses and would go about their work to the accompaniment of music ... The Little Bands would be more concerned with cultural matters, they would cultivate dress and good manners, would care for the sick and would tend the plants and vegetables."

As Michael Smith comments, though it all sounds nutty, the psychology is not at all askew. The child is given a valued social role. He then moves on to Bakunin and Proudhon. Proudhon was the craftsman son of a peasant, and both his political and educational thinking reflected this:

> Proudhon was always conscious of the fact that the children he was talking about were the children of workers. Work was going to be their life when they grew up. Proudhon saw nothing wrong with this. The work a man did was something to be proud of, it was what gave interest, value and dignity to his life. It was right, therefore, that school should prepare the young for a life of work. That is: an education that was entirely bookish or grammar-schoolish in conception, was valueless from the point of view of ordinary working-class children. Of course, an education that went too far in the other direction, which brought up children merely to be fodder for factories, was equally unacceptable. What was required was an education which would equip a child for the workplace but would also give him a degree of independence in the labour market. This could be achieved by giving him not just the basis of a trade but, as well, a whole range of marketable skills which would ensure that he

was not totally at the mercy of an industrial system which required specialisation of its workers and then discarded them when the specialisation was no
longer of interest to the firm. Thus Proudhon was led to the idea of an education that was 'polytechnical'.

You will have guessed, correctly, that Proudhon was concerning himself solely
with the education of boys, but this was not true of his successors like Kropotkin
with his opinions on the integration of brain work and manual work, nor of others like Ferrer whose approach was similarly that of education for *emancipation*
as opposed to education to meet the needs of industry or the state, which they
saw as education for *subservience*. This leads Smith to some of his most interesting pages for the English-speaking reader, when he describes 'Integral Education'
in practice through the experience of the French anarchist Paul Robin and the
school that he ran from 1880 to 1894 at Cempius. It was based on workshop training and the abandonment of the classroom in favour of what we would now call
the resource centre. Cooking, sewing, carpentry and metalwork were undertaken
by both sexes, and "the Cempius children, both girls and boys, were among the
first children in France to go in for cycling". Co-education, sexual equality and
atheism brought Robin's downfall, but another celebrated French anarchist, Se-
bastien Faure, ran a school called La Ruche (The Beehive). "Faure had learned one
very significant lesson from Robin's downfall: to stay completely out of the state
system and so be assured of complete independence". Smith takes us through the
experience of Tolstoy and Ferrer and concludes by relating the varied traditions
of libertarian pedagogy from the past, to the widely-read authors of the 1960s
and 1970s whom we lump together as the 'de-schoolers', all of them published in
widely-circulated cheap editions by Penguin Education in those days, John Holt,
Paul Goodman, George Dennison, Paulo Freire and Ivan Illich.

Finally I turn to a changing group of people who, as the Libertarian Education Collective, have published the journal *Lib ED* as "a magazine for the liberation of learning" since 1966. Files of this journal will be found in the libraries of
virtually all teacher-training institutions and an index to its contents as well as
general bibliographies and addresses are to be found in their publication *Freedom
in Education*.[55] One of their number, John Shotton, has produced a large-scale
survey of a century of educational experiment in Britain.[56] In my foreword to this
book I explained that one reason for its importance was that it was in effect the
final part of a trilogy of recent books by authors in different fields which, "through
painstaking and impeccable research, have turned the standard histories of education and their assumptions upside down". The first two were the books I have
mentioned by Stephen Humphries and Philip Gardner. For the opening section
of Shotton's book rescues from "the enormous condescension of posterity" in the
now-famous phrase of E.P. Thompson's, a whole series of local working-class libertarian schools and Sunday schools in Britain in the early years of this century.
He calls this section "The Thirst for Knowledge"—a reminder to us in the profoundly anti-educational climate of contemporary schooling that there were, and
are, times and places when schooling was and is valued for its own sake.

He goes on to describe a century of private ventures in libertarian education, with the usual names of Summerhill, Dartington Hall, Burgess Hill, Kilquhanity and Beacon Hill, and some lesser-known private adventures. This is followed by his description of a similar variety of libertarian schools for the unschoolable, and an account of efforts to introduce libertarian education into state schooling, with a description of Prestolee in Lancashire (Teddy O'Neill), St George-in-the-East in Stepney (Alex Bloom), Braehead School and Summerhill Academy in Scotland (R.F. Mackenzie) and Countesthorpe College in Leicestershire where Shotton himself was a teacher. Finally he tells the story of over a dozen examples of the 'de-schooling' movement in British cities between 1960 and 1990. Shotton makes no claims that cannot be backed up by evidence and he looks specifically for the evidence provided by children rather than by propagandists.

In the bleak climate of educational reaction in the 1990s, he draws us into unexplored territory and reminds us that experiment is the oxygen of education. It dies without it. This is why the anarchist literature on schools is important for all of us.

# 7. TOWARDS A POOR SCHOOL

*"The technological society has deliberately cultivated a careless, consumptive, egoistic and slovenly human being. The frugal society ... must start with redirecting our attitudes and re-educating our values."*

—Henryk Skolimowski

Perhaps the best-known contribution made by John Dewey to the endless debate on education was his remark that 'what the best and wisest parent wants for his own child, that must the community want for all of its children'. But perhaps the best and wisest of parents are the very ones who are least able to specify their hopes in this respect, and the more they perceive and acknowledge the uniqueness of each child, the less likely would be their hopes for any particular child to have any general relevance. Unless, that is, they take refuge in generalities of universal application. They might want their child to be happy, to be fulfilled, to be autonomous, or to 'make a contribution'. But who doesn't? What guide to individual or collective action could we derive from such aspirations?

I have a friend, a Paraguayan anarchist, whose children were named according to parental convictions. Regardless of sex or custom, the first was named Liberty, the second was called Equality, and the third was named Fraternity. (If you are wondering what the fourth child of the family was called, I have to tell you that he was called Ché.) It is hard to guess which of the family would grow up most embarrassed by this imposition of ideology on nomenclature, and I have no idea whether he sought for each child an education compatible with the slogans with which he labelled his offspring. He would be in trouble if he did, because the resounding catch-phrases we have inherited from the eighteenth century may go together marvellously on French postage stamps, but do they go together in life, or in educational policy making? Dr. Ronald Sampson of Bristol recently gave an address with the title 'The choice between inequality and freedom in education' and that title at least draws attention to one of our most agonizing and unresolved educational dilemmas.

For it often seems to me that people's social and political attitudes are determined, not on the conventional left-right spectrum, but on the relative values they place on at least the first two characters in this holy trinity. There is a quite different continuum which shapes their approaches to the politics of education as

---

Originally printed in M. Braham (ed.), *Aspects of Education*. (Chichester: John Wiley & Sons, 1982).

to everything else: that between authoritarians and libertarians. In terms of the ordinary crudities of party politics, you can, for example, place our representatives in either of the two main parties on this continuum, and you might very well find that in one of those two parties the egalitarians are always on the back benches, while in the other the libertarians are usually to be found there. In the politics of education in Britain, people's devotion to one or other of these principles leads them into some very sterile posturing, and it often lays them open to uncomfortable changes of hypocrisy since sometimes what they want for their own children is something other than what they want for all the community's children.

The pathos of the battle for equality in education is that it revolves around the principle of the quality of opportunity to be unequal. The last word on this particular issue was said many years ago in a deceptively modest little book, disguised as a satire, *The Rise of the Meritocracy*, by Michael Young. This book looks back from the twenty-first century at our own day as the period when 'two contradictory principles for legitimising power were struggling for mastery—the principle of kinship and the principle of merit'. Kinship implies that you are the child of your parents and consequently have access to the opportunities they can provide. In Michael Young's satire, Merit wins in the end, with the perfection of intelligence testing, and consequently with earlier and earlier selection a new, non-self-perpetuating elite is formed, consisting of the 'five per cent of the population who know what five per cent means'. The top jobs go to the top people, and Payment by Merit (M equals IQ plus Effort) widens the gap between top and bottom people. The people at the bottom not only are treated as inferior, they *know* they *are* inferior. But to select the few is to reject the many, and in the meritocratic society new tensions arise. By the end of the twentieth century, although the new working class no longer includes people of outstanding intellectual capacity (since they have all been creamed off by meritocratic selection), a populist movement arises, consisting of dissident intellectuals, mainly women, allied with the disruptive proletariat, declaring in the Chelsea Manifesto of the year 2000 their belief in the classless society.

Needless to say, the manifesto cuts no ice with the meritocrats of the year 2000, though it becomes a rallying point in the bitter insurrection in 2033.

The Chelsea Manifesto declared that:

> The classless society would be one which both possessed and acted upon plural values. Were we to evaluate people not according to their intelligence and their education, their occupation and their power, but according to their sympathy and generosity, there could be no classes. Who would be able to say that the scientist was superior to the porter with admirable qualities as a father, and the civil servant with unusual skill at gaining prizes superior to the lorry driver with unusual skill at growing roses? The classless society would also be the tolerant society, in which individual differences were actually encouraged as well as passively tolerated, in which full meaning was at last given to the dignity of man. Every human being would then have equal opportunity, not to rise up in the world in the light of any mathematical measure, but to develop his own special capacities for leading a rich life.

Well, my own experience is that the same people who would give an enthusiastic ideological assent to the propositions of the Chelsea Manifesto complain most bitterly when they discover that their children can earn more working for the district council's cleansing department than they can in the lower ranks of professional employment; yet in the strike of toolroom workers at British Leyland in February 1977 they would bitterly criticize the strikers who asserted that with their years of training and immense skill they would only earn the same as foremen of the lavatory cleaners. Other people's defence of pay differentials is always marked by sordid self-interest: our own is always above reproach. Education is not a path to social equality.

What do we say about liberty, the first of the holy trinity? As a political issue this is construed as parental freedom of choice in schooling for their children. As an educational issue it means, among a great many other things, the absence of coercion of the child: the goods are displayed in the educational supermarket and the customer selects or rejects. I am afraid that, with the exception of a few heroes, known by name to most of us, we are as guilty of hypocrisy in the name of this great abstraction as we are in the name of equality. In the publicly provided education system we have a book of martyrs to make the point, among them Mr Duane, Mr MacKenzie, and Mr Ellis. In the privately provided sector we know how, at some stage in adolescence, parental interest in the sacred freedom of the child diminishes until the child is removed suddenly to attend a cramming establishment to achieve whatever educational qualifications are necessary to keep open the doors to a growing number of adult careers.

Martin Buber, looking into the candid eyes of a rebellious pupil, remarked, 'I love freedom, but I don't believe in it.' His remark epitomizes the position of the modern progressive parents. They do love freedom so long as it does not interfere with the chances of their children in the occupational status race. It is nothing to do with the education system or with the philosophy of education, but it is a fact that in most high-status jobs the qualifications for entry as well as the length of training have been raised and extended to a ludicrous extent in order to up-grade that occupation. I need only to mention one occupation, that with which I am most familiar, the profession of architecture. To be accepted for professional training involves at the outset, in terms of the English education system, three 'O' levels and two 'A' levels, preferably in approved subjects, followed by six years of professional training, after which the successful aspirant finds himself preparing schedules of doors and windows for some building in the design of which he has had no hand. Now within living memory—and I think you will probably agree that architecture has been of an aesthetically and technically higher standard within the lifespan of some living people—it was totally different. Sir Clough Williams-Ellis ... confided to Sir Edwin Lutyens that he spent a term at the Architectural Association in London, learning his trade. 'A term,' said Lutyens, horrified. 'My dear fellow, it took me three weeks.' Was Lutyens a better or worse architect than the people who by a restrictive Act of Parliament are today exclusively entitled to call themselves architects? The first architect I ever worked for learned his trade at an age when we still by law imprison children in the compulsory education machine, drawing full-size details in chalk on brown paper on a barn floor here in Devon, for the building of Truro Cathedral for the man to whom he was apprenticed, Sir John Loughborough Pearson, RA. Go and look at the building and see if it leaks.

What I say of an occupation of which I have intimate knowledge applies, I am certain, to the whole range of employment. I deliberately mentioned various architectural knights to indicate that I am not generalizing from the experience of the riff-raff of the architectural profession who all, no doubt, have been through the academic tread-mill. In this I am saying, as in so many other spheres of life, professionalism is a conspiracy against the laity, and if it is the reason why we have tacitly abandoned our educational belief in liberty, we need to be quite clear that it is these external circumstances rather than our educational ideas which have forced us into this position.

For motivated families, the belief in liberty has been modified by the requirements of occupational entrance, and this view has spread from the intelligentsia to the skilled working class. Anyone from a city like Glasgow, Newcastle, or Belfast will tell you how the educational qualifications for an engineering apprenticeship have risen to impossible heights within the last decade. You need two 'O' levels to be employed with a car-washing machine in South Shields. No doubt you occasionally wash the cars lent by the Department of Education and Science to members of Her Majesty's Inspectorate so that they can get around to schools and tell teachers about the need to encourage children to aim at jobs in Britain's manufacturing industries.

Poor families and poor children interpret liberty in education quite differently. When the sociology graduate from Keele University drifts into teaching because we are overstocked with sociologists, and announces to his class that he wants them to feel free to express their own view of the situation, those amongst his conscripts who can actually hear his voice conclude with resignation that he does not really care about *them*. They conclude that in his opinion they are not worth teaching, and in their minds this is why he adopts his *laissez-faire* attitude. 'He didn't care whether we learned anything or not', is their verdict on the now-departed teacher. We have written off liberty as an educational goal.

What are we to say about fraternity as one of the aims of education? It is a concept even harder to define than the other two. Looking for a way of coming to terms with the idea, I am helped by a passage I read recently from André Malraux's book, *Lazare*. He says,

> People think they understand Fraternity because they confuse it with human warmth. But in point of fact it is something much deeper, and it was belatedly, and almost apologetically, that it was added to the blazon of the Republic, whose flag at first bore only the words Liberty and Equality ... The word Liberty has still the same ring to it, but Fraternity now stands only for a comical utopia in which nobody would ever have a bad character. Men believe that Fraternity was just tacked on, one Sunday, to feelings like Justice and Liberty. But it is not something that can be tacked on at will. It is something sacred, and it will elude us if we rob it of the irrational element that lies hidden

within it. It is as mysterious as love, it has nothing to do with duty, or with 'right thinking'. Like love, and unlike liberty, it is a provisional sentiment, a state of grace.

I am sure that Malraux betrays some ignorance of the history of ideas in his own country in making these remarks, but that is not my concern. Can we get closer to the meaning of fraternity? Peter Kropotkin chose to define it as 'mutual aid', and in his book of that name he remarks that

> to reduce animal sociability to *love* and *sympathy* means to reduce its generality and its importance, just as human ethics based on love and personal sympathy only have contributed to narrow the comprehension of the moral feeling as a whole. It is not love of my neighbour—whom I often do not know at all—which induces me to seize a pail of water and to rush towards his house when I see it on fire; it is a far wider, even though more vague feeling or instinct of human solidarity and sociability which moves me ... It is a feeling infinitely wider than love or personal sympathy—an instinct that has been slowly developed among animals and men in the course of an extremely long evolution, and which has taught animals and men alike the force they can borrow from the practice of mutual aid and support, and the joys they can find in social life.

Well, he's right, isn't he? But when the sense of fraternity, or solidarity, is cultivated in educational institutions, it is frequently in opposition to the institution itself. Teachers know that the fraternity is that of the peer group and that the values it represents are profoundly anti-educational. 'I have the greatest difficulty in restraining them from tearing up each other's work at the end of the period,' a hard-pressed secondary school teacher told me. Indeed, the closer we get to the classroom, the more diminished is our faith that the school can be the agent of social change or the vehicle for social justice. In many parts of the world there is still a hunger for schooling. Immense sacrifices are made by parents to achieve it for their children. They and their children would find unbelievable the size of education budgets in the schools of the Western world and the low esteem in which our schools are held by their scholars.

Thirteen years ago I wrote an article called 'A modest proposal for the repeal of the Education Act', and it was later blessed in the symposium 'Children's rights' as 'the first time anyone in England had dared to formulate out loud, even to a possibly friendly audience, what many of us had begun to hear as a question in our heads'. That reference to a friendly audience is important because it is easy to be misunderstood. At a time when teachers are joining the ranks of the unemployed, and when their unions as well as those of students are demonstrating under banners reading 'Fight the Education Cuts', am I not grotesquely misjudging the present climate of education in putting on my banner the slogan 'Towards a Poor School'?

Let me declare my vested interest in having rich schools. I earn half my living producing a bulletin for teachers called *BEE*, the *Bulletin of Environmental-*

*Education.* It costs £4 a year—a modest sum—and in the last year the curve of circulation growth has completely flattened, as our renewal notices keep getting returned with sad little notes saying, 'We like it very much. It's marvellously useful, but we have had to cut our spending drastically.' I always say that they ought to ask their classes to subscribe their pennies, on the grounds that getting our bulletin will improve the quality of the teaching they are subjected to, but no one takes me seriously because it is a basic educational principle, isn't it, that no one should raise a penny for his own education?

I earn the other half of my income running a project for the Schools Council, which is the body concerned with curriculum development in England and Wales. Our project is called 'Art and the Built Environment'. Can you imagine anything more frivolous, while the nation's economy goes down the drain? Not only is our project one of those marginal frills, by the standards of the education industry, but its sponsor, the Schools Council, is itself vulnerable. The notorious Yellow Paper—the report to the Prime Minister from the Department of Education and Science, which was leaked to the press—described its performance as 'mediocre'. So I have a strong interest in an education system rich enough to support marginal activities—or activities which in the eyes of the system are marginal.

In what sense do I see virtues in the idea of a poor school? There is a Polish stage producer, Grotowski, who wrote a book called *Towards a Poor Theatre*, implying that the theatre would get a new lease of life if it shed all the expensive trimmings of the proscenium, elaborate lighting and equipment: all that audio-visual gear. (Actually there is a parallel in school here. Do any of our great drama teachers—people like Dorothy Heathcote in Newcastle, for example—have any use for the elaborate theatre equipment with which many schools encumbered themselves in the days when we thought we were rich?). Similarly there is a movement, as I understand it, in the Christian church, known as 'Towards a Poor Church', a kind of echo of all those religious reformers who have haunted that religion, with their bare feet and shaggy beards, urging their fellows to abandon all that expensive architecture and ecclesiastical silverware in order to free themselves to become receptive to the Message. (Actually there is a parallel in school here, too, with those earnest members of the Church of England who think that the only thing that can save the church is disestablishment—the severing of its official connection with the state. Many teachers of what we call religious education in school believe that the only thing that can save the reputation of their subject—which in this country is the only school subject established by law and at the same time the only one we can opt our children out of—is the ending of its statutory existence as well as that of the common act of worship which is supposed to take place in morning assembly.)

Whatever we may say when we lobby against cuts in educational spending, let us reflect between friends on the implications of educational poverty. And before we get self-righteous about it, let us think about the implications of the Houghton pay award to teachers a couple of years ago. Cause and effect there may or may not be, but before Houghton, when teachers were complaining of their poverty, there was no job shortage, there was a teacher shortage. Many schools had a terrifying turnover of staff every term. In 1974 many urban schools were sending children home because there was no one to teach them. I read two items about the same city in the same newspaper on the same day that year, one of which reported the sending home of school-children for this reason while the other reported the rounding-up by the police of truants, collected off the streets. After the Houghton pay award, the huge staff turnover stopped: the oldest inhabitants of the city school became the staff once more instead of the fifth-year conscripts, and the supply of jobs dried up. As the schools became poorer, they became more stable as institutions.

The truth is that in the boom period, now over, education was oversold. Every additional bit of expenditure, every increase in student numbers at the upper and more expensive end of the system, every new development in educational technology, was a step towards some great social goal. But it has not delivered the goods. Professor A.H. Halsey, writing in *The Times Educational Supplement* (21 January 1977), remarks that

> We live today under sentence of death by a thousand cuts (that is, of all things except the body of bureaucracy). In education the position is one of extreme relative deprivation, not only because of the financial background of a sudden halt to previously mounting largesse, but also, and more seriously, because of the collapse of *belief* in education either as the best investment for national production, or the great redistributor of chances to the traditionally disadvantaged.

Nor is this simply a British phenomenon. Fred M. Hechinger, the author of *Growing up in America*, also writing in *The Times Educational Supplement* (5 November 1976) says that, 'America is in headlong retreat from its commitment to education. Political confusion and economic uncertainty have shaken the people's faith in education as the key to financial and social success.' Among the people or trends which he blames for this changed circumstance are the right-wing backlash and what he calls the 'destructive' influence of the deschoolers like Ivan Illich and the views of critics like Edgar Z. Friedenberg, John Holt, and Christopher Jencks. I think, on the contrary, that these people have had an immensely liberatory effect on our ideas about the way that the intelligentsia lapped up the deschooling literature of a few years ago—the works of Paul Goodman, Everett Reimer, and Ivan Illich—but when, at the same time, the schools were sending home pupils for lack of teachers, they failed, with a few exceptions in the 'free school' movement, to make the connection. The community did not seize the occasion to use the wonderful resources of the city to provide an alternative education for the kids who were wandering the streets. They just waited for the statistics for such offences as shoplifting, vandalism, and taking-and-driving-away, to rise—which they did. At the same time in the universities, well-educated Marxist lecturers were explaining how the education system in our society was simply a device for preparing us for our particular slot in capitalist industry. The government, as though anxious to prove them right, has set off a moral panic about the failure of the education system to meet the needs of industry ...

I do not believe that the roots of or the cure for our chronic economic malaise are to be found in the education system and, if it is true that the young do not like industrial jobs, at either a shop-floor or a graduate level (and it is symptomatic of the superficial nature of the debate that it fails to distinguish between the two), I think it ironical that instead of wanting to change the nature of industrial work, of wanting to make it an adventure instead of a penance, we should want to change the nature of the young. Actually it is not even true that we are short of graduate engineers and we are certainly not short of shop-floor fodder.

There must be many teachers who went through the boom years without even knowing that they were in them: they found themselves committed to a policy of make-do-and-mend as usual, and never got their hands on the money because it was being spent somewhere else. No one here who is a teacher will deny my assertion that the characteristic situation is for the teacher to say all year that he would like this or that set of books or piece of equipment, and be told that there was no cash, while three days before the end of the financial year the head of department would say, "You've got four hundred pounds to spend by the end of the week. Let me know what to order before the end of the afternoon because otherwise we'll lose the money.' I was in a school the other day, in an Art and Design Department, where thousands of pounds were available to spend on machinery, but the art teacher had only £38 to lay out on paper, paint, and other expendables. He could have kilns but no clay. As an advocate of the use of the local environment in education, I have often come across the situation where the teacher can easily get an illuminated terrestrial globe to suspend from the ceiling, but found that it was not in order for him to buy a class set of street maps of the locality. ...

The person who worships the state and thinks that any other mode of provision is a let-off for the state or a cop-out from the state, when faced by the politics of retrenchment, can only protest and wave his banner. There is, for example, in the world of preschool education a deep ideological division between those who believe in the provision of day nurseries and nursery schools by local education authorities, on principle, and those who believe on principle in babyminders and parent-organized playgroups. Every now and then there is a scandal about illicit babyminding, but it was left to an outsider, Brian Johnson, to think up the idea of courses in babyminding for unofficial babyminders. Now, as part of its education cuts, one English county has decided, reluctantly, to close all its nursery schools. The customers are helpless. If the local community had developed its own unofficial network of provision for the under-5s, it would have been better off today. ...

My first priority is that we should put our money at the bottom end of education rather than at the top. Now this really would be a revolutionary change in the order of things. For the greater the sums of money that are poured into the education industries of the world, the smaller the proportion which benefits the people at the bottom of the educational, occupational, and social hierarchy. The universal education system turns out to be yet another way in which the poor are obliged to subsidize the rich. A decade ago, Everett Reimer found that the children of the poorest one tenth of the population of the United States cost the public in schooling $2500 each over a lifetime, while the children of the richest one tenth cost about £35000. 'Assuming that one-third of this is private expenditure, the richest one-tenth still gets ten times as much of public funds for education as the poorest one-tenth.' In his suppressed UNESCO report of 1970, Michael Huberman reached the same conclusion for the majority of countries in the world. In Britain we spend twice as much on the secondary school life of a grammar school sixth former as on a secondary modern school leaver, while, if we include university expenditure, we spend as much on an undergraduate in one year as on a normal school child throughout his life. The Fabian tract, *Labour and Inequality*, calculates that 'while the highest social group benefit seventeen times as much as the lowest group from the expenditure on universities, they only contribute five times as much revenue'. No wonder Everett Reimer calls schools an almost perfectly regressive form of taxation. In the scramble for dwindling public expenditure on education, you may be sure that the universities are going to be almost obscenely successful by comparison with the preschool education lobby.

In re-ordering our expenditure, I would invest heavily in preschool education, and in the infant and junior school. My aim would be the traditional, and currently approved one, that every child should be literate and numerate on leaving the junior school at 11. All right, it will take up to the age of 14 to achieve this for some children, but I want to assert that the compulsory prolongation of schooling beyond such an age is an affront to the freedom of the individual and has nothing to do with the aims of education, even though it has everything to do with the restrictive practices of the job market. I mentioned earlier the entry qualifications demanded by the architectural profession. A month ago the RIBA Council solemnly sat and discussed how to make it harder still—like demanding four 'A' levels—so as to restrict entry still further. Do we have to wait until two 'A' levels instead of two 'O' levels are needed to get a car-wash job in South Shields, or do we say enough is enough: this is not what we have teachers for?

I quoted earlier the brilliant satire, *The Rise of the Meritocracy*, written by Michael Young in the 1950s. He was interviewed by one of the Sunday papers this year and explained why he feels that there is no future for secondary schools as we know them. He said,

> I think secondary schools in their present form are doomed. They haven't yet managed to reflect the new kind of family. The father used to be the fount of authority. Today, that authority is greatly diminished partly because it's shared. Schools and universities borrowed authority from the authoritarian father and now that it's no longer there to be borrowed, children in secondary schools are not going to accept it. There has to be a reduction in the school-leaving age and a move over to half-time education. People will be learning at home, at the workplace and not forced into institutions which use a bogus authority.

Dr Young has the honesty and the poor taste to bring up the subject of the crisis of authority in the secondary school: a crisis that ensures that much of our expenditure on teachers and plant is wasted by attempting to teach people what they do not want to learn in a situation that they would rather not be involved in.

A poor school could not afford such waste and frustration of both teachers and taught. The school has become one of the instruments by which we exclude adolescents from real responsibilities and real functions in the life of our society. We have in the last year of secondary schooling pathetic attempts to give 'relevance' by providing 'work experience' courses aimed at aclimatizing the young to the shock of going to work, or by providing courses in colleges of further education with such titles as 'Adjustment to Work', for the benefit of those unable or unwilling to hold down a job. The Trades Union Congress and the Confederation of British Industry have joined forces in backing a project for informing school-children about industry. Arthur Young, the headmaster of Northcliffe High School in Yorkshire, has for years been trying to find the right equation between learning and earning. He values the efforts of his pupils to earn money for themselves and has sought, within the narrowly prescribed limits of the law, to provide opportunities in and out of school for them to do so. He remarks of work experience projects that they

> have never really got off the ground because of the legal, insurance and trade union problems that hedge them around. I have always thought that the schemes proposed were phoney—the most important aspect of work experience is being neglected completely—the wage at the end of the week.

Like Michael Young, Arthur Young sees an urgent need to change the relationships in the secondary school. Describing the efforts made to provide actual cash-earning experiences for the most unlikely lads at his school, and the effect it has had on their attitudes to running their own lives, taking decisions, budgeting, fulfilling obligations, dealing with strangers, as well as such mundane things taken for granted by the middle-class child as using the telephone, he remarks,

> We have to overcome the ridiculous idea that giving children the chance to earn money in school is somehow immoral. ... In the changing situation in education, pupil-teacher relationships and roles are the essence of much heart-searching and debate. We might do well to compare the differences in an earning-learning situation between master and apprentice and in the traditional school situation, captive scholars facing chalk and talk across the barrier of the teacher's desk. The comparison of relationships between newsagent and paperboy and between paperboy and schoolmaster might also be revealing.

The carelessly rich school, greedy for resources, has no need to be a productive institution. The poor school could not afford not to be a productive workshop and belongs to a society in which every workshop is an effective school. Don't think I am denigrating or down-grading the teacher. Far from it. A poor school could not afford to have its spending kept out of the individual teacher's hands. A poor school needs to know what it is paying for. In the 1960s educational spenders were swept away on a tide of commercially inspired expensive options like programmed learning and teaching machines, which are greeted with a cynical laugh in the 1970s. The expensive hardware of educational technology has become an irrelevancy and an embarrassment in this decade. I want the school to have a clearly stated published budget with a personal allocation to each member of the staff to spend as he or she sees fit. The teacher should be responsible for his own spending. He can do it wisely or foolishly on such materials and equipment as he desires. He can pool it with others, he can carry it over to next year.

The poor school would be self-catering. Why shouldn't the school meals service be in the hands of the pupils? Why shouldn't every secondary school include a day nursery run by the pupils? The poor school would be too valuable a community asset to be open for a small part of the day and for a restricted age band. Already we are feeling our way towards such an institution through the concept of the community school and the community college. When we consider now little the massive educational spending of the last decade did to enhance the lives or life-chances of the children in what is known as 'the lower quartile of the ability range' in secondary education, we may perhaps hope that the new age of frugality will lead us to devise appropriate educational experiences in a climate where we make fewer grandiose claims for what the school can do. By settling for less, we might even achieve more.

# 8. FRINGE BENEFITS: COLIN WARD IS ALARMED AS THE CITY OF LONDON SPREADS OVER SPITALFIELDS

My friend Bobby has for 25 years had his little office in Commercial street, London E1. Nowadays he's besieged with phone calls making offers for the premises.

Bobby is always polite. He listens to the smart young speculators, gratefully accepts their offers, and just when they propose to come round with the papers, explains that he doesn't actually own the place. Receiver crashes down at the other end. I keep telling him that he's going to be bought out, squeezed out or otherwise eased out, but he goes on believing in his gentleman's agreement with the landlord, forgetting that there aren't any gentle men in the property business.

I went the other night to an exhibition called "A Farewell to Spitalfields". It was rushed together by John Shaw and Ralph Samuel of Ruskin College, from old and new photographs and testimony, to remind us of the implications of the coming closure of Spitalfields market, and its removal eastward to Temple Mills.

It's moving not because of traffic congestion or under-use, but because the annual turnover of the fruit and veg wholesalers is worth less than the "million square feet of potential office development right next door to the City of London" which will replace it.

This ancient area outside the city wall has been a market since the 14th century and a centre for the rag trade since the 15th. It is in the geographers' terms, the classic zone of transition where, as everyone knows, the Huguenots, then the Irish, then the Jews and now the Bengalis, have gained their first toe-hold in the urban economy.

It has always been a place of unlicensed factories in upper rooms, child labour, sweatshops, family solidarity and racial antagonism from outside. It has also been the hugely productive centre where the latest modes are run up for the smartest shops. And of course it houses the Petticoat Lane market, known 400 years ago as Rag Fair, and the market for birds and animals, Club Row. People have been thankful to get into it and glad to get out.

The same streets have always contained dozens of minute businesses supplying or applying the buttons, zips, fixings and trimmings or pressing, pinning and packaging for the wholesale market. What you wear either comes from a chain

Originally printed in *New Statesman and Society* (12 August 1988): 52.

of subcontractors in places like Spitalfields or from their equivalents in South East Asia.

If you don't like it you should make your own clothes. What you *shouldn't* do is to applaud the elimination of the low-rent workshop economy by the high-rent finance industry that doesn't deal with useful commodities at all, just in money.

The organisers of that little exhibition at the Bishopsgate Institute were right to say that, "The viewer is thus confronted with two versions of the enterprise culture: one of family business and small scale firms, the other of international high finance with computer screens linking the City of London to the money markets of the world."

The left, when in office, used a lot of energy in attempting to eliminate the zone of transition, which represented everything it despised about petty capitalism. The right carelessly wipes it out because low-income enterprises are automatically absurd when property as such is a much better investment. Politically neither side recognises the need for the scruffy, busy workshop economy which depends on cheap premises close to the market.

"The whole industrial economy of Spitalfields," Shaw and Samuel claim, "rests on cheap workrooms; rentals in the new office complex are some eight times greater than they are in the purlieus of Brick Lane, and with the dizzy rise in property values which will flow, accommodation of all kinds, whether for working space or home, will be beyond local people." But who cares?

# Section Five

## Influences and Alternatives

# 1. ANARCHY AND A PLAUSIBLE FUTURE

*"For the earlier part of my life I was quieted by being told that ours was the richest country in the world, until I woke up to know that what I meant by riches was learning and beauty, and music and art, coffee and omelettes; perhaps in the coming days of poverty we may get more of these ... "*
—W.R. Lethaby, *Form in Civilisation*

This book has illustrated the arguments for anarchism, not from theories, but from actual examples of tendencies which already exist, alongside much more powerful and dominant authoritarian methods of social organisation. The important question is, therefore, not whether anarchy is possible or not, but whether we can so enlarge the scope and influence of libertarian methods that they become the normal way in which human beings organise their society. Is an anarchist society possible?

We can only say, from the evidence of human history, that no kind of society is impossible. If you are powerful enough and ruthless enough you can impose almost any kind of social organisation on people—for a while. But you can only do so by methods which, however natural and appropriate they may be for any other kind of 'ism'—acting on the well-known principle that you can't make an omelette without breaking eggs, are repugnant to anarchists, unless they see themselves as yet another of those revolutionary elites 'leading the people' to the promised land. You can impose authority but you cannot impose freedom. An anarchist society is improbable, not because anarchy is unfeasible, or unfashionable, or unpopular, but because human society is not like that, because, as Malatesta put it ... 'we are, in any case, only one of the forces acting in society'.

The degree of social cohesion implied in the idea of 'an anarchist society' could only occur in a society so embedded in the cake of custom that the idea of *choice* among alternative patterns of social behaviour simply did not occur to people. I cannot imagine that degree of unanimity and I would dislike it if I could, because the idea of *choice* is crucial to any philosophy of freedom and spontaneity. So we don't have to worry about the boredom of utopia: we shan't get there. But what results from this conclusion? One response would be to stress anarchism as an ideal of personal liberation, ceasing to think of changing society, except by example. Another would be to conclude that because no roads lead to utopia no road leads

Originally printed in Colin Ward, *Anarchy in Action*, Second Edition. (London: Freedom Press, 1973).

anywhere, an attitude which, in the end, is identical with the utopian one because it asserts that there are no partial, piecemeal, compromise or temporary solutions, only *one* attainable or unattainable final solution. But, as Alexander Herzen put it over a century ago: 'A goal which is infinitely remote is not a goal at all, it is a deception. A goal must be closer—at the very least the labourer's wage or pleasure in the work performed. Each epoch, each generation, each life has had, and has, its own experience, and the end of each generation must be itself.'[1]

The choice between libertarian and authoritarian solutions is not a once-and-for-all cataclysmic struggle, it is a series of running engagements, most of them never concluded, which occur, and have occurred, throughout history. Every human society, except the most totalitarian of utopias or anti-utopias, is a plural society with large areas which are not in conformity with the officially imposed or declared values. An example of this can be seen in the alleged division of the world into capitalist and communist blocks: there are vast areas of capitalist societies which are not governed by capitalist principles, and there are many aspects of the socialist societies which cannot be described as socialist. You might even say that the only thing that makes life livable in the capitalist world is the unacknowledged non-capitalist element within it, and the only thing that makes survival possible in the communist world is the unacknowledged capitalist element in it. This is why a controlled market is a left-wing demand in capitalist economy—along with state control, while a free market is a left-wing demand in a communist society—along with workers' control. In both cases, the demands are for whittling away power from the centre, whether it is the power of the state or capitalism, or state-capitalism.

So what are the prospects for increasing the anarchist content of the real world? From one point of view the outlook is bleak: centralised power, whether that of governments or super-governments, or of private capitalism or the super-capitalism of giant international corporations, has never been greater. The prophesies of nineteenth-century anarchists like Proudhon and Bakunin about the power of the state over the citizen have a relevance today which must have seemed unlikely for their contemporaries.

From another standpoint the outlook is infinitely promising. The very growth of the state and its bureaucracy, the giant corporation and its privileged hierarchy, are exposing their vulnerability to non-co-operation, to sabotage, and to the exploitation of *their* weaknesses by the weak. They are also giving rise to parallel organisations, counter organisations, alternative organisations, which exemplify the anarchist method. Industrial mergers, and rationalisation have bred the revival of the demand for workers' control, first as a slogan or a tactic like the work-in, ultimately as a destination. The development of the school and the university as broiler-houses for a place in the occupational pecking-order have given rise to the de-schooling movement and the idea of the anti-university. The use of medicine and psychiatry as agents of conformity has led to the idea of the anti-hospital and the self-help therapeutic group. The failure of Western society to house its citizens has prompted the growth of squatter movements and tenants' co-operatives. The triumph of the supermarket in the United States has begun a mushrooming of food co-operatives. The deliberate pauperisation of those who cannot work has led to the recovery of self-respect through Claimants' Unions.

Community organisations of every conceivable kind, community newspapers, movements for child welfare, communal households have resulted from the new consciousness that local as well as central government exploit the poor and are un-responsive to those who are unable to exert effective pressure for themselves. The 'rationalisation' of local administration in Britain into 'larger and more effective units' is evoking a response in the demand for neighbourhood councils. A new self-confidence and assertion of their right to exist on their own terms has sprung up among the victims of particular kinds of discrimination—black liberation, women's liberation, homosexual liberation, prisoners' liberation, children's libera-tion: the list is almost endless and is certainly going to get longer as more and more people become more and more conscious that society is organised in ways which deny them a place in the sun. In the age of mass politics and mass conformity, this is a magnificent re-assertion of individual values and of human dignity.

None of these movements is yet a threat to the power structure, and this is scarcely surprising since hardly any of them existed before the late 1960s. None of them fits into the framework of conventional politics. In fact, they don't speak the same language as the political parties. They talk the language of anarchism and they insist on anarchist principles of organisation, which they have learned not from political theory but from their own experience. They organise in loosely associated groups which are *voluntary, functional, temporary* and *small*. They de-pend, not on membership cards, votes, a special leadership and a herd of inactive followers but on small functional groups which ebb and flow, group and regroup, according to the task in hand. They are networks, not pyramids.

At the very time when the 'irresistible trends of modern society' seemed to be leading us to a mass society of enslaved consumers they are reminding us of the truth that the irresistible is simply that which is not resisted. But obviously a whole series of partial and incomplete victories, of concessions won from the hold-ers of power, will not lead to an anarchist society. But it will widen the scope of free action and the potentiality for freedom in the society we have. But such com-promises of anarchist notions would have to be made, such authoritarian bedfel-lows chosen, for a frontal attack on the power structure, that the anarchist answer to cries for revolutionary unity is likely to be 'Whose noose are you inviting me to put round my neck this time?'

But in thinking about a plausible future, another factor has entered into the general consciousness since the late 1960s. So many books, so many reports, so many conferences have been devoted to it, that it is only necessary for me to state a few general propositions about it. The first is that the world's resources are finite. The second is that the wealthy economies have been exploiting the unrenewable resources at a rate which the planet cannot sustain. The third is that these 'devel-oped' economies are also exploiting the resources of the 'Third World' countries as cheap raw materials. This means, not only that the Third World countries can never hope to achieve the levels of consumption of the rich world, but that the rich countries themselves cannot continue to consume at the present accelerating

rate. The public debate around these issues is not about the truth of the conten-
tions, it is simply about the question: How Soon? How soon before the fossil fuels
run out? How soon before the Third World rises in revolt against international
exploitation? How soon will we be facing the consequences of the non-viability of
future economic growth? I leave aside the related questions about pollution and
about population. But all these questions profoundly affect all our futures and
the predictions we make about social change, whether we mean the changes we
desire or the ones which circumstances force upon us. They also cut completely
across accepted political categories, as do the policies of the ecology lobby or the
environmental pressure groups in both Britain and the United States.

The growth economists, the politicians of both right and left, who envisaged an
ever-expanding cycle of consumption, with the philosophy characterised by Kenneth Burke as Borrow, Spend, Buy, Waste, Want,[2] have just not caught up with
future realities. If anyone has it is that minority among the young in the affluent
countries who have consciously rejected the mass consumption society—its values
as well as its dearly-bought products—and adopted, not out of Puritanism but out
of a different set of priorities, an earlier consumer philosophy: Eat it up, wear it out,
make it do, or do without. The editor of *The Ecologist* summed up the argument
thus: 'affluence for everybody is an impossible dream: the world simply does not
contain sufficient resources, nor could it absorb the heat and other waste generated
by the immense amount of energy required. Indeed, the most important thing to
realise, when we plan our future, is that affluence is both a local and a temporary
phenomenon. Unfortunately it is the principal, if not the only, goal our industrial
society gives us.' His journal in its 'Blueprint for Survival' has the distinction of
being among the few commentaries on the crisis of environment and resources to
go beyond predicting the consequences of continued population growth and deple-
tion of resources, to envisaging the kind of physical and economic structure of life
which its authors regard as indispensable for a viable future, drawing up a timetable
for change for the century 1975–2075, to establish in that time 'a network of self-
sufficient, self-regulating communities.'[3] The authors cheerfully accept the charge
that their programme is unsophisticated and over-simplified, the implication being
that if the reader can formulate a better alternative, or a different time-scale, he
should do so. The interesting thing is that they have re-invented an older vision
of the future. Back in the 1890s three men, equally unqualified as shareholders
in Utopia Limited, formulated their prescriptions for the physical setting of a future society. William Morris, designer and socialist, wrote *News from Nowhere*;
Peter Kropotkin, geographer and anarchist, wrote *Fields, Factories and Workshops*;
and Ebenezer Howard, inventor and parliamentary shorthand writer, wrote *Tomorrow: A Peaceful Path to Real Reform*. Each of these blueprints for survival was
more influential than its original readers could have supposed, though less than
its author would have hoped. Morris's vision was totally irrelevant for the twentieth century, but his picture of a post-industrial, decentralised, state-free Britain
in the twenty-first century, certainly makes sense for the new ecologically-aware
generation, while any American will recognise the force of his backward glance at
the future of the United States: 'For these lands, and, I say, especially the northern

parts of America, suffered so terribly from the full force of the last days of civilisation, and became such horrible places to live in, that one may say that for nearly a hundred years the people of the northern parts of America have been engaged in gradually making a dwelling-place out of a stinking dust-heap ... [4]

Howard's legacy is of course the new towns: his immediate purpose was to mobilise voluntary initiative for the building of one demonstration model, confident that its advantages would set in motion a large-scale adoption of the idea of urban dispersal in 'social cities', or what the TCPA calls 'a many-centred nexus of urban communities'. Lewis Mumford notes that 'By now, our neotechnic and biotechnic facilities have at last caught up with Howard's and Kropotkin's intuitions. Howard's plan for canalising the flow of population, diverting it from the existing centres to new centres; his plan for decentralising industry and setting up both city and industry within a rural matrix, the whole planned to a human scale, is technologically far more feasible today than it was ... [5]

Kropotkin's own vision of the future, with industry decentralised, and the competition for markets replaced by local production and consumption while people themselves alternate brain work and manual work, is being realised in a political climate he hardly foresaw, in China, but is equally in harmony with the programme of the 'Blueprint for Survival':

> The scattering of industries over the country—so as to bring the factory amidst the fields, to make agriculture derive all those profits which it always finds in being combined with industry and to produce a combination of industrial with agricultural work—is surely the next step to be taken ... This step is imposed by the necessity for each healthy man and woman to spend a part of their lives in manual work in the free air; and it will be rendered the more necessary when the great social movements, which have now become unavoidable, come to disturb the present international trade, and compel each nation to revert to her own resources for her own maintenance.[6]

The authors of the 'Blueprint', having set out their analysis of the crisis of population, resources and environment, sketch out what they see as a necessary and desirable future for the human habitat. They argue for decentralisation on several grounds. Their first reason is that it would 'promote the social conditions in which public opinion and full public participation in decision-making become as far as possible the means whereby communities are ordered'. Their second reason is that, on ecological grounds, they foresee a return to diversified farming instead of prairie-type crop-growing or factory-type livestock rearing, with production for a local market and the return of domestic sewage to the land, in the setting of 'a decentralised society of small communities where industries are small enough to be responsive to each community's needs'. Thirdly, they think it significant that 'the decreasing autonomy of communities and local regions, and the increasing centralisation of decision-making and authority in the cumbersome bureaucracies of the state, have been accompanied by the rise of self-conscious individualism, an individualism that feels threatened unless it is harped upon'.

They see the accumulation of material goods as the accompaniment of this self-conscious individualism (what others would call 'privatisation') and believe that the rewards of significant relationships and mutual responsibilities in a small community will provide ample compensation for the decreasing emphasis on consumption which will be essential for the conservation of resources and the minimisation of pollution. Their final reason is that 'to deploy a population in small towns and villages is to reduce to the minimum its impact on the environment. This is because the actual urban superstructure required per inhabitant goes up radically as the size of the town increases beyond a certain point.' Affirming that they are *not* proposing inward-looking, self-obsessed, or closed communities, but in fact want 'an efficient and sensitive communications network between all communities', they conclude with the splendid declaration: 'We emphasise that our goal should be to create *community feeling* and *global* awareness, rather than that dangerous and sterile compromise which is nationalism.'[7]

But will it ever happen? Will this humane and essentially anarchistic vision of a workable future simply join all the other anarchical utopias of the past? Years ago George Orwell remarked:

> If one considers the probabilities one is driven to the conclusion that anarchism implies a low standard of living. It need not imply a hungry or uncomfortable world, but it rules out the kind of air-conditioned, chromium-plated, gadget-ridden existence which is now considered desirable and enlightened. The processes involved in making, say, an aeroplane are so complex as to be only possible in a planned, centralised society, with all the repressive apparatus that that implies. Unless there is some unpredictable change in human nature, liberty and efficiency must pull in opposite directions.[8]

This, from Orwell's point of view (he was not a lover of luxury) is not in itself a criticism of anarchism, and he is certainly right in thinking that an anarchist society would never build Concorde or land men on the moon. But were either of these technological triumphs efficient in terms of the resources poured into them and the results for the ordinary inhabitant of this planet? Size and resources are to the technologist what power is to the politician: he can never have too much of them. A different kind of society, with different priorities, would evolve a different technology: its bases already exist[9] and in terms of the tasks to be performed it would be far more 'efficient' than either Western capitalism or Soviet state-capitalism. Not only technology but also economics would have to be redefined. As Kropotkin envisaged it: 'Political economy tends more and more to become a science devoted to the study of the needs of men and of the means of satisfying them with the least possible waste of energy—that is, a sort of physiology of society.'[10]

But it is not in the least likely that states and governments, in either the rich or the poor worlds will, of their own volition, embark on the drastic change of direction which a consideration of our probable future demands. Necessity may reduce the rate of resource-consumption but the powerful and privileged will hang on to their share—both within nations and between nations. Power and privilege have never been known to abdicate. This is why anarchism is bound to be a call to revolution. But what kind of revolution? Nothing has been said in this book about the two great irrelevancies of discussion about anarchism: the false antitheses between violence and nonviolence and between revolution and reform. The most violent institution in our society is the state and it reacts violently to efforts to take away its power. 'As Malatesta used to say, you try to do your thing and they intervene, and then *you* are to blame for the fight that happens.'[11] Does this mean that the effort should not be made? A distinction has to be made between the violence of the oppressor and the resistance of the oppressed.

Similarly, there is a distinction not between revolution and reform but on the one hand between the kind of revolution which installs a different gang of rulers or the kind of reform which makes oppression more palatable or more efficient, and on the other those social changes, whether revolutionary or reformist, through which people enlarge their autonomy and reduce their subjection to external authority.

Anarchism in all its guises is an assertion of human dignity and responsibility. It is not a programme for political change but an act of social self-determination.

# 2. MARTIN BUBER (1878–1965)

Every one of my influences has had views to express about the nature of human society. The reason why I found Martin Buber to be the best explainer of everything
I believe about social organisation was precisely because he did it more simply
than anyone else. I came across Buber only because he was frequently quoted by
Herbert Read in articles in the anarchist newspaper *Freedom*. Read was a director of the publishers Routledge and in 1949 produced an English translation of
Buber's book *Paths in Utopia*. This was a re-assertion of the anarchist tradition
in socialist thought, ridiculed for decades both before and after its publication by
two kinds of state worship, that of the Fabians and that of the Marxists.

Thereafter I watched Buber's sociological thought, and was won over by his
lecture on 'Society and the State' which crystallised a range of ideas that, paradoxically, earned him only hostility. In the 1950s my friend the architect Gabriel
Epstein, whose parents chanced to live in the same street in Jerusalem as Buber,
confirmed that the then Labour Party ruling elite in Israel saw him as a saboteur,
not as a support. Thirty years later, a veteran *kibbutznik* told me that in his opinion Buber was 'just an old phoney', and, sure enough, when Buber died in 1965,
*The Guardian* reported how 'In Palestine his idea of bi-nationalism caused him to
be ostracised by the orthodox as "an enemy of the people".'[12]

A philosopher who manages to antagonise everyone, yet who was himself a
model of gentle benevolence, must have something important to say, I reflected,
and I don't think I was wrong. His reputation was as a theologian, though I can
remember him declaring to a puzzled clergyman on a BBC television programme
that 'I must confess that I don't like religion very much', and parrying the suggestion that he was a mystic with the reply that he was in fact a rationalist, and
the affirmation that rationalism was 'the only one of my world views that I have
allowed to expand into an ism'.[13]

The only time I ever saw him was in 1956 at King's College in the Strand,
where, lecturing on 'That which is common', he related his philosophy of dialogue, set out in his book *I and Thou*, with his views on community and society.
He took as his text an account of Aldous Huxley's experiments with the drug mescalin, which became, in Buber's slow and emphatic English, a parable of what he
saw as the disjointed society of western individualism. Huxley, in his escape from
the 'painful earthly world' under the influence of the drug, found that his lips, the

Originally printed in Colin Ward, *Influences: Voices of Creative Dissent*. (Bideford, Devon:
Green Books, 1991).

palms of his hands, and his genitals (the organs of communication with others, in-terpolated Buber) became cold, and he avoided the eyes of those who were present. For, said Buber, to look into the eyes of others would be to recognise that which is common. And after this flight from the self and from the ordinary environment, Huxley 'met them with a deep mistrust'. Huxley regarded his mescalin intoxica-tion as a mystical experience, but, declared Buber, those whom we call mystics, like those we call creative artists, do not seek to escape from the human situation. 'They do not want to leave the authentic world of speech in which a response is demanded. They cling to the common world until they are torn from it.'[14]

'My innermost heart,' he confessed, 'loves the world more than it loves the spirit,' and he embarrassed his chairman by leaping up the steps of the steep lec-ture theatre to question his questioners in order to discern what they really want-ed to know.

For Buber held, as Herbert Read put it, 'that the communication of any truth, of any 'lesson', depends on the existence of a condition of mutuality between the teacher and the pupil—all effective communication is a dialogue ... '[15] Buber has a different significance for different readers. For me he is a social philosopher, a soci-ologist in fact, who had grasped many decades ago the nature of the crisis of both capitalism and socialism. 'The era of advanced Capitalism,' he wrote, 'has broken down the structure of society. The society, which preceded it was composed of dif-ferent societies; it was complex and pluralistic in structure. This is what gave it its peculiar social vitality and enabled it to resist the totalitarian tendencies inherent in the pre-revolutionary centralistic State.' But socialism too, had fallen victim to state-worship, and 'if socialism is to emerge from the blind-alley into which it has strayed, among other things the catchword 'Utopian' must be cracked open and examined for its true content.'[16]

He wasn't an anarchist. He was an advocate of what he called socialist plural-ism. But socialists have not yet caught up with him, neither in the west nor the east.

Buber was born in Vienna, a child of the Jewish enlightenment and emancipa-tion, but when his parents divorced, went to live with his grandfather at Lemberg in Galicia. There he 'enjoyed his all-too-brief and trembling years of piety' and 'ceased in his formal obedience to Jewish law,'[17] but also discovered the pietistic sect, the Hasidim. As a student of philosophy in Vienna in the 1890s he encoun-tered both the anarchist poet and propagandist Gustav Landauer and the Zionist movement. He was Landauer's collaborator, and after Laundauer's murder in the massacres following the Munich 'council republic' in the wake of the first world war, his executor. Buber's relations with Zionism were stormy. For him it had nothing to do with hopes for a Jewish state: 'Although for many Zionism became the cloak of pride, the instrument of masking their alienation and lack of roots in European soil, it was for Buber the means of renewing roots, the ultimate device of re-establishing, not sundering contact, with the European tradition,'[18] as well as with the ideology of co-operative settlements propagated by secular, socialist pioneers like Aaron David Gordon.[19]

In the cataclysm that befell Germany, Buber left in 1938 and was appointed professor of social philosophy at the Hebrew University at Jerusalem. There he was more isolated, ideologically, than at any time in his life. 'During the strife that accompanied the prelude and consummation of the State of Israel, Buber assumed a position (the natural consequence of his spiritual Zionism) which alienated vast elements of the Israeli community. Arguing with Judah Magnes, Ernst Simon, and others, that the only solution to the Jewish problem a bi-national state in which the Arabs and Jews should jointly participate and share, he aroused great bitterness and resentment.'[20]

In 1951 Buber was criticised for accepting the Goethe Prize of the University of Hamburg. Was he not, it was asked, in too much haste to forgive? His reply was to accept another German prize and in doing so, to say these words:

> About a decade ago a considerable number of Germans—there must have been many thousands of them—under the indirect command of the German government and the direct command of its representatives, killed millions of my people in a systematically prepared and executed procedure whose organised cruelty cannot be compared with any previous historical event. I, who am one of those who remained alive, have only in a formal sense a common humanity with those who took part in this action. They have so radically removed themselves from the human sphere, so transposed themselves into a sphere of monstrous inhumanity inaccessible to my conception, that not even hatred, much less an overcoming hatred, was able to arise in me. And what am I that I could here presume to forgive!
>
> When I think of the German people of the days of Auschwitz and Treblinka, I behold, first of all, the great many who knew that the monstrous event was taking place and did not oppose it. But my heart, which is acquainted with the weakness of men, refuses to condemn my neighbour for not prevailing upon himself to become a martyr. Next there emerges before me the mass of those who remained ignorant of what was withheld from the German public, and who did not try to discover what reality lay behind the rumours which were circulating. When I have these men in mind, I am gripped by the thought of the anxiety, likewise well known to me, of the human creature before a truth which he fears he cannot face. But finally there appears before me, from reliable reports, some who have become as familiar to me by sight, action and voice as if they were friends, those who refused to carry out the orders and suffered death or put themselves to death and those who learned what was taking place and opposed it and were put to death, or those who learned what was taking place and because they could do nothing to stop it killed themselves. I see these men very near before me in that especial intimacy which binds us at times to the dead and to them alone. Reverence and love for these Germans now fill my heart.[21]

Buber's book *Paths in Utopia*, completed in 1945, is a defence and restatement of that stream in socialist thought that was castigated by Marx and Engels as 'utopian', and was consequently ignored in the histories and university courses on political ideas. It focusses in particular on the anarchist tradition represented by Proudhon, Kropotkin and Landauer. On the issue of *ends* and *means*, he explains that

Kropotkin summed up the basic view of the ends in a single sentence: the fullest development of individuality 'will combine with the highest development of voluntary association in all its aspects, in all possible degrees and for all possible purposes; an association that is always changing, that bears in itself the elements of its own duration, that takes on the forms which best correspond at any given moment to the manifold strivings of all.' This is precisely what Proudhon had wanted in the maturity of his thought. It may be contended that the Marxist objective is not essentially different in constitution; but at this point a yawning chasm opens out before us which can only be bridged by that special form of Marxist utopics, a chasm between, on the one side, the transformation to be consummated some time in the future— no one knows how long after the final victory of the Revolution—and, on the other, the road to the Revolution and beyond it, which road is characterised by a far-reaching centralisation that permits no individual features and no individual initiative. Uniformity as a means is to change miraculously into multiplicity as an end; compulsion into freedom. As against this the 'utopian' or non-Marxist socialist desires a means commensurate with his ends; he refuses to believe that in our reliance on the future 'leap' we have to have now the direct opposite of what we are striving for; he believes rather that we must create here and now the space *now* possible for the thing for which we are striving, so that it may come to fulfilment then; he does not believe in the post-revolutionary leap, but he does believe in revolutionary continuity.[22]

He was writing, of course, long before the 'forty wasted years' of the imposition of Marxist regimes on Eastern Europe. But when we examine capitalist society, Buber goes on, 'we see that it is a society inherently poor in structure, and growing poorer every day.' (By the structure of a society is to be understood its social content or community content: a society can be called structurally rich to the extent that it is built up of genuine societies: that is local communes and trade communes and their step by step association.) He compares Proudhon's views with those of Saint-Simon: 'Saint-Simon started from the reform of the State, Proudhon from the transformation of society. A genuine reconstruction of society can only begin with a radical alteration of the relationship between the social and political order. It can no longer be a matter of substituting one political regime for another, but of the emergence, in place of a political regime grafted upon society, of a regime expressive of society itself.'

Buber sees Kropotkin as amplifying Proudhon's thought in stating the simple antithesis between the principles of the struggle for existence and mutual help. He regards Kropotkin's earlier theory of State as historically under-substantiated and sees as more useful the later view Kropotkin expressed in the French edition of 1913 of his *Modern Science and Anarchism*: 'All through the history of our civilization, two contrary traditions, two trends, have faced one another; the Roman tradition and the national tradition; the imperial and the federal; the authoritarian and the libertarian.'

And he thinks that Gustav Landauer's step beyond Kropotkin consists in his insight into the State. For Landauer, 'The State is a condition, a certain relationship between human beings, a mode of human behaviour; we destroy it by contracting other relationships, by behaving differently.'

He examines the ideas of Marx, Engels, Lenin and Stalin, and shows how in their attitudes to co-operatives and workers' councils, as well as to the old Russian communal institutions, the *mir* and the *artel*, these are seen simply as tools in the political struggle. 'From the standpoint of Leninism,' said Stalin, 'the collective economies and the Soviets as well, are taken as a form of organisation, a weapon and nothing but a weapon.' One cannot in the nature of things, comments Buber, 'expect a little tree that has been turned into a club to put forth leaves'.

Everything about Buber's social philosophy draws him towards the co-operative movement, whether seen as consumer co-ops, producer co-ops or the idea of co-operative living. He begins with the obvious comment that

> for the most part the running of large co-operative institutions has become more and more like the running of capitalist ones, and the bureaucratic principle has completely ousted, over a wide field, the voluntary principle, once prized as the most precious and indispensable possession of the co-operative movement. This is especially clear in countries where consumer societies have in increasing measure worked together with the state and the municipalities, and Charles Gide was certainly not far wrong when he called to mind the fable of the wolf disguised as a shepherd and voiced the fear that, instead of making the State 'co-operative' we should only succeed in making the co-operative 'static'.[23]

Those of us who have spent a lifetime as members of ordinary retail co-operative societies in Britain would no doubt agree. We have seen the internal politics of the co-operative movement used as a stepping stone to office by politicians of the left. At the same time, we have watched (and this was a factor that Buber failed to observe) the local branch managers of retail co-operative societies lured away by a doubling of their wages by the capitalist chains of retail supermarkets.

But Buber moved on to examine the repeated attempts in the previous 150 years in both Europe and America to found co-operative settlements. He found that he had to apply the word *failure* not merely to those attempts, which after a short existence, either disintegrated or took on what he saw as a capitalist complexion, thus going over to the enemy camp. He also applied a similar criticism to co-operative efforts which had aimed at a wider style of co-operative living, but in isolation from the rest of the world.

> For the real, the truly structural task of the new village communes begins with their *federation*, that is, their union under the same principle that operates in their internal structure. Even where, as with the Dukhobors in Canada, a sort of federation itself continues to be isolated and exerts no attractive and educative influence on society as a whole, with the result that the task never

gets beyond its beginnings and, consequently there can be no talk of success in the socialist sense. It is remarkable that Kropotkin saw in these two elements—isolation of the settlements from one another and isolation from the rest of society—the effective causes of failure even as ordinarily understood.[24]

If the 'full co-operative' in which production and consumption are united and industry is complemented by agriculture, is to become the cell of a new society, it is necessary, Buber argues, that 'there should emerge a network of settlements, territorially based and federatively constructed, without dogmatic rigidity, allowing the most diverse social forms to exist side by side, but always aiming at the new organic whole.' He believed, in 1945, that there was one effort 'which justifies our speaking of success in the socialistic sense, and that is in the Jewish Village Commune in its various forms, as found in Palestine.' He called the Kibbutz movement a signal non-failure—he could not say a signal success, because he was too aware of the setbacks and disappointments, of the intrusion of politics, and of the 'lamentable fact that the all-important attitude of neighbourly relationship has not been adequately developed,' and of how much remained to be done.

There are two poles of socialism, Buber concluded, between which our choice lies, 'one we must designate—so long as *Russia* has not undergone an essential inner change—by the formidable name of Moscow. The other I would make bold to call *Jerusalem*.'

This polarity has not worn well. Nearly half a century later, there may well be essential inner changes in Moscow, though not in the direction Buber might have hoped. As for Jerusalem, few would see it as a beacon of socialism. It was as long ago as the 1920s that Buber warned the Zionist movement that if the Jews in Palestine did not live *with* the Arabs as well as *next* to them, they would find themselves living in enmity towards them.[25]

In 1950, as part of the celebration of the 25th anniversary of the Hebrew University of Jerusalem, Buber delivered his lecture on 'Society and the State'. He begins by citing the view of the sociologist Robert MacIver that 'to identify the social with the political is to be guilty of the grossest of all confusions, which completely bars any understanding of either society or the state'. Buber traces through sages from Plato to Bertrand Russell the confusion between the social principle and the political principle. The political principle is seen in power, authority and dominion, the social principle in families, groups, union, co-operative bodies and communities. It is the same distinction that Jayaprakash Narayan used to draw between *rajniti* (politics of the state) and *lokniti* (politics of the people). For Buber,

> The fact that every people feels itself threatened by the others gives the State its definite unifying power; it depends upon the instinct of self-preservation of society itself; the latent external crisis enables it when necessary to get the upper hand in internal crises.[26]

Administration in the sphere of the social principle, says Buber, is equivalent to government in that of the political principle. But,

> All forms of government have this in common: each possesses more power than is required by the given conditions; in fact, this excess in the capacity for making dispositions is actually what we understand by political power. The measure of this excess, which cannot of course be computed precisely, represents the exact difference between Administration and Government. I call it the 'political surplus'. Its justification derives from the latent state of crisis between nations and within every nation ... The political principle is always stronger in relation to the social principle than the given conditions require. The result is a continuous diminution in social spontaneity.[27]

Ever since I read these words I have found Buber's terminology far more valuable as an explanation of events in the real world and far more helpful than a dozen lectures on political theory or on sociology. They cut the rhetoric of politics down to size. Apply them for example to the politics of Britain in the 1980s. Governments used the populist language of 'rolling back the frontiers of the state' and of 'setting the people free', while at the same time pursuing policies of ruthless and pervasive central control, as in their war against the slightest independent policies of local authorities. Voluntary organizations too were manipulated into becoming vehicles of government policy. The blatent external crisis in the form of the Cold War or the Falklands campaign was exploited 'when necessary to get the upper hand', and when the Cold War collapsed, the Gulf became a convenient successor.

If Buber's categories are observable in a relatively free society like Britain, they apply with dramatic force to the totalitarian regimes characteristic of the 20th century, which invariably sought to destroy all those social institutions they could not themselves dominate. The importance of the Catholic church in Poland or the Lutheran church in East Germany was not a matter of religious dogma, but in fact that they were among the few remaining alternative focii of power. Buber's 'continuous diminution in social spontaneity' is a feature of the Nazi period in Germany or the Bolshevik period in the Soviet Union, or indeed of Pinochet's Chile or Ceaucescu's Romania, that every survivor records.

Like Buber, I believe that the conflict between the social principle and the political principle is a permanent aspect of the human condition. He did us a service in excavating from Kropotkin's always optimistic writings the observation that the conflict between the authoritarian tradition and the libertarian tradition are as much part of the history of the future as of the past, and Landauer's view that this is not something that can be destroyed by a revolution.

If we want to weaken the state we must strengthen society, since the power of one is the measure of the weakness of the other. Buber's exploration of the paths to Utopia, far from confirming an acceptance of the way things are, confirms, as do several of my influences, that the fact that there is no route-map to utopia does not mean that there are no routes to more accessible destinations.

# 3. THE WELFARE ROAD WE FAILED TO TAKE

Every writer produces, every now and then, a phrase, a sentence or a paragraph, which to his or her immense gratification, other people quote. I have been writing for all my adult life, for propagandist reasons, so I frequently recycle other people's words, quite apart from my own, and I too, have a most-quoted paragraph, which I first used, I think, in a letter to *The Listener* in 1960 and recycled in 1973 in my book *Anarchy in Action*, which I am happy to say is endlessly translated and reprinted.

It expresses a commonplace of social history with which a specialist audience like you will be thoroughly familiar, but which perhaps is or was less well-known in the outside world. My most-quoted paragraph was this:

> When we compare the Victorian antecedents of our publics institutions with the organs of working-class mutual aid in the same period, the very names speak volumes. On the one side the Workhouse, the Poor Law Infirmary, the National Society for the Education of the Poor in Accordance with the Principles of the Established Church; and on the other, the *Friendly* Society, the Sick *Club,* the *Co-operative* Society, the Trade *Union.* One represents the tradition of fraternal and autonomous associations springing up from below, the other that of authoritarian institutions directed from above.

Now my quotable paragraph stresses a truth that has been ignored by socialists for generations, but it also relates to a question that students of politics have been asking themselves since 1979, which is that of the failure of British socialism to win the hearts of the British public.

In this connection, the paragraph that *I* frequently quote comes from Fabian Tract No. 4 called *What Socialism Is*, published in 1886. The anonymous introduction to that text remarked that:

> English Socialism is not yet Anarchist or Collectivist, nor yet defined enough in point of policy to be classified. There is a mass of Socialistic feeling not yet conscious of itself as Socialism. But when the unconscious Socialists of England discover their position, they also will probably fall into two parties; a Collectivist party supporting a strong central administration and

Originally printed in Colin Ward, *Social Policy: An Anarchist Response.* (London: Freedom Press, 2000), 9–18.

a counterbalancing Anarchist party defending individual initiative against that administration.

I have always found that to be an extraordinarily interesting unfulfilled prophecy, not because anyone would have expected an anarchist 'party' in the ordinary sense to have emerged, but because it was evident over a century ago that there were other paths to socialism beside the electoral struggle for power over the centralised state. It is also interesting because of its assumption that anarchism was individualistic as opposed to the collectivism of Fabian socialists.

Now the one celebrated anarchist thinker with whom the early Fabians were personally acquainted was Peter Kropotkin. In fact, in that same year, 1886, he and a Fabian, Charlotte Wilson, were to start the anarchist journal *Freedom*, which of course exists to this day, and was then subtitled 'A Journal of Anarchist-Communism'. His ideology was the very opposite of individualism, and his most famous book, *Mutual Aid: A Factor of Evolution*, was a long and detailed celebration of co-operation as the condition for survival in any species, in opposition to the so-called 'social Darwinists' and the dogma of the war of each against all.

In a later book, *Modern Science and Anarchism*, he declared that "the economic and political liberation of man will have to create new forms for its expression in life, instead of those established by the State". For he thought it self-evident that "this new form will have to be more popular, more decentralised, and nearer to the folk-mote self-government than representative government can ever be", reiterating that we will be compelled to find new forms of organisation for the social functions that the state fulfills through the bureaucracy, and that "as long as this is not done, nothing will be done".

Part of Kropotkin's argument, and mine, is that in the nineteenth century the newly-created British working class built up from nothing a vast network of social and economic initiatives based on self-help and mutual aid. The list is endless: friendly societies, building societies, sick clubs, coffin clubs, clothing clubs, up to enormous federated enterprises like the trade union movement and the Co-operative movement. The question that latter-day re-discoverers of that tradition ask is, 'How did we allow it to ossify?'

The Indian politician Jayaprakash Narayan used to say that Gandhi used up all the moral oxygen in Indian, so the British Raj suffocated. In exactly the same way, I would claim that the political left in this country invested all its fund of social inventiveness in the idea of the state, so that its own traditions of self-help and mutual aid were stifled for lack of ideological oxygen. How on earth did British socialists allow these concepts to be hijacked by the political right, since it is these human attributes, and not the state and its bureaucracies, that actually hold human society together?

Politically, it was because of the implicit alliance of Fabians and Marxists, both of whom believed completely in the state, and assumed that they would be the particular elite in control of it. Administratively it was because of the alliance of bureaucrats and professionals: the British civil service and the British professional classes, with their undisguised contempt for the way ordinary people organised anything. I have been reading Ralf Dahrendorf's history of the LSE and have reached his account for the Minority Report of the Royal Commission on the Poor Law from 1909. He remarks that:

> what followed from the Minority Report was a welfare state with specialised public agencies for every need: health and housing, education and unemployment, disability and old age. There were many reasons to be sceptical. Some undoubtedly preferred the status quo to the 'socialism' of a welfare state of this kind; others abhorred the bureaucratic nightmare and the rule of unaccountable 'experts'.

However, that document set the pattern realised after 1945. The great tradition of working-class self-help and mutual aid was written off, not just as irrelevant, but as an actual impediment, by the political and professional architects of the welfare state, aspiring to a universal public provision of everything for everybody. The contribution that the recipients had to make to all this theoretical bounty was ignored as a mere embarrassment—apart, of course, from paying for it. The nineteenth century working classes, living far below the tax threshold, taxed themselves in pennies every week for the upkeep of their innumerable friendly societies. The twentieth century employed workers, as well as its alleged National Insurance contributions, pays a large slice of its income for the support of the state. The socialist ideal was rewritten as a world in which everyone was entitled to everything, but where nobody except the providers had any actual say about anything. We have been learning for years, in the anti-welfare backlash, what a very vulnerable utopia that was.

History itself was re-interpreted to suit the managerial, political and bureaucratic vision. The medical historian Roy Porter remarks that "Beatrice Webb admitted doctoring the presentation of her evidence on friendly societies for the 1909 report", as though everybody knew this. And what is taught about the origins of the welfare state implies that twentieth century state universalism replaced the pathetic unofficial or voluntary and patchy pioneering ventures of the nineteenth century. However, in the past 25 years or so, a new interest in popular history, exemplified by the History Workshop movement and the boom in local and oral history, has uncovered buried layers of our past.

Take education as an example. We have absorbed the official line that it was only rivalry between religious bodies that delayed until 1870 (and in effect 1880 or later) universal, free and compulsory elementary education. A centenary publication from the National Union of Teachers (*The Struggle for Education,* 1970) said that "apart from religious and charitable schools, 'dame' or common schools were operated by the private enterprise of people who were often barely literate", and it explained the widespread working class hostility to the school boards with the remark that "parents were not always quick to appreciate the advantages of full-time schooling against the loss of extra wages". But recent historians have shown the resistance to state schooling in a quite different light. Stephen Humphries is the author of *Hooligans or Rebels? An Oral History of Working Class Childhood and Youth*

*1889–1939* (first published by Basil Blackwell in 1981 and just reprinted). He finds that these private schools, by the 1860s, "were providing an alternative education for approximately one-third of all working-class children" and suggests that:

> This enormous demand for private as opposed to public education is perhaps best illustrated by the fact that working-class parents in a number of major cities responded to the introduction of compulsory attendance regulation not by sending their children to provided state schools, as government had predicted, but by extending the length of their child's education in private schools. Parents favoured these schools for a number of reasons: They were small and close to home and were consequently more personal and more convenient than most publicly provided schools; they were informal, tolerant of irregular attendance and unpunctuality; no attendance registers were kept; they were not segregated according to age and sex; they used individual as opposed to authoritarian teaching methods; and, most important, they belonged to, and were controlled by the local community rather than being imposed on the neighbourhood by an alien authority.

This dissenting interpretation of the history of schooling was reinforced with a mass of statistical evidence in a subsequent book by Philip Gardner, *The Lost Elementary Schools of Victorian England* (Croom Helm, 1984). He found that what he called working-class schools, set up by working-class people in working-class neighbourhoods, "achieved just what the customers wanted: quick results in basic skills like reading, writing and arithmetic, wasted no time on religious studies and moral uplift, and represented a genuinely alternative approach to childhood learning to that prescribed by the education experts". When the historian Paul Thompson discussed the implications of this book in *New Society* (6th December 1984) he concluded that the price of eliminating those schools had been "the suppression in countless working-class children of the very appetite for education and ability to learn independently which contemporary progressive education seeks to rekindle". Since he wrote, of course, the Department of Education has sought to extinguish the concept of progressive education.

Another field where the excavation of previously distorted history has yielded surprising facts is that of medicine. Now I am old enough to have been an employed worker under the pre-NHS system of panel doctors and 'approved societies', so of course I know that it was a comprehensive and free-at-the-point-of delivery system provided that you were an employed worker, with no prescription charge and no charge for dentistry for example.

I also know that it wasn't the Thatcher government which set about reorganising the NHS. It has been in a state of continuous reorganisation since its inception. Like you, I have heard former employees of the expensive consultants McKinsey's, confessing that the advice they gave was bad advice, just as I have heard Mr William Tatton-Brown, the former chief architect to the Department of Health, confessing that the advice he had given on the distribution, size and design of hospitals was also wrong.

In this area I can't improve on Ivan Illich's conclusions about the profession-alisation of knowledge:

> It makes people dependent on having their knowledge produced for them. It leads to a paralysis of the moral and political imagination ... Over-confidence in 'better knowledge' becomes a self-fulfilling prophecy. People first cease to trust their own judgement and then want to be told the truth about what they know. Over-confidence in 'better decision-making' first hampers people's ability to decide for themselves and then undermines their belief that they can decide.

Consequently, ten years ago I was happy to read the book by David Green, who had recently been a Labour councillor in Newcastle-upon-Tyne, called *Working-Class Patients and the Medical Establishment: Self-Help in Britain from the Mid-Nineteenth Century to 1948* (Gower/Temple 1986). His study of self-governing working-class medical societies showed that the self-organisation of patients provided a rather better degree of consumer control of medical services than had been achieved in post-Lloyd George and post-Bevan days. Not the least of the virtues of that book was that, as Roy Porter noted, "he takes that hallowed belief of progressives—that the improvement of the people's health hinges on state intervention—challenges its historical accuracy, and questions whether it is, in any case, a good doctrine for the Left to hold" (*New Society,* 28th February 1986).

I first met David Green only recently, at a seminar organised by Demos, and learned that there was no place for him on the political Left, since he was talking as Director of the Health and Welfare Unit at the Institute of Economic Affairs. I must add that his recent book *Reinventing Civil Society* (IEA, 1993) is a criticism, not a defence of Thatcherism. But it is also a criticism of the automatic assumptions of the political Left and its faith in the State.

Since most of us gather more information from television than from books, it is worth noting that more people were set thinking about the issues involved by Peter Hennessey's Channel 4 series called *What Has Become of Us.* In preparation for his book *Never Again* he talked to retired miners in the shadow of a statue of Aneurin Bevan. They had been members of the Tredegar Medical Aid Society, founded in 1870, which provided medical and hospital care for everyone in the district, whether or not they were among the nine million people who were members of mutual aid societies among the twelve million covered by the 1911 Act. They told Hennessey that "We thought he was turning the whole country in to one big Tredegar".

On the day I met David Green, *The Independent* (3rd April 1995) chanced to have a story about the final demise of this body. This explained that it "sustained itself through the years by voluntary contributions of three old pennies in the pound from the wage-packets of miners and steelworkers ... At one time the society employed five doctors, a dentist, a chiropodist and a physiotherapist" and of course a hospital "to care for the health of about 250,000 people".

Why didn't the whole country become, not one big Tredegar, but a network of Tredegars? The answer is that all parties became advocates of what that anony-

mous Fabian pamphleteer of 110 years ago called "a strong central administration", or what the philosopher Martin Buber called "the political surplus" of the
state over society. There is no room for self-taxation in a state where the treasury of
central government has a virtual monopoly of revenue-gathering. When every employed worker in Tredegar paid a voluntary levy of three old pence in the pound,
the earnings of even high-skilled industrial workers were below the liability to
income tax. But ever since PAYE was introduced in the second world war, the
Treasury has creamed off the cash which once supported local initiatives. If the
pattern of local self-taxation on the Tredegar model really had become the universal pattern for health provision, it would not have become the plaything of central
government financial policy.

As it is, of course, the affluent can buy private health care, though neither
BUPA not the NHS can be described as user-controlled. There once was the option of universal health provision 'at the point of service' if only Fabians, Marxists
and Aneurin Bevan had trusted the state and centralised revenue-gathering and
policy-making less, and our capacity for self-help and mutual aid more. ...

Now the standard argument against a localist and decentralist point of view,
is that of universalism: an equal service to all citizens, which it is thought that
central control achieves. The short answer to this is that it doesn't!

We have all learned how in the early 1920s George Lansbury and Poplar Borough councillors went to jail for refusing to pay the poor rate demanded from
them, when far richer boroughs paid less. Isn't it still true today that the Council
Tax is higher in London's poorest boroughs than in its richest ones? When I was
a child certain parts of the country were designated as Depressed Areas, for extra
central government aid. Later the names were changed to Special Areas or Assisted Areas. Despite decades of special redistributive policy they are still the poorest
parts of the country. Standards of provision *do* vary despite years of allegiance to
universalist policies. I live deep in the country in an affluent area, midway between
two large towns. Doctors refer patients to the big hospitals in Town A or Town
B, but you can hear from patients that they have very different reputations, which
often relate to individual departments. The same user opinion obviously applies
to schools too.

I think it is time to admit that universalism is an unattainable idea in a society that is enormously divided in terms of income and access to employment. We
would do better to look at a society which turns British assumptions upside down.
I am talking about Switzerland, which considers itself to be a welfare society rather than a welfare state. I do not suggest that the Swiss Confederation is anything
like an anarchist society. (Thanks to the fact that it has a Freedom of Information
Act, my anarchist friends there have applied for their secret police records, which
even with many blacked-out pages, are impressively long.)

But in that country, where voluntary bodies for every conceivable purpose
proliferate, the revenue-gathering body is the *commune*, large or small, grudgingly passes over some cash to the *cantons*, which passes on some to the *federal
council*. What I learn from students of the Swiss system like Ioan Bowen Rees in
*Government by Community* (Chas. Knight & Co., 1971) or Jonathan Steinberg

in *Why Switzerland?* (Cambridge, 1976, 1996), is that the civic sense there is so well-developed a tradition that the rich communes come to the rescue of the poor communes, out of a sense of social responsibility.

I attribute the fact that this is inconceivable in Britain to the fact that we stifled the localist and voluntarist approach in favour of conquest of the power of the state. We took the wrong road to welfare.

The appalling problem, for you as much as for me, is the question of how we get back on the mutual aid road *instead of* commercial health insurance and private pension schemes. We have all watched the eagerness with which Building Societies have turned themselves into banks and shed the last vestiges of their origins as mutual friendly societies. Similarly we have seen the retail co-operative movement shaking off its history faced by the inroads into its market by its capitalist rivals.

As the official welfare edifice, patiently built up by the Fabians and Beveridge, becomes merely the safety-net for the poor who can't afford anything better, the likeliest slow renewal of the self-help and mutual aid principle seems to me to emerge from the new so-called underclass of those people rejected by the economy in alliance with those déclassé people who just can't stomach current economic and social values. I am thinking of marginal activities like food co-ops, credit unions, tenant self-management, and LETS (Local Exchange Trading Systems).

Huge welfare networks were built up by the poor in the rise of industrial Britain. Perhaps they will be rebuilt, out of the same sheer necessity during its decline. What do you think?

## BIBLIOGRAPHY

(1886) *What Socialism Is*, Fabian Tract No. 4, Fabian Society: London.

Gardner, Phillip. *The Lost Elementary Schools of Victorian England*. London: Croom Helm, 1984.

Green, David. *Reinventing Civil Society*. London: Institute of Economic Affairs, Health and Welfare Unit, 1993.

———. *Working-Class Patients and the Medical Establishment: Self-Help in Britain from the Mid-Nineteenth Century to 1948*. Aldershot: Gower/Temple, 1985.

Humphries, Stephen. *Hooligans or Rebels? An Oral History of Working Class Childhood and Youth 1889–1939*. Oxford: Basil Blackwell, 1981.

Kropotkin, Peter. *Mutual Aid: A Factor of Evolution*. London: Freedom Press, 1987.

Porter, Roy. *New Society* (28 February 1986).

Rees, Ioan Bowen. *Government by Community*. London: Chas Knight, 1971.

Steinberg, Jonathan. *Why Switzerland?* Cambridge: Cambridge University Press, 1996 .

Thompson, Paul. *New Society* (6 December 1984).

Ward, Colin. *Anarchy in Action*. London: Freedom Press, 1996.

# 4. GREEN CITIES

Before the explosion in the population in the nineteenth century, cities were green. Old maps show them to be full of gardens both around and detached from the houses. Birmingham was a garden city. A historian of the years 1810–20 celebrated 'the Birmingham working man' with whom 'the cultivation of flowers was carried to great perfection' and in 1825 the author of *A Picture of Birmingham* recorded that

> ... from the west end of this area (north of the town centre) we enjoy a pleasing and lively summer-view over a considerable tract of land laid out in small gardens. This mode of applying plots of ground in the immediate vicinity of the town, is highly beneficial to the inhabitants ... They promote healthful exercise and rational enjoyment among families of the artisans; and, with good management, produce an ample supply of those wholesome vegetable stores, which are comparatively seldom tasted by the middling classes when they have to be purchased.[28]

The Georgian square, in both its grand and its humble forms, combining urbanity and greenness, was the finest architectural expression of the domestic love of foliage. Thus even in the most tightly packed streets of terraced houses the view from the rear upstairs window was of plants in pots, barrels, orange-boxes and old tin cans among the wash-houses and privies in tiny backyards. In Nottingham a century ago, when the close-packed terraces often even omitted a backyard, one family in three had an allotment on which they grew roses as well as cabbages. The urban back garden has always been one of the most cherished of amenities, being used not only as an outdoor room, a storage space, a workshop, a dump, a playpen and safe playground, but also as the one place where people can indulge in their passion for growing things. The uses change from family to family and from time to time in the same household. The important thing is that the space is there and that the space is theirs. The managers of urban space ignored these domestic priorities (which, no doubt, they automatically enjoyed themselves). Sir Ashley Bramall wisely commented that the old county of London was a city of small houses, and

Not only did the war scatter the population and destroy the homes, but it led

Originally printed in Colin Ward, *Welcome, Thinner City: Urban Survival in the 1990s.* (London: Bedford Square Press, 1989), 96–102.

to the rebuilding of London as a city of blocks of flats, of increasing height. This change has never been fully accepted by the population and there has been an increasing urge for movement to outer London and to the counties beyond, where the old pattern of street and house and garden could be recaptured.[29]

In fact it could always have been recaptured. A variation on the Georgian square developed in some places in the early nineteenth century: the hollow square. Here there was street, house and garden, but the garden opened into, or overlooked, a hidden open space which was surrounded on all four sides by streets, but gave an impression of rural seclusion. They occur not only on a grand scale behind Holland Park and Ladbroke Grove in West London, but also in a more workaday way in Fulham where, in the 1960s, there was still an enclosed smallholding surrounded by the densest pattern of streets, or in Hackney, where the neighbours in surrounding streets have colonised one of these secret gardens to provide allotments and an adventure playground. When I expressed amazement at the great green space beyond the garden of his house in Lansdowne Road, W11, the late Derek Bridgwater told me that every urban pundit from Steen Eiler Rasmussen to Lewis Mumford had been just as surprised. It is almost 80 years since Raymond Unwin demonstrated, in his pamphlet *Nothing Gained by Overcrowding!*,[30] the immense saving in development costs which this layout provided, as well as the advantages for the occupants. Happily, the Mulberry Housing Cooperative ... follows precisely the layout of the hollow square. It is a much more useful and usable form of open space than a sea of municipal grass around a housing estate.

But the provision of greenery in the urban environment is not primarily a matter of residential layout, for it depends on easy and daily access. In the nineteenth century, battles were fought to preserve ancient commons for public use, benefactors dedicated parkland to their communities and the city fathers established the tradition of public parks. In the twentieth century, planning standards were laid down to ensure that there was a certain quantity of open space per 1,000 of population. The National Playing Fields Association, which saw its function as broader than the simple provision of football fields or cricket pitches, drew attention to the overcrowded inner city areas which were inevitably under-provided for by comparison with richer or newer parts of the city.[31] Wartime bombing provided the opportunity for local authorities to convert some inner city areas back to grass in attempts to make good the deficiencies in playing field and playground space. Some very dreary and windy open spaces resulted. Official attitudes, as late as the 1960s and 1970s, were

> ... based on a hierarchical principle: parks fulfil different functions with increasing size and distance from the home. Variety of park function is thus achieved through a spatial supply of sites where the most diverse functions are offered by the largest parks. The hierarchy assumes that parks of equivalent status offer the same quality of recreational experiences and that they are equally accessible to all sections of the community.[32]

The shift in perception that contradicted this hierarchical, statistical approach to the provision of green space in the city was a result of the emergence of what is loosely called the 'environmental' movement. This has taken a variety of forms, sometimes with very different aims. One branch is the intense growth of interest in wildlife, where changes in rural life, especially in agriculture, have resulted in the paradox that, like the gypsies, wild creatures can often best be studied in the cities. Old graveyards, railway embankments, reservoirs and derelict sites became a sanctuary for both flora and fauna. This is not a new phenomenon. It was carefully recorded after the war by Robin Fitter[33] and given new topicality by Richard Mabey in the 1970s.[34] By the 1980s it was possible for Bob Smythe, an inner city councillor for five years, to publish a gazetteer of urban wildlife sites in Greater London, Bristol and South Wales, Birmingham and the Midlands, Manchester and the north-west, Yorkshire and the northeast, and Scotland.[35] The fact that he can guide us to over 300 urban wildlife sites is not only an indication of a change in perception, but also of altered professional and official attitudes in response to the incredible spread of local wildlife groups since the 1970s. Such bodies as the British Trust for Conservation Volunteers have moved from being organisers of voluntary activists who are now 'increasingly unhappy at their own diminishing influence on the Trust's affairs' to becoming large-scale employers of labour under the ever-changing regime of urban aid, 'partnership' and EEC funding. They have to exploit the sources of finance available to them, and they simply reflect the enormous interest in the greening of the cities.

Parallel with the urban wildlife movement has been the growth of city farms. We forget how within living memory, not only horses but also cows, sheep, goats, pigs and poultry were kept in inner city areas. 'Much of this husbandry was insanitary, a lot of it was downright cruel, but it is true that before the war, the East End was teeming with animals.'[36] The rediscovery of urban farming began with the initiative of Inter Action in Kentish Town in London in 1972. It has a community workshop, riding school, stable, sheep, goats, pigs, rabbits, geese, chickens, ducks and a cow. There is a conscious aim of mixing age-groups, with children and young people looking after the animals while adults, working on their own projects, are constantly around. A second such venture in the derelict Surrey Docks was the work of Hilary Peters who paradoxically remarked that 'I find farming methods in the country very cruel and difficult to stomach. Farming in London is easier and freer.'[37] The movement spread. I remember from the late 1970s the local couple, who found their ideal mission in running the Spitalfields Farm, reflecting on the educational value of sending children to the market wholesalers to scrounge fodder for the livestock they had come to cherish. The Mudchute in the Isle of Dogs is a hummocky area that originated from the dumping of waste material excavated when the Millwall Docks were first built. This 30-acre site became the biggest of all city farms, with a grant from the London Docklands Development Corporation: 'Look closely, and all of the poignant contradictions of the eighties are here, as cows graze peacefully beneath the tower blocks—the beleaguered local community, the cheerful, and expert, local history group and Community Poster Project.'[38] At the eastern end of the Docklands area, I found the Beckton

Meadows Community Smallholding in a two-and-a-half acre wedge of former allotment land where a handful of local people, convinced that animal husbandry
is an essential aspect of urban life, keep goats, geese, ducks, rabbits and a breeding
sow, with a bunch of children and teenagers to help them. Through accidents of
history, the London Residuary Body owns the site and has a statutory duty to
make the maximum financial gain from it, when the LDDC is ready to bid.

The city farm movement has spread, not through any official body but from
local enthusiasm, to every city in Britain. There are now between 50 and 60 such
ventures, linked by a quarterly journal.[39] A similar burst of new interest has arisen
in the world of the allotment or community garden. Allotment gardens have been
part of the urban scene for 200 years. They have symbolic and historical significance as the only enshrinement in law of the ancient and universal belief that every family has a right of access to land for food production. The legislation does
not say where, when or how soon the citizens can have their plots. Some local
authorities have waiting lists, others have embarrassingly empty ground. A sharp
postwar decline led the government to review policy and recommend legislative
and other changes by way of a committee chaired by Professor Harry Thorpe.[40] He
saw the allotment movement as declining, an enthusiasm of a dwindling bunch
of old men which would die with them unless radical changes were introduced.
No government has acted on his recommendations, published in 1969, but his
forebodings of inevitable decline did not come true. For, in the 1970s, the new
environmental consciousness, ideas of self-sufficiency, and the upsurge of enthusiasm for fresh and organically grown food brought a new influx of demand. It was
reported in 1979 that 'Nearly all towns and cities in Great Britain are experienc-
ing a boom in the interest shown in allotments. In England and Wales, the waiting list for allotments has gone up a staggering 1,600 per cent.'[41]

By the 1980s the demand has stabilised and allotment societies are ill-
equipped to withstand the pressures on local authorities to dispose of land for
more profitable uses, despite the statutory protection. Sometimes these pressures
have been successfully resisted but, in any case, a whole series of new initiatives,
outside the traditional allotment movement, have sought to make new gardens in
the heart of the inner cities. In Moss Side, Manchester, Bill McKeever of Playthor-
pe Street, through a total personal commitment, has established new allotments
in the Housing Action Area. In the East End of Glasgow the Barrowfield Community Association has established its own secret gardens. In Hackney, East London, a local general practitioner, Jon Fuller, has persuaded the council to release
and fence a whole series of pocket-sized sites for the New Hackney Allotment Society. In Newcastle upon Tyne the activities coordinated by Voluntary Initiatives
in Vacant Areas (VIVA) have created a variety of new gardens. In Sparkbrook,
Birmingham, the Ashram Asian Vegetable Project has turned abandoned land
into food production for the local community. In Islington a group of residents
made use of the council's Partnership Programme to make the Culpepper Community Garden.

These initiatives, like dozens of others, are not co-ordinated and, in fact, there
is no reason why they should be. For they depend absolutely upon local enthusi-

asm and energy, and on the ability to make use of the range of grants and special funding, as well as of temporary work funded by the Youth Employment Scheme or now-abandoned Community Programme. The reliance on short term funding and job-creation projects brings its own difficulties, but has also enabled local groups to establish new permanent work in city greening and in associated activities, such as recycling waste products, insulating houses and other environmental improvements.[42] The greening of the cities, in thousands of little local projects, is a genuinely popular movement[43] made possible by the thinning-out of the overcrowded industrial city. Yet these values emerging from the daily lives of city dwellers are consistently undervalued by politicians and professions. Jonathon Porritt reports that 'greenery seems to have become irrevocably entangled in the barbed wire of class antagonism by being perceived as being overwhelmingly middle class'.[44] On the other hand, when Jacquelin Burgess and Carolyn Harrison of the geography department of University College, London, attended a conference on public perceptions of the countryside, they reported with dismay that 'Throughout the proceedings the general public was portrayed as insensitive, ignorant and passive; as people who do not share the same insights, knowledge or active concerns of the committed few.'[45]

Doctors Harrison and Burgess were entitled to be dismissive, as for years they had been conducting an extensive series of interviews and group discussions to discover the concepts, beliefs and values about the green environment among residents of different neighbourhoods in several inner city areas ranging from a white working-class district, through a group of Asian women, to a middle-class community.

They found that these groups, regardless of social class, income or residence, 'gained great pleasure from the natural world', less in parks or playing fields than in daily life. The sensuous experience of encountering the natural world gave enormous pleasure in 'walks along the riverside', round the houses and on the way to school; waste places seen from the top of a bus or used by children; streams and scrubby bits; farmland, woodland, golf courses, cemeteries and squares in shopping centres. All these spaces, especially 'the wild bits', and most especially among people living in estates without gardens, were highly valued because they provide places 'where children can have adventures, experience independence for the first time, enjoy the companionship of other children, and discover the natural world'.

This view of the social role of the urban green was given great stress by the Asian women, 'separated from their childhood by geographical distance as well as age', and whose ordinary experiences of open spaces include racial abuse and physical harassment. Indeed, since everyday fears, especially of more wooded and secluded places, include assault and violence, sexual dangers for women and children, vandalism, glue-sniffing and every kind of contemporary horror, Doctors Harrison and Burgess stress the need for more *social* management of these places which have a *social* meaning.[46]

They tried to find a concept that really reflected the aspirations of the inner city groups whose green values they explored, which embraced the sensory experience of contact with nature, the wonderland of adventurous play for the young, and a shared experience with children, families, neighbours and friends.

The memorable phrase which occurred to them was outside the vocabulary of the parks department, the director of leisure services and even, I fear, that of the conservation lobby. It was 'gateways to a better world'.

# 5. ANARCHIST SOCIOLOGY OF FEDERALISM

## THE BACKGROUND

That minority of children in any European country who were given the opportunity of studying the history of Europe as well as that of their own nations, learned that there were two great events in the last century: the unification of Germany, achieved by Bismarck and Emperor Wilhelm I, and the unification of Italy, achieved by Cavour, Mazzini, Garibaldi and Vittorio Emanuale II.

The whole world, which in those days meant the European world, welcomed these triumphs. Germany and Italy had left behind all those little principalities, republics and city states and papal provinces, to become nation states and empires and conquerors. They had become like France, whose little local despots were finally unified by force first by Louis XIV with his majestic slogan 'L'Etat c'est moi', and then by Napoleon, heir to the Grande Revolution, just like Stalin in the twentieth century who build the administrative machinery to ensure that it was true. Or they had become like England, whose kings (and its one republican ruler Oliver Cromwell) had successfully conquered the Welsh, Scots and Irish, and went on to dominate the rest of the world outside Europe. The same thing was happening at the other end of Europe. Ivan IV, correctly named 'The Terrible', conquered central Asia as far as the Pacific, and Peter I, known as 'The Great', using the techniques he learned in France and Britain, took over the Baltic, most of Poland and the west Ukraine.

Advanced opinion throughout Europe welcomed the fact that Germany and Italy had joined the gentlemen's club of national and imperialist powers. The eventual results in the present century were appalling adventures in conquest, the devastating loss of life among young men from the villages of Europe in the two world wars, and the rise of populist demagogues like Hitler and Mussolini, as well as their imitators, to this day, who claim that 'L'Etat c'est moi'.

Consequently every nation has had a harvest of politicians of every persuasion who have argued for European unity, from every point of view: economic, social, administrative and, of course, political.

Needless to say, in efforts for unification promoted by politicians we have a multitude of administrators in Bruxelles issuing edicts about which varieties of vegetable seeds or what constituents of beefburgers or ice cream may be sold in the shops of the member-nations. The newspapers joyfully report all this trivia.

Originally printed in *Freedom* (June 27, 1992 and July 11, 1992).

The press gives far less attention to another undercurrent of pan-European opinion, evolving from the views expressed in Strasbourg from people with every kind of opinion on the political spectrum, claiming the existence of a Europe of the Regions, and daring to argue that the Nation State was a phenomenon of the sixteenth to nineteenth centuries, which will not have any useful future in the twenty-first century. The forthcoming history of administration in the federated Europe they are struggling to discover is a link between, let us say, Calabria, Wales, Andalusia, Aquitaine, Galicia or Saxony, as regions rather than as nations, seeking their regional identity, economically and culturally, which had been lost in their incorporation in nation states, where the centre of gravity is elsewhere. In the great tide of nationalism in the nineteenth century, there was a handful of prophetic and dissenting voices, urging a different style of federalism. It is interesting, at the least, that the ones whose names survive were the three best known anarchist thinkers of that century: Pierre-Joseph Proudhon, Michael Bakunin and Peter Kropotkin. The actual evolution of the political left in the twentieth century has dismissed their legacy as irrelevant. So much the worse for the left, since the road has been emptied in favour of the political right, which has been able to set out its own agenda for both federalism and regionalism. Let us listen, just for a few minutes, to these anarchist precursors.

## PROUDHON

First there was Proudhon, who devoted two of his voluminous works to the idea of federation in opposition to that of the nation state. They were *La Federation et l'Unite en Italie* of 1862, and in the following year, his book *Du Principe Federatif.*

Proudhon was a citizen of a unified, centralised nation state, with the result that he was obliged to escape to Belgium. And he feared the unification of Italy on several different levels. In his book *De la Justice* of 1858, he claimed that the creation of the German Empire would bring only trouble to the Germans and to the rest of Europe, and he pursued this argument into the politics of Italy.

On the bottom level was history, where natural factors like geology and climate had shaped local customs and attitudes. "Italy," he claimed, "is federal by the constitution of her territory; by the diversity of her inhabitants; in the nature of her genius; in her mores; in her history. She is federal in all her being and has been since all eternity ... And by federation you will make her as many times free as you give her independent states." Now it is not for me to defend the hyperbole of Proudhon's language, but he had other objections. He understood how Cavour and Napoleon III had agreed to turn Italy into a federation of states, but he also understood that, per esempio, the House of Savoy would settle for nothing less than a centralised constitutional monarchy. And beyond this, he profoundly mistrusted the liberal anti-clericalism of Mazzini, not through any love of the Papacy but because he recognised that Mazzini's slogan, 'Dio e popolo', could be exploited by any demagogue who could seize the machinery of a centralised state. He claimed that the existence of this administrative machinery was an absolute threat to personal and local liberty. Proudhon was almost alone among nineteenth century political theorists to perceive this:

> Liberal today under a liberal government, it will tomorrow become the formi-
> dable engine of a usurping despot. It is a perpetual temptation to the executive
> power, a perpetual threat to the people's liberties. No rights, individual or
> collective, can be sure of a future. Centralisation might, then, be called the
> disarming of a nation for the profit of its government.

Everything we now know about the twentieth century history of Europe, Asia, Latin America or Africa supports this perception. Nor does the
North American style of federalism, so lovingly conceived by Thomas Jeffer-
son, guarantee the removal of this threat. One of Proudhon's English biog-
raphers, Edward Hyams, comments that: "It has become apparent since the
Second World War that United States Presidents can and do make use of the
Federal administrative machine in a way which makes a mockery of democracy." And his Canadian translator paraphrases Proudhon's conclusion thus:

> Solicit men's view in the mass, and they will return stupid, fickle and violent
> answers; solicit their views as members of definite groups with real solidarity
> and a distinctive character, and their answers will be responsible and wise.
> Expose them to the political 'language' of mass democracy, which represents
> 'the people' as unitary and undivided and minorities as traitors, and they will
> give birth to tyranny; expose them to the political language of federalism, in
> which the people figures as a diversified aggregate of real associations, and
> they will resist tyranny to the end.

This observation reveals a profound understanding of the psychology of
politics. Proudhon was extrapolating from the evolution of the Swiss Confederation, but Europe has other examples in a whole series of specialist fields. The
Netherlands has a reputation for its mild or lenient penal policy. The official
explanation of this is the replacement in 1886 of the Code Napoleon by "a genuine Dutch criminal code" based upon cultural traditions like "the well-known
Dutch 'tolerance' and tendency to accept deviant minorities". I am quoting the
Netherlands criminologist Dr Willem de Haan, who cites the explanation that
Dutch society 'has traditionally been based upon religious, political and ideological rather than class lines. The important denominational groupings created their own social institutions in all major public spheres. This process ... is
responsible for transporting a pragmatic, tolerant general attitude into an absolute social must."

In other words, it is diversity and not unity, which creates the kind of society
in which you and I can most comfortably live. And modern Dutch attitudes are
rooted in the diversity of the medieval city states of Holland and Zeeland, which
explained, as much as Proudhon's regionalism, that a desirable future for all Europe is in accommodation of local differences.

Proudhon listened, in the 1860s, to the talk of a European confederation or a
United States of Europe. His comment was that:

By this they seem to understand nothing but an alliance of all the states which presently exist in Europe, great and small, presided over by a permanent congress. It is taken for granted that each state will retain the form of government that suits it best. Now, since each state will have votes in the congress in proportion to its population and territory, the small states in this so-called confederation will soon be incorporated into the large ones ...

## BAKUNIN

The second of my nineteenth century mentors, Michael Bakunin, claims our attention for a variety of reasons. He was almost alone among that century's political thinkers in foreseeing the horrors of the clash of modern twentieth century nation-states in the First and Second World Wars, as well as predicting the fate of centralising Marxism in the Russian Empire. In 1867 Prussia and France seemed to be poised for a war about which empire should control Luxemburg and this, through the network of interests and alliances, "threatened to engulf all Europe". A League for Peace and Freedom held its congress in Geneva, sponsored by prominent people from various countries like Giuseppe Garibaldi, Victor Hugo and John Stuart Mill. Bakunin seized the opportunity to address this audience, and published his opinions under the title *Federalisme, Socialisme et Anti-Theologisme*. This document set out thirteen points on which, according to Bakunin, the Geneva Congress was unanimous.

The first of these proclaimed: "That in order to achieve the triumph of liberty, justice and peace in the international relations of Europe, and to render civil war impossible among the various peoples which make up the European family, only a single course lies open: to constitute the United States of Europe." His second point argued that this aim implied that states must be replaced by regions, for it observed: "That the formation of these States of Europe can never come about between the States as constituted at present, in view of the monstrous disparity which exists between their various powers." His fourth point claimed: "That not even if it called itself a republic could a centralised bureaucratic and by the same token militarist State enter seriously and genuinely into an international federation. By virtue of its constitution, which will always be an explicit or implicit denial of domestic liberty, it would necessarily imply a declaration of permanent war and a threat to the existence of neighbouring countries." Consequently his fifth point demanded: "That all the supporters of the League should therefore bend all their energies towards the reconstruction of their various countries in order to replace the old organisation founded throughout upon violence and the principle of authority by a new organisation based solely upon the interests needs and inclinations of the populace, and owning no principle other than that of the free federation of individuals into communes, communes into provinces, provinces into nations, and the latter into the United States, first of Europe, then of the whole world."

The vision thus became bigger and bigger, but Bakunin was careful to include the acceptance of secession. His eighth point declared that: "Just because a region has formed part of a State, even by voluntary accession, it by no means follows that it incurs any obligation to remain tied to it forever. No obligation in perpetuity is acceptable to human justice ... The right of free union and equally free secession comes first and foremost among all political rights; without it, confederation would be nothing but centralisation in disguise."

Bakunin refers admiringly to the Swiss Confederation "practising federation so successfully today", as he puts it and Proudhon, too, explicitly took as a model the Swiss supremacy of the commune as the unit of social organisation, linked by the canton, with a purely administrative federal council. But both remembered the events of 1848, when the Sonderbund of secessionist cantons were compelled by war to accept the new constitution of the majority. So Proudhon and Bakunin were agreed in condemning the subversion of federalism by the unitary principle. In other words, there must be a right of secession.

## KROPOTKIN

Switzerland, precisely because of its decentralised constitution, was a refuge for endless political refugees from the Austro-Hungarian, German and Russian empires. One Russian anarchist was even expelled from Switzerland. He was too much, even for the Swiss Federal Council. He was Peter Kropotkin, who connects nineteenth century federalism with twentieth century regional geography.

His youth was spent as an army officer in geological expeditions in the Far Eastern provinces of the Russian Empire, and his autobiography tells of the outrage he felt at seeing how central administration and funding destroyed any improvement of local conditions, through ignorance, incompetence and universal corruption, and through the destruction of ancient communal institutions which might have enabled people to change their own lives. The rich got richer, the poor got poorer, and the administrative machinery was suffocated by boredom and embezzlement.

There is a similar literature from any empire or nation-state: the British Empire, the Austro-Hungarian Empire, and you can read identical conclusions in the writings of Carlo Levi or Danilo Dolci. In 1872, Kropotkin made his first visit to Western Europe and in Switzerland was intoxicated by the air of a democracy, even a bourgeois one. In the Jura hills he stayed with the watch-case makers. His biographer Martin Miller explains how this was the turning point in his life:

> Kropotkin's meetings and talks with the workers on their jobs revealed the kind of spontaneous freedom without authority or direction from above that he had dreamed about. Isolated and self-sufficient, the Jura watchmakers impressed Kropotkin as an example that could transform society if such a community were allowed to develop on a large scale. There was no doubt in his mind that this community would work because it was not a matter of imposing an artificial 'system' such as Muraviev had attempted in Siberia but of permitting the natural activity of the workers to function according to their own interests.

It was the turning point of his life. The rest of his life was, in a sense, devoted to gathering the evidence for anarchism, federalism and regionalism.

It would be a mistake to think that the approach he developed is simply a matter of academic history. To prove this, I need only refer you to the study that Camillo Berneri published in 1922 on 'Un federaliste Russo, Pietro Kropotkine'. Berneri quotes the 'Letter to the Workers of Western Europe' that Kropotkin handed to the British Labour Party politician Margaret Bondfield in June 1920. In the course of it he declared:

> Imperial Russia is dead and will never be revived. The future of the various provinces which composed the Empire will be directed towards a large federation. The natural territories of the different sections of this federation are in no way distinct from those with which we are familiar in the history of Russia, of its ethnography and economic life. All the attempts to bring together the constituent parts of the Russian Empire, such as Finland, the Baltic provinces, Lithuania, Ukraine, Georgia, Armenia, Siberia and others under a central authority are doomed to certain failure. The future of what was the Russian Empire is directed towards a federalism of independent units.

You and I today can see the relevance of this opinion, even though it was ignored as totally irrelevant for seventy years. As an exile in Western Europe, he had instant contact with a range of pioneers of regional thinking. The relationship between regionalism and anarchism has been handsomely, even extravagantly, delineated by Peter Hall, the geographer who is director of the Institute of Urban and Regional Development at Berkeley, California, in his book *Cities of Tomorrow* (1988). There was Kropotkin's fellow-anarchist geographer, Elisee Réclus, arguing for small-scale human societies based on the ecology of their regions. There was Paul Vidal de la Blache, another founder of French geography, who argued that "the region was more than an object of survey; it was to provide the basis for the total reconstruction of social and political life." For Vidal, as Professor Hall explains, the region, not the nation, which "as the motor force of human development: the almost sensual reciprocity between men and women and their surroundings, was the seat of comprehensible liberty and the mainspring of cultural evolution, which were being attacked and eroded by the centralised nation-state and by large-scale machine industry."

## PATRICK GEDDES

Finally there was the extraordinary Scottish biologist Patrick Geddes, who tried to encapsulate all these regionalist ideas, whether geographical, social, historical, political or economic, into an ideology of reasons for regions, known to most of us through the work of his disciple Lewis Mumford. Professor Hall argued that:

> Many, though by no means all, of the early visions of the planning movement stemmed from the anarchist movement, which flourished in the last decades of the nineteenth century and the first years of the twentieth ... The vision of these anarchist pioneers was not merely of an alternative built form, but of an alternative society, neither capitalist nor bureaucratic-socialistic: a society

based on voluntary co-operation among men and women, working and living in small self-governing communities.

## TODAY

Now in the last years of the twentieth century, I share this vision. Those nine-teenth century anarchist thinkers were a century in advance of their contempo-raries in warning the peoples of Europe of the consequences of not adopting a regionalist and federalist approach. Among survivors of every kind of disastrous experience in the twentieth century the rulers of the nation states of Europe have directed policy towards several types of supranational existence. The crucial issue that faces them is the question of whether to conceive of a Europe of States or a Europe of Regions.

Proudhon, 130 years ago, related the issue to the idea of a European balance of power, the aim of statesmen and politician theorists, and argued that this was "impossible to realise among great powers with unitary constitutions". He had ar-gued in *La Federation et l'Unite' en Italie* that "the first step towards the reform of public law in Europe" was "the restoration of the confederations of Italy, Greece, the Netherlands, Scandinavia and the Danube, as a prelude to the decentralisa-tion of the large states and hence to general disarmament". And in *Du Principe Federatif* he noted that "Among French democrats there has been much talk of European confederation, or a United States of Europe. By this they seem to un-derstand nothing but an alliance of all the states which presently exist in Europe, great and small, presided over by a permanent congress." He claimed that such a federation would either be a trap or would have no meaning, for the obvious rea-son that the big states would dominate the small ones.

A century later, the economist Leopold Kohr (Austrian by birth, British by nationality, Welsh by choice), who also describes himself as an anarchist, pub-lished his book *The Breakdown of Nations*, glorifying the virtues of small-scale societies and arguing, once again, that Europe's problems arise from the existence of the nation state. Praising, once again, the Swiss Confederation, he claimed, with the use of maps, that "Europe's problem—as that of any federation—is one of division, not of union."

Now to do them justice, the advocates of a United Europe have developed a doctrine of 'subsidiarity', arguing that governmental decisions should not be taken by the supra-nation institutions of the European Community, but pref-erably by regional or local levels of administration, rather than by national gov-ernments. This particular principle has been adopted by the Council of Europe, calling for national governments to adopt its Charter for Local Self-Government to formalise commitment to the principle that government functions should be carried out at the lowest level possible and only transferred to higher government by consent.

This principle is an extraordinary tribute to Proudhon, Bakunin and Kropot-kin, and the opinions which they were alone in voicing (apart from some absorbing Spanish thinkers like Piy Margall or Joaquin Costa), but of course it is one of the first aspects of pan-European ideology which national governments will choose to ignore. There are obvious differences between various nation states in this respect. In many of them—for example Germany, Italy, Spain and even France—the machinery of government is infinitely more devolved than it was fifty years ago. The same may soon be true of the Soviet Union. This devolution may not have proceeded at the pace that you or I would want, and I will happily agree than the founders of the European Community have succeeded in their original aim of ending old national antagonisms and have made future wars in Western Europe inconceivable. But we are still very far from a Europe of the Regions.

I live in what is now the most centralised state in Western Europe, and the dominance of central government there has immeasurably increased, not diminished, during the last ten years. Some people here will remember the rhetoric of the then British Prime Minister in 1988:

> We have not successfully rolled back the frontiers of the State in Britain, only to see them reimposed at a European level, with a European super-state exercising a new dominance from Brussels. [Margaret Thatcher, address to the College of Europe, Bruges, 20th September 1988.]

This is the language of delusion. It does not relate to reality. And you do not have to be a supporter of the European Commission to perceive this. But it does illustrate how far some of us are from conceiving the truth of Proudhon's comment that: "Even Europe would be too large to form a single confederation; it could form only a confederation of confederations."

The anarchist warning is precisely that the obstacle to a Europe of the Regions is the nation state. If you and I have any influence on political thinking in the next century, we should be promoting the reasons for regions. 'Think globally—act locally' is one of the useful slogans of the international Green movement. The nation state occupied a small segment of European history. We have to free ourselves from national ideologies in order to act locally and think regionally. Both will enable us to become citizens of the whole world, not of nations nor of trans-national super-states.

## REFERENCES AND SOURCES

Bakunin, Michael & Lehning, Arthur (ed.). *Selected Writings*. London: Jonathan Cape, 1973.

Berneri, Camillo. *Peter Kropotkin: His Federalist Ideas*. London: Freedom Press, 1942.

Council of Europe, *The Impact of the Completion of the Internal Market on Local and Regional Autonomy*. Council of Europe Studies and Texts, Series no. 12, 1990.

de Haan, Willem. *The Politics of Redress*. London: Unwin Hyman, 1990.

Hall, Peter. *Cities of Tomorrow: An Intellectual History of Urban Planning and Design in the Twentieth Century*. Oxford: Basil Blackwell, 1988.

Hyams, Edward. *Pierre-Joseph Proudhon*. London: John Murray, 1979.

Kohr, Leopold. *The Breakdown of Nations*. London: Routledge, 1957.

Miller, Martin. *Kropotkin*. Chicago: University of Chicago Press, 1976.

Proudhon, Pierre-Joseph & Edwards, Stewart (ed.). *Selected Writings*. London: Macmillan, 1970.

Proudhon, Pierre-Joseph & Vernon, Richard (ed.). *The Principle of Federation*. Toronto: University of Toronto Press, 1979.

Wistnch, Ernest. *After 1982: The United States of Europe*. London: Routledge, 1989.

# 6. DEADSVILLE REVISITED

*"Get into the habit of seeing things as they are, with the dirt, strewn paper, and orange peel thrown in; don't acquiesce, don't be content ... It is the deadness of our town life which produces the deadness of our architecture: the unutterable deadness which has come over English cities and villages in the last forty years, the stagnation and daily dying of the towns up and down the country ... For the earlier part of my life I was quieted by being told that ours was the richest country in the world, until I woke up to know that what I meant by riches was learning and beauty, and music and art, coffee and omelettes. Perhaps in the coming days of poverty we may get more of these."*

—W. R. Lethaby, *Form in Civilisation* (1922)

In Market Street, Deadsville, the market has gone. The new shopping centre has drained away the multiple groceries, although some of the shops there are still unlet. (Two of them are held rent-free by the Deadsville Pre-school Playgroup Association.) But so are the old shops in Market Street too, and this was probably why the Education Committee was able to secure a lease on the old Co-op premises in that street to turn the building into their Streetwork Centre. It was cheaper than the proposed Sixth Form Centre at Deadsville County Secondary School, which had been pushed back, year after year, in the Department of Education and Science's building programme. It is a deep, double-fronted shop with two storeys above and an extension behind, and the decision to take the lease was based on the square-footage available for a relatively low outlay.

On the left of the main entrance, in what used to be the home furnishings department, is now the Omelette House, run by the Community Industry, which couldn't help being a success as it is the only place for decent food in Deadsville. People enjoy the continually changing mural on the wall, the decor of old griddles and grids (cast 120 years ago in this very street at the foundry down by the bridge), as well as the menu with its twenty-five different egg dishes. You will recognise the waiters and the cooks: last year's—or is it this year's?—fifth form. You will recognise the group too, playing in the evening. Wasn't that boy, singing the songs that Cecil Sharp noted down in this area sixty years ago, in your English class two years ago? Did he learn them from you? Did you know he played the guitar? Where did he learn those tough American railroad songs, at the very time when

---

Originally printed in Colin Ward and Anthony Fyson, *Streetwork: The Exploding School.* (London: Routledge and Kegan Paul, 1973), 114–121.

they are proposing to close down Deadsville Central? Does he see the irony? Did this enter into your scheme of work?

But our interest is on the other side of the main entrance, in what used to be the grocery department. Today it houses the Egg Head, which involves not only the sixth form centre, but is also the ROSLA headquarters, for it had been decided that there was no reason why the two should be separate. The Egg Head is becoming more and more the focus of upper school work in Deadsville, and various groups can be seen there in the morning, discussing their assignments with their tutors over coffee.

The English group are preparing a feature 'What's Under Your Back Garden' for next week's *Bugle*. Their task is to put into layman's language the findings of a number of Mode Three projects in history, commerce, geology and geography which related to the eighteenth- and nineteenth-century coal workings around the town, using the evidence from the sites and from the maps in the county library and the National Coal Board archives. Another group—the cartographers—is preparing the map which will illustrate the feature article, superimposing a street map of Deadsville onto the geological survey.

*Bugle* was started by the Neighbourhood Council which had been set up a few years earlier, when people in the town realised that the changes in the structure of local government in 1974 had made government even less local than it had been before.[47] *Bugle* is printed on the offset litho printing machine operated by the Community Industry in what used to be the gents working footware department at the back of the Egg Head. A lot of printing is done there for a variety of local enterprises including the school, which uses the same premises for its art department, whose output of silkscreen posters has become famous. Some of their collectors' items are sold by post from the Community Shop, further down Market Street. Children from the lower school sell *Bugle* from door to door every Friday, on a commission basis.[48] The result is that *everybody* in Deadsville, including the kids, reads *Bugle*.

The history group, upstairs in the Egg Head, are working through the papers of the old Urban District Council under the direction of the County Archivist, this being thought better than burying them in the vaults of the new District Council. They are preparing a monograph on public health in Deadsville 1888–1973. The work is sometimes tedious, but the students are conscious that they are handling materials which no historian has touched before.

But for us as visitors, the most stimulating of the projects going on at the Egg Head is the one everyone calls futurology, although it is officially known as the planning group. They are engaged in long-term strategic planning. The futurology project mushroomed from the preoccupations of two members of staff. One of them, who was charged with the task of giving careers advice, was continuously perplexed and depressed by the lack of useful answers to the question constantly put to him, 'Well Sir, *is* there any future for this part of the world?' He and another teacher had been up to the Newcastle-Upon-Tyne Festival in 1972 and attended the conference on 'Planning for People', where they heard a talk by Robert Allen of *The Ecologist* magazine on the subject 'Has the North-East a Future?' Allen was appealing for people and organisations in the region to form committees to set out their plans for the development of the North-East, looking ahead to 2073. He got a cool reception from his audience in Newcastle, it seemed to them at the time, but the implications struck a responsive chord in those teachers from Deadsville.

The problems which they tried to cope with, and to find an answer for, were very similar to those of the North-East, and they went back home excited by Mr Allen's propositions, so it is worth quoting them at length:[49]

> The problems of the North-East are well known: unemployment, declining heavy industry, the abandonment of long-established mining communities, pollution and dereliction.
>
> Are they being tackled properly?
>
> Will the solutions to one problem make any of the others worse? Take unemployment. In the period 1960–1970, the percentage of unemployed went up from 2·9 to 4·8, as against the national average which went up from 1·7 to 2·7. The North of England has a higher percentage of unemployed than any other region of the UK except Northern Ireland.
>
> What is the conventional solution to this and related problems? It was expressed succinctly enough six years ago in the foreword to the Northern Economic Planning Council's publication, *Challenge of the Changing North*: 'it is immediately clear that success in meeting the challenge that faces the region will come only by the continued expansion of its industry and commerce'.
>
> When these words were published, unemployment stood at 35,100. By 1970, it had risen to 63,300, an increase of 80·3 per cent. During the same period, public investment in new construction (the most readily available index of economic expansion) rose from £107·6 million to £181·2 million, an increase of 68·4 per cent. This increase was unable to prevent a worsening of the situation, let alone bring about an improvement.
>
> It is not difficult to understand why. A major key to economic expansion is the maximisation of labour productivity, so that a given investment will provide fewer and fewer jobs. The proposed new steel complex for Teesside is a typical example of this. As BSC's deputy chairman, Dr. M. Finniston, has pointed out: 'We produce 120 tons for every man-year in the corporation. But the Japanese are producing nearly four times that, and any single plant of modern design will produce 750 tons per man, or six times as much, so to produce the required tonnage of steel, you need one sixth of the manpower. You are investing only to reduce the manpower. BSC is not the way out for this area.'
>
> He is quite right. The relationship between industrial expansion and social betterment is unproven to say the least. Worse, expansion of any kind is not a process which can continue for very long. Sooner or later we will run out of the raw materials required to sustain such expansion, and the best available evidence indicates that it will be sooner. Also, the increasing consumption of raw materials and energy leads inevitably to greater pollution, which not only damages human health but also jeopardises those ecological networks on which we all depend for life.

As long as growth come-what-may is seen as the answer to the ills of the North-East, the region will continue to suffer from heavy unemployment and pollution, and any solution to either problem is likely to fail, or to aggravate the other problem, or both. Indeed, within today's social and economic context the 'jobs versus beauty and health' dichotomy is an irrelevant diversion. Industrial expansion can give us none of these.

This is not to say that the problems of the North-East are insoluble. Quite the contrary. But the solutions must reflect basic social needs and recognise real bio-physical limitations. More important than industrial expansion is a sustainable society ...

It is very difficult for people to envisage what such a society might be like or how it might be achieved. What is needed, therefore, is an exercise in popular planning and public imagination. All sections of the community must look at the problems of this region in a new light, and together work out the kind of society they would like their children to be able to enjoy.

This is the object of 'NE 2073–A Future for the North-East'. Farmers, housewives, industrialists, trades unionists, planners, lawyers, scientists, miners, factory-workers—anybody and everybody, professionally or privately—in Northumberland, Durham and the North Riding of Yorkshire are invited to form committees to develop a 'Blueprint' for the North-East. They will imagine that the North-East is a semi-independent region, with sufficient self-government to formulate its own agricultural, educational, development, employment, housing, transport and urban renewal policies—in other words free to do what it likes in all those areas that would not have direct effect on other regions. The committees will discuss how the region could meet 'basic' demands—for food, shelter, health, etc., and how to stabilise and contain 'surplus' demands—more and bigger roads, reservoirs and so on. They will try to decide the optimum population for the North-East, how satisfying employment can be given to its citizens without causing ugliness and ill-health, and what social reforms are necessary—what is the best social structure for the North-East.

It will be an exciting exercise, but above all it will be a useful one, for three reasons.

(1) Everyday decisions by local government are taken with a number of limited futures in mind, and sometimes none at all. This is why they betray so little imagination or insight. If you want to change the decisions, big or small, you've got to change the framework in which they're taken. Show the local authorities you have a different future in mind. This is the way to do it.

(2) Many politicians, national and local, including a high proportion of those in Government, are well aware that the serious social and environmental problems we face today can't be solved without radical change. The trouble is that they are afraid to initiate it until they *know* the public are behind them. This is the way to show them.

(3) If you want a decent future for you and your children, we must begin to plan with a difference. This will only happen by public demand. This means that people must know about the problems *and* the solutions.

You can see, can't you, why this proposal so excited those teachers from Deadsville? It spoke to their condition. They spent a week-end feverishly re-writing it in terms of their own region and their own town. Then they discussed their version with their colleagues at Deadsville County Secondary School, and evolved a plan for building a great deal of the school's work around a strategic plan for *Deadsville 2073*. By the time the futurology project members were meeting this morning, several reports on alternative strategies had already been produced and published, and had been, and still are, the subject of acrimonious disputes in the correspondence columns of the *Deadshire Echo*, and of course in *Bugle*. One group is making a journey to London tomorrow, as it is involved in conducting a feasibility study for Deadsville Carbon Fibres, a prospective firm in the district. It is going (staying at the London Environmental Studies Centre at Clapham, of course) to gather information from the managers and employees of the Morganite Carbon Company. On the following day, following the traditional split between the sciences and the humanities, one segment will conduct a statistical survey of waiting times for lifts in high flat blocks in Southwark, while the other conducts a graffiti survey in Battersea.[50]

The other group from the futurology project have a more home-spun mission. They are concerned with the long-term productivity study of Goods Yard Holdings Ltd, another joint, mutually supportive venture of the Education Department and the Community industry. When British Rail shut down the goods yard, and the branch line to Dedington (unwisely in the view of the futurology project), the Education Department stepped in,[51] and acquired not only the site of the branch line, but the goods yard too. The disused railway land on the way to Dedington has become one of the first urban nature trails, and the school's part in Tree-Planting Year, 1973, was not only to plant in Market Square and on the Jack Lawson Estate in Deadsville itself, but to plant forest trees, and protect them, along the Dedington linear nature reserve.

This is not the only trail in Deadsville of course. After the school had perfected its town trail, it developed the Industrial Museum which really is a museum without walls, unless you count the Visitor's Centre housed in the pit-head baths, ('a little gem of art deco', as the guide says) built by the Miners' Welfare Commission in 1936, and lovingly restored to house an introduction to the rise and decline of Britain's basic industries in the form of a dramatic 'photo-play' of slides and tapes made in the school, followed by a guided itinerary showing how water, coal and iron shaped the town.

But on the way, what is this alien corn blowing in the wind in the front yard of Arnold Weinstock Close? It's part of the project's experiment in the horticultural treatment of cereals. Each of those transplanted wheat plants is expected to produce between 600 and 1000 grains of wheat, and the project has set itself the onerous task of counting each over a period of years. You can tell that Mr Compost, of the School's rural science course, is gathering material for his paper, *Intensive Agriculture: A Horticultural Approach* (Community Publications, Deadsville, 1977). When we arrive at the goods yard—what a spectacle! There are roosters on the roof of the station. It is like one of those old Ealing comedies, except that the station is glistening with newly applied paint, and so are the chicken houses. For much of the goods yard has become a free-range chicken run, and there they are, scratching around in the ballast and dog-daisy, supplying the needs of the Omelette House and the Egg Head. They even produce a surplus which is sold at the first stall in the market place since—after such a battle—it was closed to traffic. Pretty soon their productivity will meet the whole town's needs. But what will the supermarket in the shopping centre say about that?

The school's involvement in food production goes further. The train shed has become a piggery. Swill collection, something which the older generation recalls from the past, is suddenly relevant again. Just lately they have got a couple of cows, and are talking of making Deadsville cheese.[52] They already have a firm bid from the Omelette House for everything they can produce.

All this has been a delight to Mr Compost, who always maintained that urban and rural studies were one, but even he has been surprised at the latest turn of urban study work in the sixth form. Inquiring into housing, landownership, industry, jobs and incomes in Deadsville, they found that the majority shareholders in all these respects are public authorities. The state, or a government department, or a public corporation, or a nationalised industry, or the local authority, control just about everything in Deadsville. Now, since this is so, say the sixth form, why hasn't recent development here been in the interests of the inhabitants, instead of working against them? The issue came to a head over the Coal Board houses. The Board found them an embarrassment and decided to sell them off—but to a private bidder, to the local authority, to the sitting tenants, or to a housing association? This practical issue, which vitally affected many of the town's inhabitants, was debated in *Bugle* and in the sixth form forum. The way in which these political issues were traditionally presented seemed irrelevant to them. The polarisation of private and public enterprise was unreal: they saw it as a matter of the politics of dependence or of community action.

At the mucky end of the goods yard, known as the dump, students from the technical department of the school are busy experimenting in car recycling. They had seen the days when old cars stood around in the streets because it was worth nobody's while to haul them away, and they had seen on television the giant machine which compresses all that delicate mechanism into a few cubic feet of old metal for the melting pot. Surely, they thought, all this gadgetry could be used for something? So they tried stripping down the useful ends of the old cars into their components. They found that they could link the dynamo with a propeller (rather beautifully carved from an old pit prop) and, by mounting the assembly in a place which caught the wind, generate electricity. This explains those windmills scattered around Deadsville, and the more sophisticated structures they are now building for this purpose. They also found that the delicate filigree of the radiators could be used as a ready-made component in a heat pump. This is the basis of some of the house heating devices which they have developed with the support of the Schools Council Project Technology, and of the experimental 'eco-houses' which the Community Industry is building in Deadsville.[53]

Environmental studies in Deadsville have taken some paths which were scarcely imagined when their programme began, but which led to a deeper and deeper involvement in the community's future, and which obliterated the differences between urban and rural studies, and between the study of what is and what might be. The head of the County Secondary School is delighted. In the past his best students automatically left Deadsville just as soon as they could, while the ordinary ones joined the ranks of the permanently unemployed. Now he finds them involved in one way or another, thanks to the direction taken by the school's concern with a whole spectrum of environmental issues, and to the continuity provided by the growth of the Community Industry, in the whole future of the town. They and the school have been thrust into the centre of a campaign to make Deadsville habitable. Could he ask for more than that?

# 7. AN ANARCHIST APPROACH TO URBAN PLANNING

Forty years ago, when the *Rivista Volontà* was edited in Naples by my friends Giovanna Berneri and Cesare Zaccaria, they published an article about housing and planning by a young architect Giancarlo De Carlo, which I laboriously and, no doubt, inaccurately, translated for the English anarchist journal *Freedom*.[54]

Then, as now, anarchist propaganda has been impeded by its insistence that nothing can happen until everything happens. The destruction of both capitalism and the state were the prerequisites for the building of a free society. The problem is that neither De Carlo nor me, nor the millions of people actually involved, then or now, can actually wait for these revolutionary changes. Ask yourself whether they are nearer or further than they were forty years ago.

In looking for alternative approaches, he examined building co-operatives, tenants' co-operatives, rent strikes, and "squatting", the illegal occupation of empty houses. Now we have seen over these 40 years since 1948 that every one of these techniques of direct action by poor citizens, whether in Italy, Britain or the United States, has led to a wider involvement in urban planning. And in the part that citizens can demand.

All those years ago, De Carlo went on to consider the possible anarchist attitudes to town planning:

> It is possible to adopt a hostile attitude: "The plan must necessarily emanate from authority, therefore it can only be detrimental. Changes in social life cannot follow the plan—the plan will be the consequence of a new way of life."

Or, he suggested, an attitude of participation could be adopted: "The plan is the opportunity for liquidating our present social order by changing its direction, and this changed *aim* is necessarily the preliminary for a new social structure".

> The first main attitude is based on two principle arguments. Firstly that authority cannot be a liberating agent—perfectly true; secondly, that man [and

Originally printed in Colin Ward, *Talking Houses*. (London: Freedom Press, 1990), 123–132. Address to a Joint Seminar of CoSA (Architecture Students Centre) and the Centro Studio Libertari G.Pinelli, Milan, 17 September 1988.

of course today he would say man and woman] can do nothing until he is free—a mistaken view. Man cannot be liberated, he must liberate himself, and any progress towards that liberation can only be the conscious expression of his own will. The investigation of the full extent of the problems of region, city and home, is such an activity. To find out the nature of the problems and to prepare their solutions is a concrete example of direct action, taking away the powers of authority and giving them back to men [and women].

The attitude of hostility that really means "waiting for the revolution to do it", does not take into account the fact that the social revolution will be accomplished by clear heads, not by sick and stunted people unable to think of the future because of the problems of the present. It forgets that the revolution begins in the elimination of these evils so as to create the necessary conditions of a free society.

Giancarlo De Carlo was arguing two important propositions. Firstly that whatever kind of society they live in, it is important for the anarchist to push forward those approaches to personal and social needs which depend on popular initiatives and which present alternatives to dependency on capitalism and the state. Secondly that "urban planning *can* become a revolutionary weapon if we succeed in rescuing it from the blind monopoly of authority and in making it a communal organ of research and investigation into the real problems of social life."

For me, this point of view from forty years ago, has always been important and helpful, because I am convinced, and I am still, that one of the tasks of the anarchist propagandist is to propagate solutions to contemporary issues which, however dependent they are on the existing social and economic structures, are *anarchist* solutions: the kind of approaches that would be made if we were living in the kind of society we envisage. We are much more likely to win support for our point of view, in other words, if *we* put anarchist answers which can be tried here and now, than if we declare that there are no answers until the ultimate answer: a social revolution which continually disappears over the horizon.

Let me take the first of Giancarlo's points of 40 years ago: the importance of the Squatter's Movement: the illegal seizure of empty housing. At the time when he was writing, we had been through the post-war eruption of squatting in Italy, in Britain and elsewhere. Its history and its lessons were forgotten. Then, many years later, in the 1960s, it became important again, in Turin, in London, in Berlin and in Copenhagen, and in dozens of European and American cities. Not only was the squatters' movement successful as a tactic for housing oneself, it was also a political education.[55] And it is a fact that the most successful of the housing cooperatives that have flourished in Britain in the past decade, started life as illegal "squats".[56]

A second point of interest in his argument of 1948 was his use of the phrase "an attitude of participation". Now the word "participation" was not part of the vocabulary of architects and planners in the 1940s, nor in the 1950s. It crept into the language after the phase of post-war reconstruction in the cities of Britain and the United States which was known as "urban renewal".

As we all understand by now, "urban renewal" meant in practice, "driving the poor out of town" and it also meant the destruction of the traditional working class culture of the cities. We have a huge library of books on the implications of this. There are the famous American studies by Robert Goodman and Jane Jacobs[57] and there are English equivalents, of which just one was the work of a socialist councillor, not an anarchist, who declared that:

> Planning in our society is in essence the attempt to inject a radical technology into a conservative and highly inegalitarian economy. The impact of planning on this society is rather like that of the education system on the same society: it is least onerous and most advantageous to those who are relatively powerless or relatively poor. Planning is, in its effect on the socio-economic structure, a highly regressive form of indirect taxation.[58]

So there grew up a new 1960s ideology of "participation" which was populist, socialist, and to a small but important extent, *rediscovery*, by people who had never heard of anarchism, of anarchist values. One of the most important attempts to measure the actual worth of these exercises in participation was made by an American planner, Sherry Arnstein, in what became known as Arnstein's Ladder of Participation.[59] The rungs of her ladder, climbing up from the bottom, were:

*Citizens Control*
*Delegated Power*
*Partnership*
*Placation*
*Consultation*
*Informing*
*Therapy*
*Manipulation*

I have always found Arnstein's Ladder a very useful measuring-rod which enables us to get behind the barrage of propaganda and decide whether any particular exercise in "public participation" is merely manipulation or therapy, or often *deception* (which found no place on Arnstein's ladder—but should have done).

Naturally the anarchist aim is the very top rung of Arnstein's Ladder, that of Full Citizen Control. It's something worth aiming at, whatever kind of society we live in. We may not win the economic battles, but we can sometimes win the environmental battles! There have been histories of success in the cities of the United States, of Britain, and of Italy, as well as exhausting failures.

But we do have to ask ourselves whether "participation" was one of those words of the 1960s and 1970s which has been quietly abandoned in the 1980s. You will know that the governments of both Britain and the United States, with their ideology of the New Right, when they talk about the cities at all, talk in terms of partnership of business and government. They do not speak of "participation" of ordinary citizens.

The word "renewal", having been discredited, is replaced by new equivalents, like "regeneration" and "revitalisation". We are all invited to see the regeneration of the cities of the United States. I was invited to a conference in Pittsburgh, USA on the theme of "Remaking Cities". There was one speaker there, Alan Mallach of New Jersey, who addressed himself to the issue that concerns you and me. He said,

> The concept of a public/private partnership as a relationship between two sectors— government and the private market—is flawed by its exclusion of a third, essential actor—the residents of the community affected. Self-congratulatory messages about entrepreneurial successes and the proliferation of shiny downtown office buildings obscure the reality that many people do not benefit from all this success, and many are deeply and permanently harmed.[60]

In other words, the battle for local citizen participation has to be fought continually, everywhere. Giancarlo De Carlo was right, all those years ago.

But there is a different aspect of the city that needs to be discussed from an anarchist point of view. Anarchism has shared with other political ideologies of the Left, certain assumptions about the growth of the modern industrial city and the modern industrial proletariat. Marx and Engels, whatever the virtues or defects of their concept of history, based it on the first country, Britain, to experience the industrial revolution: the mushroom growth of industrial cities like Manchester, Birmingham, Leeds or Glasgow, and the proletarianisation of the displaced peasantry and so on.

To fit the real world into this theory, they minimised the survival of the English equivalent of the European peasant economy,[61] and dismissed the huge small-workshop economy as a tedious survival of the "petty trades" of the middle ages. Kropotkin, in his book *Field, Factories and Workshops,* attempted to correct this view and to remind us that the vast industrial city was a temporary phenomenon, which happened to begin in Britain. Thus he argued in 1899 that decentralisation was both inevitable and desirable:

> The scattering of industries over the country—so as to bring the factory amidst the fields, to make agriculture derive all those profits which it always finds in being combined with industry and to produce a combination of industrial with agricultural work—is surely the next step to be taken ... This step is imposed by the necessity for each healthy man and woman to spend a part of their lives in manual work in the free air; and it will be rendered the more necessary when the great social movements which have now become unavoidable, come to disturb the present international trade, and compel each nation to revert to her own resources for her own maintenance." [62]

Now Kropotkin was, like me, an optimist. But he had grasped a big truth about the industrial city and about industrial employment. About the industrial city, Kropotkin's contemporary, the Garden City pioneer, Ebenezer Howard, declared in 1904 that

> I venture to suggest that while the age in which we live is the age of the great closely-compacted city, there are already signs, for those who can read them, of a coming change so great and so momentous that the twentieth century will be known as the period of the great exodus ... [63]

Whether or not it happened in the way that Howard anticipated, ordinary demographic statistics of British cities support his view. A British economist, Victor Keegan, remarked a few years ago that

> the most seductive theory of all is that what we are experiencing now is nothing less than a movement back towards an informal economy after a brief flirtation of 200 years or so with a formal one. [64]

The huge industrial city, the vast concentrated factory with its army of the proletariat, are a brief episode in the history of cities, in the history of production and in the history of work. You have only to visit the dying industrial cities of Britain or the United States to become convinced of this.

We have a characteristic Anglo-American divide in discussing this particular Italian economic miracle. For example, a British author, Fergus Murray, provides an absorbing account of the recent changes in Italian industry with the explanation that

> In the late 1960s labour militancy in many Italian industries reached levels that directly threatened firm profitability, and management undertook a series of strategies designed initially to reduce the disruptiveness of militant workers. [65]

One of these strategies was the decentralisation of industrial production into a local, self-employed, small workshop economy. So we can see this whole recent evolution as a conspiracy by the capitalists.

Predictably the same industrial changes were seen quite differently from the United States. The American architect Richard Hatch, whom both Giancarlo De Carlo and I remember as a pioneer of participatory planning in that toughest of all environments, Harlem, New York, [66] wrote much more recently that,

> A new form of urban industrial production in Italy is giving new meaning to its historical form. It is based on a large number of very small, flexible enterprises that depend on broadly skilled workers and multiple-use, automated machinery. Essentially intermediate producers, they link together in varying combinations and patterns to perform complex manufacturing tasks for widening markets. These firms combine rapid innovation with a high degree of democracy in the workplace. They tend to congregate in mixed-use neighbourhoods where work and dwelling are integrated, Their growth has been the objective of planning policy, architectural interventions, and municipal investment, with handsome returns in sustained economic growth and lively urban centres. [67]

Well of course, lively urban centres are one of the aims of the urban planning profession, and which it has been singularly unskilled in providing, ever since the 1940s. Those of us who are concerned with urban planning have every reason to observe what is happening in Italy.

There was, for example, an Italo-American anarchist, the late George Benello, who found in the "industrial renaissance" of north-eastern and central Italy,

> a model that worked, creating in less than three decades, not hundreds but literally hundreds of thousands of small scale firms, out-producing conventionally run factories, and providing work which called forth skill, responsibility, and artistry from its democratically organised workforces.[68]

I learn from the same source, that Benello was

> Amazed at the combination of sophisticated design and production with human scale work-life, and by the extent and diversity of integrated and collaborative activity within this network. Small cities, such as Modena, had created "artisan villages"—working neighbourhoods where production facilities and living quarters were within walking or bike range, where technical schools for the unemployed fed directly into newly created businesses, and where small firms using computerized techniques, banded together to produce complex products.[69]

By this point I am sure that many people here, whether they are anarchists, workers, or urban planners, will be acutely embarrassed at the idealised picture I have given you of *Italia artigianata* and will complain that daily reality has little relation to this view. Well, I have to embarrass you one stage further, since my subject is an anarchist approach to urban planning. George Benello's own conclusion was that

> Italy has taught the world perhaps more than any other nation about urban life and urban form. Once again it is in the forefront, creating a new economic order, based on the needs of the city and on human scale.[70]

Now, even making allowances for sentimental Anglo-American Italophilia, there is a sense in which this comment is absolutely true. Go, not to the cities of northern Italy, but to those of Britain and the United States, and you will certainly find the ruins of a factory culture of monopolistic employers who have fled or diversified, and of work-forces dependent upon social security hand-outs, or upon the various alternatives to work devised for British or American cities: garden festivals, museums of our industrial heritage, or shopping malls and aquaria. Anything, in fact, except the opportunity to be involved in productive work.

Comparing the experience of car workers in, say Coventry or Birmingham, and Turin, I was told by a British historian that in English factories, a third generation of skilled industrial workers have been "moulded in worker-resistance to industrial capitalism", knowing nothing except employment for big capitalists, whereas in Torino, with its high "generation-turnover" of new industrial workers from the South, the artisans and peasants who moved north were not "crushed by factory capitalism", and have consequently found it easier to become self-employed workers, or members of co-operatives or employees of small-scale, high-technology entrepreneurs, or to drop out of industrial work almost completely and pick up a living from small-scale horticulture.

Now we anarchists are not Marxists. We belong to a different tradition from the one which saw the steam-engine and the consequent concentration of industrial production as the ultimate factor in human history. We belong to a different tradition which includes, for example, Proudhon's faith in the self-governing workshop and Kropotkin's concern with the decentralisation of production and its combination with horticulture.

It is *our* tradition which corresponds more closely to the actual experience, both of our grandparents and of our grandchildren. One of the people from a different tradition who has thought seriously about this issue is André Gorz, who argues that the political Left has been refrigerated in authoritarian collectivist attitudes that belong to the past. He says that

> As long as the protagonists of socialism continue to make centralised planning the lynchpin of their programme, and the adherence of everyone to the "democratically formulated" objectives of their plan the core of their political doctrine, socialism will remain an unattractive proposition in industrial societies. Classical socialist doctrine finds it difficult to come to terms with political and social pluralism, understood not simply as a plurality of parties and trade unions but as the co-existence of various ways of working, producing and living, various distinct cultural areas and levels of social existence ... Yet this kind of pluralism precisely conforms to the lived experience and aspirations of the post-industrial proletariat, as well as the majority of the traditional working class.[71]

Now this would be perfectly well understood in the urban fringes of Torino, or of Modena or Bologna or in all the workshop-villages of Emilia-Romagna or, I imagine, here in Milano.

And of course it has its implications in the world of the physical planning of the environment. It implies a plan which is modest, tentative and flexible, which assumes *dweller control* as the first principle of housing and which also assumes that the householder has access to a garden, whether this garden is used for horticulture or as a playspace for the children, or as a workshop or a commercial asset. And I take it for granted that there is a nursery and a junior school close at hand, and room for self-governing workshops all around. These are such simple demands that even as anarchists in a society which is hostile to anarchism, we should be able to achieve them!

# 8. A PEOPLED LANDSCAPE

Our perceptions of our surroundings are as subject to changes in fashion as our attitudes to any human artefact. In the early 18th century, when Defoe travelled to Westmorland, he found it *'a country eminent only for being the wildest, most barren and frightful of any that I have passed over in England.'* For it lacked the signs of human activity, ingenuity and well-being that mattered to him. A century later, the Lake poets sanctified that district as a place where, in the words Bishop Heber used for another tourist attraction, *'every prospect pleases, and only man* is *vile'*.

The paradoxical result of this cult of 'wild' nature combined with misanthropy towards mere humans was that by 1995 it was possible for Jonathan Croall ... to visit Cumbria and report that *'the sole path up the spine of Helvellyn had gradually been widened by the pressure of walkers, so that it begins to resemble a trunk road.'*[72] Tourism dominates while productive activity declines. Discussing the economic problems of small hill farmers, as opposed to factory farmers, Fay Godwin, a close observer of the rural scene, asks, *'Do we want these lived-in landscapes to become cloned theme-parks regulated by the heritage industry?'* For she argues that:

> current government thinking will lead not only to rural depopulation, but also to the loss of many of our most valued landscapes, whose character has been informed by small farmers over thousands of years, unlike the wilderness national park areas in other countries.[73]

She is right to stress that ours is a landscape constructed by human activity over centuries. Peter Kropotkin, geographer and anarchist described how over a century ago he took a knapsack and went on foot out of London and saw empty fields within ten miles of Charing Cross in a city supplied with Flemish and Jersey potatoes, French salads and Canadian apples. When he asked why, the explanation was 'Heavy Clay', with no recognition (Kropotkin complained) that

> ... in the hands of man there are no infertile soils; that the most fertile soils are not in the prairies of America, not in the Russian steppes; that they are in the peat-bogs of Ireland, on the sandy downs of the northern seacoast of France, on the craggy mountains of the Rhine, where they have been made by man's hands.[74]

Originally published in Ken Warpole (ed.), *Richer Futures: Fashioning a New Politics.* (London: Earthscan, 1999), 83–98.

In the Weald of Kent and Sussex too, he saw no one in the fields:

> I could walk for twenty miles without crossing anything but heath or wood-
> lands, rented as pheasant-shooting grounds to "London gentlemen", as the
> labourers said. "Ungrateful soil" was my first thought; but then I would oc-
> casionally come to a farm at the crossing of two roads and see the same soil
> bearing a rich crop; and my next thought was *"tel seigneur, telle terre"*, as the
> French peasants say.[75]

Kropotkin argued for a peopled landscape and his book *Fields, Factories and
Workshops* is not only an exploration of the economic consequences of the hu-
manization of work, but an anticipation of changes made possible by technologies
which did not exist when he wrote. For he was writing at a time when Britain was
still regarded as 'the workshop of the world', and when it was assumed by economists of both right and left that huge centralized factories were the industrial
norm for the future. But Kropotkin argued that there is an inevitable trend for
industry to disperse throughout the world, that the scramble for overseas markets
is consequently futile, and that small-scale production for a local market is the
pattern of future industry.

He concluded that intensive small-scale farming could meet the basic food
needs of a country like Britain and that the dispersal of industry in combination
with agriculture is rational and desirable and would provide a reduction of working hours and greater individual fulfillment. Education should equip every child
for a working life that combined brain work and manual work. Kropotkin was
endlessly optimistic, and prophecies seldom fulfill the prophets' anticipations.
Certainly industry was globally dispersed, but for a global rather than a local
market. Certainly Britain could be agriculturally self-sufficient, but through the
opposite of the labour-intensive bio-dynamic farming he envisaged. On the other
hand, as Lewis Mumford stressed,

> Almost half a century in advance of contemporary economic and techni-
> cal opinion, he had grasped the fact that the flexibility and adaptability of
> electric communication and electric power ... had laid the foundations for a
> more decentralised urban development in small units. Responsive to direct
> human contact, and enjoying both urban and rural advantages ... Kropotkin
> understood these implications before the invention of the motor car, the ra-
> dio, the motion picture—though each of these inventions further confirmed
> his penetrating diagnosis by equalising advantages between the central me-
> tropolis and the once peripheral and utterly dependent small communities.
> With the small unit as a base, he saw the opportunity for a more responsible
> and responsive local life, with greater scope far the human agents who were
> neglected and frustrated by mass organisations.[76]

Another observer of the depopulated rural landscape of a century ago was Ebenezer Howard, shorthand-writer and inventor. His book *Tomorrow: A Peaceful Path*

*to Real Reform* was also published a century ago, and has been reprinted continually under the title *Garden Cities of Tomorrow*. Howard was familiar with the appalling problems of the over-crowded Victorian city and put together a combination of proposals for outward movement. A body should be formed to buy rural land at the depressed land values of his day and develop a town surrounded by a green belt, to give the citizens the benefits of both town and country as listed in his famous Three Magnets diagram. The town would belong to its inhabitants; since, as Peter Hall explains,

> The citizen would pay a modest rate-rent for their houses or factories or farms, sufficient to repay the interest on the money originally borrowed, to provide a sinking fund to repay the capital, and then—progressively, as the money was paid back—to provide abundant funds for the creation of a local welfare state, all without need for local central taxation, and directly responsible to the local citizens.[77]

## LAND VALUES

It is important to stress that his intention was to find a solution to the intractable problems of the Victorian city. He was convinced that once the site values of the inner city had been 'demagnetized', since large numbers of people had been convinced that '*they can better their condition in every way by migrating elsewhere*,' the bubble of the monopoly value of inner-city land would burst. Needless to say, the capitalist property-market ensured that this was not to happen. But Howard was attempting to cope with an issue that has been quietly dropped from the political agenda: the recouping for the community rather than for a landowner the 'unearned increment' in site values that is generated simply by the community's existence.

In this connection, Howard declared that he had drawn 'much inspiration' from Henry George's famous book *Progress and Poverty*. The planning historian Dennis Hardy explains that

> It was the idea of land values properly belonging to the community which appealed to Howard, although he did not share George's enthusiasm for a centralised State system as the right way to appropriate and re-allocate the benefits. Howard accepted the kernel of the book, but rejected anything that might lead to more centralisation, as opposed to basically communal forms of organisation.[78]

The centralized state has been no more successful. The Town and Country Planning Act of 1947 provided for a Central Land Board which nationalized the betterment value of land and imposed development charges. But legislation in the late 1950s abandoned these provisions. In the 1960s a Land Commission was introduced by another Labour government imposing a betterment levy on land, but another Conservative government abolished the Commission in 1971. In the 1970s, the Community Land Act was equally short-lived.

Our failure to develop the social will to tackle the issue of land valuation has, paradoxically, been worsened by the planning system. Planning permission for housing development can multiply the value of farm land tenfold, while its agricultural value has already been advanced by the prospect of subsidy, even though that subsidy may be paid as a reward for growing nothing. In the south-east of England, 60 per cent of the cost of building a house in 1997 was the price of the land. Similarly, Ray Thomas of the New Towns Study Unit at the Open University, introducing the most recent edition of Howard's book, comments that:

> ... as far as land in old cities is concerned, the effect of the planning system has been to maintain prices in spite of the exodus of population. Derelict urban land for which no buyer can be found remains as a capital asset for its owners. The land remains an unused eyesore, but when there is any question of acquisition of the land for public purposes, the price is usually in terms of hundreds of thousand pounds per acre. The implementation of Howard's ideas for what would nowadays be called the greening of the city has become exorbitantly expensive to the public purse.[79]

Another of Howard's famous diagrams, only restored in recent editions of his book, explained his concept of the Social City. Howard was not, as his detractors claim, presenting a suburban ideal. His garden cities were envisaged with much higher residential densities than that of the kind of urban expansion that became known as 'suburban sprawl'. They were conceived as a cluster, separated by a green belt, around a central city providing those facilities that individual towns could not supply, in a polynucleated settlement pattern of city regions: a peopled landscape. And although Howard was writing on the eve of the century when the internal combustion engine was to transform the urban environment, his transport priorities precisely fit those we are aspiring to for the 21$^{st}$ century.

Howard's book inspired the two pioneer garden cities that he initiated in Britain, Letchworth and Welwyn, and many such ventures abroad. It led in post-war Britain to the government's New Towns Act of 1946 and to the building of 28 New Towns, admired and emulated in other countries, and criticized, usually for the wrong reasons, at home.[80] In comparison with other forms of development in the post-war decades, especially the disastrous adventure with tower blocks for the city poor, the New Towns had many virtues, were a lucrative investment of public funds and were more economical in the use of land. The choice of government corporations as the engines of development. and the subsequent disposal of public assets in the private market destroyed, as Professor Peter Hall noted,

> the essence of Howard's plan, which was to fund the creation of self-governing local welfare states. Top-down planning triumphed over bottom-up; Britain would have the shell of Howard's garden city vision without the substance.[81]

Both Howard and Kropotkin, the prophets of a peopled landscape, were astute in their perceptions of the issues that would pre-occupy us at the end of the 20th century. A note prefixed to the 1919 reprint of *Fields, Factories and Workshops* stressed that '*It pleads for a new economy* in *the energies used in supplying the needs of human life, since these needs are increasing and the energies are not inexhaustible.*' In the same year, Kropotkin urged that,

> ... after the cruel lesson of the last war, it should be clear to every serious person and above all to every worker, that such wars, and even crueller ones still, are inevitable so long as certain countries consider themselves destined to enrich themselves by the production of finished goods and divide the backward countries up amongst themselves, so that these countries provide the raw materials while they accumulate wealth themselves on the basis of the labour of others ... We should not forget that at the moment it is not only the capitalists who exploit the labour of others and who are "imperialists". They are not the only ones who aspire to conquer cheap manpower to obtain raw materials in Europe, Asia, Africa and elsewhere....[82]

These two observations remain immensely relevant to our approach to today's global economy and our search for alternatives, and nowhere more obviously than in the production and distribution of food, as Tim Lang reminds us. ... In Britain five giant supermarket firms control more than two thirds of the retail food market and roam the world market for producers, always to the detriment of the local food market whether in Britain or in Africa and Latin America, where export crops may dominate the demand for scarce and precious resources like water.

In an American context the economist Paul Hawken urges a shift from the Free Trade enshrined in current dogma and in treaties like GATT to the concept of Most Sustainable Nation tariffs.[83] Jeffrey Jacob explains the implications of this proposal:

> It is possible that the Most Sustainable Nation tariffs could remove the profitability from a Third World agriculture that relies on the application of chemicals banned in North America and wages calculated to do no more than reproduce a subservient labour force. If, however, sustainability requirements in the North were to cripple export agriculture in the underdeveloped South, the beneficiaries would be the masses of rural and urban Third World poor. With the dissolution of plantation-style agriculture, peasants would be free to turn their attention to growing basic grains in order to address the long-standing calorific deficit from which they and the urban poor suffer, rather than producing luxury crops for First World consumers. In addition, without the power and wealth that comes from the ownership of cash-crop export operations, Third World elites would no longer have automatic access to the resources of oppression ... Consequently, in underdeveloped countries whose economies are heavily dependent on export agriculture, the loss of North American and Western European markets could create an opening for democratic movements, movements that in the past have been routinely crushed by the planter class.[84]

## THE GREAT EXODUS

Kropotkin's reflections remind us of dilemmas we have failed to resolve, and Ebenezer Howard too, the 'heroic simpleton' as Bernard Shaw called him when writing his obituary in 1928, was given to astute prophecy. More far-sighted than most social and demographic observers, he remarked in 1904 that

> while the age we live in is the age of great closely compacted, overcrowded cities, there are already signs, for those who can read them, of a coming change so great and so momentous that the twentieth century will be known as the great exodus.[85]

This was good news, because a century ago there was a growing public and official concern about the consequences of urban overcrowding, where any redevelopment at lower densities brought greater pressures of the dispossessed on neighbouring districts, and of rural depopulation. A report to the Council for the Protection of Rural England in 1997 studied the Great Exodus today and found that:

> The available statistics certainly indicate that the urban exodus, while long-established in terms at local suburbanisation around older urban cores, is now the dominant feature of population redistribution across Britain as a whole ... On the other hand, the scale of the urban exodus does fluctuate over time and it is important to recognise that it is by no means a one-way process. Net out-migration from the main conurbations fell to 78,000 in 1982 before rising to 125,000 in 1987 and then falling back sharply to 65,000 in 1989, since when it has moved back up to around its long term average of 90,000 a year.[86]

It is not surprising to learn from this report that *'Districts with a higher density of people per hectare have a greater tendency to lose their residents to non-metropolitan areas, all other things being equal.'* Earlier in the 20th century, movements of population were still in the opposite direction, and were thought alarming. One report on the exodus from the villages stressed that,

> In some parts of the country we find villages from which the majority of the younger able-bodied men have emigrated, and it is generally the most capable and energetic who go. Side by side with emigration, for the last thirty years and more, there has been a huge exodus of labourers into the towns, especially the large towns ... [87]

But of course the 19th-century exodus was composed of the rural poor, while the 20th-century exodus has been composed of the urban affluent. One of the seldom-discussed virtues of the post-war New Town programme was that with a single exception, the New Towns were the only official mechanism by which city dwellers with low incomes could join the outward movement of population from the cities which, just as Howard forecast, has characterized this century. The exception was the parallel Town Development programme by which an 'exporting' city's local authorities could undertake 'overspill' development in agreement with a cooperating 'importing' town eager for growth.[88] But in rural parishes, there is not merely no place for low-income newcomers, there is no place for the adult children of long-established local families who have been priced out of the housing market and are obliged to rent rooms in the nearest town.

## RURAL HOUSING
In the 1970s the historian of the canals and of the railway network, L.C.T. Rolt, wrote a third volume of autobiography in which he described changes in the village where he lived:

> Because of mis-application of the well-intentioned Slum Clearance Act by a zealous Medical Officer of Health, most of the old village cottages I knew were condemned on grounds of their low ceilings, or lack of through ventilation. Even with the aid of the available local authority grants, their occupants could not afford alterations which would conform with load regulations. Consequently, such houses have been acquired by those who could afford reconstruction, executives or retired business men. With the result that they have been 'prettified' beyond recognition and embellished with such things as bogus wrought iron work of welded steel strip, carriage lanterns or wooden wheelbarrows filled with flowers. Meanwhile, such old village families as have survived this upheaval live in council houses on the village outskirts from whence they are collected and delivered daily by special coaches which take them to work in the near factories.[89]

The span of time between the writing and the publication of Rolt's book is a reminder of several aspects of recent history. The first is that those pathetic and neglected cottages were demolished by the thousand in the early post-war decades as unfit for human habitation before they were redefined as precious relics of vernacular architecture. The second is that their inhabitants were thankful to be allocated one of these raw new council houses, with all the modest facilities that had been beyond their reach for years. And the third is that by the 1990s most of those council houses have been sold on instructions from central government and no more have been built. All attempts to provide 'affordable housing' for rent in village England have to surmount the soaring price of land, an impenetrable thicket of legislation and the vehement opposition of the present occupants of those picturesque cottages. ...

There is a curious irony about the fact that in the first 40 years of this century it was possible for poor city dwellers (often only two generations away from the country in their own family history) to buy a patch of the empty fields that every observer deplored a century ago. Scattered around on the coast and in the country there are little patches of makeshift development with grass-track roads leading to bungalows whose origins in First World War army huts or in converted railway coaches can still be discerned behind additions and improvements. Or they are weather-boarded chalets whose asbestos-cement roof-tiles were salmon-pink in the 1920s but have now, through attracting mosses and lichens, become the colour and texture of Cotswold stone. Some of these settlements are famous, like Peacehaven or Jaywick Sands. Others, hidden in the landscape of Kent, Essex and the Thames Valley, are known only to their residents and to the planning authorities, where many hours of professional labour have been devoted to eliminating, controlling or improving them. They are described collectively as the 'plotlands' because when land was 'dirt cheap' in the agricultural depression, it was parcelled up into plots by speculators and sold, often for £5 or less for a plot, to people who wanted to live out their dreams of a place in the country.

The pre-war literature of planning rural conservation was full of righteous anger about the 'bungaloid growth' creeping over the face of the Home Counties, and demanding precisely the kind of control over development that was introduced in post-war planning legislation. The real offence was that low-income families were gaining the freedom to move into a more spacious life that was taken for granted by their betters. And the result was to turn the derelict farmland of ruined barns, dockweed and thistles into an improvised world of make-and-mend, resembling Barrie Trinder's characterization of the pre-industrial rural scene with its bustling activity as *'a landscape of busy-ness'*.[90]

## OUR PLOTLAND HERITAGE

Needless to say, by the end of the century, the plotlands themselves have become part of our heritage. At Basildon, one of the few remaining bungalows called 'The Haven' at Dunton Hills has become a plotland museum. At Dungeness in Kent, a plotland site was designated as a Conservation Area to preserve it from redevelopment, as was the site called 'Holt's Field' in Swansea Bay. But when Dennis Hardy and I attempted to collect the history of the plotlands in SE England, we were in time to gather the experiences of the original settlers.[91]

When we met Mrs Sayers of Peacehaven, she had lived there since 1923. Her husband, severely wounded in the First World War, was urged to live in a more bracing, upland climate than that of Tottenham. They sought somewhere to rent in the Surrey Hills and found them far beyond their reach. Through the publicity (on the back of London tram tickets) of the flamboyant speculator who started Peacehaven on the south coast, they bought three plots and obtained title to the land in 1921. They built on it in 1922 and in the following year opened a branch post office and grocery shop, and lived there happily for many decades.

Mr. Fred Nichols of Bowers Gifford in Essex was in his seventies. He had a poverty-stricken childhood in East London and a hard and uncertain life as a casual dock worker. His plot, 40 ft wide and 100 ft long, cost him £10 in 1934. First he put up a tent which his family and friends used at week-ends, and he gradually accumulated tools, timber and glass which he brought to the site strapped to his back as he cycled the 25 miles from London. For water he sank a well in the garden. His house was called 'Perseverance'. The view of those plotland pioneers was summed up for us by Mrs Granger from Laindon who told us how *'I feel so sorry for young couples these days, who don't get the kind of chance we had'*. She was right. None of those settlers from the 1920s and 30s would have qualified for a mortgage loan. And our rigid planning laws and building by-laws have ensured that there is no place for them in today's rural England.

What we witness now is a semi-theological debate conducted by the professional employees of various interest groups on the relative proportions of the new housing needs forecast for the early 21$^{st}$ century that should be built on 'brownfield' sites in urban areas and on 'green-field' sites in the country. What is missing is any discussion of which sections of the population the debate is about. Who is to be housed, how and by whom? Do the would-be rural dwellers of the new century have the same demands as those of the double-garage Range-Rover families who move there today? There is a growing number of people, especially among the young, who are concerned with environmental issues, who reject what they see as the socially useless forms of employment the job market offers, but yearns to live on the land. They are interested in alternative approaches to food production, in alterative technology, and building for themselves the most rudimentary of dwellings, in the expectation that their homes will evolve and improve over time. The numbers of these alternative citizens are going to increase in the next century, as environmental crises impinge more and more on people's lives. One such person is Simon Fairlie, who explains how:

> When, with friends, I rented a house with a sizeable garden on a country estate, we were thrown out after three years to make way for a golf course. I lived in a van for two years and eventually, with some other people, bought a bare-land small-holding. To accommodate ourselves we pitched tents on our land. In the two years since we moved onto our land, we have been through almost the entire gamut of planning procedure: committee decision, enforcement order, stop notice, Article 4 application, Section 106 agreement, appeal, call in by the Secretary of State and statutory review in the High Court. All this for seven tents!

The experience obliged him to master the complexities of the planning system and examine how very slight changes could accommodate *'the radical new forms of development that the quest for sustainability demands.'*

## A VERY DIFFERENT KIND OF RURAL SOCEITY
The key argument of Fairlie's outstanding book on *Low Impact Development* is that:

> If permission to build or live in the countryside were to be allocated, not just to those who can afford artificially inflated land prices, but to anyone who could demonstrate a willingness and an ability to contribute to a thriving local environment and economy, then a very different kind of rural society would emerge. Low-impact development is a social contract, whereby people are given the opportunity to live in the country in return for providing environmental benefits. Planners will recognize this as a form of what they call "planning gain". The mechanisms to strike such a bargain are for the most

part already written into the *English* planning system and there is thus no need for any major structural changes.[92]

Fairlie is not bitter about the planning system because he also knows that without it speculative developers would have completed the destruction of the countryside begun by the farmers subsidized to destroy woodlands, wetlands, hedges and wildlife. He knows that most of us demand a more luxurious but ecologically friendly environment than the one that suits him, and he realizes that all living environments are enhanced out of earnings over time. So he wants to make just a few changes to the planning machinery so that local authorities can actually foster experiments in low-impact rural development, '*some of them carried out at the margins of society, others designed to cater for more conventional people.*'

There is, however, a huge need for changes in attitudes, not only in adopting concepts of fairness and social justice instead of greed, but also in accepting the desirability of a peopled landscape. An important ally is the economic historian Joan Thirsk, who edited the massive *Cambridge Agrarian History of England and Wales*. In a new book she traces the various phases of alternative agriculture in our history, from the period after the Black Death onward.

She traces different causes for each of these times of searching for alternate crops and for our current situation of over-production resulting from heavily-subsidized environmental destruction. Thirsk pays particular attention to those turn-of-the century reformers like Kropotkin who sought the repopulation of the empty countryside through the combination of labour-intensive horticulture and small workshop industry:

> Since far-sighted individuals have forecast the impossibility of restoring full employment now that modern technology is daily reducing the work required, we plainly await another Peter Kropotkin to pronounce the same lesson all over again. The continuing obsessive drive to foster technology and shed labour at all costs belongs appropriately to the phase of mainstream agriculture, and not to the alterative phase ... [93]

All too often a concern for the protection of the countryside is a concern for the exclusive enjoyment of it by the mobile affluent classes and a determination to keep out any other aspirants to rural life. Yet the potentiality to retain or revive vital village services: the bus, the school, the shop and the post office, depend upon the re-creation of a peopled landscape....

# NOTES

## PREFACE AND INTRODUCTION

**1**  Ward draws the phrase 'Seeds Beneath the Snow' from Ignazio Silone's novel *The Seeds Beneath the Snow* (Harper, 1932).

**2**  Ward won the Angel Literary Award for non-fiction in 1985 and was given the Charles Douglas Home Memorial Trust Award to write *Welcome, Thinner City*.

**3**  As Paul Barker has observed. See Paul Barker, "Anarchy in the suburbs," *Prospect Magazine* Issue 43 (20 July 1999).

**4**  Maurice Blanchot (translated by Susan Hanson), "Everyday Speech," *Yale French Studies* No. 73 (1987): 12–20.

**5**  To use the phrase of Pickerill and Chatterton. See Jenny Pickerill and Paul Chatterton, "Notes Towards Autonomous Geographies: Creation, Resistance and Self-Management," *Progress in Human Geography* 30 (2006): 738.

**6**  Cited in Colin Ward, *Anarchy in Action*. (London: Freedom Press, 1973), 121.

**7**  Colin Ward, *Influences, Voices of Creative Dissent*. (Green Books, 1991), 11.

**8**  This non-dogmatic quality of Ward's writings has undoubtedly helped spread its influence and facilitated numerous successful collaborative writings projects with colleagues as varied in interests and professional background as the novelist Ruth Rendell and the urban planner Peter Hall, the art educationalist Eileen Adams and the geographers David Crouch and Dennis Hardy—writers who clearly share some of his general sympathies to decentralization and the virtues of self organization without being fully committed anarchists.

**9**  Colin Ward, *The Child in the City*. (London: Bedford Square Press, 1990), 18.

**10**  Ibid., 19.

**11**  Colin Ward, *Talking Houses* (London: Freedom Press, 1990), 124–125.

**12**  Ibid., 9.

**13**  The links between Ward, Lefebvre and Gramscian strategies have yet to be made, yet they clearly exist. Compare Ward's *Anarchy in Action* with H. Lefebvre, *The Production of Space* (Oxford: Blackwell, 1992). Ward was very influential in some of the left-libertarian currents in Italy, and as such there are links to be made here with these movements and practices that have been so influential politically in recent decades.

**14**     We are indebted here to the excellent essays of David Goodway for this bio-graphical information. See David Goodway 'Introduction' in Colin Ward and David Goodway, *Talking Anarchy*. (Nottingham: Five Leaves, 2003), 1–20; and David Goodway, 'Colin Ward' in *Anarchist Seeds Beneath the Snow: Left-Libertarian Thought and British Writers from William Morris to Colin Ward*. (Liverpool: Liverpool University Press 2006).

**15**     Ward, *Influences, Voices of Creative Dissent*, 91.

**16**     See Colin Ward, "Anarchy and Architecture" in Jonathan Hughes and Simon Sadler (eds.), *Non-Plan: Essays on Freedom, Participation and Change in Modern Architecture and Urbanism*. (London: Architectural Press, 2000).

**17**     *War Commentary: For Anarchism* was the title used by *Freedom* during the Second World War years. It reverted to the title *Freedom* after 1945.

**18**     Colin Ward wished the journal to be called *Autonomy – A Journal of Anarchist Ideas*. This title was thought to be inappropriate by others members of the editorial board of Freedom Press.

**19**     The Town and Country Planning Association was started by Ebenezer Howard as the 'Garden Cities Association' in 1899.

**20**     See David Goodway 'Introduction to Talking Anarchy' in *Talking Anarchy*, 2–3.

**21**     Ibid., *Talking Anarchy*, 2.

**22**     See Ward "Anarchy and Architecture" in *Non-Plan*.

**23**     See Goodway in *Talking Anarchy*, 4. Read, Herbert (1945), *Freedom: Is it a crime? The strange case of the three anarchists jailed at the Old Bailey, April 1945*, London: Freedom Press. See also: http://robertgraham.wordpress.com/2009/06/06/herbert-read-war-revolution-1945. Ward was called as a witness for the prosecution to testify against the editors of *War Commentary* between January and April 1945, who were accused of trying to seduce members of the armed services from their duties. He was an unproductive witness and he subsequently became firm allies and friends with the group. See *Talking Anarchy*, 29–31 for an account of the affair.

**24**     See David Stafford "Anarchists in Britain Today" in David E. Apter and James Joll (eds.), *Anarchism Today*. (London: Macmillian, 1971), 89.

**25**     See Colin Ward, "After a Hundred Issues," *Freedom* (14 June 1969), republished in Colin Ward (ed.), *A Decade of Anarchy*. (London: Freedom Press, 1987), 277.

**26**     Brock Millman, *Managing Domestic Dissent in First World War Britain*. (London: Routledge, 2000).

**27**     Basildon in Essex was a former Plotland that was incorporated into the New Towns project.

**28**     See http://www.essex.ac.uk/human_rights_centre/hrc/projects/dalefarm.aspx.

**29**     See, for example, Guy Julier, *The Culture of Design*. (London: Sage Publications, 2008); Harvey Molotch, *Where Stuff Comes From*. (London: Routledge, 2005).

**30**     For a few exceptions to this see Nigel Whiteley, *Design for Society*. (London: Reaktion Books, 1993); Charles Leadbeater and Paul Miller, *The Pro-Am Revo-*

*lution.* (London: Demos, 2004); N. Wakeford (ed.), "Innovation through people centred design—Lessons from the USA". (London: DTI, 2004).

31    See, for example, Bernard Rudofsky, *Architecture without Architects: A Short Introduction to Non Pedigreed Architecture.* (Albuquerque: University of New Mexico Press, 1987); Eiko Komatsu, Athena Steen and Bill Steen, *Built by Hand: Vernacular Buildings Around the World.* (Utah: Gibbs Smith, 2003); Marcel Vellinga, Paul Oliver and Alexander Bridge *Atlas of Vernacular Architecture of the World.* (London: Routledge, 2008).

32    See Lucien Kroll, "Anarchitecture," in R. Hatch (ed.), *The Scope of Social Architecture.* (New York: Van Nostrand Reinhold, 1984).

33    See http://www.segalselfbuild.co.uk

34    See Ward, *Anarchy in Action*, chapter 7.

35    See J. Huizinga, *Homo Ludens.* (London: RKP, 1947); Lewis Mumford, *The Myth of the Machine.* (London: Secket & Warburg, 1967); Chris Rojek, *Leisure and Culture.* (Basingstoke: MacMillan, 2000); Pat Kane, *The Play Ethic- A Manifesto for a Different Way of Living.* (London: Macmillian, 2005).

36    He, along with contributors to the journal *Anarchy* has also been criticised by some fellow anarchists, such as Albert Meltzer, for being part of a 'Failed Mandarin' group who were not active enough themselves in actual struggles (see Abert Meltzer, *I Couldn't Paint Golden Angels.* (Edinburgh: AK Press, 1996).

37    See Stafford, "Anarchists in Britain Today" in *Anarchism Today.*

38    See Paul Barker "Anarchy in the Suburbs," *Prospect Magazine* Issue 43 (20 July 1999).

39    Stuart White, "Making anarchism respectable? The social philosophy of Colin Ward," *Journal of Political Ideologies* Volume 12, Issue 1 (Feb 2007): 11–28.

40    See Ward and Goodway, *Talking Anarchy*, 49–53.

41    Such criticisms have been made by Ken Worpole and Alison Ravetz in Ken Worpole (ed.), *Richer Futures.* (London: Earthscan, 1999), 63–79.

42    See, for example, Manuel Castells, *The Rise of the Network Society.* (Oxford: Blackwell, 1996). For an interesting critique of the use of 'network' metaphors and imaginary in contemporary social theory, see Andrew Barry, *Political Machines.* (London: Athlone Press, 2001).

43    See the work of the late Paul Hirst: *Associative Democracy.* (London: Polity Press, 2006).

44    It has been well documented, though, that many developing countries cannot choose to develop effective welfare systems because, as preconditions of loans, they are forced to accept IMF and World Bank structural adjustment policies (as they were until recently known), which still follow the chaotic neo-liberal policies that have driven the latest global recession.

45    See Ash Amin and Nigel Thrift, *Cities: Reimagining the Urban.* (Cambridge: Polity Press, 2002); Hilary Wainwright, *Reclaim the State: Experiments in Popular Democracy.* (London: Verso, 2003); J.K. Gibson-Graham, *A Postcapitalist Politics.* (Minneapolis: University of Minneapolis Press, 2006).

**46**     Luc Boltanski and Eve Chiapello, *The New Spirit of Capitalism*. (London: Verso, 2005). A similar argument has been made by Richard Sennett in *The Corrosion of Character*, W.W. Norton & Company, Inc. (New. York, 1998).

**47**     See Leadbeater and Miller, *The Pro-Am Revolution*; Don Tapscott and Anthony D. Williams, *Wikinomics: How Mass Collaboration Changes Everything*. (London: Penguin Books, 2006).

**48**     See Worpole, *Richer Futures*, 171.

**49**     Elinor Ostrom, *Governing the Commons: The Evolution of Institutions for Collective Action*. (Cambridge: Cambridge University Press, 1990).

**50**     See Doreen Massey, *For Space*. (Cambridge: Polity Press, 2005).

**51**     See Chapter Five of this anthology.

**52**     The suppression of the 'political' in radical politics has been a long-standing theme of radical political thought in recent decades. For some expositions of this line of thought see C. Pierson, *Marxist Theory and Democratic Politics*. (Cambridge: Polity Press, 1986); Chantal Mouffe, *The Return of the Political*. (London: Verso, 1993).

**53**     Of the kind argued by the right-wing libertarian Robert Nozick, see *Anarchy, State, and Utopia*. (New York: Basic Books, 1977).

**54**     It could be observed here that there are interesting tensions in Ward's writings about the state. In his theoretical writings, he tends to follow anarchist orthodoxies in treating the state in essentialist fashion, as a singular thing with transhistorical properties. Yet, in his applied writings there are moments where he recognizes that the state is actually a much more complex terrain of struggle with its competing elements and layers that are open to engagement in different ways and recognizes also that different elements of the state have capacities to aid self organization in civil society as well as destroy civil society. Ward's pragmatism here often emerges in the sentiment that 'the state just needs to get out of the way', but in other writings, addressed to policy-making audiences, the state is clearly given a much more specific creative role as facilitator and protector of self management. For example, if we go back to the DIY new town it could be argued that ensuring such a venture met minimum standards of safety and social and environmental health would draw state-like agencies back into the picture.

**55**     A related matter here is the extent to which Ward fully grapples with the fact that the achievement of certain large social goals—civil rights, gender politics, environmental preservation, just conditions of employment and so on—have often required mass collective action to secure mandated agreements that can be enforced. Ward's work is obviously an important corrective to the view that this approach is always optimal. At the same time though, premising all social relations on self-organization and voluntary agreements can generate free rider problems, refusals to comply, etc. It is difficult to see how voluntarism, self-management and mutual aid could have dealt with demands for civil rights for African Americans in the 1960s, for example. To take a more recent example, can one assume that voluntarism, mutual aid and self-organization can deal with issues like climate change? Such ideas, at present, are becoming increasingly common as lifestyle change is emphasised above and beyond the debate for industry to be brought under regulatory frameworks with mandated and enforced emission cuts.

**56**     It would be fair to recognise that Ward's writings are heavily dependent on his influences, sometimes too much so. Readers of this anthology will quickly become aware of the extent to which Ward recycles a favoured quote or observation from a key thinker across multiple writings generating a high degree of thematic duplication. Ward can debatably be read as a supplement to Foucault, providing almost genealogical accounts of the micro-politics of self-organization to counter the micro-politics of governmentality. Yet, it would have to be recognised that his work is by no means as theoretically sophisticated as Foucault's. More generally, readers might find that Ward's unrelenting optimistic reading of certain social forces fails to meet the test of time. It is not clear how enduring Ward's preferred forms of self-organization have been, and at times his work has been marked by a lapse of judgment (for example, in viewing in relatively benign terms China's experiment with industrial decentralisation in the 1970s).

**57**     Ward's work could be additionally criticised for being a-theoretical, yet such a criticism is somewhat misleading. Theory is present in Ward's work—but what his writings are not informed by, is what we might call 'Grand Theory', the search for a comprehensive synthesis of critical thought that will yield up a thick explanatory theory of society and a supposedly clear path for action. Rather, theory in Ward's writings is much more modestly deployed, both in explaining and recommending. It is always simply a set of propositions that may or may not be found useful in the material world. Ward's work by its very raison d'être cannot function as Grand Theory because it recognises human plurality and seeks to give voice to lay practices and to create room for creative acts of self-organization by other people in serious ways. To engage in grand theory where all is worked out in advance would be to contain too much of the future and the spirit of libertarian practice, which ultimately is to encourage forms of communalist self-organization. In this respect, Ward's skepticism of grand theory makes for an interesting contrast with the other major figure of the libertarian left in the 20th century: Murray Bookchin. See Damian F. White, *Bookchin: A Critical Appraisal*. (London: Pluto Press, 2008).

**58**     Cited in Ward, *Talking Houses*, 13.

**59**     See Anne Power, "Neighbourhood management and the future of urban areas" (CASE077, Centre for Analysis of Social Exclusion, London School of Economics and Political Science, London, 2004). To take the politics of housing associations, many would argue this shift in housing policy has a mixed legacy. Many (but by no means all) of these Housing Associations often ended up raising rents and acting even more like private landlords, and remained remote from tenants with Boards of Trustees that were often from the wealthier classes and who had no idea what tenants lives were actually like.

**60**     To use Paul Barker's vivid phrase. See Paul Barker, "Anarchy in the Suburbs," *Prospect Magazine*, 62.

**61**     See Ward, Colin, *Reflected in Water: A crisis of Social Responsibility*. (London: Cassell, 1997), 15–30.

**62**     For a development of this theme see Damian White and Chris Wilbert (eds.) *Technonatures*. (Waterloo: Wilfred Laurier University Press, 2009).

**63**     See Ward, *Talking Houses*, 8.

**64**     Colin Ward, "High Density Life," *Prospect* (July 2000): 41.

**65**     See "In the Sandbox of the City" Section 4 of this anthology.

**66**     See Frank Furedi, *Paranoid Parenting: Why Ignoring the Experts May Be Best for Your Child*. (Chicago: Chicago Review Press, 2002).

**67**     See Worpole, *Richer Futures*, 10.

**68**     See Colin Ward, "Fringe Benefits," *New Statesman & Society* (1988) on Spitalfields in London, for example—reproduced in Chapter 4.

**69**     See Roberto Unger, *What Should the Left Propose?* (London: Verso, 2006).


## SECTION ONE:

**1**     Editors' Note: A general grocer.

**2**     Sydney Caulfield—who himself had studied under Edward Johnson, Eric Johnson and W.R. Lethaby at the Central School of Arts and Crafts (see Goodway, in *Talking Anarchy*, 2).

**3**     See the excerpt "Allied Military Government," *War Commentary* (Mid-December 1943) in this chapter.

**4**     See Chapter 2, "The People Act."

**5**     Vernon Richards was arrested in Feb 1945 along with two other members of the *War Commentary* editorial group and charged with attempts to create disaffection in the armed services. Richards received nine months in prison as a result of this.


## SECTION TWO:

**1**     Colin Ward, *Talking Houses*. (London: Freedom Press, 1990).

**2**     Dennis Hardy and Colin Ward, *Arcadia For All: The Legacy of a Makeshift Landscape*. (London: Mansell, 1984).

**3**     Clough Williams-Ellis, *England and the Octopus*. (London: Geoffrey Bles, 1928).

**4**     G.M. Trevelyan, "Amenities and the State," in Clough Williams-Ellis (ed.), *Britain and the Beast*. (London: J.M. Dent, 1937), 183–186.

**5**     Patrick Abercrombie, *Greater London Plan 1944*. (London: HMSO, 1945).

**6**     Anthony D. King, *The Bungalow: The Production of a Global Culture*. (London: Routledge & Kegal Paul, 1984).

**7**     *The Times*, 15 November 1957, quoted in Paul M. Hopkins (ed.) *The Long and the Short and the Tall; Half a Lifetime of the Arts in Harlow by the People Who Have Lived It* (Harlow Arts Council, 1983).

**8**     Publisher's note on the cover of Angus Wilson, *Late Call* (London: Penguin Books, 1992).

**9**     Leslie Lane, "Reshaping our Physical Environment," Danes Memorial Lecture

(London: Civic Trust, 1966).

**10**    "Paradise Mislaid," *The Times*, 24 January 1992.

**11**    David Hall: letter to *The Times*, 30 January 1992.

**12**    See a continuous literature from Norman Dennis, *People and Planning*. (London: Faber and Faber 1968) to Frances Heywood and Mohammed Rashid Naz, *Clearance: The View from the Street*. (Birmingham: Community Forum, 1990).

**13**    David Hall, letter to *The Times*.

**14**    *New Town, Home Town*, directed by David Heycock, BBC2, February 1980.

**15**    Ebenezer Howard, opening the discussion of a paper by Patrick Geddes on "Civics as Applied Sociology," London School of Economics, 18 July 1904, reprinted in Helen Mellor (ed.), *The Ideal City*. (Leicester: Leicester University Press, 1979).

**16**    Harry Hopkins, *The New Look: A Social History of the Forties and Fifties*. (London: Secker and Warburg, 1963).

**17**    Lord Taylor and Sidney Chave, *Mental Health and Environment in a New Town*. (London: Longman, 1964), quoted in Frank Schaffer, *The New Town Story*. (London: Paladin 1972).

**18**    Wilfred Burns, at the seminar of the Artist Placement Group, Royal College of Art, 1978.

**19**    Parker-Morris Report, "Homes for Today and Tomorrow." (London: HMSO, 1961)

**20**    J. M. Richards, Gordon Cullen, et al. "Failure of the New Towns," *The Architectural Review* (July 1953).

**21**    Robin H. Best, *Land for New Towns*. (London: TCPA, 1964).

**22**    G. P. Wibberley, *Agriculture and Urban Growth*. (London: Michael Joseph, 1959).

**23**    *A Design Guide for Residential Areas* (Chelmsford: Essex County Council, 1973); *Housing: Roads* (Chester: Cheshire County Council, 1976); Department of the Environment and Department of Transport, *Residential Roads and Footpaths*. (London: HMSO, 1977).

**24**    Arnold Whittick in Frederic J. Osborn and Arnold Whittick, *The New Towns: The Answer to Megalopolis*. (London: Leonard Hill, 1963).

**25**    Quoted in Garry Philipson, *Aycliffe and Peterlee New Towns 1946–1988*. (Cambridge Publications for Companies, 1988).

**26**    Ibid.

**27**    Ian Colquhoun and Peter G. Fauset, *Housing Design in Practice*. (Harlow: Longman, 1991).

**28**    Jeff Bishop, "Milton Keynes: The Best of Both Worlds: Public and Professional Views of a New City." Occasional Paper 24, School for Advanced Urban Studies, 1986.

**29**    Ibid.

**30**     Ibid.

**31**     Channel 4, *Hard News*, 7 April 1992.

**32**     Lewis Silkin, "Housing Layout in Theory and Practice," *Journal of the Royal Institute of British Architects* (November 1948).

**33**     Frederic J. Osborn, letter of 10 Feb 1956, in Michael Hughes (ed.), *The Letters of Lewis Mumford and Frederic J. Osborn* (Bath: Adams and Dart, 1971).

**34**     See, for example, Vanessa Houlder, "New Towns Show Their Age," *Financial Times*, 27 March 1992.

**35**     Terence Bendixson and John Platt, *Milton Keynes: Image and Reality*. (Cambridge: Granta Editions, 1992).

**36**     George Woodcock, *Pierre-Joseph Proudhon: A Biography*. (London: Routledge & Kegan Paul, 1956), 45.

**37**     Christopher Hill (ed.), *Gerrard Winstanley: The Law of Freedom and Other Writings*. (Harmondsworth: Penguin Books ,1973).

**38**     David Mittrany, *Marx Against the Peasant: A Study in Social Dogmatism*. (New York: Collier Books ,1961), 80–81. For an anarchist account, see Voline (V.M. Eichenbaum), *The Unknown Revolution*. (London: Freedom Press, 1955).

**39**     Robert Service, *A History of Twentieth-Century Russia*. (London: Allen Lane 1997), 183.

**40**     Ibid., 181.

**41**     J.P. Cole, *A Geography of the USSR*. (Harmondsworth: Penguin Books, 1967), 167.

**42**     Oliver Rackham, *Trees and Woodlands in the British Landscape*. (London: J.M. Dent, 1976), 165.

**43**     Simon Schama, *Landscape and Memory*. (London: Harper Collins, 1995), 144.

**44**     Hugh Stretton, *Capitalism, Socialism and the Environment*. (Cambridge: Cambridge University Press, 1976).

**45**     Martin Walker, "The Seeds of a Revolution," *The Guardian,* 14 May 1985. See also David Crouch and Colin Ward, *The Allotment: Its Landscape and Culture*. (London: Faber & Faber, 1997).

**46**     Ian Hamilton, "Spatial Structure in East European Cities" in R.A. French and Ian Hamilton (eds.), *The Socialist City: Spacial Structure and Urban Policy*. (Chichester: John Wiley, 1979).

**47**     L.C.T. Bolt, *Landscape with Figures*. (Stroud: Alan Sutton, 1992).

**48**     Mark Shucksmith, *Exclusive Countryside? Social Inclusion and Regeneration in Rural Britain*. (York: Joseph Rowntree Foundation, 2000).

**49**     Simon Fairlie, *Low Impact Development Planning and People in a Sustainable Countryside*. (Oxfordshire: Jon Carpenter, 1996), x.

**50**     Richard Body, "Countryside Planning," *Town & Country Planning Summer School*. (London: Lancaster Report, RTPI, 1993), 62–66.

**51**     Peter Hall and Colin Ward, *Sociable Cities: The Legacy of Ebenezer Howard*. (Chichester: John Wiley, 1998), 107–108.

**52**     "Rio Declaration," Agenda 21, cited in Simon Fairlie, *Defining Rural Sustainability: Fifteen Criteria for Sustainable Developments in the Countryside*, 1999.

**53**     Editorial in "Chapter 7," News No. 5, Autumn 2000, 2.

## SECTION THREE:

**1**     John F.C. Turner and Robert Fichter (eds.), *Freedom to Build*. (New York: Collier MacMillan, 1972).

**2**     Janine Bailly-Herzberg (ed.), *Correspondance de Camille Pissarro*, 5 volumes, (Paris: Presses Universitaires de France, et Pontoise: Editions du Valhermeil, 1980–91).

**3**     Colin Ward, 'Preface' to John F.C. Turner, *Housing by People: Towards Autonomy in Building Environments*. (London: Marion Boyars, 1976).

**4**     John Turner in John F.C. Turner and Robert Fichter (eds.), *Freedom to Build: Dweller Control of the Housing Process*. (New York: Macmillan, 1972).

**5**     Colin Ward, *Welcome, Thinner City*. (London: Bedford Square Press, 1989).

**6**     John McKean, *Learning from Segal*. (Basle: Birkhauser Verlag, 1989).

**7**     Jon Broome and Brian Richardson, *The Self-Build Book*. (Devon: Green Books, 1991).

**8**     Colin Ward, *Talking Houses*. (London: Freedom Press, 1990).

**9**     Walter Segal, *Self Build Trust*, 57 Chalton Street, London NW1 IHIJ.

**10**    George Woodcock, *Pierre-Joseph Proudhon: A Biography*. (London: Routedge & Kegan Paul, 1956).

**11**    J.P. Cole, *A Geography of the USSR* (Harmondsworth: Penguin Books, 1967).

**12**    Hugh Stretton, *Capitalism, Socialism and the Environment*. (Cambridge: Cambridge University Press, 1976).

**13**    Ian Hamilton, "Spatial Structure in East European Cities" in *The Socialist City*.

**14**    Peter Kropotkin, *Prisons and their Moral Influence on Prisoners* (1877), reprinted in R. N. Baldwin (ed.) *Kropotkin's Revolutionary Pamphlets* (New York: Vanguard Press, 1927; Dover Press, 1971).

**15**    For the British experience, see Dennis Hardy, *Alternative Communities in Nineteenth Century England*. (London: Longman, 1979).

**16**    Peter Kropotkin, letter published, with his permission, in *Newcastle Daily Chronicle*, 20 February 1895, quoted in Colin Ward, "Colonising the Land: Utopian Ventures," in *The Raven* Anarchist Quarterly 17, Volume 5, No. 1 (January–March 1992).

**17**    Stewart Brand, *How Buildings Learn*. (New York and London: Penguin Viking, 1994).

**18**    See, for example, the books by John Turner, listed above. In a British context see Dennis Hardy and Colin Ward, *Arcadia for All: The Legacy of a Makeshift Landscape*. (London: Mansell, 1984).

**19**    Dolores Hayden, *The Grand Domestic Revolution: A History of Feminist*

*Designs for American Homes, Neighborhoods and Cities.* (Cambridge, Massachusetts: MIT Press, 1981).

**20**     Every European language has its own literature on this theme.

## SECTION FOUR:

**1**     *Holiday Camp Review* was published monthly from April to September 1938, and from May to September 1939.

**2**     Editorial, *Holiday Camp Review*, Volume 1, No. 1 (April 1938).

**3**     Editorial, *Holiday Camp Review*, Volume 1, No. 2 (May 1938).

**4**     Ibid.

**5**     Letter from C. T. Norman, *Holiday Camp Review*, Volume 2, No. 1 (May 1939).

**6**     Ibid.

**7**     A note from the President to explain the Association was included in the *Holiday Camp Review*, Volume 1, No. 2 (May 1938).

**8**     From "Looking Backwards H. E. Potter of Hopton Beach tells you his story," *Holiday Camp Review*, Volume 2, No. 1 (May 1939).

**9**     "What we want from Campers," *Holiday Camp Review*, Volume 1, No. 3 (June 1938).

**10**     Information from Mr. Victor Dodd.

**11**     Hardy and Ward, *Arcadia for All: The Legacy of a Makeshift Landscape*.

**12**     Philip Wren, "Holiday Shanties in Britain" (Unpublished dissertation, Hull School of Architecture, 1981).

**13**     Edith Sellers, "For England's Sake and their Children's," Comhill, February 1927.

**14**     Dr. Innes, Chief Education Officer for Birmingham, reported in *Holiday Camp Review*, Volume 2,

**15**     *Wheatsheaf,* Coventry Edition, July 1930.

**16**     Harold Worthington, personal communication, August 1985. See also Coventry and District Co-operative Society (1967): *A Century of Service*.

**17**     *Holiday Camp Review*, Volume 1, No. 4 (July 1938).

**18**     "Leisure as an Architectural Problem," *The Architectural Review* (December 1938).

**19**     Elizabeth Brunner, *Holiday Making and the Holiday Trades*. (Oxford: Nuffield College, 1945).

**20**     W. J. Brown. *So Far.* (London: Allen and Unwin, 1943).

**21**     *Red Tape* (Journal of the CSCA) (August 1924).

**22**     Alec Spoor, *White Collar Union: Sixty Years of NALGO* (1967).

**23**     "Holiday Facilities—Future planning policy" (NALGO Conference White Paper, 1970).

**24**    George Newman, *Path to Maturity: The History of NALGO 1965–1980* (1982).

**25**    "Holiday Camps: Some Notes on Recent Suggestions," *Industrial Welfare* (February 1939).

**26**    Lord Dawson of Penn, speaking on the Second Reading of the Camps Bill in the House of Lords, 1939.

**27**    George Lansbury, *Holiday Camp Review* Volume 1, No. 1 (April 1939).

**28**    "First Time at a Camp but Going Back for More," *Holiday Camp Review* Volume 1, No. 2 (May 1938).

**29**    "Holiday Camps and Why We Go There," *Holiday Camp Review*, Volume 2, No. 3 (July 1939).

**30**    International Working Meeting on Environmental Education in the School Curriculum, Nevada, 1970.

**31**    D. G. Watts, *Environmental Studies*. (London: Routledge & Kegan Paul, 1969).

**32**    Arthur Razzel, *Juniors*. (London: Penguin, 1969).

**33**    "Environmental Education" (Report of the Council for Environmental Education presented to the Standing Committee of 'The Countryside in 1910', 1910).

**34**    Paul Goodman, *Compulsory Miseducation*. (Horizon Press, 1962; Penguin, 1971). Everett Reimer, *School is Dead: An Essay on Alternatives in Education*. (Penguin, 1971). Ivan D. Illich, *Deschooling Society*. (Calder & Soyars, 1971). Keith Paton, *The Great Brain Robbery*. (20p from Freedom Press, 84a Whitechapel Hill Street, London E1, 1971).

**35**    "School without Walls," *Bulletin of Environmental Education*, No. 11 (March 1972).

**36**    William S. Helsel, "Teaching School Children About Planning" (unpublished thesis. Graduate School of Planning. Architectural Association, London, 1972).

**37**    "Metro Education Montréal," *L'Architecture d'Aujourd'hui* (December 1970–January 1971).

**38**    Report of the Conference on Social Deprivation and Change in Education (University of York, April 1972).

**39**    Peter Kropotkin, *Anarchism and Anarchist Communism*, edited by Nicolas Walter (London: Freedom Press, 1987).

**40**    Leonard Krimerman and Lewis Parry, *Patterns of Anarchy*. (New York: Doubleday Anchor, 1966).

**41**    Colin Ward, "The Educational Thought of William Godwin" (unpublished special study, Garnett College, London SW15, 1965).

**42**    Peter Marshall, *William Godwin*. (London: Yale University Press, 1984); and *The Anarchist Writings of William Godwin*. (London: Freedom Press, 1986).

**43**    Colin Ward, *Influences: Voices of Creative Dissent*. (Devon: Green Books, 1991).

**44**    William Godwin, *The Enquirer: Reflections on Education, Manners and Literature*. (London: G.G. and J. Robinson, 1797; facsimile reprint New York, Augustus J. Kelley, 1965). His school prospectus is reprinted in William Godwin,

*Four Early Pamphlets*, edited by B. R. Pollin. (Gainsville, Florida: 1965).

**45**     William Godwin, *Enquiry Concerning Political Justice*. (London: G.G. and J. Robinson, 1793; reprint of third edition by Isaac Kramnick, Harmondsworth: Penguin Classsics, 1976). I should mention that the task of scholars has been eased by the availability in university libraries of Marilyn Butler and Janet Todd (eds.) *The Complete Works of Mary Wollstonecraft* six volumes. (Pickering, 1989); Mark Philp et al. (eds.) *The Collected Novels and Memoirs of William Godwin* eight volumes. (Pickering & Chatto, 1992); and Mark Philip et al. (eds.) *The Political and Philosophical Writings of William Godwin* seven volumes. (Pickering & Chatto, 1994).

**46**     National Union of Teachers, *The Struggle for Education*. (London: NUT, 1970).

**47**     Stephen Humphries, *Hooligans or Rebels? An Oral History of Working-Class Childhood and Youth 1889–1939*. (Oxford: Basil Blackwell, 1981).

**48**     Philip Gardner, *The Lost Elementary Schools of Victorian England*. (London: Croom Helm, 1984)

**49**     Paul Thompson, "Basic Skills," *New Society* (6 December 1984).

**50**     For general histories of anarchism, see George Woodcock, *Anarchism: A History of Libertarian Ideas and Movements*. (Harmondsworth: Penguin, 1963) and Peter Marshall, *Demanding the Impossible: A History of Anarchism*. (London, Harper Collins, 1992). For the American impact of Francisco Ferrer, see Paul Avrich, *The Modern School Movement: Anarchism and Education in the United States*. (New Jersey: Princeton University Press, 1980).

**51**     Michael Bakunin, *God and the State*. (London: Freedom Press, 1910; New York: Dover Publications, 1970.)

**52**     Reported in *The Teacher* (8 April 1972).

**53**     Jonathan Croall, *Neill of Summerhill: The Permanent Rebel*. (London: Routledge & Kegan Paul, 1983); Jonathan Croall (ed.) *All the Best, Neill: Letters from Summerhill*. (London: Andre Deutsch, 1974).

**54**     Michael P. Smith, *The Libertarians and Education*. (London: Allen & Unwin, 1983).

**55**     *Freedom in Education: A Do-It-Yourself Guide to the Liberation of Learning*. (Libertarian Education, Phoenix House, 170 Wells Road, Bristol BS4 2AG, 1992).

**56**     John Shotton, *No Master High or Low: Libertarian Education and Schooling 1890–1990*. (Bristol: Libertarian Education, 1993).

## SECTION FIVE:

**1**     Alexander Herzen, *From the Other Shore* (London: George Brazzilier, 1956).

**2**     Kenneth Burke, "Recipe for Prosperity," *The Nation* (8 September 1956).

**3**     "Blueprint for Survival," *The Ecologist* (January 1972).

**4**     William Morris, *News From Nowhere*. (London: Routledge, 1972).

**5**     Lewis Mumford, Introduction to the post-war edition of Ebenezer Howard,

*Garden Cities of Tomorrow* (London, 1945).

**6**    Peter Kropotkin, *Fields, Factories and Workshops Tomorrow*, edited by Colin Ward. (London, Freedom Press, 1985).

**7**    "Blueprint for Survival," *The Ecologist* (January 1972).

**8**    George Orwell, in *Poetry Quarterly* (Autumn 1945).

**9**    See Colin Ward, "Harnessing the Sun," *Freedom* (23 March 1957); "Harnessing the Wind," *Freedom* (13 July 1957); "Power from the Sea," *Freedom* (1 March 1958); Lewis Herber, "Ecology and Revolutionary Thought," *Anarchy* 69 (November 1966); "Towards a Liberatory Technology," *Anarchy* 78 (August 1967)—both of the latter are reprinted in Murray Bookchin, *Post-Scarcity Anarchism* (Berkeley: Ramparts Press, 1971). See also Victor Papanek, *Design for the Real World* (London: Pantheon Books, 1972).

**10**   Peter Kropotkin, *Fields, Factories and Workshops Tomorrow*.

**11**   Paul Goodman, *Little Prayers and Finite Experiences* (New York: Harper & Row, 1972).

**12**   Obituary in *The Guardian*, 14 June 1965.

**13**   Television interview with Vernon Sproxton, *The Listener*, 18 April 1962.

**14**   This lecture was printed as Martin Buber, "What is common to all, *The Review of Metaphysics* (March 1958).

**15**   Herbert Read, *Anarchy and Order: Essays in Politics*. (London: Faber 1953).

**16**   Arthur A. Cohen, *Martin Buber*. (Bowes & Bowes, 1957).

**17**   *Ibid.*

**18**   Martin Buber, *Israel and Palestine*. (East and West Library, 1951).

**19**   Cohen, *Martin Buber*.

**20**   Martin Buber, *Pointing the Way*. (London: Routledge & Kegan Paul, 1957).

**21**   Martin Buber, *Paths in Utopia*. (Beacon Hill, 1960).

**22**   Ibid.

**23**   Ibid.

**24**   Maurice Freedman, *Martin Buber: The Life of Dialogue*. (London: Routledge & Kegan Paul, 1955).

**25**   Martin Buber, "Society and the State," *World Review* (May 1951).

**26**   Martin Buber, *Pointing the Way*.

**27**   Ibid.

**28**   James Drake, *A Picture of Birmingham*, cited in *The Allotment: Its Landscape and Culture* (Faber, 1988).

**29**   Asley Bramall, in *Education* (3 December 1976).

**30**   Raymond Unwin, *Nothing Gained by Overcrowding!* (Garden Cities and Town Planning Association, 1912). This rare pamphlet is partly reprinted in Walter Creese (ed.), *The Legacy of Raymond Unwin: A Human Pattern for Planning*.

(Cambridge, Mass: MIT Press, 1967). Its key argument is illustrated in Peter Hall, *Cities of Tomorrow* (Oxford: Basil Blackwell, 1988).

**31**  Peter Heseltine and John Holborn, *Playgrounds: The Planning, Design and Construction of Play Environments* (Mitchell Publishing, 1987).

**32**  Jacquelin Burgess, et al. "People, parks and the urban green: a study of popular meanings and values for open spaces in the city," *Urban Studies* Volume 25 (1988).

**33**  R.S.R. Fitter, *London's Natural History.* (Collins, 1945).

**34**  Richard Mabey, *The Unofficial Countryside.* (Collins, 1973).

**35**  Bob Smythe, *City Wildscapes.* (Hilary Shipman Ltd., 1987).

**36**  Nigel Winfield, interviewed in William Hatchett, "The greening of the cities," *New Society* (11 July 1986).

**37**  Hilary Peters, *Docklandscape* (Watkins, 1979).

**38**  Hatchett, "The Greening of Cities."

**39**  *City Farmer,* published from The Old Vicarage, 66 Fraser Street, Bedminster, Bristol BS3 4LY.

**40**  *Report of the Departmental Committee of Inquiry into Allotments*, Cmnd. 4166 (HMSO, 1969).

**41**  Pete Riley, *Economic Growth: The Allotments Campaign Guide.* (Friends of the Earth, 1979). For subsequent history see *The Allotment.*

**42**  Joan Davidson, *How Green Is Your City?* (London: Bedford Square Press, 1988).

**43**  David Nicholson-Lord, *The Greening of the Cities.* (Fontana, 1988).

**44**  Jonathan Porritt, *The Coming of the Greens.* (Fontana, 1988).

**45**  Jacquelin Burgess and Carolyn Harrison, "Qualitative research and open space policy," *The Planner* (Journal of the Royal Town Planning Institute) Volume 74, No. 11 (November 1988).

**46**  Ibid. and Carolyn Harrison, Melanie Limb and Jacquelin Burgess, "Nature in the city—popular values for a living world," *Journal of Environmental Management*, Volume 25 (1987).

**47**  They got the idea of the Neighbourhood Council because a member of the Deadsville Tenants and Residents Association went to a conference and picked up a copy of *The Hornsey Plan: A Role for Neighbourhood Councils in the new Local Government* by John Baker and Michael Young (50p from Association for Neighbourhood Councils 18 Victoria Park Square London E2).

**48**  They got this idea from the *Tuebrook Bugle* in Liverpool.

**49**  Robert Allen: "NE 2073, A Future for the North-East" at the Planning for People Conference of Tyneside Environmental Concern, 21 October 1972. For follow-up details read *The Ecologist.*

**50**  For the methodology, they consulted Pearl Jephcott, *Homes in High Flats.* (Oliver & Boyd, 1971).

**51**  They consulted DOE circular 72/71 (Welsh Office circular 156/71).

52    They were inspired by an old book: A. C. Hilton and J. E. Audric, *The School Farm*. (Harrap, 1945), which Mr. Compost got from the county education library, and a new one: *The Backyard Dairy Book* (Whole Earth Tools, Mill Cottage, Swaffham Road, Bottisham, Cambridgeshire 1972, 40p) which his pupils got through the underground network.

53    They consulted Andrew McKillop of the Department of Environmental Studies, University College, London, as well as a fascinating book, *Survival Scrapbook 1: Shelter* (Unicorn Books, 50 Gloucester Road, Brighton, Sussex, 1972), which discusses, among other aspects of house-building, materials and techniques for do-it-yourself housing. (Has your class yet built a geodesic dome in the playground?) Needless to say, *The Last Whole Earth Catalogue* (Penguin, 1972) is another of their bibles.

54    Giancarlo De Carlo, "The Housing Problem in Italy," *Freedom* (12 June and 19 June 1948).

55    Colin Ward, *Housing: An Anarchist Approach*. (London: Freedom Press, 1976, 1983).

56    Johnston Birchall, *Building Communities the Co-Operative Way*. (London: Routledge & Kegan Paul, 1988).

57    Robert Goodman, *After the Planners*. (Simon & Schuster, 1972). Jane Jacobs, *The Death and Life of Great American Cities*. (Random House 1961)

58    John Gower Davies, *The Evangelistic Bureaucrat*. (Tavistock Publication, 1972).

59    Sherry R. Arnstein, "A Ladder of Citizen Participation in the USA," *Journal of the American Institute of Planners* (July 1969).

60    Alan Mallach, talking on the final day of the "Remaking Cities" conference organised by the American Institute of Architects and the Royal Institute of British Architects, Benedum Theatre, Pittsburgh, 5 March 1988.

61    Mick Reed, "The Peasantry of Nineteenth Century England: a Neglected Class?," *History Workshop* No. 18 (Autumn 1984).

62    Peter Kropotkin, *Fields, Factories and Workshops*.

63    Ebenezer Howard, at the London School of Economics, 18 July 1904.

64    See Colin Ward "Anarchism and the Informal economy" *The Raven* Anarchist Quarterly 1 (1987).

65    Fergus Murray ,"The Decentralisation of Production—the Decline of the Mass-Collective Worker?" in R. E. Pahl (ed.) *On Work, Historical Comparative and Theoretical Approaches*. (Oxford: Basil Blackwell, 1988).

66    C. Richard Hatch Associates *Planning for Change* (Ginn &. Co and Architects Renewal Committee for Harlem 1969)

67    C. Richard Hatch "Italy's Industrial Renaissance: An American Cities Ready to Learn?," *Urban Land* (January 1985).

68    C. George Benello quoted in *Changing Work* No. 7 (Winter 1988).

69    Len Krimerman, "C. George Benello: Architect of Liberating work" in *Changing Work* No. 7 (Winter 1988).

**70**    C. George Benello quoted, Ibid.

**71**    André Gorz, *Farewell to the Working Class: An Essay in Post Industrial Socialism.* (London: Pluto Press, 1982).

**72**    Jonathan Croall, *Preserve or Destroy.* (London: Gulbenkian Foundation, 1995).

**73**    F. Godwin, "Dear Tony ... " *Guardian,* 16 January 1988.

**74**    Peter Kropotkin, *Fields, Factories and Workshops.* (London: Hutchinson. Modem reprint, London: Allen &: Unwin 1974, Freedom Press 1985).

**75**    Ibid.

**76**    Lewis Mumford, *The City in History.* (London: Secker & Warburg, 1961).

**77**    Peter Hall, *Cities of Tomorrow.* (Oxford: Basil Blackwell, 1988).

**78**    Dennis Hardy, *From Garden Cities to New Towns* (London: E & FN Spon, 1991).

**79**    R. Thomas, Introduction to Howard's *Garden Cities of To-morrow.* (Builth Wells: Attic Books, 1985).

**80**    Colin Ward, *New Town. Home Town: The Lessons of Experience.* (London: Gulbenkian Foundation, 1993).

**81**    Peter Hall, *Cities of Tomorrow*, Note 6.

**82**    Peter Kropotkin, Postscript to Russian edition of *Words of a Rebel* (Petrograd & Moscow: 1921) translated by Nicholas Walter in *Freedom Anarchist,* Pamphlet No. 5 (London: Freedom Press, 1970).

**83**    Paul Hawken, *The Ecology of Commerce: A Declaration of Sustainability.* (New York: Harper Business, 1993).

**84**    Jeffrey Jacob, *New Pioneers: The Back-to-the-Land Movement and the Search for a Sustainable Future.* (University Park, PA: Pennsylvania State University Press, 1997).

**85**    Ebenezer Howard (1904), opening the discussion of a paper by Patrick Geddes at the LSE, reprinted in Helen Mellor (ed.), *The Ideal City.* (Leicester: Leicester University Press, 1979).

**86**    A. Champion, "Urban Exodus: A Report for the Council for the Protection of Rural England," University of Newcastle, Dept. of Geography, 1997.

**87**    Land Committee Enquiry, *The Land* Volume 1 (London: Hodder & Stoughton, 1913).

**88**    Stephen Potter, *The Alternative New Towns: The Record of the Town Development Programme 1952–1984.* (Milton Keynes: Open University Social Science Publications, 1984.

**89**    L.C.T. Rolt, *Landscape with Figures.* (Stroud: Alan Sutton, 1992).

**90**    Barrie Trinder, *The Making of the Industrial Landscape.* (London: JM Dent, 1982).

**91**    Hardy, D and Ward C (1984) *Arcadia for All: The Legacy of a Makeshift Landscape.* London: Mansell.

**92**    Simon Fairlie, *Low Impact Development: Planning and People in a Sustainable*

*Countryside.* (Oxford: Jon Carpenter, 1996).

**93**   Joan Thirsk, *Alternative Agriculture, A History from the Black Death to the Present Day.* (Oxford: Oxford University Press, 1997).

# SUPPORT AK PRESS!

AK Press is one of the world's largest and most productive anarchist publishing houses. We're entirely worker-run and democratically managed. We operate without a corporate structure—no boss, no managers, no bullshit. We publish close to twenty books every year, and distribute thousands of other titles published by other like-minded independent presses from around the globe.

The Friends of AK program is a way that you can directly contribute to the continued existence of AK Press, and ensure that we're able to keep publishing great books just like this one! Friends pay a minimum of $25/£15 per month into our publishing account. In return, Friends automatically receive (for the duration of their membership), as they appear, one free copy of every new AK Press title. Friends are also entitled to a discount on everything featured in the AK Press Distribution catalog and on the website, on each and every order.

There's great stuff in the works—so sign up now, and let the presses roll!

Won't you be our friend? Both our US and UK offices maintain a Friends of AK membership program, so please email friendsofak@akpress.org or ak@akedin.demon.co.uk for more info. Or visit us online: http://www.akpress.org/programs/friendsofak.

Would you like to contribute a larger sum? Or perhaps sponsor a book? Get in touch!